THE LIMITS OF DÉTENTE

The Limits
of
Détente

The United States, the Soviet Union, and
the Arab-Israeli Conflict, 1969–1973

CRAIG DAIGLE

Yale UNIVERSITY PRESS

NEW HAVEN AND LONDON

Yale University Press books may be purchased in quantity for educational,
business, or promotional use. For information, please e-mail sales.press@yale.edu
(US office) or sales@yaleup.co.uk (UK office).

Set in Electra type by IDS Infotech, Ltd.
Printed in the United States of America.

Library of Congress Cataloging-in-Publication Data

Daigle, Craig.
The limits of détente : the United States, the Soviet Union, and the Arab-Israeli conflict,
1969–1973 / Craig Daigle.
p. cm.
Includes bibliographical references and index.
ISBN 978-0-300-16713-9 (clothbound : alk. paper)
1. Middle East—Foreign relations—United States. 2. United States—Foreign relations—Middle
East. 3. United States—Foreign relations—Soviet Union. 4. Soviet Union—Foreign relations—
United States. 5. Cold War. 6. Arab-Israeli conflict. I. Title.
DS63.2.U5D34 2012
956.04—dc23   2012016446
A catalogue record for this book is available from the British Library.

This paper meets the requirements of ANSI/NISO Z39.48–1992
(Permanence of Paper).
10 9 8 7 6 5 4 3 2 1

For
Jack Benson and Fred Engel

CONTENTS

CONTENTS

ACKNOWLEDGMENTS

The notion that I would ever write a book remains a somewhat foreign concept to me. Not that long ago it seems that I was getting kicked out of classes in middle and high school for poor behavior, struggling to get into college, and scoring below 400 on the verbal portion of graduate admissions exams (yes, it's possible). Thus, countless number of teachers, colleagues, friends, and family members have helped get me to this point and deserve mention for their role in helping produce this book.

My interest in the history of American foreign relations dates from my undergraduate studies at the University of Maryland, where I benefited from the guidance of Professor Shu Guang Zhang. Not only did Professor Zhang broaden my understanding of the US role in the world and the connection between American foreign and domestic policies, but he taught me important and valuable historical methodical techniques without which I could not have completed this book. It was also at Maryland that I had the great fortune to have Matt Wasniewski, now the Historian of the House of Representatives, as my graduate teaching instructor. I thank Matt for helping me develop needed skills as a researcher and a writer and for insisting that I become a more focused and engaged reader. I am also profoundly indebted to Matt for encouraging me to pursue my graduate studies at his alma mater, James Madison University—the best decision I made in my many years of education.

The two years I spent as a graduate student in history at JMU were invaluable in teaching me the craft of becoming a professional historian and for improving my analytic abilities. Thanks especially to Professors Caroline Marshall, Lee Congdon, Steve Guerrier, David Owusu-Ansah, Skip Hyser, Sidney Bland, Chris Arndt, and Philip Riley. I am also grateful that I spent my two years in Harrisonburg with a number of other graduate students who were good friends and wonderful intellectual partners. Thanks to Bradley Arnold, Susan Dawson, Timothy Layne, Andrew Bell, Geoff Suiter, Christian Cotz, Elizabeth Warner, and especially Jamie Ferguson, whose warm heart and passion for history still inspire me.

I continued my graduate studies at George Washington University, where I fortunately arrived at a time when the History Department expanded its emphasis on the study of Cold War international history. During my first semester, Jim Hershberg encouraged me to explore the Nixon presidential tapes that were being declassified at the National Archives. It was in those tapes that this project first began, and I am forever indebted to Jim for his guidance, support, and enthusiasm for this project and for challenging me to study the Cold War from multiple perspectives. I further developed my work on the tapes, and what would largely become chapter 5 of this book, in Leo Ribuffo's research seminar on the 1970s. I benefited not only from Leo's constant skepticism and prodding but also from the many talented graduate students in the class who offered valuable advice on how to better structure the chapter. These include Hunter Hammond, Heather Masterton Shapiro, Brazell Carter, Ken Borgoff, and Phil Muehlenbeck. I also owe profound thanks at GW to Hope Harrison, Jim Goldgeier, and Gregg Brazinsky for their direction of George Washington University's Cold War Group, which provided an important venue to present many of the ideas in this book, and to Professor Tyler Anbinder for years of advice about the historical profession and for setting an example as a scholar and teacher that I have long sought to emulate.

My former colleagues at the State Department Historian's Office, many of whom have moved on to new endeavors, were extremely helpful and encouraging throughout the many years of work on this book. Thanks to Ted Keefer, John Carland, Erin Mahan, Laurie Van Hook, Monica Belmonte, David Nickles, Jamie Van Hook, Adam Howard, Robert Krikorian, Doug Selvage, Jim Siekmeier, Brad Coleman, Kathy Rasmussen, Amy Garret, Myra Burton, Bill McAllister, Linda Qaimmaqami, Carl

Ashley, Todd Bennett, Chris Tudda, Alex Weiland, Scott Wilson, Edmund Pechaty, Renee Goings, Vicki Futscher, and Susan Weetman. I owe a special debt of gratitude to Steve Galpern for not only sharing his own expertise on this subject but for pointing me to many documents and resources along the way. And I am particularly indebted to David Geyer, who continually pushed me to scour every source I could find, spent many hours of his own time assisting me with the production of Nixon tape transcriptions, translating documents and memoirs for inclusion in this manuscript, and encouraging me to think more deeply about the Nixon period.

Several former Nixon era officials were kind enough to grant me interviews and share their thoughts and expertise on the many topics covered in this book. Thanks especially to Joseph Sisco, Harold Saunders, and Leonard Garment. I also want to express my warm thanks to Dale Rogers Marshall and the entire Rogers family for being so receptive to a young researcher who wanted to learn more about their father. Although this is not the study on William Rogers that I envisioned at the beginning of my research, the private collection of family letters, and the Rogers family's generosity in responding to email inquiries have helped shape my views on their father, which had a significant contribution to this project. Claire Germain and the Cornell University Law School kindly provided me funding and a place to stay while examining a collection of Rogers's materials donated there in 2001.

A number of colleagues have read all or parts of this work and offered thoughtful comments on conference papers or dissertation chapters drawn from the manuscript. Many thanks to Salim Yaqub, Bill Burr, Jim Hershberg, Hope Harrison, Dina Khoury, Leo Ribuffo, Walter Hixson, and Tim Naftali. Mircea Munteanu, formerly of the Cold War International History Project, has been invaluable at tracking down documents in Eastern European archives and for generously translating several of the Romanian documents used in this book. Artemy Kalinovsky assisted with the translation of several of the Russian documents and offered important advice on Soviet foreign policy during the Brezhnev years. Sarah Snyder helped with this project from its early inception to the final footnote. I am enormously grateful for her advice, friendship, hospitality during several research trips to London, and, especially, putting up with all my complaining during the process of writing this book.

As I completed this book, the History Department at the City College of New York has provided a warm and collegial environment in which to work. Thanks especially to Darren Staloff and Cliff Rosenberg, my department chairs, as well as to Judith Stein, Beth Baron, Andreas Killen, Danian Hu, Greg Downs, Adrienne Petty, Anne Kornhauser, Emily Greble, Barbara Syrrakos, and John Gillooly, many of whom read and commented on portions of the manuscript. Deans Fred Reynolds and Geraldine Murphy provided invaluable research assistance and institutional support during the final stages of this project. I'd also like to thank several of my students at City College who consistently challenged and improved my thinking on the link between the Cold War and the Arab-Israeli conflict, and for constantly reminding me of why I chose to pursue this profession. These include: Don Gomez, Briana Broberg, Fidel Tvarez, Rene Cordero, Damon McCool, Aleksandra Dybkowska, Johari Harris, Betsy Marmol, Anthony Decosta, Jonathan Hill, Morgan Hess, and Paula Russo.

At Yale University Press, Laura Davulis graciously helped move this book to publication and was always understanding of everything that slowed me down along the way. Laura Jones Dooley assisted greatly with copyediting the manuscript and significantly improved my prose throughout the book. I was extremely fortunate that the Press chose two talented historians and authors to review the manuscript. Thanks to Nigel Ashton of the London School of Economics, who offered valuable comments and suggestions for improvement and whose scholarship was extremely important to my understanding of the period. And special thanks to Doug Little of Clark University not only for offering extensive commentary to make this a better book than it otherwise would have been but for being kind enough to spend several hours with me in Worcester, Massachusetts, teaching me how to better craft the manuscript. He will recognize the stronger portions of the book for his contributions and will I hope forgive the remaining problems that he told me to correct.

During my work on this book I was fortunate to have a number of good friends who provided companionship and encouragement and who often gave me a much-needed break from the manuscript. Warm thanks to

Mahyar Abousaeedi, Stephanie Wood, Saam and Lilly Farhang, Karl and Caroline Zwick, Jon and Deb Szumny, Jeremy and Kristin Zeid, Kevin Marckx and Susie Stirling, Mike and Emily Liedtke, Kori Shaiman, and Christina Vander Vegt. Benjamin and Cathy Deneault have graciously treated me as part of their family for many years, and I cannot thank them enough for their love and support and for always thinking to include me in everything they do.

By far the best part of working on this book and becoming a historian was meeting Chris Morrison along the way. In the past decade, Chris has lived through every phase of this project and devoted countless hours of his time to making this a better book. He has graciously endured endless phone calls and emails about William Rogers, Henry Kissinger, and Golda Meir and never complained about the many times I imposed on him to proofread chapters on short notice. Chris and his wife, Yvonne, have opened their home to me on numerous occasions, supported me through personal and professional challenges, and sustained me with their love and generosity. Without their friendship, I would never have completed this book.

When I arrived in Maryland to begin my undergraduate studies, and through the many years that I worked on this book, Gus, Cheryl, Stephanie, and Amy Siekierka provided a warm home away from home for which I will always be grateful. Steve, Judy, Stephanie, Chad and Tania Beguin, Kevin and Nicole Dipasquale, and Jeff Druck have been my extended family for many years, and I cannot thank them enough for their unwavering support and constant encouragement, and especially for all the additions to their families that have so enriched our lives: Connor, Lauren, Cooper, Tasher, Zander, and Keira.

Words fail to convey what my family's contribution has meant to this project. I may not have inherited my dad's artistic talents and enduring patience, but he taught me the importance of finding a career you enjoy and to pursue it with passion and dedication. He has assisted with this project in countless ways—from drawing the wonderful maps in the book to shuttling me to the airport in the middle of the night on many research trips. I cannot thank him enough for his boundless encouragement, steadied guidance, and constant love. My mom has sustained me with loving support and comfort and has cheered me on when I needed it most. She has always encouraged me to pursue my dreams and supported me in my every decision. Scott, Verena, Abigail, and Andrea Daigle provide me far more love than I deserve and have been extremely patient with me during the many hours I spent reading books and documents on our family vacations when I should have been spending time with them. My grandmothers, Elaine Hirschman and Jo Daigle, are constant sources of inspiration and love. I hope they know that I cherish the memories of my grandfathers and try to make them proud in everything I do.

Finally, I would like to thank Jack Benson and Fred Engel, my history teachers at Cherry Creek High School in Englewood, Colorado. In all my years of education, they are two of the finest historians and teachers I have had the good fortune to know. They taught me long ago that history could be a rewarding profession and what it truly means to be an effective teacher: have passion for your students, bring enthusiasm to the classroom, and never take yourself too seriously. Working with a below-average student, they inspired me to be serious about my studies, challenged me to become a better writer, and gave me the opportunity to succeed at levels I could never have imagined. The following pages are a culmination of work that began in their classes and the product of their lessons that I continue to draw on to this day. I dedicate this book to them, with gratitude.

ADST	Association for Diplomatic Studies and Training, Foreign Affairs Oral History Project, Library of Congress, Washington, DC
AVP RF	Archive of Foreign Policy of the Russian Federation, Moscow
CAB	Cabinet Papers
CF	Country Files
CIA	Central Intelligence Agency
CT	*Chicago Tribune*
CWIHP	Cold War International History Project
DSB	*Department of State Bulletin*
DSNA	Digital National Security Archive
EUR	Europe
FBIS	Foreign Broadcast Information Service
FCO	Foreign and Commonwealth Office, United Kingdom
FO	Foreign Office, United Kingdom
FRUS	*Foreign Relations of the United States*
H-Files	National Security Council Institutional Files
HAK	Henry A. Kissinger
HAKOF	Kissinger Office Files
HHSF	Harold H. Saunders Files
IFR	*Israel's Foreign Relations*
ISA	Israel State Archives, Jerusalem

JJS	Office Files of Joseph J. Sisco
LAT	*Los Angeles Times*
LOC	Library of Congress, Washington, DC
ME	Middle East
MENF	Middle East Negotiating Files
MFA	Ministry of Foreign Affairs, Israel
NARA	National Archives Records Administration, Washington, DC
NPMS	Nixon Presidential Materials Project
NSA	National Security Archive, Washington, DC
NSC	National Security Council
NSCF	National Security Council Files
NYT	*New York Times*
PC	Presidential Correspondence
POF	President's Office Files
PREM	Prime Minister's Office
PTF	President's Trip Files
SF	Subject File
TNA	The National Archives of the United Kingdom, Kew Gardens
UAR	United Arab Republic
WHT	White House Tapes
WHY	Henry Kissinger, *White House Years* (Boston: Little, Brown), 1979
WP	*Washington Post*
WPR	Office Files of William P. Rogers
WSAG	Washington Special Actions Group
YoU	Henry Kissinger, *Years of Upheaval* (Boston: Little, Brown), 1982

THE LIMITS OF DÉTENTE

Israel and the occupied territories, 1967

The war came as a complete surprise.

Shortly past 6:00 a.m. on Saturday, October 6, 1973, Secretary of State Henry Kissinger was sound asleep in his suite at the Waldorf Towers in New York, his headquarters for the annual session of the United Nations General Assembly, when Joseph J. Sisco, assistant secretary of state for Near Eastern and African affairs, barged into his bedroom. "Israel, Egypt, and Syria are about to go to war," Sisco said as he watched the secretary force himself awake. Sisco had just received an urgent message from the American ambassador in Israel, former senator Kenneth Keating, warning that Egyptian and Syrian troop movements, which had earlier been perceived by Israel and the United States as routine military exercises, had "suddenly taken a threatening turn."[1]

Hours earlier, Israeli prime minister Golda Meir had informed Keating that her government had received from "totally reliable sources" information that Syria and Egypt were planning a coordinated attack against Israel to begin later that afternoon and that Soviet naval vessels had been seen departing from Egyptian ports, a clear signal that Moscow had decided to get out of the way of the pending strike. At first, said Meir, the government of Israel thought the Soviet evacuation from Syria might mean a break in diplomatic relations, but considering that many Soviet military advisers remained in Cairo, it soon became apparent what was about to happen. Before the meeting concluded, she assured the American ambassador that

Prime Minister Golda Meir and Chief of the Southern Command General Shmuel Gonen visit an IDF outpost in the Sinai Peninsula, October 1973. *(Yehuda Tzioin, Israel Government Press Office)*

her government did not intend to launch a preemptive strike, as they had done during the 1967 war, and requested that American officials quickly pass this information along to leaders in Cairo, Damascus, and Moscow.[2]

Kissinger refused to believe the news. Not only had US and Israeli intelligence recently determined that an Arab attack remained unlikely, but as Kissinger later wrote, it was "extraordinary" for an Israeli leader to be at work on that day—for it was Yom Kippur, the Day of Atonement, the holiest day of the Jewish year.[3] Moreover, the secretary of state did not believe that a war with Israel made any sense from the Arab standpoint. Even with the arrival of Soviet-made tanks and aircraft following the Six-Day War, as well as the SA-3, the most sophisticated of the Soviet antiaircraft defense system, Egyptian and Syrian armies were no match for the Israeli Defense Forces. "Every Israeli (and American) analysis before October 1973 agreed that Egypt and Syria lacked the military capability to regain their territory by force of arms" and therefore would not attack, Kissinger confessed in his memoirs. "The premises were correct," he said, "the conclusions were not."[4]

Within minutes Kissinger had Anatoly Dobrynin, the Soviet ambassador to the United States, on the telephone trying to figure out what had occurred during the night and hoping to get matters under control before the shooting began. "We have information from the Israelis that the Arabs and Syrians are planning an attack within the next 6 hours and that your people are evacuating civilians from Damascus and Cairo," Kissinger said, clearly concerned about the global consequences of a Middle East war. On behalf of Israel's leadership, the secretary of state stressed that Israel had no intentions to move against Egypt or Syria but warned that in the event of a foreign attack, Israel would "successfully defend itself."[5]

Kissinger's call to Dobrynin—the first of more than fifty telephone calls made to Israeli, Egyptian, Syrian, Jordanian, and United Nations officials on the first day of the October War—was a telling sign that he believed a Middle East war was just as much a contest between the United States and the Soviet Union as it was between Israel and its Arab neighbors. Throughout his numerous calls with Dobrynin on October 6, he informed the ambassador that the United States and the Soviet Union had a "special responsibility" to restrain their respective clients and made a plea to the ambassador to not let the outbreak of another Arab-Israeli war damage détente: "I would like to tell you as you no doubt [know]—that this is very important for our relationship, that we not have an explosion in the Middle East right now."[6]

During the next three weeks, Kissinger worked in his capacity as both secretary of state and national security adviser to end the fighting and preserve the relationship with the Soviet Union that he and President Richard M. Nixon had built during the previous four and a half years. On October 20, at the height of the crisis and amid the unfolding events of Watergate, Kissinger made a special trip to Moscow to negotiate an Arab-Israeli cease-fire with Soviet leaders and then stopped in Israel to discuss the cease-fire and the fate of the encircled Egyptian Third Army. When Soviet leader Leonid Brezhnev threatened "unilateral" Soviet intervention in the Middle East to prevent Israeli violations of the cease-fire agreement on October 24—in Kissinger's estimate "one of the most serious challenges" to an American president by a Soviet leader—the secretary of state urged Nixon to call the Soviet bluff by placing US military forces on high alert. Kissinger then drafted a letter to President Anwar Sadat of Egypt under

Nixon's name warning that should Soviet forces appear in the region, the United States would have to resist them on Egyptian territory. "I ask you to consider the consequences for your country if the two great nuclear countries were thus to confront each other on your soil," the letter stated as the crisis quickly abated.[7]

In their respective memoirs, both Kissinger and Dobrynin argued that it was a testament to détente that they could negotiate an end to the war and open a period of active diplomacy in the region. "The crisis demonstrated that tension could be localized and prevented from disrupting relations between Washington and Moscow," said Dobrynin, as "the two countries found themselves deeply involved . . . as partners seeking the earliest possible end to the war."[8] Kissinger was even more emphatic in his assessment: "I believe détente mitigated the succession of crises that differences in ideology and geopolitical interest had made nearly inevitable; and I believe we enhanced the national interests in the process."[9]

Kissinger and Dobrynin were not alone in the belief that détente had passed a significant test. On the morning after the military alert, the *Washington Post* and the *New York Times* ran lengthy editorials suggesting that the result of the crisis was "the single most significant vindication of détente" and proof that the relationship Nixon and Brezhnev had created "served both of them well in their contest." On an ideological level, moreover, the *Post* argued that the crisis helped shape and define détente not as "an easy solvent of great power tension" but rather as "an attitude, an understanding, a frame of mind in which the two great powers could pursue their various political interests, and conduct their rivalry, with some sense of the need for pulling back on this side of the brink."[10]

It is certainly true that détente had both created the mindset in which Washington's and Moscow's first instinct was to prevent disruptions in great power relations and provided the foundation on which Soviet and American officials could conduct the negotiations needed to end the war. Nevertheless, these comments obscure the fact that the October War was in large part a product of Soviet-American relations and decision-making during the previous four and a half years. Although through détente the Soviet Union and United States reached agreements on the limitation of strategic arms and the prevention of nuclear warfare, established scientific and cultural exchanges and trade agreements, and formalized treaties to curb rivalries and tensions in Eastern Europe, Western Europe, and Berlin, détente rarely, if ever, extended to the Middle East.

Indeed, both Soviet and American officials resisted attempts to place pressure on their respective clients to agree to a Middle East peace settlement and continually adopted policies that brought their two countries closer to confrontation in the region. In 1969–1970 the Soviets rejected a US peace proposal (which they helped construct) and responded by moving more than ten thousand military personnel into Egypt. After the United States successfully brokered an Egyptian-Israel cease-fire agreement in August 1970, ending the War of Attrition, the Soviets exploited the terms of the agreement by helping Egypt build a missile shield against Israeli aircraft along the Suez Canal. For its part, the United States continued to send Israel its most advanced weapons, attempted to broker separate deals with the Egyptians, and sought to remove the Soviet military presence from the region. "After all," said Kissinger, "a principal purpose of our own Mideast policy was to reduce the role and influence of the Soviet Union, just as the Soviets sought to reduce ours."[11]

When in 1972 the superpowers agreed to place their difference in the Middle East on ice and accepted the status quo in the region for the benefit of détente, Egypt's Anwar Sadat felt compelled to launch a war against Israel. After months of failed diplomacy with Secretary of State William P. Rogers and Israel's repeated rejections of his peace overtures, Sadat concluded that his only hope of recovering the territories seized by Israel in June 1967 was to create a "crisis of détente" by attacking Israel and drawing the superpowers into a regional confrontation.

Through the years, historians and political scientists have devoted considerable attention to the Soviet-American "jockeying" during the October War, especially to Kissinger's role during the crisis and to the shuttle diplomacy that followed. Many have subscribed to the notion that Kissinger's handling of the crisis was "a model of crisis management" and proved that the cease-fire ending the war resulted in large part from Washington and Moscow's mutual desire to preserve détente.[12] Others have underlined the fracture in Soviet-American détente evident during the negotiations and the

October 24–25 military alert, as well as Kissinger's desire to leave the Soviets out of the postwar negotiations.[13]

By devoting so much attention to the war and the ensuing diplomacy, however, historians have largely ignored the US and Soviet involvement in precipitating the conflict. William B. Quandt's *Decade of Decisions* was the first significant study to examine American policy toward the Arab-Israeli conflict during the presidencies of Nixon and Gerald Ford, and his revised *Peace Process* is still widely considered the authoritative account of American diplomacy in the Arab-Israeli conflict. But Quandt's study lacks archival documentation, and as a former National Security Council staffer under Kissinger, Quandt is quick to dismiss State Department efforts to bring about peace in the Middle East.[14] Several former American diplomats serving in the Middle East have written studies on the great power diplomacy during the Egyptian-Israeli War of Attrition that highlight the effects of Arab-Israeli tensions on détente, but these studies generally conclude during the summer of 1970 and thus do not address the three critical years leading to the October War, including Anwar Sadat's rise on the Egyptian scene.[15]

The ending of the Cold War and the subsequent opening of former Soviet and Eastern European archives gave rise in recent years to a number of studies focusing on the Soviet intervention in the War of Attrition. These accounts are significant for understanding Soviet decision-making and have shed important light on Moscow's decision to introduce Soviet military units into Egypt—dubbed Operation *Kavkaz*—in February 1970. Yet these authors do not place the Soviet decision to intervene in the War of Attrition in the broader context of détente, nor do they adequately address how the Soviets' experiences during this conflict influenced their behavior in the Middle East before and during the October War.[16] The preponderance of more recent US-Soviet and détente studies have also failed to grasp the role that the Middle East played in contributing to and limiting détente.[17]

Studies on the Middle East and the Arab-Israeli dispute have ignored détente's role in contributing to the outbreak of the 1973 October War. Although a consensus has emerged in recent years that Sadat's objectives during the war were largely political in that he wanted to give the peace process a "jolt," not embark on large-scale reconquest of Arab territory, most studies focus on Sadat's desire to move the Israelis off their frozen position rather than on how he was trying to budge the United States and the Soviet Union off their rigid adherence to the status quo.[18]

This book fills this historiographic gap by presenting the first detailed survey of US-Soviet relations in the Middle East in the era of détente. In it, I reveal not only that the Arab-Israeli conflict repeatedly caused problems for détente to the point of risking a US-Soviet confrontation but also that détente exacerbated Arab-Israeli tensions. I begin by demonstrating how, during the early months of the Nixon presidency, both Washington and Moscow viewed Arab-Israeli peace discussions as a needed venue to ascertain each other's intentions and willingness to negotiate on a broader scale. For both countries the successful completion of an Arab-Israeli peace agreement would eliminate a potential arena for a superpower confrontation and prove to officials in both capitals that bilateral negotiations on major areas could succeed and overcome differences in the Third World. Nixon's authorization of the "Two Power" talks with the Soviets in the first month of his presidency to discuss an Arab-Israeli agreement reflected his larger concept of "linkage." According to Nixon, "The great issues are fundamentally interrelated," and linkage thus represented a way to convey to the Soviets that they "cannot expect to reap the benefits of cooperation in one area while seeking to take advantage of tension or confrontation elsewhere."[19]

In chapter 2, I place the Rogers Plan squarely in the context of Soviet-American relations. Although traditionally interpreted strictly through the lens of the Arab-Israeli conflict, the Rogers Plan was primarily a closing chapter of the "test" of Soviet intentions in the Middle East, which the president had ordered at the beginning of his administration, rather than a definitive statement of what the Nixon administration believed would ultimately constitute a long-term peace agreement between Egypt and Israel.

In chapters 3 through 5 I discuss the consequences of the Soviet decision to intervene in the War of Attrition, perceived by Kissinger as the "first Soviet threat" to the Nixon administration. Not only did the Soviets threaten the chances for détente by directly intervening in the War of Attrition, but they attempted to undermine the Egyptian-Israeli cease-fire agreement of August 1970. In chapter 5, "Fighting for Sadat," I explore the rise of Anwar el-Sadat on the Egyptian scene and show how the United States and the Soviet Union each exploited the transfer of power in Egypt following

President Gamal Abdel Nasser's death to improve its strategic position in the region relative to its rival.

In a broader sense, though, *The Limits of Détente* helps explain the roots of the 1973 October War. The war resulted largely from policies adopted in Washington and Moscow as much as it did from the competing interests between Arabs and Israelis: it was thus a *consequence* of détente. As I argue in chapters 6–8, the United States and the Soviet Union, in a genuine effort to promote détente and avoid a potential superpower confrontation in the Middle East, accepted agreements in 1972 and 1973 that solidified an untenable status quo in the region rather than promote a lasting Arab-Israeli peace agreement. Moreover, both superpowers largely ignored Sadat's threats that he would take his country to war with Israel if Washington and Moscow did not actively attempt to resolve the dispute. By effectively telling Arab leaders that Israel would indefinitely retain possession of their land, the Soviets alienated their clients in the Middle East and pushed the Egyptians and Syrians into another war.

In choosing to take his country to war, as I demonstrate in chapter 9, Sadat's primary objective was not to defeat Israel militarily, which he knew he could not do, but rather to reignite the stalled political process by creating a "crisis of détente"—drawing the superpowers into a regional conflict and forcing leaders in Washington and Moscow to forego the "no war, no peace" situation that had been produced in the Middle East as a result of their burgeoning détente.

In no way does this book imply that there were no other constraints on détente. America's continued involvement in the Vietnam War, the US effort to exploit the Sino-Soviet rift by establishing ties with the People's Republic of China, and the Soviet-American rivalry that erupted during the India-Pakistan War of 1971 all demonstrated the limits of détente. In 1973–1974, the Jackson-Vanik Amendment, which denied most favored nation status to nonmarket economies that restricted emigration rights, highlighted the domestic constraints of détente, while differences over the 1975 Helsinki Accords, US and Soviet involvement in Angola, and the Soviet intervention in Afghanistan all contributed to détente's eventual collapse.

Few if any of these conflicts, however, brought the United States and the Soviet Union closer to military confrontation than did the Arab-Israeli conflict.

The Soviet-American rapprochement, a centerpiece of American foreign policy during the Nixon and Ford presidencies, failed to reach its full potential owing to the ongoing competition between Washington and Moscow for control of the Middle East. Although détente relaxed tensions and improved relations between the United States and the Soviet Union at the global strategic level during the early 1970s, at the regional level, détente undermined progress toward an Arab-Israeli peace settlement and in so doing helped trigger the October War.[20]

ONE

From Confrontation to Negotiation,
January–September 1969

As the dusk settled over the Sinai Peninsula on Saturday, June 10, 1967, signs of the colossal destruction of Egypt's army were everywhere. Hundreds of smashed trucks and tanks stretched bumper to bumper for miles. The shattered frames of dozens of Russian-built MiG-21s were tossed across the expansive desert. Forward air bases were littered with blackened craters along their runways. Guns, armor, and ammunition lay strewn across the sizzling sand. Piles of bedding, tents, mess equipment, and shoes covered the narrow roads, a sign of the army's hurried retreat. Bloody remains of the some of the fifteen thousand Egyptian soldiers killed in action were left rotting under the hot sun.[1] "Nobody had been prepared for defeat on such a shattering scale," wrote Mohamed Heikal, the influential editor of the Cairo daily *Al-Ahram*. "Everybody was shocked . . . [and] in a state of total confusion."[2]

Along the Golan Heights overlooking the Upper Galilee on the Syrian-Israeli border, the scene was equally devastating. A UPI correspondent trailing Israeli soldiers up the snow-capped Mount Hermon range observed charred remains of Syrian troops killed on their way to battle. Smoke billowed from bomb-blasted concrete bunkers that once protected artillery used to shell Israeli settlements on the other side of the border. Long lines of prisoners, some blindfolded with their own *keffiyeh* headdresses, were whisked away in Israeli military vehicles. Wheat fields still afire up the Golan foothills and near the Israeli settlement of Ein Gev cast a "ruddy glow" over the Sea of Galilee that could be seen from the town of Tiberias on the western shore.[3]

On the West Bank of the Kingdom of Jordan, the ruin from the war was perhaps most pronounced. Burned-out Jordanian tanks and jeeps littered the road from Jerusalem to Bethlehem, along with taxis, trucks, and other vehicles mired in the crossfire.[4] Down the highway to the Dead Sea valley, several bodies of unburied Jordanian fighters were still visible, a slimmer of the seven hundred soldiers who died in battle and the nearly six thousand wounded or missing. Most notably, tens of thousands of Arab civilians caught up in the tides of war crowded the streets and poured over the Jordan River into what remained of the kingdom's East Bank, containing the seeds of a new refugee problem.[5] "Our losses were tremendous, but we are proud of the fact that we fought honorably," said a despondent King Hussein, whose Hashemite dynasty once again teetered on the brink of collapse.[6] "If our men had known from the beginning that they could not expect support from either Egypt, Syria, or Iraq our strategy would have been different."[7]

The third Arab-Israeli war lasted only six days—132 hours—but in that brief period, the landscape of the Middle East changed forever.[8] With its stunning victory over the Arabs, Israel now occupied territory three times its size. It conquered the Sinai Peninsula and the Gaza Strip from Egypt. It seized the strategic Golan Heights from Syria. And it secured the West Bank from Jordan, leaving the Old City of Jerusalem and its holy sites entirely under Israeli control, an event of "unimaginable significance" to the Israelis.[9] For the first time since the establishment of the state, Jews could pray at the Western Wall, the last remnant of their holy Temple and their historic past. "We have returned to the holiest of our holy places, never to depart from it again," said the charismatic, one-eyed major general Moshe Dayan, who served as Israel's defense minister during the war.[10]

The conquest brought Israel obvious advantages. With expanded borders, Israel secured a much-needed buffer against its Arab neighbors, whose artillery was always in range of its most populous cities. Unobstructed passage through the Strait of Tiran and the Gulf of Aqaba, and possession of Sharm el-Sheikh, near the tip of the Sinai Peninsula, also ensured that Israeli ships could safely reach the port of Eilat. And control of the Golan Heights meant that Israel could neutralize its most troublesome border and remove the threat to the Jordan River water supply, on which future development depended.[11] At the same time, however, the victory also brought with it numerous challenges. In addition to having to secure more than twenty-six thousand square miles of territory previously in Arab hands, a major strain on Israel's largely reserve army, the Israelis assumed responsibility for nearly 1.3 million Arabs, most of whom remained hostile to the Jews. "The Palestinian population was a demographic time bomb for Israel," the historian David W. Lesch has written, "as their higher birth rates would make them the majority within forty to fifty years in Israel if it held onto the occupation."[12]

What to do with the occupied Arab territories quickly emerged as the central question facing Israeli leaders immediately after the war. Should the land be settled by Jews, expanding well beyond the borders that the United Nations had allocated to the Jewish state in its resolution of November 1947, or should some or all of the land be returned to the Arabs in exchange for meaningful peace agreements? Would the Israelis annex the West Bank of the Jordan, taking in great numbers of Arabs whose loyalties would be unpredictable? Or would they make the West Bank a "protected state"—neither Jordanian nor Israeli—managed by international authorities? Should the Golan Heights be returned to Syria with the hope that its leaders would quell the violence along the border and recognize Israel's sovereignty, or would Israel hold on to the land indefinitely to protect its citizens and natural resources in the north? Some Israelis, chiefly in the military, wanted to retain most of the territory they took for security purposes, while many of Israel's top political leaders were prepared to leverage the land for a peace treaty that recognized the state of Israel.[13]

One thing was certain, however: Israel would never agree to a *complete* return to the June 4, 1967, borders. Soon after the fighting ended, Israeli leaders made constant references and comparisons to the aftermath of the 1956 Suez-Sinai war, when their forces withdrew within their boundaries with only paper guarantees that the Arabs would make peace.[14] The Israelis did not intend to repeat the scenario. Prime Minister Levi Eshkol declared before the Knesset (parliament) on June 12 that his government no longer recognized the 1949 armistice agreements, which had been used as "time-gaining expedients" to prepare for renewed aggression, and he denounced

Egyptian and Jordanian claims to Arab Palestine, since both areas had been taken by the Arabs in 1948 "as the result of military aggression and occupation."[15] It was equally unlikely that his government would return Sharm el-Sheikh to Arab hands, lest there be another blockade of the Gulf of Aqaba, nor would Israel ever agree to a divided Jerusalem, a fact that was dramatically asserted by the cabinet's vote on June 18 to annex East Jerusalem and its surrounding area.[16]

"Be under no illusion that the state of Israel is prepared to return to the situation that reigned up to a year ago," declared Eshkol. "Alone we fought for our existence and our security. We are entitled to determine what are the true and vital interests of our country and how they should be secured. The position that existed until now shall never again return. The land of Israel shall no longer be a no man's land, wide open to acts of sabotage and murder."[17]

As determined as Eshkol was to use the newly acquired occupied territories to Israel's advantage, the Arab states were equally determined to get their land back—by force if necessary. Meeting in Khartoum in August 1967, Arab leaders supported a resolution to continue the state of belligerency against Israel. "This will be done within the framework of the main principles by which the Arab states abide, namely, *no* peace with Israel, *no* recognition of Israel, *no* negotiations with it, and the insistence on the rights of the Palestinian people within their own country." The resolution, often referred to as the "three noes of Khartoum," confirmed to many Israelis that the Arabs had learned nothing from the recent conflict and that there was little point to give back the land if they were unwilling to live in peace with Israel.[18]

In November 1967, hoping to reconcile the differences between the two sides, the United Nations Security Council passed Resolution 242, which established a "land for peace" formula. But even this resolution, though accepted by both Arabs and Israelis, was left intentionally vague and further added to the difficulty in bridging their long-standing disagreements. On one hand, the resolution clearly established the principle of the "inadmissibility of the acquisition of territory by war"; by this definition Israel could not retain any of the occupied territories. On the other hand, it deliberately omitted a requirement for Israeli forces to return to the lines of

June 4, 1967. Instead the text called for Israel to withdraw only "from territories occupied in the recent conflict"—not *all* territories or *the* territories, just "territories." By intentionally leaving out the definitive article before the word "territories," the United Nations allowed each side to interpret the resolution to its liking. The Arabs and their supporters repeatedly asserted that the resolution meant "all" territories, and this is reflected in Arabic translation of the resolution. But the British (English) version—the one voted on in the Security Council and therefore the only text that holds international standing—omitted these words and thus left little doubt that part of these territories could remain in Israeli hands.[19]

With both sides holding firm to their interpretation of Resolution 242, and the United Nations seemingly unable to resolve the deadlock, the Arab-Israeli dispute quickly became a focus of the politics and diplomacy of the Cold War. For the Soviet Union in particular, Israel's victory in 1967 and its occupation of Arab territory was a significant setback to its strategic position in the Middle East and an even larger blow to its prestige. In just six days of war, the Israeli Defense Forces had effectively erased a decade of Soviet military aid to the Arab states, demonstrating to Soviet allies around the world that their weapons were no match for what the United States provided Israel. Although Premier Alexei Kosygin had threatened military intervention to defend the Arabs and severed diplomatic relations with Israel on the last day of the conflict, the Soviets largely stood helplessly by, "watching through field glasses," as the vastly superior Israeli forces destroyed its heavy Middle Eastern investment.[20] The question for Moscow, according to Israel's foreign minister Abba Eban, was whether any of its allies would take the Soviet Union seriously in the future.[21]

Hoping to demonstrate Moscow's loyalty to its Arab friends, Kosygin requested an emergency session of the UN General Assembly to consider the "grave and dangerous" situation caused by Israel's continued "aggression" and "crimes" against the Arab states. Speaking before the assembly on June 19, he condemned Israel as an "unbridled aggressor" and demanded Israel's immediate and unconditional withdrawal from Arab territory. "The Arab states are entitled to expect that their sovereignty, territorial integrity, legitimate rights and interests . . . will be reconstituted in full and without delay," said the sixty-three-year-old premier. This was a bold claim coming

14

from the leader of a nation that had built its empire after World War II by ignoring the sovereignty and territorial integrity of its "allies" in Eastern Europe. But Kosygin apparently did not see the contradictions. "As long as the Israeli troops continue to occupy the seized territories, and urgent measures are not taken to eliminate the consequences of the aggression," he cautioned, "a military conflict can flare up any minute."[22]

In addition to lending its political support, the Soviet Union became the primary source of financial and military aid for rebuilding the shattered Arab armies. In the first six months following the war, almost 80 percent of the aircraft, tanks, and artillery Egypt had lost in the June war had been replaced by the Soviet Union, and more than five thousand Soviet "advisers" were sent to Cairo in all phases of training, planning, and air defense. These weapons allowed Egypt to rebuild its military quickly and helped lessen the humiliation left over from the war.[23] According to political scientist Alvin Rubinstein, "The magnitude of the Soviet commitment [to Egypt] was unprecedented, surpassing in both quantity and quality the aid given to North Vietnam and exceeding the rate at which aid had hitherto been given to allied or friendly countries."[24]

Despite its heavy military investment in the Middle East, however, Moscow remained interested primarily in a political settlement to the Arab-Israeli conflict. Soviet leaders feared that if another Middle East war erupted because the differences from the 1967 conflict were left unresolved, their forces would be unable to stand on the sidelines again. This would certainly lead to a superpower confrontation in the region and had the potential to unleash a nuclear war. Desperate to avoid this nightmare scenario, the Soviets, in September 1968, presented the United States with a detailed plan for an Arab-Israeli peace settlement that called for a staged Israeli withdrawal from the occupied territories in exchange for Arab declarations to end the state of war; recognition of Israel's right to live in peace, within "safe and recognized" boundaries; and respect for and recognition of the sovereignty, territorial integrity, and political independence of each "state" in the region. Dean Rusk, President Lyndon B. Johnson's secretary of state, described the proposal as a "constructive" move in Soviet policy toward the Middle East, but with only two months before the next presidential election, the Johnson administration could do little to help deliver the agreement. The Soviet proposal, therefore, was left to Johnson's successor.[25]

With Richard Nixon's election to the presidency in November 1968, the Soviets were, surprisingly, presented with an opportunity to move this proposal forward. Nixon had long believed that Washington had tilted its policy too heavily in Israel's favor at the expense of US security interests in the Middle East. This resulted, in part, from the "enormous influence" of the American Jewish lobby, he argued, but many Americans supported Zionist aspirations in Palestine after the United States failed to respond more aggressively to the Holocaust.[26] A mutual desire to curb Gamal Abdel Nasser's popularity in the aftermath of the Suez Crisis, and contain the spread of Arab nationalism in the late 1950s, drove the United States and Israel closer together.[27] Before leaving office early in 1961, Dwight D. Eisenhower agreed to sell Israel ten million dollars' worth of sophisticated military equipment, a policy that accelerated during the Kennedy and Johnson administrations.[28] "The United States," President John F. Kennedy told Golda Meir in 1962, "has a special relationship with Israel in the Middle East really comparable only to that which it has with Britain over a wide range of world affairs."[29]

Although President Johnson tried to prevent the Israelis from launching a preemptive strike against the Arabs before the 1967 war, repeatedly telling Foreign Minister Abba Eban on May 26 that "Israel will not be alone unless it decides to do it alone,"[30] and refused to replenish Israeli arsenals during the crisis, the perception by the Arabs was that the United States had "colluded" with Israel to destroy the "revolutionary Arab regimes which had refused to be part of the Western sphere of influence."[31] Nixon, too, believed that the Arab's humiliating defeat in the Six-Day War would have significant consequences for both Israel and the United States. After visiting the region immediately after the war, Nixon concluded that Israel's victory "left a residue of hatred among their neighbors that I felt could only result in another war, particularly if the Russians were to set up military aid to their defeated Arab clients."[32]

For Nixon, however, US support of Israel was only half the problem. The United States, in his view, had made too many mistakes regarding its policies in the Arab world. As vice president, he objected to Secretary of State John Foster Dulles's decision in 1956 to withdraw American funding

Israeli foreign minister Abba Eban at the White House with President Lyndon B. Johnson before the Six-Day War. Johnson warned Eban: "Israel will not be alone unless it decides to go alone." *(LBJ Library)*

to Egypt for the building of the Aswan Dam, and he believed that the United States had "totally closed our eyes to the terrible condition of Arab refugees."[33] All this needed to change in his administration. Although he would not abandon Israel as an ally, he felt that it was clearly in America's interest to "halt" the Soviet domination of the Arab Middle East; to do so would require broadening US relations with the Arab countries.[34] "Where on the analysis the question becomes primarily one of the interests of Israel and the interests of Israel's neighbors, Egypt, Jordan, et al, then we should have a totally even-handed policy," Nixon told Secretary of State William Rogers. "I believe that an even-handed policy is, on balance, the best one for us to pursue as far as our own interests are concerned."[35]

In line with this "even-handed" policy, Nixon was receptive to the Soviets' idea of holding discussions on an Arab-Israeli peace settlement. The president understood that in the wake of the Arab defeat, Moscow needed a "face-saving formula" to help its allies get their land back while reducing the risk of confrontation with the United States.[36] But joining the

Kremlin in these negotiations, he reasoned, could also help him achieve his larger foreign policy objectives. First, Nixon expected that in return for Washington's efforts to get the Israelis to withdraw from the occupied territories, Moscow would reduce its military aid to North Vietnam. This would weaken Hanoi's ability to prolong the Vietnam War and give the president increased leverage to deliver on his promise of an "honorable" end to the war.[37] Second, persuading Israel to moderate its position and return the Arab territories would also improve US standing in the Arab world and potentially reduce Soviet influence in the Middle East.

Perhaps most important, though, a joint US-Soviet effort to secure an Arab-Israeli settlement would demonstrate Nixon's commitment to détente. Indeed, despite his long history of anticommunism and his sometimes open hostility toward the Kremlin, Nixon entered office eager to change America's relationship with the Soviet Union. During the campaign, he made it clear that the "era of confrontation" between Washington and Moscow needed to end and that the United States could live in peace with the Soviet Union. "Where the world's super powers are concerned, there is no acceptable alternative to peaceful negotiation," he said. An administration under his authority would begin with the proposition that if the United States wanted to live in peace, it must negotiate with its adversaries. "The years just ahead can bring a breakthrough for peace," he said, "they must be a time of careful probing, of intensive negotiations, of a determined search for those areas of accommodation between East and West on which a climate of mutual trust can eventually be built."[38]

Thus, in the first months of the Nixon administration, discussions surrounding the Middle East and the search for a resolution to the ongoing Arab-Israeli conflict in particular preoccupied officials in Washington and Moscow. Between March and July 1969, the United States and the Soviet Union devoted more time to and held more discussions on the Middle East than any other topic. Negotiations were conducted in Washington in the form of the Two Power talks with Secretary of State William P. Rogers, Assistant Secretary Joseph J. Sisco, and the Soviet ambassador to the United States, Anatoly Dobrynin, and sometimes in the confidential "backchannel" between Dobrynin and Henry Kissinger, Nixon's national security adviser. Although it would be a stretch to say that leaders in either the

United States or the Soviet Union viewed Arab-Israeli negotiations as a *central* component in paving the way for détente, both sides believed that these discussions were a needed venue to ascertain each other's intentions and willingness to negotiate.

If the Two Power talks failed to bring about an Arab-Israeli peace agreement, as seemed likely since neither the United States nor the Soviet Union appeared willing to place the necessary pressure on its client to deliver such an agreement, both understood that it would not preclude them from engaging in substantive and successful negotiations in other areas of mutual concern. If, on the other hand, the talks succeeded and an Arab-Israeli peace agreement followed, it would not only eliminate a potential arena for a superpower confrontation but would prove to officials in both capitals that bilateral negotiations on major areas could succeed and differences in the Third World could be overcome. Either way, both Washington and Moscow viewed the talks as the opening "test" on the road to détente.

Nixon, the Middle East, and the Origins of Détente

"After a period of confrontation, we are entering an era of negotiation." With these words in his inaugural address on January 20, 1969, President Nixon heralded a period of US-Soviet cooperation unmatched during the Cold War. Following a decade of often contentious and bitter rivalry between the two superpowers, which led to a nuclear confrontation over the presence of Soviet missiles in Cuba, crises over the status of Berlin, communist control of Eastern Europe, and proxy wars in Africa, Latin America, and Indochina, Nixon believed that the time had come for rapprochement. To America's adversaries, he called for "peaceful competition," cooperation to "reduce the burden of arms," and "years of patient and prolonged diplomacy." He offered his "sacred commitment" to devote his office and energies to "the cause of peace" and to join with the communist world to "explore the reaches of space" and to "lift up" the poor and the hungry. "Let all nations know that during this administration our lines of communication will be open," he declared. "We seek an open world—open to ideas, open to the exchange of goods and people—a world in which no people, great or small, will live in angry isolation."[39]

These calls for "peaceful negotiation" and "prolonged diplomacy" with the Soviets were somewhat surprising coming from the man who had built his political career as a staunch anticommunist. Running for Congress in 1946, he accused his opponent, Representative Jerry Voorhis, a popular Democrat who had earned a record as one of the nation's better known New Dealers, as being soft on communism because he received support from the radical California Political Action Committee.[40] Nixon won the election by more than fifteen thousand votes and never forgot the lesson of impugning his political opponents with the "communist" label. In 1948, as a member of the House Un-American Activities Committee, he aggressively investigated Alger Hiss, a former State Department official accused of passing government secrets to the Soviets during the 1930s.[41] And in 1950, during his Senate campaign against Helen Gahagan Douglas, Nixon gave speeches coupling the liberal congresswoman's name with that of Hiss and distributed "pink sheets" showing that Douglas and Vito Marcantonio, a socialist-leaning congressman from East Harlem, had cast 254 identical votes in the House of Representatives. Nixon had also sided with Marcantonio more than one hundred times, but it did not matter. The tactic earned Douglas the label of "The Pink Lady" and vaulted Nixon into the senate.[42]

As the vice presidential candidate on the 1952 Republican ticket, moreover, Nixon continued to employ his red-baiting tactics. In speeches and appearances across the country he accused the Truman administration, and particularly Secretary of State Dean Acheson, of suffering from "colorblindness, a form of pink eye towards the communist threat in the United States," and accused Adlai Stevenson, the Democratic presidential nominee, of having received a "PhD from Dean Acheson's College of Cowardly Communist Containment."[43] Yet it was his "Kitchen Debate" with Soviet Premier Nikita Khrushchev that truly cemented Nixon as a fierce anticommunist and cold warrior. Touring the opening of a US exhibition in Moscow in 1959, the vice president stood virtually toe-to-toe with the Soviet leader, at one point prodding his finger in Khrushchev's chest for emphasis, arguing the merits of capitalism over the communist system. Although the outcome of the "debate" was largely inconclusive, the American people hailed Nixon for standing his ground against the Soviet dictator.[44]

Less than a decade after his impromptu exchange with Khrushchev, however, Nixon had largely softened his anticommunist rhetoric. Traveling the world as a private citizen and witnessing repeated crises with the Soviet Union and their allies had convinced the former vice president that the American people were living in a "new world"—a world with new leaders, new people, and new ideas. The giants of the postwar era—Winston Churchill, Konrad Adenauer, Joseph Stalin, Jawaharlal Nehru, Khrushchev, and Sukarno—had all left the stage. No longer was Western Europe economically and militarily dependent on the United States, as it was for nearly a decade after the war, nor could the communist world be seen as "monolithic," given the public rift between the Soviet Union and the People's Republic of China. Most important, the United States had lost its atomic monopoly and had pursued an unpopular war in Southeast Asia, causing it to lose much of its international prestige. "Twenty years ago, after our great World War II victory, we were respected throughout the world," Nixon said in 1967, but "today, hardly a day goes by when our flag is not spit upon, a library burned, an embassy stoned some place in the world. In fact, you don't have to leave the United States to find examples."[45]

Taking the "long view," Nixon believed that the United States needed a fundamental reappraisal of its foreign policy, particularly in moving toward more normal relations with the Soviet Union. Among the many reasons that impelled this change was the fact that by the late 1960s the Soviets had reached strategic parity in nuclear weapons with the United States. Both superpowers, therefore, needed to resolve their differences through negotiation and avoid crises that could lead to US-Soviet conflict. Equally important, Nixon believed, was the fact that the Kremlin had vastly increased its influence around the word while the United States appeared to be losing friends. The Soviets, for example, had a major presence in the Arab states while the United States had none, and important American allies, led by West Germany and France, increasingly sought to improve their relations with Moscow. The Soviets, moreover, still possessed considerable influence in Fidel Castro's Cuba, a constant thorn in America's side, while Eastern Europe remained largely under Soviet control.[46]

But it was Nixon's desire to extricate America from Vietnam, perhaps more than any factor, that necessitated a strategy of détente. By any objective analysis, there was simply no way to end the Vietnam War without Soviet cooperation. As late as 1968, the Soviets were providing 100 percent of the oil and 85 percent of all "sophisticated" military equipment for the North Vietnamese forces, including such modern weapons as surface-to-air missiles (SAMs), fighter airplanes, and tanks. The Soviets also had several thousand technicians and "advisers" supporting the Vietnamese communists, some of them operating antiaircraft batteries and shooting down US aircraft.[47] As long as Moscow continued to supply Hanoi with these weapons and send its forces to the region to assist North Vietnam, the Vietnam War could continue indefinitely. "It was often said that the key to a Vietnam settlement lay in Moscow and Peking rather than Hanoi," Nixon later wrote. "Without continuous and massive aid from either or both of the communist giants, the leaders of North Vietnam would not have been able to carry on the war for a few months."[48]

Although Nixon clearly had his own reasons for improving relations with Moscow, détente had its antecedents elsewhere. President Eisenhower, for example, invited Khrushchev to Camp David and his private Gettysburg farm in an effort to lesson Cold War tensions.[49] After the Cuban Missile Crisis, President Kennedy began negotiations with Moscow that led to a Nuclear Test Ban Treaty.[50] And President Johnson had called for discussions with Moscow on such issues as arms control, mutual and balanced force reductions in Germany, scientific and cultural exchanges, and the liberalization of trade and travel restrictions between East and West. He also held a major summit with Premier Kosygin at Glassboro, New Jersey, to improve the prospects for a lasting peace with the Soviet Union.[51] European leaders, moreover, including France's Charles de Gaulle and Germany's Willy Brandt, had pursued rapprochement with the Eastern bloc in response to domestic pressure for change.[52] By 1968, in fact, with domestic unrest spreading globally, world leaders had a "common urge" for international stability.[53]

But unlike these earlier efforts, which often collapsed at the first sign of disagreement, Nixon made détente a priority. He realized when he entered office that there were unique circumstances, including the militarization of the Sino-Soviet split and the Kremlin's need to expand trade with the United States and the major Western powers, which allowed for improvement in US-Soviet relations that were unavailable to his predecessors. Soon after his election, he informed President Nikolai Podgorny that the American and Soviet people must work together "in a spirit of mutual respect" and "on the basis of special responsibility for the peace of the world," and had his national security adviser, Henry Kissinger, convey to Soviet officials that under Nixon this would be "an era of negotiation not confrontation."[54]

Although many of the president's critics, especially from his own Republican party, argued that negotiating with the Soviet Union demonstrated America's weakness, Nixon and Kissinger maintained that negotiations with the Kremlin were the most effective means of "containing" the Soviet Union. Whereas the Truman and Eisenhower administrations had treated power and diplomacy as two distinct elements in phases of policy and had often failed to negotiate from positions of strength, and the Kennedy and Johnson administrations had relied heavily on "crisis management," Nixon and Kissinger wanted to use negotiations with the communist world to lay the foundation for a "long-range" American foreign policy. They understood that the limits of the nuclear era meant that negotiations with a nuclear power could no longer wait until one side achieved the unattainable "situation of strength." As the historian John Lewis Gaddis has succinctly described the Nixon-Kissinger strategy, negotiations were not in themselves a sign of weakness. "Properly managed," wrote Gaddis, "with a view to the identification of common interest as well as the frank recognition of irreconcilable antagonisms, they could become the primary means of building a stable world order, not simply a luxury to be enjoyed once stability had been achieved."[55]

Nixon did not offer a blueprint for what issues would be at the center of US-Soviet negotiations, but it was clear that discussions regarding a Middle East peace settlement would play an important role in improving relations with Moscow. True, by itself an Arab-Israeli peace agreement could not bring about US-Soviet détente. Even if Washington and Moscow succeeded in producing a settlement, it would not necessarily improve US-Soviet relations. But the absence of Arab-Israeli peace, and a superpower confrontation in the Middle East, which was extremely likely if another war erupted in the region, meant that progress on the issues central to détente's success—arms limitation, the prevention of nuclear warfare, scientific and cultural agreements, trade, Berlin and Vietnam—would come to an end.

Détente, therefore, was held hostage to the politics of the Arab-Israeli conflict.

From the outset of his administration, therefore, Nixon made it clear that he viewed the problems in the Middle East not just as a conflict between Arabs and Israelis but between the Soviets and Americans as well. "I consider it a powder keg—very explosive—it needs to be defused," he said during his first press conference on January 27, "because the next explosion in the Middle East I think, could involve a confrontation between the nuclear powers—which we want to avoid.[56] Helmut Sonnenfeldt, a Soviet expert on the NSC staff, concurred with the president's analysis. "The US needed to remain in touch with the Soviets on the Middle East," he wrote in a briefing paper to the president, "because it may be one . . . way of preventing renewed large-scale hostilities with a potential for a direct US-Soviet military clash," and because the Soviets possessed "great influence" with Egypt, "the key to any tranquilization of Middle East tensions and dangers."[57]

Nixon, therefore, made one of his first priorities as president to engage Moscow in negotiations leading to a Middle East settlement. During two NSC meetings in February 1969, wide agreement emerged that the United States should respond favorably to a December 30 proposal by the Soviets to begin a bilateral dialogue on an Arab-Israeli settlement.[58] This move would clearly be resisted by Israeli leaders, who would see this as the beginning of an effort to impose a settlement on the parties, and it would mean that Washington and Moscow would take over the critical part of the negotiations from the United Nations. But there were few better alternatives available to produce an agreement. "The rationale for the [Two Power] approach is that the parties will not otherwise move," an NSC study concluded. "Such bilateral discussions are essential to lessen the risk of misunderstanding and miscalculation . . . and that there may be terms of settlement which are just, reasonable, and tolerable to the moderates on both sides."[59]

Following an NSC meeting on February 1, Kissinger sent Nixon a follow-up memorandum summarizing the policy recommendations made at the meeting. He made it clear that the Two Power forum, while not a perfect venue for resolving Arab-Israeli disagreements, would "position the

Middle East into the whole context of East-West relations with maximum control and linkage to other negotiations such as those on force limitations." Kissinger then urged the president to particularly concentrate on US-Soviet arrangements, "which would slow the pace of the Near Eastern arms race and serve as a restraining influence on the nations in the area—at least arrangements which would assure U.S.-U.S.S.R. disengagement if hostilities broke out again."[60]

Nixon's decision to move forward with the Two Power talks was not simply the best of three bad options when dealing with the Middle East, as Kissinger somewhat implied in his memoirs, nor did Nixon choose this avenue to avoid a confrontation over policy with the State Department so early in his administration. Rather, the decision reflected Nixon's view that the Arab-Israeli dispute could be solved only by the participation of the superpowers. "I believe that the willingness of our two countries to exert a responsible and beneficial influence in the Middle East is an essential element in building the confidence that must be the basis of serious and productive negotiations," he wrote Soviet leaders after making his decision to proceed with the Two Power talks.[61] The decision was also an indication of the president's broader strategic vision of how negotiations with the Soviet Union were going to be conducted as the two countries moved "from con-frontation to negotiation." As Nixon told Secretary of State Rogers, whom he had selected to lead the Two Power dialogue, when dealing with the Soviet Union the "crucial issues" of the day—by which he meant Vietnam, the Middle East, and arms control, among others—were "fundamentally interrelated."[62]

In the Spirit of Glassboro

In Moscow, Nixon's calls for an "era of negotiation" and eagerness to discuss the Middle East were naturally received with considerable skepti-cism. The Politburo, in fact, unanimously believed that his "classic anticommunism" would mean "hard times" for Soviet-American relations.[63] The Soviet ambassador to the United States, Anatoly Dobrynin, also had his doubts about the new president's commitment to détente. Having served as Moscow's ambassador in Washington since 1962, Dobrynin knew that

Nixon's career "was imbued with anti-Sovietism, anti-communism, and militarism, and he had skillfully used irresponsible and demagogic attacks on his political rivals and others he considered fair game to advance his position."[64] However, instead of rejecting Nixon's call for negotiations, Soviet leaders recognized the need for a thaw in superpower relations, even while questioning whether Nixon was the man they could work with to bring about such changes. To Nixon's call for an "era of negotiations," Foreign Minister Andrei Gromyko replied later in the year that "we for our part our ready."[65]

Foremost among Soviet reasons for pursuing détente with Nixon was the growing threat of China to its far east. Although China was once an important ally to Moscow, the Sino-Soviet alliance collapsed between 1956 and 1966 due to substantive differences regarding Marxism-Leninism, disagreements over "peaceful coexistence" with the capitalist West, and competition for leadership of the socialist world.[66] In its infancy, the Sino-Soviet rivalry remained a largely ideological and political affair, but by the end of the 1960s, the split turned "hot," as border clashes erupted between the armies of two communist giants along the Ussuri River.[67] By 1969, the Soviets had placed twenty-five heavily armed divisions on the border with China, far beyond the requirements for border security, suggesting to CIA analysts that Moscow may initiate "offensive operations" against north China "should the need arise."[68] That same year, General Secretary Leonid Brezhnev condemned the Chinese as not merely "renegades" but "open enemies of the Soviet state."[69]

Facing continued tension on its border with China, the Soviets believed that hostility toward the United States and the West should be muted. In part this decision stemmed from the fact that the Kremlin wanted to attract new allies in order to "contain" the Chinese.[70] But the Soviets also feared that if they failed to normalize relations with Washington, the United States would soon find ways to use the Sino-Soviet rivalry against Moscow.[71] This concern was not entirely without foundation. Following the Ussuri River incident there were calls inside the White House for the United States to recognize Albania, which supported the PRC during the Sino-Soviet split, and to promote West German contact with Communist China as a means of making the Soviets "nervous" over a possible US-Chinese deal.[72]

Recognizing the US would exploit the situation, Gromyko circulated a telegram to Soviet embassies around the world making clear the need to avoid "pressure on the USSR from two flanks—NATO and China"; Soviet policy henceforth should "manifest restraint, moderation, and flexibility in relations with the US, [and] to refrain from complications with her which are not dictated by our important national interests."[73]

In addition to using détente to contain the Chinese threat, the Kremlin also viewed negotiations with the new president as an effective way to improve its global image following its invasion of Czechoslovakia in August 1968. In the short term, Soviet officials viewed the use of force to suppress the "Prague Spring"—the reform efforts to de-Stalinize Czechoslovakia and purse an independent course from Moscow—as a necessary move to reassert Soviet control over the Eastern bloc and to prevent "falling dominoes" in Central Europe.[74] But in the long run, the overwhelming force and the blatant disregard for Czechoslovakia's sovereignty did more to cripple Soviet foreign policy than it did to strengthen it. Many communist countries, including China, condemned the use of troops against a socialist country, and the invasion soured the emerging US-Soviet détente. President Johnson canceled his impending visit to the Soviet Union and, according to historian Thomas Schwartz, issued a "clear warning" to Moscow to discontinue the "Brezhnev Doctrine" by taking action against either Romania or Yugoslavia, countries that had both split from the traditional orthodoxy of Moscow's foreign policy.[75]

Finally, there were a number of economic pressures pushing the Soviets in the direction of a détente with the United States. The financial burden of the nuclear arms race and the high costs of maintaining large armies in both the east and the west were no longer sustainable. Many Soviet leaders, moreover, wanted to purchase Western technology to help modernize their chemical and automobile industries and sought to increase the rate of Western investment for future growth.[76] And there was recognition among the top echelons of the Politburo that the Kremlin needed to be more receptive to popular demands for material improvement, especially in the areas of food and housing.[77]

Faced with the overwhelming combination of foreign and domestic pressures to improve relations with Washington, the Kremlin undertook a

President Johnson learns from Soviet ambassador Anatoly Dobrynin of the Soviet Union's invasion of Czechoslovakia to crush the Prague Spring uprising, August 20, 1968. (*Corbis*)

major reassessment of its foreign policy objectives to better meet these challenges. On September 16, 1968, Gromyko presented the Politburo with a paper entitled "An Assessment of the State of Foreign Policy and the State of Soviet-American relations," which in effect outlined the future Soviet foreign policy doctrine. The document called for a combination of "firmness with flexibility" with the United States and for "actively using means of diplomatic maneuver." Under certain conditions, Gromyko explained to his colleagues, a "dialogue" could be initiated with the United States on a broad range of issues, preparations for which "should be conducted systematically and purposely even now."[78] The Politburo unanimously approved the paper and presaged the course of Soviet foreign policy and the scope of Soviet-American relations during the Nixon years.[79]

Following Nixon's election, and in line with Gromyko's call for "flexibility" in Moscow's relations with Washington, Soviet leaders took a number of steps to signify their desire to improve relations with the United States. They instructed their media to avoid personal attacks on the president-elect; invoked "the sanction of Lenin" on the need for friendly US-Soviet relations; and indicated their readiness to discuss strategic weapons limitation.[80] On December 30, in response to Nixon's early signals to Moscow to begin an era of negotiations, Soviet chargé Yuri Tcherniakov presented Robert Ellsworth, senior adviser to the president-elect, a proposal for an Arab-Israeli peace agreement that could be arranged jointly between Washington and Moscow. Although the proposal maintained the extreme Arab line that Israel should withdraw its forces from all Arab territories, to the borders "prior" to June 5, 1967, and showed no flexibility for any modification of frontiers, the plan demonstrated to the new administration that the Soviets viewed Arab-Israeli discussions as a venue to test America's willingness to engage Moscow on areas of mutual concern.[81] Moreover, by offering the proposal so soon after Nixon's election, the Soviet officials wanted to demonstrate that they remained committed to the views expressed by Kosygin and Johnson during the Glassboro summit the previous year, which highlighted the prospects for détente.

Two days later, emphasizing the importance Moscow attached to Tcherniakov's proposal, the Soviet leadership sent Boris Sedov, a KGB agent masquerading as counselor of the Soviet embassy, to meet privately with Kissinger at the Pierre Hotel in New York, headquarters of Nixon's transition team. Sedov explained that the Soviets' recent overture on the Middle East should be viewed "as a sign of good faith" toward the new administration and an indication of his government's determination to begin an era of "peaceful coexistence." Moscow realized that fundamental theoretical and practical differences remained between their two countries, but that should not interfere with the gradual achievement of agreements on a number of problems, including the Middle East, disarmament, and ratification of the nonproliferation treaty. Before the meeting ended, the KGB operative requested some reference to "open communications" be included in Nixon's inaugural address as a signal that the president would carry through on his promises to begin a new era of relations with the Soviet Union.[82]

After hearing Nixon's call on January 20 that "our lines of communication" will be open to "all" nations, the Kremlin moved aggressively to respond in kind.[83] In early February, during a "special review" of Soviet-American relations held at a government dacha outside Moscow, Soviet leaders drafted a message for Nixon that intended to show they "were full of goodwill and eager to move forward on a broad front." The Soviet leadership indicated their willingness to answer questions on Vietnam, or "any other political problem on [your] mind," and urged the president to begin joint negotiations on the Middle East to avoid "most undesirable consequences" in the region.[84] "We are confident that if the Soviet Union and the United States . . . make full use of their possibilities and influence in order to find just and lasting settlement in the Middle East it will also greatly contribute to the general relaxation of international tensions."[85]

When Dobrynin brought the message to the White House on February 17, there could be little doubt that Nixon shared Moscow's desire to begin negotiations not just on the Middle East but on other areas of joint concern, including arms control, Vietnam, and a summit. According to Dobrynin, Nixon nodded his head "vigorously" to the passages in the Soviet note that "expressed our readiness to conduct a comprehensive exchange of views with him and our readiness for a joint, constructive dialogue," and he noted that it was apparent that, on the whole, Nixon liked the "balanced, constructive tone" of the Soviet statements. "Those views, he said, fully correspond to his own thoughts on the main point: the leaders of the two great powers must maintain a frank dialogue based on mutual trust and an understanding of the complex and important role that both our countries play in the modern world."[86]

After Nixon read the Soviet note, Dobrynin emphasized that his government would use its "influence" on the Arab states to arrive at a solution to the ongoing problem in the region and reiterated the Soviet desire to begin talks with the United States on the Middle East. Under no circumstances did the Soviet government believe a solution could be achieved overnight, he assured Nixon, but a beginning should be made. "While other subjects might be discussed," said Dobrynin, "the Middle East and arms control . . . were among the most important which should engage our early attention."[87]

Nixon, Rogers, and Kissinger

Given the importance the Soviets attached to the bilateral discussions on the Middle East, Nixon's decision to let the State Department, not Kissinger, lead the Two Power talks was somewhat surprising. From his time as vice president, Nixon had developed a strong antipathy toward the State Department and members of the Foreign Service. Kissinger recalled that during his initial interview with Nixon in November 1968, the president-elect told him that the Foreign Service had "disdained" him as vice president and "ignored him the moment he was out of office."[88] But Nixon's contempt for the Foreign Service went even deeper. He believed that the department was riddled with Ivy League liberals who voted Democratic, were prone to leaks, and had no loyalty to him. He made it clear to Kissinger that as president he would "take the responsibility for cleaning up the State Department" and did not hide the fact that before he left office, his "one legacy is to ruin the Foreign Service. I mean ruin it—the old Foreign Service—and to build a new one. I'm going to do it."[89]

Nixon's distrust of Foggy Bottom was so palpable that in the early weeks of his administration he not only restructured the NSC system to ensure that institutional power in foreign policy shifted to the White House[90] but instructed Kissinger to establish a private channel of communication directly with the Soviet embassy to avoid having to involve State Department bureaucrats in confidential exchanges between the White House and the Kremlin. According to Dobrynin, the president stressed that he attached "special significance" to "confidential channels" through which he and the Soviet government could exchange views "frankly and informally on various delicate and complex matters" and that would be known to only a "very small circle" of people on the US side. Of course, Nixon professed that the establishment of "The Channel," as it became known, did not mean he was "downplaying" the role of Secretary of State Rogers. "He is my closest aide for foreign policy affairs," he assured Dobrynin, and "what's more, he is a long-time personal friend of mine, from whom there will be no secrets in the area of relations with the Soviet government."[91] But Dobrynin had been in Washington long enough and, as an experienced diplomat who had often dealt with presidential emissaries rather than the

President Richard M. Nixon, Secretary of State William P. Rogers, and National Security Advisor Henry A. Kissinger aboard Air Force One. *(NARA)*

secretary of state, could see right through Nixon's remarks.

Scholars have often speculated that in turning the Middle East over to Rogers, Nixon believed that Kissinger "could not be sufficiently objective about Israel" because of his Jewish origins and that any participation in the intense negotiations of the Arab-Israeli conflict raised "uncomfortable questions" about his loyalties.[92] This view is not entirely without foundation. In his memoirs, Nixon confessed that he made this decision "partly" because he felt that Kissinger's Jewish background would "put him at a disadvantage during the delicate negotiations" for the reopening of diplomatic relations with the Arab states.[93] Others have correctly noted that the president often "associated" Kissinger with the Jewish political lobby in the United States, groups he vehemently distrusted.[94] Even Kissinger acknowledged that as a Jew who had lost thirteen members of his family during the Holocaust, he could hardly "do anything that would betray Israel."[95]

It is also fair to point out that Nixon, a Quaker from the West Coast, was uneasy about Kissinger's Jewish background. "Kissinger had to walk a tightrope, accentuating the general 'lessons' of his personal experience without mentioning the specific attributes that helped to shape it," historian Jeremi Suri concluded. "He had to articulate the wisdom derived from his life as a German Jew, without explicit reference to German and Jewish characteristics. Nixon contributed to the difficulty of this endeavor. . . . Although he made frequent (usually negative) references to Kissinger's Jewish background, he encouraged Kissinger to remain silent about his Jewishness for fear of the reactions among the public and among his patron."[96]

Although Kissinger's "Jewishness" may have contributed to Nixon's decision to leave the initial Middle East discussions to Rogers, it was not a *deciding* factor and thus has been overstated by scholars. Nixon had other Jews on his staff, including Arthur Burns, his chief domestic counselor (and later appointed by Nixon as the chairman of the Federal Reserve); Herbert Stein, head of the Council of Economic Advisors; Ed David, chief science adviser; Leonard Garment, the president's cultural adviser and, in Garment's words, representative "for all things Jewish"; and speechwriter William Safire. Safire recalled that Nixon did not prevent him from writing policy statements regarding Israel because he was Jewish and argued that "linking the attitude of Jews towards Nixon and vice versa to a separate subject like Israel is unfair and exaggerated."[97]

Nor did leaders of the Arab states, who would have been the most concerned about Kissinger's religious affiliation, display any hesitation about meeting with Kissinger or indicate that Kissinger should not partake in the discussions that dealt with Israel. In fact, the records are quite clear that throughout 1969, and in the midst of the Two Power talks, Arab leaders, including King Hussein of Jordan and Egyptian foreign minister Mahmoud Riad, often met privately with Kissinger at the White House and would come to Kissinger when they felt they could not get what they wanted out of the State Department. Egyptian president Anwar Sadat acknowledged that he preferred to deal with Kissinger instead of Rogers and worked aggressively to establish his own private channel with Kissinger.[98]

Several factors, therefore, led Nixon to place the Middle East negotiations in Rogers's hands. First, the president knew that with Kissinger almost entirely preoccupied with trying to extricate the United States from Vietnam, engaged in disarmament talks with the Soviet Union, and attempting to pave the way for the rapprochement with the People's Republic of China, he simply would not have the necessary time to be involved in the day-to-day Arab-Israeli negotiations. "I felt that the Middle East required full time and expert attention," Nixon admitted in his memoirs. As he told Kissinger, "You and I will have enough on our plate."[99] Nixon also believed, however, that because the chances of getting an Arab-Israeli settlement were remote, especially when the Arabs refused to hold direct discussions with Israel, he felt it best to distance the White House from the negotiations. During a trip to Europe in February 1969, Nixon confessed to France's Charles De Gaulle that he was "somewhat pessimistic on the Middle East" and fearful that even with a settlement, "Radical Forces" could scuttle an agreement.[100]

Nixon also knew that Kissinger opposed the idea of the Two Power forum to resolve the Arab-Israeli dispute and therefore felt it best to leave the discussions to State Department officials who would purse the talks more aggressively. As part of the president's concept of "linkage," Kissinger argued that the United States should proceed slowly on the Middle East in order to pressure the Soviets on Vietnam. Since Moscow needed an agreement for their Arabs clients far more than Washington needed a settlement for Israel, the Soviets would have to show some flexibility.[101] This, Kissinger believed, could be done in the informal "backchannel" negotiations with Dobrynin where Moscow had more room to maneuver. But the State Department, in its eagerness to achieve an Arab-Israeli settlement and deliver an early accomplishment to Nixon's foreign policy agenda, wanted to keep Arab-Israeli issues on a separate track so as not to allow US-Soviet disagreements on Vietnam or disarmament from thwarting a Middle East peace agreement.

More serious than the choice of forum, Kissinger maintained, was the "fundamental premise" behind the Two Power talks that the United States would have to deliver Israeli agreement.[102] "The Arabs assume—wrongly but irrevocably—that we can make Israel do what we wish," he explained to Nixon on March 5, while the Soviets, who knew the limits of their own influence in Cairo and Damascus, and therefore understood the limits of American influence in Jerusalem, would nevertheless "find too much propaganda advantage in our support for Israel to admit the truth publicly."[103] Even if Washington and Moscow succeeded in composing a joint peace plan, based on or near the frontiers of June 4, 1967, it was bound to "blow up" with both sides. "The borders were certain to be unacceptable to Israel, and the Arabs, in Nasser's current frame of mind were not ready to make the necessary commitments to peace," Kissinger argued. "It would not improve our relations with the Arabs; it would strengthen the position of the Soviets . . . [who] would first get credit for having pushed us this far and then accuse us of not going far enough and not delivering Israel on what we had promised."[104]

It should also be noted that in leaving the Two Power talks to Rogers, the president had every confidence in the secretary of state's abilities to negotiate with the Soviets and deal with the delicate negotiations of the Middle East. Nixon had known Rogers for more than twenty years and had often sought Rogers's counsel at pivotal moments in his political career. Rogers, for example, had encouraged Nixon to pursue Alger Hiss in 1948, helped him write the "Checkers" speech in 1952, and was by his side following Eisenhower's heart attack in 1955. Having witnessed him in times of "great crisis," Nixon knew Rogers was best when the "going was hardest," felt he was a "superb negotiator," and had faith in his sound judgment. "I would put him up against any man in the world today that I have met, around the world in my many travels" Nixon declared in 1968.[105] Bryce Harlow, a senior adviser to Nixon, similarly recalled that when Nixon contemplated naming Rogers secretary of state, it was agreed that Rogers would be able to handle the discussions with the Russians, Arabs, Israelis, Vietnamese, or whoever faced him across the table. "He's cold, mean, and tough," Harlow maintained. Asked years later by journalist Seymour Hersh why, then, did Rogers eventually allow the State Department to be "over-run" by Kissinger, Harlow simply replied: "Rogers didn't try. He could have whipped Kissinger easily."[106]

Rogers, though, would not be handling the Two Power talks alone. With him was Joseph J. Sisco, his indefatigable assistant secretary of state for Near Eastern and South Asian Affairs (NEA). A twenty-year veteran of the State Department by the time he took over NEA, Sisco possessed an intimate knowledge of both the Soviet Union and the Arab-Israeli dispute. He grew up in Chicago, the son of Italian immigrants, and later studied history at

Knox College in Galesburg, Illinois. After serving in the army during World War II, he earned a doctorate in Soviet affairs from the University of Chicago and then spent a year as a CIA analyst before joining the State Department's United Nations Bureau. In 1965, Secretary of State Dean Rusk appointed Sisco assistant secretary for International Organization Affairs. In that capacity, he spent six months in 1967 at the United Nations as Ambassador Arthur Goldberg's principal assistant working on the draft of United Nations Security Council Resolution 242, and the following year he became the chief US mediator in the Middle East.[107]

Sisco wanted to leave the State Department at the end of the Johnson administration, but he accepted Rogers's invitation to stay on and take over NEA. Although he only knew the incoming secretary of state from a brief stint Rogers served as a UN delegate on the South-East Asia committee in 1967, Sisco quickly became one of Rogers's most trusted advisers. Not only was he Rogers's point man on the Middle East, but he played an important role of resolving many of the bitter disagreements between the White House and the State Department during the Nixon administration. "He probably spent as much time mediating between Rogers and me as between the Arabs and Israelis," Kissinger recalled."[108] Sisco had a reputation as a fierce and "ruthless" negotiator, and according to Kissinger, his "fits of enthusiasm" and boundless energy often made him a "menace" in his job.[109] For all the complaints, though, Sisco was the right man for the job, and proved to be an asset to Nixon, Rogers, and Kissinger.

The principal drawback to leaving the Two Power talks to the State Department was that it raised doubts inside the Kremlin whether Nixon took the negotiations seriously. Indeed, having closely observed the first six weeks of the Nixon administration, Dobrynin quickly concluded that a "clash of views" as well as a "struggle for influence" for Nixon's ear existed between Rogers and Kissinger. By virtue of his previous experience as a professor and specialist in international affairs and having at his disposal a certain "stock" of ideas with respect to the principal direction of US foreign policy, Kissinger was the "prime moving force" in shaping foreign policy in the administration, Dobrynin argued: "His conduct is marked by maneuvering and by a noticeable desire not to aggravate the situation, in both international and domestic political affairs, and to maintain good relations with everybody as long as possible." Thus, it was possible that by engaging Rogers instead of Kissinger on the Middle East, the Soviets were embarking on a wasted effort.[110]

Still, Dobrynin held out hope that even though Rogers's views carried less weight than Kissinger's, the Two Power talks would afford Washington and Moscow the opportunity to conduct a "concrete, business-like" exchange of views that could lead to further cooperation between the two countries down the road. In no way did he believe that the Middle East was the subject of "greatest interest" inside the White House—that, of course, being left to Vietnam—nor did he believe that the Kremlin should overestimate Washington's readiness for a quick resolution of the Middle East issue, since experience showed that the new US government continued to "look over its shoulder" at Israel. But unlike negotiations on Vietnam, or even disarmament, Dobrynin believed the Two Power talks gave Moscow "certain opportunities for influencing Nixon" that could not be ignored. With bilateral relations between the United States and the USSR in a "suspended" state, "substantial progress" toward a US-Soviet détente could not be made until "positive results" had been achieved in resolving at least some major problems, such as the Middle East.[111]

The Two Power Talks

For all the good intentions heading into the negotiations, the Two Power talks were bound to fail. Although Washington and Moscow clearly wanted an agreement to promote détente and avoid the possibility of a superpower confrontation in the Middle East, neither the Arabs or the Israelis appeared interested in having of a "big power" solution "imposed" on the parties. For Israel, the timing of the negotiations was particularly bad. In February 1969, Prime Minister Levi Eshkol died of a sudden heart attack, making it virtually impossible for Israeli leaders to make any concessions to the Arabs heading into a new election cycle. Eshkol's successor, Golda Meir, also had bitter memories from the events of 1957, when, after the Suez-Sinai war, the US and USSR had compelled Israel to withdraw its forces from the Sinai Peninsula without concessions from the Arabs in return. She was "justly apprehensive" that the Soviet leadership could be expected to "indulge a strongly pro-Arab bias" while the United States would at best be "evenhanded."[112]

On March 4, Yitzhak Rabin, Israel's ambassador to the United States, raised concerns about the proposed Two Power talks to Henry Kissinger. A hero of the 1967 war, Rabin did not mince words, and he generally brooded over every effort the United States made to get involved in the Arab-Israeli dispute. "Yitzhak Rabin had many extraordinary qualities," Kissinger later wrote, "but the gift of human relations was not one of them."[113] Yet Rabin had a point on this occasion. Not only did the Two Power formula violate Israel's desire to negotiate directly with the Arabs, but Israel had "no faith whatsoever in outside guarantees." Specifically, Rabin felt that Moscow would tolerate Arab violations of any agreement while the Nixon administration, in its effort to avoid creating obstacles for détente, would "hesitate" to confront the Soviets directly in such a situation.[114] More important, the ambassador argued that there was no way to achieve a settlement without it being "imposed" on Israel from the outside." Said Rabin: "We knew perfectly well that if an agreement were reached between the two powers, each would be obliged to 'induce' its 'client' to accept it."[115]

Foreign Minister Abba Eban echoed Rabin's remarks when he arrived in Washington for talks with Nixon, Rogers, and Kissinger two weeks later. Eban took "vigorous exception" to the very concept of the Two Power talks on the ground that "the deck" would be stacked against Israel. He stressed that by its very participation in such negotiations, the United States precluded the one Israeli demand that was a prerequisite for any peace agreement—the insistence on direct negotiations and a joint peace treaty with the Arab states. During several meeting at the State Department in mid-March, Rogers and Sisco attempted to assuage the foreign minister by assuring him the United States favored maintaining the cease-fire lines until they could be replaced by a "permanent peace" and that they did not see themselves "as merely your lawyers, and we don't want the Soviets to be the Arabs' advocates."[116] But Eban was not convinced. "What is the purpose of all of this exercise?" he asked Rogers. "Nothing good will come of it."[117]

For their part, the Egyptians seemed more interested in taking back their land by force rather than have the Soviets negotiate a settlement on their behalf. In March 1969, President Gamal Abdel Nasser renounced the UN-decreed cease-fire that ended the Six-Day War and unleashed a heavy artillery bombardment against Israeli forces in the Suez Canal zone, beginning the seventeen-month War of Attrition. The move came as a direct response to Israel's construction in the winter of 1968–1969 of the "Bar-Lev Line"—a chain of heavily fortified bunkers built along the east bank of the Suez Canal and named after army chief of staff Chaim Bar-Lev. Nasser viewed the defensive line as Israel's attempt to convert the Canal into a de facto border, and he reasoned that if he did not quickly destroy the fortifications, it would be nearly impossible for Egyptian forces to cross the Suez in the event of another war.[118]

The fact that Nasser renewed hostilities less than two years after the Six Day War and only days before the Two Power talks commenced also signaled that Egypt had no confidence in the Soviets' ability to deliver a favorable agreement to the Arab states. Indeed, if the discussions regarding Resolution 242 after the 1967 war had taught the Arabs anything, it was that Moscow would compromise their interests to avoid a confrontation with the United States. The Egyptians, moreover, were well aware that the Soviet leadership, facing increased problems with China to the east, and seeking improved relations with the US, would be eager to reach a compromise with Washington at the expense of their Arab clients. According to Dr. Mahmoud Fawzi, special adviser to Nasser on foreign affairs, the Kremlin seemed to have reached a point of "diminishing returns" in its relationship with the Arabs. "When a friend can't help his friend either by making peace or by the use of force, then he gradually loses his credibility," he said.[119]

The objections to the Two Power talks from both Arabs and the Israelis, however, did not stop the negotiations. Beginning on March 18, Sisco and Dobrynin held their first formal meeting at the State Department. From the outset, it was clear that the Soviet ambassador, despite a strong reputation as a "highly intelligent" negotiator with an "exceptional analytic ability,"[120] did not have a firm grasp of the delicate Arab-Israeli issues. He was a "cautious" negotiator, according to one study, "and it became obvious that Moscow was holding him on a tight leash."[121] Dobrynin often spoke in generalities, failed to offer any concrete proposals of what the Arabs states were prepared to offer in exchange for Israel's withdrawal from the occupied territories, and refused to commit the Soviets to anything beyond their December 30 proposal. Sisco was not much better. He, too, avoided specifics on how far the Israelis should withdraw, believing that the final borders could only be settled directly between the parties. Dobrynin complained to Moscow that the assistant secretary "was always speaking in the abstract about secure and recognized borders" and asserted that "talking to Sisco was getting to be a waste of time."[122] At one point during the discussions, Dobrynin directly asked Nixon to press for more cooperation from Sisco: "Why is your representative (Sisco) stubbornly avoiding concrete discussion of this issue during the current consultations?"[123]

Despite their initial frustrations, however, Sisco and Dobrynin continued to meet at least twice a week for more than two months. Although common ground emerged on moving toward a "just and lasting peace," direct participation of the parties in a future agreement, and Israel's right to exist as an independent state, large differences remained; the United States refused during the first six weeks to present a specific peace plan and feared that the Soviets were trying to build "loopholes" into any settlement. In the midst of the discussions, Harold Saunders, the Middle East expert on the NSC staff, explained to Kissinger that although the Sisco-Dobrynin channel seemed "useful," it also demonstrated the difficulty in getting the Kremlin to abandon the "face-saving legal fiction which makes it appear that the Arabs have committed themselves to nothing until the Israelis have withdrawn." In Saunders's estimate, the effort to achieve this fiction "feeds natural suspicion that Moscow is trying to build escape hatches into the settlement for later Arab use."[124]

The negotiations with Sisco also left Moscow frustrated that the talks were not having the desired impact on improving US-Soviet relations, nor did they appear to be easing Middle East tensions. On April 14, Dobrynin complained to Kissinger that while Moscow wanted to come to an understanding on the Middle East "as rapidly as possible," the Two Power talks were proceeding "too abstractly" and needed more concrete proposals. The Kremlin wanted the United States to produce a detailed plan—which would be kept in "strictest confidence" and could eventually be turned into a "joint offer" to both sides—that would spell out its position on the nature of Israeli troop withdrawals and "border rectification." Dobrynin insisted that his government would not haggle over the Golan Heights or the Gaza Strip, or whether the borders were thirty miles east or west of these territories, so long as both sides agreed. But "you must be specific," he said. "Why don't you write out a paragraph that tells us exactly what you want Nasser to say and if we agree with it, we will try to get them to accept it."[125]

The feeling on the US side appeared just as bleak. In mid-April, before an NSC review of Middle East policy, Secretary Rogers informed Nixon that although Dobrynin had conveyed Moscow's view "from the top" that the Soviets wanted the Two Power talks to succeed, it remained uncertain "just what the Soviets are up to." Rogers acknowledged that Dobrynin had introduced "certain modifications" to the December 30 Soviet plan that appeared on the surface to move toward the US position. But even with these minor concessions, he concluded, Washington and Moscow were "still some distance apart on such potentially critical questions," including the size of areas to be demilitarized and, more important, meeting Israel's "minimal requirements" of complete peace based on a contractual agreement with the Arab states.[126]

To avoid an early impasse, Rogers suggested that during the next round of Sisco-Dobrynin meetings the United States should surface a detailed plan for an Egyptian-Israeli settlement that would spell out US positions on borders, refugees, and enforcements provisions. Given Israel's opposition to many of the specific proposals, along with Arab objections to direct negotiations and their ambivalence about reconciling themselves to permanent peace with Israel, Rogers conceded that the odds were against the success of the proposed approach. At the same time, however, he believed that if the Americans and Soviets did not move forward with a proposal, the chances of the Arab-Israeli situation getting "out of control with a potential for ultimate US-Soviet involvement" would increase. "Even if we try and fail, we will be better off," Rogers concluded, "since we would have avoided the twin dangers of being isolated in support of Israel and of having a major break with Israel over failure to support her basic requirements of a contractual peace."[127]

After discussing the issue at an NSC meeting on April 25,[128] Nixon authorized the State Department to present its plan to the Soviets. The proposal, as meticulously unfolded by Sisco during three meetings with Dobrynin in early May, was strictly limited to an Egyptian-Israeli settlement. The Americans felt that there was no point in including Syria in any peace plan until its leaders accepted Resolution 242, and the United States could deal with Jordan separately since it was an American ally. Sisco made it clear that the main objectives of the settlement would be based on UN Resolution 242, a formal state of peace would exist, all claims or states of belligerency would end, including "terrorist raids," and the parties would agree to abide by the UN charter in settling future disputes.[129]

The main thrust of the proposal, however, had to deal with the withdrawal of Israeli forces from the occupied territories, future borders, and provisions for direct negotiations. Here, the US plan came up short on specifics and demonstrated that the Americans were unwilling at this point to take a clear stand on the location of the final frontiers. Although Sisco made it clear that the United States "would not support Israeli territorial aggrandizement" and that the former Egypt-Palestine border "is not necessarily excluded as the future border," the "outside powers," he argued, should not relieve Egypt and Israel from the responsibility of determining their own borders. In other words, the United States would leave the fundamental issue of the location of the secure and recognized boundary between Egypt and Israel directly to the parties. This may have fulfilled Israeli demands for direct negotiations with the Arabs, but it left Soviet leaders wondering why they had participated in two months of tedious negotiations if the US position boiled down to letting Egypt and Israel resolve everything instead of the Two Powers.[130]

Only on the issue of Sharm el-Sheikh did Sisco offer a concrete position. He informed the Soviet ambassador that because of Nasser's history of broken commitments about the free passage of through the Straits of Tiran, the United States expected Israel to maintain control of Sharm el-Sheikh in order to keep the Gulf of Aqaba open. Sisco told Dobrynin that this is a "critical point" to which the parties must find an answer. "The US does not want to return to 1967 when Nasser broke commitments obtained by the US and closed the straits."[131]

The State Department considered this only a "preliminary document" to be further developed with the Soviets and then presented as a "joint" US-USSR document to Egypt and Israel. Nevertheless, the proposal immediately met opposition from all sides because it was so abstract, omitted crucial details of the locations of the future Egyptian-Israeli borders, and contained no timetable for Israel's withdrawal. Rabin told Sisco on May 7 that the points were "generally negative, do not spell out what peace is, and contain no positive Arab obligation to peace."[132] Dobrynin, similarly, seized on the many weaknesses in the proposal, making it clear that Moscow would not consider a separate Egyptian-Israeli settlement if it were not linked to agreements for the Arabs, and insisting that the United States had omitted the "most important" question — withdrawal and boundaries. "All of Israel's demands are clearly stated," he said, but there were no important concessions to the Arabs. Egypt's reaction would be negative, and Moscow would almost certainly be unwilling to support a document that did not include guarantees that Israel would make similar agreements with the other Arab states.[133] "So far, the US document reflected the views of only one side — the Israelis — and if there is no more substance in our other points," he stressed, "we will be back where we were two months ago."[134]

The Kremlin kept the United States waiting in limbo for nearly six weeks while they consulted with the Egyptians and considered how to respond to the American proposal.[135] On June 17, the Soviets came back to the State Department with their own plan, their first since the beginning of the talks in March.[136] The counterproposal consisted largely of a recasting of the December 30 Soviet paper and showed little movement. After three months of discussions, the Kremlin still refused to agree to direct negotiations between the parties, a prerequisite for the Israelis; did not accept the US proposal for an acknowledgment by both sides to a formal state of peace; rejected the Arab obligation to control the fedayeen; dropped the US effort to end Arab sanctions against Israel; and stuck to their familiar position that Israel would have to withdraw to the pre–June 5, 1967, lines.[137]

Still, there were a few encouraging signs in the document. Moscow agreed that the Arabs would "respect and recognize Israel's sovereignty, territorial integrity, inviolability, and political independence," as well as Israel's right "to live in peace in secure and recognized boundaries without being subjected to threats or use of force." They affirmed Israeli passage through the Straits of Tiran and the Suez Canal and agreed to the stationing of UN troops in Gaza and Sharm el-Sheikh "on a fairly extended basis." These were much closer to the US and Israeli positions. On the whole, however, the document fell far short of what the United States had hoped and, as Saunders explained to Kissinger after his review of the proposal, left unanswered basic questions whether Moscow and Cairo were willing to "pay any serious price" for Israeli withdrawal from the occupied territories.[138]

After studying the counterproposal for several days, both the White House and the State Department concluded that the Soviets left "barely enough" room for further talks and therefore agreed to send Sisco to Moscow for another round of negotiations, this time with Foreign Minister Gromyko.[139] During their first session on July 14, Gromyko stressed the "very serious" Soviet intentions to make progress and made it clear that finding a "common language" on the Middle East would have a positive effect on US-USSR relations. In the meeting, Gromyko hinted that differences on refugees and the Suez Canal could be resolved and, to Sisco's surprise, did not make any "pitch" for total withdrawal of Israeli forces from the occupied territories.[140]

Still, when it came down to specifics, Sisco appeared to get no more out of Gromyko than he had with Dobrynin. According to the report he sent back to Washington, Gromyko "revealed no discernable give" on the two "fundamental issues"—namely, the need for Arab commitment to direct negotiations at some stage and to specific Arab obligations flowing from the establishment of a state of peace. Regarding arms limitations to the Middle East, Gromyko refused to discuss the issue so long as Israel continued to occupy Arab territory, and he adhered to the Soviet notion of equating an end of belligerency with a formal state of peace. Gromyko also would not provide any details of the mood and views he found during his recent trip to Cairo and "gave no explicit clue" as to how seriously the Kremlin viewed the current violence in the Middle East and the risks involved.[141]

Although it appeared to be an exercise in futility, Sisco spent three more days searching for areas of mutual agreement. Out of these discussions, the Soviets and Americans were able to compose a "common document" that combined views on a number of areas of mutual concern but also demonstrated large difference on key issues. The texts disclosed that Moscow and Washington agreed that war should bring no territorial gain; a final peace should take the form of one package binding Israel to withdraw from occupied lands and the Arabs to recognize and live in peace with Israel. The Two Powers also agreed that the Suez Canal should be opened to ships of all nations, including Israel, and that the entire settlement should be agreed upon before any part of it is executed.[142]

Even with these agreements, however, their differences remained too vast to believe that any lasting Arab-Israeli peace agreement would emerge from the talks. Both sides remained at odds over the eventual form of the peace talks; the nature of the final peace contract; Egyptian obligations in respect to opening the Straits of Tiran; negotiations of "secure and recognized" frontiers; and Israel's obligations toward Arab refugees. The Soviets also insisted that any agreement should be "multilateral," meaning that Syria and Jordan should be included, whereas the United States remained exclusively interested in securing an Egyptian-Israeli settlement. Sisco left Moscow with the conviction that the Soviets were not going to push Cairo hard in the immediate future and that they would only continue to try to chip away at the US position until the beginning of the UN General Assembly in September.[143]

On his return to Washington, Sisco stopped in Romania, where Nixon was on a state visit, to brief the president on his discussions with the Soviet leaders. Nixon had carefully studied all of Sisco's reports from Moscow and reached the same conclusion that the Two Power talks were at an impasse. "Joe," he said, "the goddamn Russians don't seem to want a settlement."[144] Sisco could not argue. He, too, remained "skeptical" about Soviet "flexibility" and "intentions," and said that he found "no evidence that the Soviets were prepared to press Nasser on the key issues of peace and direct negotiations." Moscow, he added, had decided to "sit tight" and "erode our position to a point where we were prepared to impose their terms on Israel."[145]

Sisco concluded that the administration should do nothing more in the Two Power talks until the opening of the United Nations General Assembly in late September when the foreign ministers of the Soviet Union, Egypt, and Israel would all be in New York for possible discussions. Nixon agreed: "The ball was in the Soviet court. . . . It was up to the Russians to make the next move."[146]

Conclusion

By any reasonable analysis, the Two Power talks were an abject failure. After five months of discussions, Washington and Moscow remained miles apart on producing a joint document that could lead to an Arab-Israeli settlement. Both sides showed during the negotiations that they would not place pressure on their respective clients and had accepted the status quo in the region. The Americans were frustrated that the Soviets wanted a settlement on their terms so they could keep Nasser "as their own tool."[147] The Soviets, for their part, appeared equally disappointed. In their view, they had made "important concessions" in their June 17 paper and had expected the State Department to be more forthcoming during the Moscow talks in terms of the final Egyptian-Israeli borders. Instead, Sisco had nothing more to offer Gromyko than he did to Dobrynin, and neither side could claim to have made any important substantive headway.[148]

American standing in the Arab world suffered as result of its participation in the Two Power talks. Egypt spread the view throughout the region that the US proposals reflected the "total" Israeli position.[149] This was a deliberate misrepresentation of the American viewpoint, but Rogers and Sisco had only themselves to blame. By failing to spell out clearly the location of the final Egyptian-Israeli boundaries, they left the impression that Washington supported Israel's acquisition of substantial Arab territory. The United States could not beat the Soviet position—total withdrawal of Israeli forces from all the occupied territories to the pre-June 5 lines—but the State Department could have convinced the Arabs that the Nixon administration had adopted an "evenhanded" policy in the Middle East by supporting only minor adjustments to the final frontiers.

When he returned from his state visit in Bucharest and a trip through Asia, Nixon held an important NSC meeting on the Middle East to review the US position in the Two Power talks. Visibly agitated by the lack of progress, the president demanded to know why Moscow refused to demonstrate more flexibility when the Arabs had suffered the defeat in the recent war and need US assistance to get the Israelis to cooperate. "What does the USSR want?" he asked Rogers and Sisco. "Don't the Soviets know [the]

Arabs will be beaten in another war?" Sisco assured Nixon that the Soviets were trying to be "responsive" to Nixon's call for an "era of negotiation" and also needed to continue talking with the United States to show the Arabs they are trying to help. But the president had his doubts. "In 1967, Soviets looked unready to help Arabs," Nixon said. "If this happened again, Soviets don't want to be in that position. Do they really believe—given that fact—that they consider this worth a US-USSR confrontation?"[150]

Nixon's frustrations in the Two Power talks, however, were only indicative of the larger problems in US-Soviet relations. Although he entered office eager to reach agreements with Moscow on a range of issues, détente remained a distant prospect. In addition to the "mechanical phase" of the Arab-Israeli discussions, the Soviets had failed to provide a response to the US Strategic Arms Limitation Treaty (SALT) proposal, remained stationary on Vietnam and Laos, and refused to loosen its grip over Eastern Europe. The United States, meanwhile, sought ways to exploit the Sino-Soviet split by playing the "China card" against the Soviets, delayed the start of the SALT talks, and refused to relax its trade policies. As Jacob Beam, the US ambassador in Moscow, commented on August 11, "The conduct of our relations with the USSR seemed to have reached a 'marking-time stage.'"[151]

In the coming months, it would be left to Rogers and Sisco to find a way out of the Two Power talks while trying to avoid another regional war in the Middle East. Neither wanted the talks to fail, but both understood that Nixon's "test" of Soviet intentions could not go on forever. Rogers looked to advance the Two Power talks by making a major policy address on the Middle East that would not only reflect the views expressed by the United States and the Soviet Union in their bilateral discussions but would largely define his tenure in the State Department.

TWO

The Rogers Plan,
October–December 1969

On December 9, 1969, Secretary of State William P. Rogers publicly unveiled his blueprint of a plan for an Arab-Israeli peace settlement that had been in the works with the Soviet Union for the better part of eight months. Speaking before the Galaxy Conference on Adult Education at the Sheraton Park Hotel in Washington, DC, Rogers declared that the United States had adopted a "balanced and fair" policy in the Middle East consistent with UN Security Council Resolution 242. He argued that the Arabs must accept a "permanent peace" with Israel based on a "binding agreement" and maintained that any settlement between Israel and the Arabs must contain a "just settlement" of the Palestinian refugee question. Most important, though, Rogers put the United States on record as supporting Israel's withdrawal from the Arab territories occupied in the 1967 Six-Day War. "We believe that while recognized political boundaries must be established and agreed upon by the parties, any change in the pre-existing lines should not reflect the weight of conquest and should be confined to insubstantial alterations required for mutual security," said Rogers. "We do not support expansionism. We believe troops must be withdrawn."[1]

To many observers, the "Rogers Plan," as it was quickly dubbed, was a "sincere effort to find a proposition the Arabs and Israelis could both accept." Although the proposal left the final status of Jerusalem unresolved, it took into account Israel's security concerns by insisting that its withdrawal from the occupied territories would only come after its Arab neighbors accepted

Israel's "territorial integrity," while at the same time addressing the needs of the Egyptians and Palestinians by calling on the Israelis to grant partial control of Jerusalem to the Arabs and work toward a solution to the Palestinian refugee problem. According to Richard B. Parker, a former Foreign Service officer with extensive service in northern Africa and the Middle East, the Rogers Plan was "watered down in the name of realism" and, in retrospect, looked considerably more favorable to the Arabs than to Israel. The *New York Times* also acknowledged that the secretary of state's speech was the most "definitive" and "comprehensive" statement yet offered of what the United States was trying to achieve between Arabs and Israelis. And moderate Arab states, such as Saudi Arabia and Morocco, "drew warm expressions of appreciation" to Secretary Rogers's plan.[2]

To the parties directly affected by the new proposals, however, the Rogers Plan landed with a thud. Israeli prime minister Golda Meir insisted that it would be "suicidal" for Israel to accept the plan and argued that any Israeli leader who approved the initiative would be guilty of treason. Her foreign minister, Abba Eban, called it "one of the major errors of international diplomacy in the postwar era," and the Israeli ambassador to the United States, Yitzhak Rabin, told Henry Kissinger that the plan was a "great mistake" and "undermined" Israel's position in future negotiations with its neighbors. The Egyptians, moreover, while far more receptive to the ideas than the Israelis, believed that the Rogers Plan was simply an "American maneuver" to split the Arab world by inducing President Gamal Abdel Nasser into a separate peace agreement with Israel. And the Soviet Union, though a partner in the talks that produced the American proposal, scoffed at the idea, calling it "one-sided" and "pro-Israeli" and maintaining that it could not "facilitate finding ways of settlement in the Middle East."[3]

Of course, most of the accusations coming out of Israel and Egypt were exaggerated, and the Soviets were obviously reluctant to support an American-led, rather than a Soviet or even a joint, proposal. But if their accusations were true, why would Rogers put forward such a proposal knowing in advance that the reaction to it would be universally negative? And why did President Nixon allow Rogers to go public with the plan when even he believed that "it could never be implemented" and had "absolutely no chance of being accepted by Israel"?[4] Was it simply because it was important for the Arab world to know that the United States did not automatically dismiss its case regarding the occupied territories, as Nixon argued in his memoirs, or could it have been that the president was unwilling to overrule his secretary of state on a critical foreign policy initiative so early in his administration?

At the time, many commentators believed that the root of the Middle East peace plan could be found in Rogers's desire to make a name for himself as secretary of state, especially in light of the increasing role Henry Kissinger continued to play in shaping foreign policy in the Nixon administration. In fact, if there was one complaint about the secretary after his first year at the State Department, it was that he had not asserted himself more forcefully as the architect of American foreign policy. "Rogers's voice was so muffled that it seemed, at times, unheard," Marilyn Berger wrote in the *Washingtonian* toward the end of his first years at State. One Foreign Service officer, moreover, remarked that for the first half-year Rogers "was all but invisible, as far has his impact on the building goes," emphasizing that Undersecretary Elliot Richardson made a much deeper impact on morale and management. And the longtime *New York Times* reporter, Max Frankel, wrote in late 1969 that even though Rogers had the longest personal relationship with Nixon, it was Attorney General John Mitchell who had emerged as the "strong man" in the cabinet.[5]

Although Rogers had hardly made a name for himself as secretary of state in the way that George C. Marshall, Dean Acheson, or John Foster Dulles had during their first years in the department, the Rogers Plan was not motivated by personal aggrandizement. Nor was it driven purely by Arab-Israeli tensions. Rather, the Rogers Plan should be seen primarily as a closing chapter of the "test" of Soviet intentions in the Middle East, which Nixon had ordered at the beginning of his administration. Indeed, after eight months of tedious negotiations with the Soviet Union that had produced no tangible results, the Rogers Plan offered the United States the surest way out of the Two Power talks while at the same time maintaining its credibility with both the Soviets and the Arabs. If the plan was accepted by the parties, which even the State Department knew was highly unlikely, the Nixon administration would be praised for taking the initiative of finding a settlement between Egypt and Israel and reducing the likelihood of a superpower confrontation in the Middle East. If the plan was rejected, the administration could stand firmly on the proposal, and it would provide the parties with a solid foundation for negotiations if and when they began. Either way, the Rogers Plan put an end to the Two Power talks with the Soviet Union and proved to be the move that paved the way for the United States to take a unilateral role in the Arab-Israeli conflict in the years ahead.

Golda Meir and the "Trauma of 1957"

Few foreign leaders presented more difficulties for Secretary of State Rogers than Israeli prime minister Golda Meir. Meir had a difficult personality and possessed a domineering streak. Although she spent a decade as Israel's foreign minister, she had little patience for diplomatic protocol and disdained foreign leaders she found "too polished." She would dominate conversations with American leaders, had little concern for larger US strategic interests, and often showed contempt for American officials. "Mrs. Meir treated Secretary Rogers as if the reports of his views could not possibly be true," Kissinger wrote in his memoirs. "She was certain that once he had the chance to explain himself the misunderstandings caused by the inevitable inadequacy of reporting telegrams would vanish; she then promised forgiveness." Kissinger's relationship with Meir was more personal, given their European Jewish background and shared experience of escaping anti-Semitism, but Meir often tried to exploit that connection to her advantage. "To me," said Kissinger, "she acted as a benevolent aunt toward an especially favored nephew, so that even to admit the possibility of disagreement was a challenge to family hierarchy producing emotional outrage."[6]

Part of Meir's toughness and rigid personality stemmed from the hardships of poverty, hunger, and fear she felt as a child in Eastern Europe and a long political and diplomatic career struggling to sustain the Zionist vision of a Jewish state. Born Golda Mabovich in Kiev, Ukraine, in 1898, Meir witnessed firsthand the wave of anti-Semitic pogroms that swept Europe in the late nineteenth and early twentieth centuries.[7] In 1921, she emigrated to Palestine, fulfilling her dream of becoming an active participant in the Zionist movement, and she soon became involved in the newly formed

Prime Minister Meir in her office in Tel Aviv, 1969. *(Micha Bar-Am, Magnum Photos)*

Histadrut, the General Federation of Labor, one of the most important organizations for Jews living in Palestine.

In 1946, after more than two decades as part of Histadrut's inner circle, Meir was selected by David Ben-Gurion to replace Moshe Sharett as acting head of the political department of the Jewish Agency when Sharett and many of the Jewish community's senior leaders were interned by the British authorities. From then on she played an integral part both in internal Labor Zionist politics and in diplomatic efforts, including serving as Israel's first ambassador to the Soviet Union, minister of labor and national insurance, foreign minister, and secretary-general of Mapai and then of the newly formed "Alignment." Meir retired from active politics in 1966, but when Prime Minister Levi Eshkol suffered a fatal heart attack in February 1969, the Labor party selected Meir as the "consensus candidate" to succeed Eshkol rather than endure a fierce tug-of-war between Defense Minister Moshe Dayan and Deputy Prime Minister Yigal Allon for control of the party. "I honestly didn't want the responsibility, the awful stress of being Prime Minister," she admitted in her autobiography. But "I had no choice. . . . It was enough that we had a war with the Arabs on our hand; we could wait for that to end before we embarked on a war of the Jews."[8]

Meir's selection to succeed Eshkol was hardly greeted enthusiastically inside Israel. For more than twenty years Israel had been ruled by its founding fathers — the generation that emigrated from Eastern Europe in the decade before World War I — and many felt it was time for the younger generation of Israelis, who were seen as more adept with dealing with Israel's Arab neighbors, to take control. Dayan later wrote that he did not consider Meir "the kind of personality that would open new vistas in the leadership of the state and the party" and abstained from the party vote that elected her. Others, like Foreign Minister Abba Eban, believed that Allon's "expansive, cheerful, and optimistic" personality inspired leadership, in stark contrast to Meir, and felt Allon would do a better job of managing the party and reaching out to the Arab states, given his understanding and respect of Arab culture. After Allon successfully and skillfully managed the cabinet debates in the wake of Eshkol's death, Ma'ariv, the leading Israeli daily newspaper, ran a political cartoon of Allon sitting in the prime minister's chair with a caption that read: "Why not leave him there?"[9]

The problem for the United States in dealing with Meir was that her vision of foreign policy and relations with the Arab states was shaped largely by what Secretary Rogers later called the "trauma of 1957," when as foreign minister in David Ben-Gurion's government, she painfully watched Israeli forces withdraw from the Sinai Peninsula and Gaza Strip under pressure from Eisenhower, Khrushchev, and the United Nations, without any promise that Egypt, in return, would enter negotiations with Israel or guarantee the lifting of the blockade of the Straits of Tiran. Unlike many on the Israeli right who wanted to annex the land or expand settlements in "Judea and Samaria," Meir had little interest in maintaining possession of the occupied territories, but she resisted calls for Israeli withdrawal from Arab land without firm guarantees that Israel's neighbors would accept its right to live within secure and recognized boundaries, less she repeat the mistakes made after the Suez Crisis. "I . . . couldn't get through to the Americans . . . that our very life depended on adequate guarantees, real guarantees with teeth in them," Meir recalled of her discussions with the "cold, gray" John Foster Dulles in early 1957. "I . . . tried to swallow my sense of bitterness and sense of betrayal," she added, but "the U.S. State Department had won its battle against us, and the Egyptian military government, with its garrison was going to return to Gaza. There was nothing I could do or say. I just sat there, biting my lip. . . . It was not one of the finest moments of my life."[10]

Meir's sense of bitterness and betrayal of the events of 1957 left her strongly opposed to UN Security Council Resolution 242, which she believed had been "thoroughly distorted" by the Arabs and the Russians. For Meir, Resolution 242 did not say that Israel must withdraw from "all" territories, nor did it say that Israel must withdraw from "the" territories. "But it does say that every state in the area has a right to live within 'secure and recognized boundaries,' and it does specify a termination of belligerency," she insisted.[11] Technically, this was true; 242 called for Israeli withdrawal only "from territories" occupied during the Six-Day War. Yet only the Israelis interpreted the resolution to mean that it required insubstantial alternations from their current positions. But that made no difference to Meir. "We were perfectly agreeable to the 1967 borders in 1967," she would later tell Secretary of State Rogers. "The fact that they demand to be given back what they have destroyed in war is absurd."[12]

In the six months since she had assumed the premiership, Meir gave little indication that she had overcome the events of 1957. She strongly opposed US participation in the Two Power talks, fearing that once again Israel would be forced to swallow an agreement that benefited superpower interests but largely ignored Israeli security concerns, and she resisted calls by Nixon and Rogers to enter negotiations with the Arab states. In June 1969, during a series of meetings with British prime minister Harold Wilson in London, Meir stressed that Israel would not agree to withdraw from *any* Arab territory until she was satisfied that she could agree to all the elements of a "package solution." But she did not know what would be in the package.[13]

Despite Meir's reluctance to withdraw Israeli forces from the occupied territories, when she arrived in the United States for her first official visit as prime minister in September 1969, Secretary of State Rogers believed that the escalating military violence on Israel's borders left Meir with little choice but to seek accommodation with the Arabs based on the formulations he and Sisco had discussed with the Soviets during the preceding months. Since March, when Egyptian president Nasser rescinded the cease-fire ending the 1967 war and launched the War of Attrition against Israeli forces in the Sinai, the Israelis had suffered almost two hundred casualties along the Suez Canal. For many countries such losses would seem insignificant, but for Israel, with a small population, these were major losses. Egyptian artillery, moreover, continued to shell the recently constructed Bar Lev Line—the hundred-mile string of underground forts and minefields along the Canal named after Israel's chief of staff Chaim Bar-Lev—while incidents on the Jordanian front continued at a high level, forcing King Hussein to temper his pro-Western posture. Even Lebanon, which once stood aside from Arab-Israeli fighting, had become more engaged in the raid-and-retaliation cycle that embodied the situation on the Egyptian front.[14]

The Israelis did little to temper the violence, increasing the likelihood that the Soviets would intervene to protect their Arab clients. In late June and early July, Israeli Mirages downed nine Egyptian MiG-21s, demonstrating its vast superiority in airpower and making it clear to Nasser that he had little chance to recover the land lost to Israel during the Six-Day War through the force of arms. Two weeks later, in separate operations on July 20 and July 22, the Israeli Air Force struck again, this time against Soviet-installed SA-2 surface-to-air missiles sites along the Canal, paving the way for the air force to begin deep-penetration raids of the Egyptian hinterland.[15]

Israel's continued success on the battlefield emboldened Meir to take a firm stance in her conversations with Rogers when the two met at the State Department on September 25. She insisted that there could be no substitute for forcing the Arabs to face up to the choice of war or peace and that the "test" of Arab desire for peace was whether they would negotiate with Israel with no "preconditions" on either side. Referring to the events of 1957, Meir made it clear that Israel did what was "demanded" of it after the Suez Crisis, but it was now time for the Arab leaders to face their responsibilities. "Either they make war and pay the consequences," the prime minister stated, "or they face up to making peace."[16]

Rogers acknowledged that he, too, shared Israeli doubts about the Egyptian and Soviet commitment to peace, but he also felt there was an opening to get negotiations started based on the "Rhodes formula" of 1949. On the Greek island of Rhodes following the first Arab-Israeli war, both indirect and direct negotiations took place under the mediation of special UN envoy Ralph Bunche. The parties met together with Bunche during the first session but thereafter broke into their own delegations, with Bunche shuttling from one delegation to another, listening to what they had to say and then reporting on what the others had said. This procedure, Rogers believed, would satisfy the Arabs, who favored physical separation between them and the Israelis with a mediator shuttling back and forth, while also giving the Israelis the chance to sit down with the Arabs and thrash matters out.[17]

Rogers had discussed the idea with Foreign Minister Mahmoud Riad, a member of the Egyptian delegation at Rhodes, and Riad found the idea acceptable.[18] The Israelis also appeared amendable to Rhodes-style negotiations, so long as there was agreement as to what actually occurred at Rhodes and that the talks would not take place before withdrawal. Yitzhak Rabin, who was also present at the Rhodes talks in 1949, explained to Rogers that there were at least two meetings of direct negotiations, not including the signing ceremonies of the armistice agreements, and that Israel would expect as much from the Egyptians in any future negotiation. Meir agreed. In her view, what was needed was a "psychological breakthrough." How can people really want peace and yet refuse to meet together? she asked Rogers. "Nasser has indoctrinated his people with the idea that Israel must be destroyed," said Meir. "He must now sit down with Israel to demonstrate that this is no longer the case."[19]

When the two met again five days later, this time in New York during the annual meeting of the United Nations General Assembly, Rogers and Assistant Secretary of State Joseph Sisco tried to shift the focus away from the procedural issues and wanted instead to focus on finding acceptable language for Israel's withdrawal from the occupied territories. Sisco, who had been intimately involved of the drafting of Resolution 242 after the Six-Day War, could not understand why, only two years later, the prime minister now refused the language calling on Israeli withdrawal to "agreed boundaries" when Israel had accepted the same language as part of Resolution 242. "I am asking this as an American who still doesn't have an answer to this question," Sisco stated, pleading for a reasonable explanation.

"Because there was a withdrawal in 1957 based on 'aspirations, expectations, etc.,' but look where it led us to," Meir shot back. "I understand this sounds illogical . . . [but] we are sensitive to the word 'withdrawal.' Say it in Israel and everybody in Israel stiffens up. . . . We must never be responsible for something like 1957."[20]

Meir's two conversations with Rogers were rather unproductive, but she had better luck when she met with Nixon at the White House the same week. Although she had never met the president before, Meir found him to be "warm" and "welcoming" and hailed him as an "old friend" of the Jewish people. Such comments came as "startling news to those of us more familiar with Nixon's ambivalences on that score," Kissinger later admitted, "but it gave him a reputation to uphold." Whereas Rogers and Sisco had pressured Meir on withdrawal, Nixon repeated his pledge to the prime minister that he would never ask the Israelis to withdraw from the Golan Heights. He also left the prime minister the impression that the United States would respond favorably to her request for twenty-five Phantoms and eighty Skyhawk jets, as well as two hundred million dollars in low-interest loans during the next five years.[21]

President Nixon and Prime Minister Meir share a light moment during their farewell meeting at the White House, September 26, 1969. *(Moshe Milner, Israel Government Press Office)*

What was also clear from the meeting was that the prime minister had obviously convinced the president that her government would not endorse any proposal that emerged from the Two Power talks, and therefore it was time that the discussions with the Soviets on a Middle East settlement come to an end. Two days after her meeting with the president, Nixon told Kissinger over the telephone that he was now convinced "we can't deliver" the Israelis, and he was loathe to leave the Soviets holding the cards. "The Summit and trade they can have but I'll be damned if they get the Middle East," he said. He believed that the State Department had "talked themselves out of the ballgame" and promised to "cool off" Rogers on the Middle East.[22]

The Joint US-USSR Working Paper

Nixon's message to "cool off" Rogers apparently did not reach the State Department. Less than two weeks after Meir left Washington, Rogers informed Nixon that he intended to move forward with presenting the

Soviets a formal Arab-Israeli peace proposal that was based on the positions their two governments had refined over eight months of negotiations. The proposal he had in mind was designed to take advantage both of the atmosphere created by the recent round of talks with the Soviets, Egyptians, and Israelis and of the "more favorable climate" now existing for getting "Rhodes-type" negotiations started, to see whether real movement toward a settlement was possible. "Even if, as seems more likely, the present impasse continues for the foreseeable future," Rogers explained, "I believe this course of action is the right one, because it will enable us to avoid total isolation with Israel and will put us on record as supporting a position which, however much the Arabs and Israelis do not like it, will be defensible and generally viewed as equitable in world public opinion."[23]

The proposal that Rogers intended to bring to the Soviets contained a separate Egyptian and Jordanian package. The Egyptian package called for negotiations to begin under the auspices of Gunnar Jarring, the Swedish ambassador assigned by the UN secretary-general to oversee the Arab-Israeli talks, using both the indirect and direct means followed at Rhodes in 1949 in an effort to reach "acceptance of the principle of withdrawal of Israeli forces from Egyptian territory to the pre-June 5 line conditioned on Egypt's willingness to negotiate with Israel." Rogers also sought a commitment to "practical security arrangements" in the Sharm el-Sheikh area of the Sinai and Gaza, agreement on where demilitarized zones would be established and how demilitarization would be enforced, freedom of passage through the Straits of Tiran and Suez for all vessels, including Israel, and Arab recognition of Israel's right to exist and live in peace in the area.[24]

As for the Jordanian part of the proposal, the State Department intended to concentrate on this part of the settlement in two ways. First, Charles Yost, the US ambassador to the United Nations, would engage in general discussions at the United Nations, concentrating initially on refugees and Jerusalem. Second, in early November, either Rogers or Sisco would raise with Israel and Jordan whether they would agree to the United States playing a "singular, middle-man role" between them to see whether an agreement can be hammered out. "We do not want to engage the Soviets in a bilateral context on the Jordanian aspect as we have on the UAR part of the settlement," as this would provide the Soviets "too good an opportunity to become the lawyer for our friend, Jordan." Hussein, in fact, personally requested Sisco, in whom he apparently had confidence, to negotiate directly with Zaid Rifai, his personal secretary, and Yacob Herzog, Golda Meir's secretary, together in his presence "at some secret place" to see what could be done.[25]

In forwarding the two papers to the president, Rogers acknowledged that "only an unabashed optimist can predict agreement between ourselves and the USSR on the above proposition, let alone agreement of the parties." But he also believed that moving forward with the joint paper was "clearly in our interest" whether or not the Soviets decided to cooperate. "It is a position that both sides will criticize, but neither can really assail effectively," he argued. "It is a position we can stand on both in Israel as well as in the Arab world as reasonable. Israel does not want us to be specific on the UAR-Israeli border question, but we would now only be coming to a position on the border question which the previous Administration conveyed to the Egyptians in November 1968."[26]

Rogers had a strong case to stand on. After seven months of negotiations, this would be the first time the United States took an official position on the Egyptian-Israeli border question since Nixon came into office. The Soviets had regarded the absence of an American stand on future borders as a missing link in the Two Power talks, leading to a stalemate in the ongoing negotiations. This would also be an important sign to the Arab world that the United States was not acting as Israel's lawyer but rather sought to adopt positions more consistent with larger American interests in the Middle East. Finally, if the Soviets accepted the proposal, there was a strong chance of getting Arab-Israeli negotiations started, and it would be a strong signal from both superpowers of their continued interest in détente.

Still, the "Rogers Plan" touched off an intense debate inside the Nixon administration over whether this was the proper course of action. Not surprisingly, Kissinger strongly opposed the move. In his estimate, it was a tactical mistake to offer Moscow the American "fallback position" without receiving concessions from the Kremlin on Vietnam in return. Sisco tried to reason with Kissinger, telling him that the proposal would advance the Two Power talks, give the United States a more "balanced position" between the Arabs and Israelis, and benefit "our overall interests in the areas." But

Kissinger was not convinced. "I had my doubts about this 'progress,'" he later admitted. "I thought the Soviets were using the Middle East . . . to make the President rethink his threatened November 1 'deadline' over Vietnam."[27]

Harold Saunders, Kissinger's Middle East expert on the NSC staff, disagreed. Based on Nixon's recent commitment to Meir of more economic and military aid, Saunders believed that the US Middle East policy was dangerously on the verge of shifting too heavily in support of Israel. On October 22, Saunders expressed his concerns to Kissinger in what he called the "most important" memo he had written since Nixon took office. In addition to helping Israel build up its defense industry, Saunders pointed out that there were several plans on the table to cover Israel's foreign exchange gap amounting to over a billion dollars, becoming Israel's sole supplier of military equipment, acquiescing in Israel's possession of a nuclear deterrent, and allowing the Israeli government to redraw its map. The problem was also exacerbated by the delivery to Israel of the first American F-4 Phantom aircraft in September, which sent the Arab world into a "ferocious protest."[28] "If I assume correctly that we do not want to go this route, then the main issue is to find a way to establish a position independent of Israel with minimum damage to the President's policies across the board."[29]

For Saunders, the Rogers formula, as expressed in the joint working paper, offered a way to provide needed distance between Washington and Jerusalem. The proposal would put Washington on record as saying that the United States did not believe Israel should keep any part of the Sinai provided that Egypt would negotiate satisfactory security arrangements for Sharm el-Sheikh and the Sinai along with a final Arab government for Gaza. "This may weaken Israel's negotiating position," he acknowledged, "but the US interest is in Israel's *security*, not its *expansion*." He also argued that the Rogers Plan was "a necessary step" if the United States was going to move toward a position consistent with US interests—and not move to a position tied exclusively to Israel. "I believe, too, that it is a defensible stand to take in this country to say that we will support Israel's security wholeheartedly but not Israel's expansion."[30]

Saunders sent an additional memo to Kissinger on October 27, the day before Sisco planned to deliver the proposal to Dobrynin, this time trying to be less of an "advocate" for the Rogers Plan. The drawback of presenting the Soviets with the joint working paper, he argued, was that the plan was so "heavily conditioned" that it asked of the Soviets at least as much as it gave. "Moscow would have every reason to judge that the US is simply trying to shore up its position with the Arabs with words while continuing to back Israel's position with hardware." He also conceded that the Soviets, sensitive to their inability to get Nasser's territory back, would hardly consider the move enough of a concession to justify their paying a price in Vietnam. Even with those reservations, however, Saunders still sided in favor of moving forward with the Rogers Plan. "The tide is running against the US in the Mid-East perhaps irreversibly," he said. "But with a settlement, the US would still have a competitive chance to turn the tide. . . . The US cannot afford not to make any reasonable effort to achieve a settlement. Until the US at least takes a stand on the terms of a settlement consistent with its own interests, the US cannot claim to have made a reasonable effort."[31]

Even former secretary of state Dean Acheson weighed in on the Middle East situation. Acheson was no stranger to Arab-Israeli problems. While serving as deputy secretary of state under George Marshall in 1947–1948, Acheson had been actively involved in the debates inside the Truman administration regarding whether the United States should extend recognition to the Jewish state following the termination of the British Mandate in Palestine. As secretary of state, moreover, Acheson observed the armistice talks taking place under Ralph Bunche and watched Nasser's Free Officers Movement come to power during the Egyptian Revolution of 1952. Although the former secretary of state wanted to see a Middle East settlement, he was reluctant to encourage further US involvement in the region and found the Rogers Plan "abortive," recommending that it "should be abandoned at once." During a meeting with Nixon at the White House on October 27, he argued that while events were building up to a renewal of the fighting on a scale larger than that of border raids, the United States should not intervene either directly or by supplying military items to such a conflict. He was sure that the United States could find ways of letting the Soviets know that its purpose would be greatly facilitated by their adopting a similar course.[32]

Nixon's position was more ambivalent. On the one hand, he agreed with Rogers that it was time for the United States to present its position on borders and security arrangements and see the Two Power talks come to an end. He was angry with the Soviet government for adopting a "very hard-line position" in the talks by demanding that Israel give up everything it had obtained at a heavy cost in the 1967 military conflict, and even accused the Soviet ambassador of being "uncompromising" in his numerous discussions with Sisco.[33] At the same time, however, the president was reluctant to place the needed pressure on Israel to withdraw from the occupied territories, as the Rogers Plan would certainly require. "After all," Nixon told Dobrynin during a meeting at the White House on October 20, "it was Israel, not the UAR that ultimately achieved success in the war. Israel therefore wants to hold on to its gains until an agreement is reached that satisfies it and ensures its future security."[34]

The timing of proceeding with the Rogers Plan was also less than desirable from Nixon's perspective. Since Meir had left Washington at the end of September, the president had been almost entirely preoccupied with events in Vietnam. Nixon was on record as saying that if substantial progress was not made at the Paris Peace talks by November 1—the one-year anniversary of Lyndon Johnson's bombing halt—he would be forced to take "strong action" against the North Vietnamese. He intended to deliver a "major speech" to review Vietnam policy on November 3, and he did not want any issue interfering with the administration's planning for the speech, nor did he want Middle East issues distracting the Soviets from the message he wanted to get across on Vietnam.[35]

When Kissinger informed Nixon on October 25 that Sisco intended to present the Rogers Plan to Dobrynin before the end of the month, Nixon made it clear that he wanted the State Department to delay. He instructed Kissinger to "command" Sisco that there be no further contacts with the Soviets "on any subject" until he had given his November 3 speech on Vietnam.[36] But when Sisco protested, Kissinger recalled, the president, having little stomach for a fight with the State Department, yielded reluctantly and agreed to let Rogers move forward with his new formula.[37]

Thus, on October 28, Sisco met with Dobrynin and presented to the Soviet ambassador the text of a ten-point, joint US-USSR working paper, which reflected the "mutual" and "common" US-Soviet positions developed during the Two Power talks. The paper called for full Israeli withdrawal to the international border established between Egypt and British Mandate Palestine after World War II, for a binding contractual agreement ending the state of war and prohibiting "acts inconsistent with the state of peace between them," and for "a fair settlement" to the Palestinian refugee problem. To solve such questions such as the future of the Gaza Strip, security arrangements at Sharm el-Sheikh, and demilitarized zones, Egypt and Israel would hold "Rhodes-type" negotiations, though the State Department formula was specifically vague as to whether that meant the Israeli or Egyptian interpretation of the Rhodes Formula. The State Department paper also called on Egypt to agree to the freedom of passage through the Straits of Tiran and Suez for all Israeli vessels and Arab recognition of Israel's right to exist and live in peace in the area.[38]

In giving the working paper to Dobrynin, Sisco made it absolutely clear that the document was the result of the process that had begun between the two countries back in March, and he asked the ambassador to report to Moscow that the United States did not consider the revised formulations as elements of any new US document. "What we have tried to do is basically reflect what we hope is concrete U.S.-Soviet understanding reached orally on particular points," he explained. Dobrynin, though, hardly seemed impressed by what Sisco was telling him, nor did he believe that the working paper accurately reflected Soviet positions. He remarked that the plan "seems rather different than what Soviets had in mind," and he wanted more concessions from the United States on the timing of the Israeli withdrawal and the nature of the peacekeeping force. Dobrynin also added that the document appeared rather "short" and left several important questions unclear. "The question for the Soviets is whether it is wise to move with so many open formulations," Dobrynin told the assistant secretary. "A basic judgment would have to be made, and the Soviets might decide it is wiser to try to clarify some of these open questions."

But Sisco refused to budge. "The fact of the matter is [that the] US has now gone as far as it can substantively," he replied to the Soviet ambassador, visibly disturbed by his comments. The "rubber band had been stretched to the fullest extent."[39]

The Galaxy Speech

The joint working paper appeared dead on arrival. Just three days after Sisco handed Dobrynin the text, the Soviet government accused Washington of using "diplomatic corridors to cover up their support for Israel and its aggressive actions" and squarely blamed the United States for the lack of any "tangible results" in the Two Power talks. "The reason lies in the obstructionist line of Israel and the one-sided attitude taken by representatives of some western states who assume that Israel should benefit from the aggression it committed," the Soviets charged. A separate editorial in *Pravda*, the Communist party newspaper and voice of the Soviet government, similarly accused Washington with "duplicity" and "bad faith" by agreeing to provide more arms to Israel while at the same time talking peace with the Soviets.[40]

On November 6, in the first official response to the joint working paper, Georgy Korniyenko, chief of the Soviet Foreign Ministry's American desk and one of the principal Soviet Middle East negotiators, told Ambassador Beam in Moscow that his government viewed the proposal as "unbalanced and unacceptable." Specifically, Korniyenko said that the Kremlin objected to the fact that the United States tied its language on borders to other issues—Gaza, Sharm el-Sheikh—and which, he argued, must be worked out between parties. Although Korniyenko agreed that the Two Power talks should continue, Beam reported, "He left me with the impression that the Soviets see no possibility of arriving at agreed US-USSR position."[41]

To counter the Soviet charges, Sisco wanted Rogers to get out publicly. On November 6, he encouraged Rogers to make a "major policy speech" on the Middle East, which would expose the substantive positions the United States had taken during the past months. These, he believed, were far more balanced than the impression the world had of them. "From a public point of view," he explained to Rogers, "we have suffered in [the Middle East] because we have not revealed more of the substance, while the Soviets have pegged out the most extreme position publicly—total withdrawal of Israeli forces from all of the occupied territories to the pre-June 5 lines." Although a speech of this magnitude would probably not satisfy the Arabs and would no doubt draw flak from an Israeli government that had objected to the US provisions in the Two Power talks at every point, making the American position public, Sisco maintained, would "ease some of the increasing pressures in the Arab world and take a little sting out of the emotionalism."[42]

According to the draft of the speech Sisco had in mind, he wanted it on the record that the Nixon administration had adopted a "balanced" policy in the Middle East—one that seriously took into account the principle and legitimate concerns of both sides to the conflict. He pointed out that in the early weeks of the Nixon presidency there had been a strong effort on behalf of the White House and the State Department to resume relations with Egypt "without conditions" and maintained that the United States did not support Israeli expansionism.

Addressing the Soviet Union, Sisco included tough language that would get the attention of officials in Moscow. He accused the Kremlin of repeatedly spurning opportunities for cooperation with the United States on arms control, ending the Vietnam War, and curbing the arms race in the Middle East. He argued that Moscow had falsely accused Washington of "interference" in the recent Lebanese crisis while at the same time asserting its right of interference in the affairs of the states of Eastern Europe. Most important, though, he put the onus of the success of the Roger Plan squarely on the shoulders of Soviet officials. "Our talks will help determine if the Soviets want a stable peace or whether they would prefer to live with the risks involved in the current unstable conditions in the area. We will continue these talks only as long as there is hope; we want no part of talk just for the sake of talk."[43]

Sisco's call to go public with the Rogers Plan entailed enormous risks to US-Soviet relations and the future of détente. To announce the plan at a time when leaders inside the Kremlin were still contemplating its substance ran the risk of angering Soviet officials, whose cooperation was needed in getting Egypt to accept the plan. Moreover, exposing the substance of the plan after Israeli leaders had repeatedly expressed their opposition to it meant that the only way that Israel could accept the initiatives outlined in the joint working paper was for them to be "imposed" upon Israel by

Washington. For Sisco, however, these risks were secondary. The speech, he explained to the secretary of state, would give the United States a "solid basis" to stand on for some time to come. "I believe the current document is defensible everywhere," he argued, "and whichever direction this whole matter moves, it is important that more and more of our substantive position be revealed to the public so that it can be demonstrated that ours is a *balanced* and not a *one-sided* approach."[44]

Despite the inherent risks of moving forward with the speech, Rogers strongly agreed with Sisco. The fact that Rogers had said nothing of substance on the Middle East since the Two Power talks began in March left many wondering exactly where the Nixon administration stood on the major questions regarding a final Arab-Israeli settlement—borders, refugees, and the status of Jerusalem. After examining the draft of the speech, he sent Nixon a letter emphasizing the importance of getting the elements of the American proposal for an Arab-Israeli settlement on the public record to make clear that it was a balanced position and not simply a "carbon copy" of Israeli views. "Such an effort will not satisfy the Arab extremists," he conceded, "but it will be difficult for either side or world opinion to criticize objectively and will be of some help to our beleaguered friends in the Arab world."[45]

If there were any objections from within the administration for moving ahead with the speech on the Middle East, they once again came from Henry Kissinger. In a telephone conversation with Sisco not long after Rogers had sent the draft over to the White House, he emphasized that he did not see the advantage of giving it, and argued that the State Department was off on the wrong track.[46] Later, when transmitting the draft of the speech to President Nixon, Kissinger again repeated, by his own admission, his now "tiresome refrain" that all of these exercises were doomed to failure. "No scheme was conceivable that would bridge that gap between the two sides," he argued. "It cannot produce a solution without massive pressure on Israel. It is more than likely going to wind up antagonizing both sides. It may produce a war." He also feared that Israel, out of frustration, might strike the Arabs preemptively, or that the Arab countries would shift to hostility when Washington failed to impose its proposals.[47]

Kissinger's resistance to Rogers's speech, though certainly not without its merits, revealed much about the emerging split between the White House and the State Department over the fundamental direction of US policy in the Middle East. Not only did he believe that it was a mistake for the State Department not to extract concessions from Moscow in return for calling on Israel to withdraw from the occupied territories, but he argued that Rogers had mistakenly focused on a settlement with Egypt first on the theory that Nasser's agreement would make Hussein's easier. "I have long felt that we should shift focus," he wrote in a memo to President Nixon in mid-November. In Kissinger's estimate, there was a far greater interest in Hussein than in Nasser, and what was even more important, he argued, the State Department approach completely ignored the Syrian factor. "While I hesitate to say this because of the complications it raises, there will be no settlement until Syria comes into the process. In essence, the roots of the 1967 war lay in Syrian support for fedayeen attacks on Israel. There is no reason not to expect that to continue."[48]

Kissinger was not alone in these views. In fact, much of his argument about finding an agreement on other fronts was also conveyed to Secretary Rogers in a telegram from Egyptian foreign minister Mahmoud Riad. Riad believed there were many "positive points" in the joint working paper the State Department had presented to Dobrynin, the most important of which was the provision calling for Israel's total withdrawal to the international boundaries. Like Kissinger, however, Riad believed that settlements with Jordan and Syria must be included in the package. On November 16, he explained to Rogers the necessity of formulating "a comprehensive settlement" wholly on the basis of Security Council Resolution 242. "What we have received are several projects, in different formulas, which ultimately seek to effect partial settlement with Egypt only," he said. "Therefore, I am sure you will appreciate that our final position cannot be defined until we examine the integrated formula for integrating the Security Council Resolution [242] of 22 November 1967."[49]

The following day, the Israelis added their weight to the list of objections to the State Department approach. During a meeting with Kissinger, Ambassador Rabin explained that Prime Minister Meir believed that the United States had made a "great mistake" and "undermined" Israel's position in future negotiations by becoming more specific on October 28 about the Egyptian-Israeli boundary. Drawing an "exact map," Rabin protested, "even in the context of peace, is subject for negotiations between the parties." Moreover, the Israeli stressed, much to Kissinger's delight, that the State Department's approach to the Soviets was "basically wrong." If the real purpose was to find out if the Soviets wanted a compromise, then it was a mistake to "give in" without concession from them. "You should know better than we," he argued, that the United States can "only move as they move toward you."[50]

Despite concerns raised by Kissinger, Rabin, and Riad, the State Department decided to proceed with the speech. Sisco, in particular, was concerned about an upcoming Arab summit, at which he believed the Arabs were going to be extremely critical of the American positions and would galvanize opposition to distort the American position to their respective countries. The only way to get out in front of the Arabs and the Soviets was to publicize the American positions as soon as possible.

It is important to point out, though, that while Rogers and Sisco were eager to expose the substance of their plan, they did so with President Nixon's approval. Through the years there has been wide speculation, advanced mainly by Henry Kissinger, that Rogers went ahead with the speech without Nixon's knowledge or approval. Recently declassified evidence from Kissinger's own records, however, confirms that this was not the case. In a telephone conversation between the national security adviser and Joe Sisco on December 4, Sisco made it clear that Rogers would not move forward on the speech until he got a "general go-ahead" from the president, to which Kissinger replied, "It's in the President's office now." Even Harold Saunders readily admitted that the White House was not caught unaware by Rogers's speech. "I remember being in the doorway of the Cabinet room when Nixon was informed of Rogers' desire to give a speech on the Middle East," Saunders said in an interview years later. "I think most likely the actual draft text was given to the President. Nixon and Kissinger discussed it, so it seemed clear to me that the White House was aware of Rogers' plans and at least did not object."[51]

On December 9, therefore, the secretary of state spelled out in detail the provisions of the October 28 joint working paper before the Galaxy Conference on Adult Education. Responding to the Soviet critique that the working paper presented to Dobrynin was "one-sided," Rogers made it

Secretary of State William P. Rogers (*Corbis*)

absolutely clear that the State Department plan would require Israel to withdraw from Egyptian territory to the international border that existed before the Six-Day War in return for a specific commitment from President Nasser to make peace with Israel and negotiate on the basis of the Rhodes formula and insisted that there could be no lasting peace without a "just settlement" to the Palestinian refugee question. "To call on the Arabs to accept peace without Israeli withdrawal would be partisan toward Israel," he stated. "Therefore, our policy is to encourage the Arabs to accept a permanent peace based on a binding agreement and to urge the Israelis to withdraw from occupied territory when their territorial integrity is assured. Such an approach," he maintained, "directly addresses the principal national concerns of both Israel and the UAR. . . . We believe that this approach is *balanced* and fair."[52]

Rogers also used the Galaxy speech as an opportunity to address the allegations from the Soviets that the United States had been using the Two Power talks to "divide" the Arab states by urging Egypt to make a separate peace with Israel. "These allegations are false," he said in no uncertain terms. He pointed out that both the United States and the Soviet Union opted to start with the Israeli-Egyptian aspect because of its "inherent importance" for future stability in the area, and simply because one must start somewhere. Any suggestion that the United States wanted a separate peace treaty at the expense of Jordan and Syria was completely unfounded. "It is a fact that we and the Soviets have been concentrating on the questions of a settlement between Israel and the United Arab Republic," Rogers said. "We are under no illusions; we are fully conscious of past difficulties and present realities."[53]

In the four and a half years Rogers served as secretary of state, this was by far most important—and controversial—speech he would make. The *New York Times* editorialized that Secretary Rogers's "forthright statement" of American policy in the Middle East "sounds a clear call to reason and fair play in an area where passion and bias for too long have obstructed settlement of the 21-year-old Arab-Israeli conflict." The *Washington Post* similarly argued that the Rogers Plan was "sound and fair" and stated that, "unlike the Soviet Union, the United States is taking the responsible tack of searching for middle ground." And Peter Grose, foreign correspondent of the *New York Times*, maintained that the guidelines for a Middle East settlement publicized by the secretary of state was "the most definitive and comprehensive statement yet offered of what this country has been trying to achieve between Arabs and Israelis, between Washington and Moscow, over the past eight months."[54] More than that, though, the "Rogers Plan," as it was quickly dubbed, defined the direction of American policy in the Middle East for the following decade. The formulations Henry Kissinger used as secretary of state in his "Shuttle Diplomacy" talks following the 1973 Middle East war and the Camp David Accords President Jimmy Carter brokered between Egypt and Israel in 1978–1979 were largely based on the fundamental principles outlined in the Rogers Plan.[55]

Still, while the press found every reason to endorse the Rogers Plan, the following morning, Wednesday, December 10, Rogers found himself aggressively defending his speech before a meeting of the National Security Council. With the exception of Sisco and Charles Yost, US ambassador to the United Nations, almost everyone sitting around the table inside the Cabinet Room of the White House—the president, Kissinger, CIA director Helms, Defense secretary Melvin Laird, and Wheeler—objected to the strategy Rogers had outlined in his speech the previous evening. The president, in particular, believed the State Department was losing ground in region. He pointed out that in the eleven months since he had taken office, the Soviets had significantly strengthened their position in the Middle East, while the American position with the moderate Arab states had rapidly deteriorated. "I do not mean to say that we have not done all we could do," he added, but "the danger of war seems greater." Particularly upsetting to the president was the fact that by calling on Israel to withdraw from the Arab territories, the Kremlin was rewarded for their obstinate position in the Two Power talks. "If the UAR comes out of a settlement whole and gives only vague obligations to peace in return, the Soviets come out looking good and Israel has little in return."[56]

The president, though, was not the only one who saw this problem. Kissinger quickly added that the State Department was headed down a "slippery slope" by pressing Israel to withdraw from the occupied territories. In his estimate, "the longer Israel holds its conquered Arab territory, the longer the Soviets cannot deliver what the Arabs want." As that time dragged on, he reasoned, the Arabs would conclude that friendship with the Soviet Union is "not very helpful—that it led to two defeats, one of which the U.S. rescued the Arabs from, and to continued impotence in regaining what they have lost."[57]

Rogers believed Nixon and Kissinger's sentiments to be a little disingenuous. Less than a year earlier, the president had authorized the State Department to begin negotiations with the Soviets specifically to find a solution to the Arab-Israeli conflict and avoid a potential superpower confrontation in the Middle East, which would threaten Nixon's goal of cooperation with the Soviet Union on a host of other issues. To suggest now that the administration should back away from calling on Israel to withdraw from the Arab territories not only flew in the face of his earlier comments, but only increased the likelihood that another Arab-Israeli war would erupt.

"Our position has deteriorated because we are seen as the principal supporters of Israel," the secretary countered. "We send planes and economic aid. Unless we want to change that policy, our position will continue to deteriorate." Charles Yost quickly jumped to Rogers's defense. As someone who had studied the Arab-Israeli conflict from its inception, Yost believed that the administration's deteriorating position in the Middle East was inherent in the situation and argued that even if the administration pulled out of the talks with the Soviets, people would still look to Washington to deliver Israel. "We would, in fact, be even more isolated than we are now, because we would have created the impression that we do not care."[58]

The president, though, remained unconvinced. Although he sought a balanced policy in the region, he also wanted to ensure that Moscow would not achieve a strategic advantage. If the United States was going to have to "put the squeeze" on Israel, he believed, then the administration should seek as much as possible from the Kremlin in return. "The Soviets should not come out ahead," he insisted. "The Arabs played a substantial part in bringing on the [Six-Day] war, and the Soviets should pay some price for picking up the pieces."[59]

If Rogers thought the reaction to his speech from within the administration was bad, he quickly found that there was virtually no support for its provisions anywhere else. In Congress, members who feared to take any position that unnecessarily placed pressure on Israel lambasted the Rogers Plan. Former vice president Hubert Humphrey condemned the Rogers Plan as "a sacrifice of Israel's interest to gain accord with the Soviet Union" and accused the secretary of state as being unrealistic in expecting an Israeli withdrawal "in return for not more than what the administration describes as a 'binding agreement' from the Arab nations." Senators Jacob Javits and Edward Brooke both expressed criticism of the plan, maintaining that the Soviet Union "has now made it clear that its policy in the Mideast is to take a mile every time the United States gives an inch." Only Senator J. William Fulbright, the chairman of the Senate Foreign Relations Committee, publicly endorsed the proposal, saying that he believed the speech was "an outstanding example of a balanced and sensible approach, in the interests of the United States and in the interests of peace."[60]

In Cairo the reaction was equally bad. Foreign Minister Mahmoud Riad fiercely objected to the State Department's insistence that Egypt agree to direct negotiations with Israel at a time when Israel still occupied Egyptian land. "Would you, as an American, have accepted your government negotiating with the Japanese after its attack on Pearl Harbor?" Riad asked

Rogers. "Was de Gaulle at fault when he refused to negotiate with the Nazis while they still occupied part of France? We find ourselves in the same position now. If we were to accept negotiations with Israel while its forces still occupy even one square foot of our territory, then we would be taking the round of no return."[61]

For their part, the Israelis were absolutely incensed by every aspect of the Rogers Plan. In Jerusalem, Prime Minister Meir stated flatly that the prospects for peace "will be seriously marred if states outside the region continue to raise territorial proposals and suggestions on subjects that cannot promote peace and security."[62] Her foreign minister, Abba Eban, similarly argued that Israel insisted upon remaining at Sharm el-Sheikh and therefore could not accept the October 28 formulations as outlined to the Soviet Union in the joint working paper.[63] And Rabin's deputy, Shlomo Argov, met with the president's former law partner and special liaison to the American Jewish community, Leonard Garment, at the White House to convey his government's anger at the administration. According to the record of the meeting, Argov believed that the Rogers Plan put the United States and Israel on a "collision course" and argued that this was part of a "deliberate process" on behalf of the State Department that could only lead to a future "arrangement" with Syria regarding the Golan Heights. He also said that Prime Minister Meir felt betrayed by the administration, describing the recent moves as a "scandal," "calamitous," and a "national and personal tragedy."[64]

The Israelis took particular exception to the statement in Rogers's speech calling on Israel to accept only "insubstantial" modifications in its future borders with Jordan.[65] "Never, in any of its decisions, has the Israeli government consented to withdraw from the West Bank," Ambassador Rabin fumed to Rogers's deputy, Elliot Richardson, shortly after learning of the plan. He pointed out that the cabinet's decision on June 19, 1967, referred only to the Sinai and the Golan Heights, and even there, "withdrawal to the international frontiers was made conditional upon security arrangements that would satisfy Israel."[66] That same week, in a meeting between Secretary Rogers and Foreign Minister Eban at the State Department, Eban left little doubt that his government planned on "substantial" changes along the West Bank, not merely the "insubstantial" modifications Rogers had called for in his speech. "Although our proposals have not yet proved acceptable to Jordan, if the United States publicizes its view that Israel must withdraw from the all the territories—including those on the Jordanian border—that will put an end to those contacts."[67]

Fearing that the Nixon administration would continue to press Israel to accept the provisions outlined in Rogers's speech, Rabin was called back to Israel during the third week of December, and returned to Washington within days with instructions to "launch a public campaign against the Rogers Plan." On December 24, he held a background press briefing at the Israeli embassy in Washington at which he called the Rogers Plan "an abrupt reversal of the principle that U.S. policy has hitherto proclaimed" and maintained that US policy, as unfolding, "undermines the principle of negotiation" and "comes close to the advocacy and development of an imposed settlement."[68] He also met again with Kissinger to put matters clearly on the line: "Let me tell you in complete frankness, you are making a bad mistake. In taking discussion of peace settlement out of the hands of the parties and transferring it to the powers, you are fostering an imposed solution that Israel will resist with all her might. I personally shall do every-thing within the bounds of American law to arouse public opinion against the administration's moves."[69]

The Soviet Reply

As much as Israel's "public campaign" against the Rogers Plan was sinking any possibility that it might succeed, the final blow came on December 23, when Dobrynin delivered the official Soviet reply. In a somewhat bizarre statement, Moscow again characterized the US proposal as being of a "one-sided" and "pro-Israeli nature" that could not "facilitate finding ways of settlement in the Middle East." The official Soviet text, handed to Rogers by Dobrynin, alleged that some of the US provisions altered the position taken earlier by the American side and therefore that the Soviets believed there were insufficient grounds to continue to work for a joint Soviet-American document based on the October 28 formula. At the same time, the Soviets also objected that the American draft did not mention anything about what they deemed the "essence of the key question," Israeli withdrawal from occupied Arab territories, an utterly ridiculous statement consider the plan specifically called for Israel to withdraw from the land conquered during the Six-Day War.[70]

Equally troubling from the American vantage point, the Soviet statement retreated from Moscow's earlier commitment to have the parties negotiate under the Rhodes formula. In his meeting with Rogers and Sisco, Dobrynin remarked that although the Soviet side had no objection to the Rhodes formula per se, they now felt this formula should not be used in view of public comments made by various parties. Moscow was nevertheless willing to try to go beyond "neutral formulations" where possible in an attempt to find more precise language regarding some of the issues—for example, demilitarized zones, passage through waterways, and security provisions. But the chances for a lasting peace agreement negotiated through his government, he conceded, were slim.

Rogers did not mask his disappointment to what he clearly interpreted as a "retreat" from Moscow's earlier position. In response to Dobrynin's presentation, he emphasized that the United States had gone as far as it could possibly go and that it was now time for the parties to begin a process of negotiations. Any more precise formulations from either Washington or Moscow, he argued, would suggest an attempt to "impose" a settlement, which the United States was simply unwilling to do. Sisco, too, chided the Soviet ambassador for the "unresponsive" statement he had delivered on behalf of his government. The Kremlin's most recent position seemed more a reflection of its position of the previous June than what Rogers and Gromyko had discussed in New York in September, and almost a complete reversal on their agreement to having the parties negotiate under the Rhodes formula.[71]

Rogers and Sisco had every reason to be disappointed. The Rogers Plan may have been many things—ill-timed, ill-advised, and highly controversial for sure. But "pro-Israeli" and "one-sided" as the Soviets maintained, it was not. The US position to commit itself to a near total Israeli withdrawal from the Sinai to the international border was hardly in Israel's interest, nor was the provision in the plan stipulating that Israel must accept a "just settlement" to the Palestinian refugee problem, which the Arabs would certainly interpret as the "right of return" for those Palestinians whom the wars of

1948 and 1967 made homeless. One need only to look at the remarks of Prime Minister Meir to her cabinet on December 22 to understand that the Kremlin had far overreached in its condemnation of the Rogers Plan. "If [the] U.S. proposal were implemented, it would be suicidal and would mean destruction of Israel," she declared. "Any Israeli government which approved this proposal would be guilty of treason."[72] Following the meeting with Dobrynin, Rogers sent a memo to President Nixon that concluded that the Soviet reply to the American formulations on an Israel-Egypt settlement was "negative" and "unresponsive" and "provides no serious basis for continuing those talks."[73]

Even members of the National Security Council staff, many of whom had been the State Department's strongest critics in putting forth a formula that included a firm position on Israel's borders, were astounded by the "cavalier nature" of the Soviet reply. "After actively discussing a joint document" Kissinger's Middle East expert, Harold Saunders, wrote, "they simply turned aside our October 28 formula—containing the position they wanted from us on boundaries—as providing no basis for a joint document." It was possible, Saunders believed, that the Soviets were testing whether a flat rejection would cause Washington to make a few last concessions or that Moscow simply did not have the power to make Nasser accept the proposal. But more likely, he argued, the Kremlin was content with the present situation. "In any case, the December 23 response is such a step backward that it warrants a sharp rebuff and even telling Dobrynin that we have nothing more to say."[74]

Kissinger, though, did no such thing. Just six days after receiving the official reply to the Rogers Plan from Moscow, he met again with the Soviet ambassador with hardly a mention or a condemnation of the fact that his government had flatly rejected a serious peace offer on the Middle East that had taken into account the views expressed by the Kremlin during the eight months of negotiations in the Two Power talks. Instead, as a reward for their intransigence, Kissinger welcomed future Soviet cooperation on a range of bilateral issues with Moscow, including European security, SALT, and Vietnam, and said that both he and President Nixon would prefer that matters of "great importance" be discussed in the private channel between him and Dobrynin, leaving "routine matters" to the State Department.[75]

That Kissinger did not support the Rogers Plan was evident by now. But that he was so willing to reward the Kremlin for its lack of cooperation on an issue that President Nixon had deemed in the first week of his administration to be of "vital importance" showed that his motives in this issue were almost completely selfish. As long as he was not directing Middle East policy, and as long as there was a chance for him to make progress with Moscow in other bilateral issues, Kissinger was willing to disregard Soviet behavior in other areas, especially the Middle East. This is not to suggest that there were not legitimate policy grounds for objecting to the Rogers Plan. Calling for an Israeli withdrawal from the Arab territories arguably rewarded Nasser for provoking the Six-Day War and initiating the War of Attrition. It also unnecessarily put pressure on America's most important ally in the Middle East when Moscow continued to send the Arabs weapons and technology to resist the Israeli army. Still, had Kissinger showed even a hint of frustration to Dobrynin over the lack of progress on the Middle East or indicated that there could be no cooperation on other issues until this issue was resolved, it is hard to believe that Moscow would not have put the needed pressure on Egypt to make an agreement under the terms spelled out in the joint US-USSR working paper.

Conclusions: The End of the Two Power Talks

It is certainly easy to look back on the nine months of negotiations between Washington and Moscow on the Middle East and blame the Soviet Union for the demise of the Two Power talks and the failure of the Rogers Plan. Moscow's refusal to bring Egypt any closer to an agreement at a time when President Nasser was virtually dependent on Soviet economic and military aid to keep his country afloat demonstrated that the Kremlin was hardly committed to finding a resolution to the conflict between Israel and its Arab neighbors. The Soviet decision, too, to distort the American position in the Arab world and retreat from the many commitments made to the United States during the Two Power talks only undermined the negotiating process along the way. But for all of Moscow's faults—and there were many—the failure of the Rogers Plan was a result of many factors.

First and foremost was the continued Cold War rivalry. Even though both Nixon and Brezhnev called for a period of negotiation between their two countries, the Soviet-American rivalry was still too sharp to believe that the two superpowers could reach an agreement on such fundamental importance as the Arab-Israeli conflict. "Mutual trust was lacking," Assistant Secretary Sisco later conceded. There were times when the Soviets were sometimes active and helpful in containing violence at certain junctures when they thought it could lead to a confrontation, but they were never helpful in terms of negotiating peace. While both the United States and the Soviet Union wanted to avoid a confrontation in the region, neither seemed willing to put enough pressure on its client to accept a peace agreement, and both continued to adopt policies that escalated the arms race in the region and allowed the War of Attrition to continue. "The operational assumption of the United States of the test of Soviet intentions proved faulty," said Sisco. "The Soviets gave Nasser a veto. They would not endorse anything he did not accept."[76]

Second, the State Department's refusal to coordinate its proposals with the Israeli government throughout the negotiations left little possibility that Jerusalem would accept an "imposed" settlement. Prime Minister Meir steadfastly maintained that the United States had no business taking a position on what constituted Israel's "secure and recognized" boundaries and argued that any peace agreement must be worked out directly through the parties, not through the superpowers. The fact, too, that Rogers offered a Jordan-Israel settlement without even informing Israel ahead of time only exacerbated the growing sense of mistrust between Washington and Jerusalem. Of course, it was not likely that the Israeli government, sitting in its most strategically secure position since 1949, was going to endorse the peace proposal, even one that left the definition of Israel's borders highly ambiguous.

Finally, there was the matter of internal US policy. The lack of cohesion between the White House and the State Department on an issue of such strategic importance undermined the negotiations and allowed the Soviet Union to extract concessions from one which they could not get from the other. The rivalry between Rogers and Kissinger, though still in its infancy, sent conflicting signals to Moscow over who was really in charge of US Middle East policy. In his memoirs, Dobrynin recalls that the divided authority in Washington left his boss, Foreign Minister Andrei Gromyko, "thoroughly unnerved" after his visit to the United States in the fall of 1969. "I was dealing with Sisco, who was shrewd, knowledgeable, and very stubborn. He took all his orders from Kissinger, who remained in the shadows, while officially working for Rogers and doing what he could to accommodate him."[77] Sisco, too, remembers that throughout much of the first year of the Nixon administration he spent as much of his time negotiating between Kissinger and Rogers as he did on the problem itself.

In many cases, the differences between the State Department and the White House were very real. As evidenced during the nine months of discussions, Nixon and Kissinger saw the Middle East primarily in broad strategic terms; any agreement, they believed, must be negotiated with the larger goal of détente in mind and "linked" to progress in other areas. Kissinger, in particular, was adamant that the United States could not let American arms in the Middle East be defeated by Soviet arms. "If the Soviets are going to put in anti-aircraft missiles, we have to counter this with more aircraft for the Israelis," said one former State Department official of Kissinger's views.[78] The State Department, by contrast, was far more concerned with trends in the region that could threaten American interests. Rogers and his staff viewed the Arab-Israeli dispute primarily as a regional dispute that, if left unresolved, could threaten American access to vital oil reserves. Yet in either case, Sisco later argued, it was naive to think that the State Department or the White House was oblivious to one or the other of the dimensions. "It was a matter of weight and emphasis," he said, "and Nixon, interestingly enough, agreed with both views."[79]

President Nixon's own ambivalence on the Middle East also weakened the prospects for a peace agreement. At times, he was for an active policy. He encouraged the State Department early on to work with the Soviets in finding a solution to the conflict that would prevent a superpower confrontation in the region. Yet as soon as Rogers offered a plan to the Soviets that took into account their concerns, as well as adhered to Security Council Resolution 242, Nixon did little to support it and even went out of his way to undercut the plan. Not once after Rogers delivered his December 9 speech did Nixon come out publicly and endorse the proposals, nor did he send any signal to Moscow and Jerusalem that the plan was *his* and not just Rogers's. Moreover, the president routinely maintained that because he received less than 8 percent of the Jewish vote in the 1968 election, he was not subject to the pressures from the American Jewish community and would squeeze Israel into an agreement if and when the time was necessary. But in his numerous meetings with Golda Meir and Yitzhak Rabin during his first year in office, he only reinforced the view that he would continue to provide for Israel's military and economic needs.

That the Rogers Plan did not bring about an end to the fighting between the Arabs and Israelis, however, did not necessarily mean that it was a complete failure. If anything, it gave the United States a firm position to stand on and demonstrated to the Arab world that the United States was prepared to take tough positions against Israel. Not since the United States endorsed the UN partition plan for Palestine in 1947 had the United States taken such a firm position on Israel's borders, and never had Israel been at such odds with the United States, even including when President Eisenhower condemned Israeli government for its behavior during the 1956 Suez Crisis. At the same time, moreover, the Rogers Plan, despite its many flaws, provided the parties the necessary framework for negotiations if and when the talks resumed, a fact that was evident during the negotiations between Egypt and Israel in the Camp David accords of the late 1970s.

To say, also, that the inability of the two superpowers to reach an agreement on the Middle East diminished the possibilities of Soviet-American cooperation in other areas would be premature. As Kissinger's conversation with Dobrynin on December 29 demonstrated, Moscow and Washington remained very interested in discussing ways in which their governments could cooperate in areas such as Vietnam, arms control, and European security, and the parties still held out the possibility that they could "regulate their different interests in the Middle East apart from the Arab-Israeli conflict." President Nixon even proposed sending American astronauts to Moscow as a sign of mutual cooperation between the two countries in the wake of the collapse of the Two Party talks and held out the possibility that the Kremlin would consider a summit with the United States to discuss the limitation of armaments.[80]

Still, if the Two Power talks and the Rogers Plan were considered the first test of the Soviet-American détente, they must be considered a failure. Even factoring in Vietnam, both Washington and Moscow understood that the

Middle East posed the most serious threat for a superpower confrontation and that, therefore, the conflict needed a quick resolution. Yet after nine months of tedious negotiations, the two countries appeared further apart than before. According to former secretary of state Dean Acheson, who was actively following the details of the negotiations, Rogers's effort to produce any movement toward peace or any effect in enhancing the prestige of the United States in the Arab world was "a complete failure," and he argued that the effort indicated only "the futility of attempting through bilateral talks with the Russians . . . to guide the parties to a peaceful settlement."[81]

Following the Soviet rejection of the Rogers Plan, Assistant Secretary Sisco prepared a memorandum which was sent through Secretary of State Rogers to President Nixon in which he stated in no uncertain terms that the Soviets had "failed the test" that the president had given the State Department in the first weeks of his administration. "They have not been able to produce for whatever reason their concerns, or the Egyptian, or a combination thereof," he explained, and he advocated that from hereon in, in the peace process, "the United States should seek to do this unilaterally." The paper went to the White House in the first week of January, and Sisco was traveling aboard Air Force One when the president called him into his compartment to discuss the memo. "Joe, I agree fully with this recommendation," the president said. "From now on, we're going to go at it alone in the peace process. The Soviets have had their opportunity."[82]

THREE

The First Soviet Threat, January–May 1970

At approximately 2:00 p.m. on January 7, 1970, three squadrons of Israeli F-4 Phantom IIs crossed over the west side of the Suez Canal, headed deep into the Egyptian hinterland. The stated military objectives of the mission were, first, to reduce Egyptian military pressure in the forward Canal area by bombing military bases and supply depots in the rear and disrupting logistical support to Egyptian forces stationed along the Canal; second, to disrupt Egyptian military planning for launching a full-scale war against Israel; and third, to bring the War of Attrition to an end by compelling Nasser to observe the UN-decreed cease-fire that had ended the Six-Day War.[1] Of course, there were also unstated objectives of the mission, which no Israeli leader would publicly acknowledge. In striking the Egyptian heartland, there could be no question that the Israelis intended to punish Nasser severely for having launched the War of Attrition in March 1969 and potentially bring about a change in the Egyptian regime.

The Israeli fighter planes struck that afternoon at three targets: a training camp at Dahsur, just south of Cairo and less than ten miles from the industrial suburb of Helwan; a military airfield at Tel el-Kebir in the eastern Delta; and the atomic energy research facility at Inshas, not far from Cairo. The attacks were followed within days by another round of strikes at military installations at el-Khanka, Huckstep, Jabal Hawf, and along the Cairo-Suez road. All planes returned safely to Israeli bases without incident setting up more attacks of the Egyptian heartland in the following weeks and months.[2]

To the casual observer, the Israeli air attacks that began in January 1970 were just a continuation of the cycle of violence that had resumed in July 1969, and only further indication of Israel's vast air superiority in the Middle East. The Israeli government did little to highlight the success of the missions, nor did press accounts draw attention to the fact that this was the first time the Israeli Air Force had struck Egyptian targets significantly west of the Canal line since 1967. The attacks, however, marked a distinct change in Israel's military strategy in the War of Attrition. In the ten months since Nasser had formally declared war on Israel, the Israeli government had confined its counterbombardments to the area around the Suez Canal, fearing that to strike deep inside Egypt ran the risk of drawing Soviet intervention and would alienate support in Washington while Israel anxiously awaited Nixon's response to a request for twenty-five more Phantoms and one hundred additional Skyhawks.[3]

The change in Israel's strategy was spurred in large part by Yitzhak Rabin, the Israeli ambassador to the United States. For months, Rabin had urged leaders in Jerusalem to step up attacks against Nasser. A former chief of staff of the Israeli Defense Forces, and the man who helped guide Israel to victory in 1967, Rabin believed that the American position in the Two Power talks, calling for Israel to withdraw to the international boundary, was directly linked to Israel's misguided handling of the War of Attrition. In September and October 1969 he sent numerous cables to Jerusalem arguing that only by undertaking deep-penetration raids and striking military targets in the Egyptian heartland could Israel induce the Egyptians to halt the war and reverse the direction of American policy.[4]

For Rabin, moreover, attacks beyond the Canal line would be viewed as a welcomed development in the United States. Despite pressure from the State Department to agree to a diplomatic solution, the ambassador firmly believed that the White House wanted Israel to escalate the military pressure on Egypt to undermine Nasser's standing with his people and to weaken the Soviet position in the region. "A man would have to be blind, deaf, and dumb not to sense how much the administration favors military operations," he explained in a cable to the prime minister in the fall of 1969. Some circles in Washington, he argued, were even encouraging Israel to destroy the Egyptian army in a large-scale offensive, and many wanted officials in

Israeli ambassador Yitzhak Rabin talks to reporters as he leaves the State Department after a two-hour meeting with the acting secretary of state, Elliot Richardson, on February 13, 1970. Rabin had been summoned to the State Department to discuss the Israeli bombing of an Egyptian factory near Cairo. *(Bettman/Corbis)*

Jerusalem to initiate a full-scale offensive that could bring down Nasser's regime. "Sources have informed me that our military operations are the most encouraging breath of air the administration has enjoyed recently," he continued. "The willingness to supply us with additional arms depends more on stepping up our military activity against Egypt than reducing it."[5]

Rabin's calls for deep-penetration bombing of the Egyptian heartland touched off a fierce debate among the Israeli leadership. The question was not over Israel's military capabilities to carry out the missions. Even those who opposed the escalated bombardment recognized that with the recent arrival from the United States of more than a dozen F-4 Phantom aircraft, which surpassed anything technologically that the Soviets could offer Egypt, there was little the Egyptian military could do to prevent the Israeli Air Force from penetrating deep inside Egyptian territory. Rather, the concern centered on what the US reaction would be to the increased attacks at a time when Washington wanted improved relations with the Arab world and the Soviet Union. Other Israeli officials raised questions regarding the potential Soviet response to seeing Moscow's client repeatedly attacked with American-made weapons. And if the attacks forced the collapse of Nasser's government, was Israel prepared to live with a new, and possibly more hostile, Egyptian regime on its border?

Deputy Prime Minister Yigal Allon, a longtime ally of Rabin's dating back to the 1940s when Rabin had served under Allon's command in the Palmach, the elite "strike force" unit of the Haganah, strongly supported the bombing. In speeches and writings, Allon argued that it was "inconceivable" the Soviets would send to Egypt an expeditionary force large enough to counter the bombing given that Moscow had never sent forces to a non-communist government beyond the Warsaw Pact. Nor, Allon maintained, would the Kremlin risk a confrontation with the United States over differences in the Middle East when it was clear that Nasser had initiated the war.[6] General Ezer Weizman, who recently joined the cabinet as minister of transportation, concurred, arguing that Israel needed to "use our power to the utmost, so as to win the War of Attrition and to remove any doubt as to who was the victor."[7]

Defense Minister Moshe Dayan and Foreign Minister Abba Eban led the opposition to the bombings. Dayan was not opposed to limited bombing around Cairo, but he did not share Allon's confidence that the Soviet Union would turn a blind eye to increased attacks on their ally and watch indifferently as Nasser's regime collapsed. Eban, by contrast, felt certain that Rabin was leading the cabinet down a dangerous path by suggesting without "sufficient evidence" that the United States supported the bombardment of Egypt in depth. At a cabinet meeting on December 21, 1969, in which Rabin returned from Washington to advocate for the deep-penetration raids, Eban disputed the ambassador's analysis of the American position. When it appeared that his argument fell on deaf ears, Eban took the dramatic step of publicly criticizing Rabin's position in an article of January 2, 1970, in the daily paper *Ha'aretz*: "If fate wills it that Nasser should fall . . . I presume that there will be no mourning in Israel," he wrote. "But one should not conclude from this that the U.S. encourages actions taken deliberately in order to overthrow him. That is no sign of a U.S. desire for an energetic increase of activity beyond the cease-fire lines if Egypt does not force us into this."[8]

Eban was certainly correct to challenge Rabin's claims. No evidence has surfaced suggesting that the Nixon administration welcomed the increased attacks or favored Nasser's removal. But Eban's opinion did not hold the weight in the Meir government that it formerly held under Levi Eshkol and David Ben-Gurion. Meir, moreover, appeared prepared to live with the consequences of the escalated attacks. "We shall not go into mourning if Nasser falls," she said in an interview in the newspaper *Davar* shortly after the cabinet voted to initiate the deep-penetration raids. "I don't know if Nasser's successor would be any better than he is, but I don't think he could be much worse."[9]

The deep-penetration raids that began on January 7 continued unfettered until April 13, 1970. During those three months, the Israeli Air Force conducted more than three thousand sorties and dropped an estimated eight thousand tons of ordinance on Egyptian territory, inflicting heavy casualties on both military and civilian populations. They struck major supply depots for the Egyptian air force, attacked military bases around Cairo, and destroyed the Canal line air defense systems installed by the Soviet Union after the 1967 war. On January 28, in perhaps the most brazen attack of the entire deep-penetration campaign, Israeli fighter planes deliberately hit a main training center near Cairo full of Soviet personnel, killing and wounding dozens.[10]

Yet although the attacks were militarily successful, the deep-penetration campaign must be judged a political failure. Not only did the attacks fail to compel Nasser to end the War of Attrition immediately, but the Israelis grossly miscalculated the Soviet response. Between February and May, Moscow responded to the deep-penetration raids by sending to Egypt more than ten thousand of their own "instructors" and "advisers." Soviet pilots, moreover, became active participants in the Egyptian air defense, flying reconnaissance missions and intercepting Israeli aircraft, while additional Russian units manned the new SA-3 surface-to-air missile systems installed along the Suez Canal. The Kremlin also bolstered its naval presence in the Mediterranean, rivaling what the United States had in the region as part of its Sixth Fleet. "It is a unique turn of Soviet policy," wrote NSC staffer William

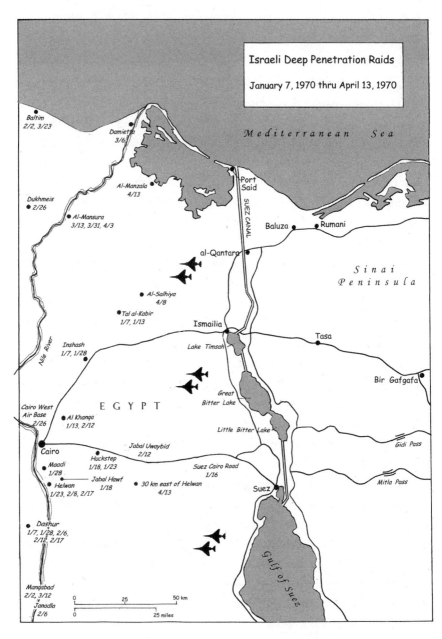

Israeli deep-penetration raids, January 7–April 13, 1970

Hyland of the Soviet move. "Never before have the Soviets put their own forces in combat jeopardy for the sake of a non-communist government."[11]

The Soviet decision to intervene in the War of Attrition, however, did not just affect the military situation in the Middle East. By choosing to send forces to Egypt, Moscow unleashed an arms race in the Middle East that would have far-reaching implications on US-Soviet relations and the future of détente. Instead of turning 1970 into year of "promoting US-Soviet relations on a mutually acceptable basis,"[12] as many in the upper echelons of the Soviet leadership had wanted, Moscow and Washington repeatedly made decisions that inched the superpowers closer to a confrontation in the Middle East, proving that détente was still very much on hold.

The Kosygin Letter

Around 8:30 p.m. on January 31, 1970, the Soviet ambassador to the United States, Anatoly Dobrynin, arrived on short notice at Henry Kissinger's office in the White House with a letter addressed to President Nixon from Premier Alexei Kosygin. Dobrynin had become a frequent visitor at the White House in the first year of the Nixon presidency. Since establishing the back channel with Kissinger in February 1969, the two men had forged a strong working relationship, often meeting at odd hours and almost always in private, without interpreters or secretaries. During their conversations, which generally took place in the Map Room of the White House, Kissinger and Dobrynin discussed topics as far-ranging as arms control, Vietnam, Berlin, the Middle East, and Soviet-American trade. In part, this reflected Nixon's desire of "linkage," whereby progress on each issue, particularly issues of importance to the Soviet Union, would depend on progress on several others. Yet it also ensured, according to Kissinger, that the "major negotiations" with the Soviet Union would be conducted from the White House, under the president's direct supervision.[13]

The success of "the channel" rested in large part on the confidence their leaders placed in their private meetings and the faith that both Kissinger and Dobrynin had in each other's ability to speak directly, without polemics, and hold their discussions in the "strictest confidence." Kissinger described Dobrynin as "highly intelligent," possessing an exceptional analytic ability. "Within the scope of discretion granted him by his government," said Kissinger, "he was flexible, skillful and reliable . . . devoted to the improvement of US-Soviet relations. I respected his human qualities." Dobrynin, similarly, believed that in Kissinger he had found a negotiating partner with whom he did not have to resort to ambiguities or avoid specific problems. "He could give you a big headache," Dobrynin later wrote of Kissinger, "but he was clever and highly professional, and never dull or bureaucratic."[14]

For the Soviet ambassador, moreover, the private meetings with Kissinger were a refreshing change of pace from the more formal discussions he often had with the State Department officials, especially Assistant Secretary of State Joseph Sisco, whose meetings he once described as "like throwing beans against the wall."[15] Kissinger and Dobrynin, by contrast, conducted their dialogue in "a polite and at times even jocular manner," which enabled the channel to emerge by 1971 as the "principal venue for Soviet-American relations," producing a number of agreements, including the Anti-Ballistic Missile agreement and the Strategic Arms Limitation Treaty that would largely symbolize the period of détente.[16]

The letter Dobrynin brought with him on the evening of January 31, however, could hardly be described in the spirit of détente. In this letter, confined exclusively to the Middle East, Kosygin launched into a four-page diatribe against Israel's recent bombing of Egyptian territory, which he claimed violated United Nations Security Council resolutions. He argued that the Israeli Air Force had deliberately targeted civilian populations, brought destruction to Arab towns, villages, and industrial installations, and exacerbated "tension" in one of the most important areas of the world. "The aims of these adventurist actions are clear," declared the Soviet premier, "to force the neighboring Arab countries into accepting the demands which are put forward by Israel."[17]

In addressing the United States, Kosygin's comments were equally blunt. He accused Nixon of conspiring with Israel to attack Egypt and insisted that it was the responsibility of the United States to "compel" Israel to cease its attacks and to agree to the "speediest withdrawal" of "all" the occupied territories. More important, though, the Soviet premier made it clear to Nixon that if Israel's attacks continued, not only would Israel face "highly risky consequences" but, he added, the Soviet Union would have no choice but "to see to it that the Arab states have means at their disposal with the help of which a due rebuff to the arrogant aggressor could be made."[18]

The decision to send Kosygin's letter came after weeks of intense discussion inside the Kremlin's political and military circles over how to respond to Israel's deep-penetration bombing of Egypt. Much like the Israeli debate to initiate the bombings, Soviet officials wrestled with the idea of what defending Egypt would entail and if the bombings warranted the risk to get further entrenched in the Middle East less than two years after having forcefully intervened in Czechoslovakia. The Politburo also considered whether Soviet forces would have to be introduced into Egypt covertly and how the introduction of Soviet forces would affect Moscow's relationship with the United States.[19]

At a more basic level, though, the Israeli bombings forced Soviet leaders to reassess its strategic relationship with Egypt. In less than three years, Nasser had inadvisably launched two separate wars against Israel, leaving the Soviet Union largely responsible for picking up the pieces of Egypt's broken army. The Soviets were partly to blame in 1967 for giving Nasser faulty information that the Israelis were preparing to attack and encouraging him to mobilize the Egyptian army.[20] Yet few Kremlin officials welcomed Nasser's decision to launch the War of Attrition and believed that with the deep-penetration raids Nasser got what was coming to him.

On January 22, two weeks into the deep-penetration campaign, Nasser arrived in Moscow for secret meetings with Kosygin, General Secretary Leonid Brezhnev, and Soviet president Nikolai Podgorny to plead his case for massive Soviet military assistance to defend Egyptian cities against the Israeli attacks. "The fate of the whole Middle East," he said, "was going to be decided in the strip of land about 30 kilometers [nineteen miles] either side of the Suez Canal." Nasser remained particularly concerned with the fate of Alexandria, Egypt's only remaining functional port, and stressed that his people felt "naked" to the Israeli bombardments. He requested that the Soviets send to Egypt its new SA-3 surface-to-air missile systems to replace the SA-2, which he argued proved ineffective against aircraft flying below sixteen hundred feet.[21]

The Soviet leadership put up some resistance to Nasser, insisting that Nasser's request required approval by a full meeting of the Politburo. Yet by the time Nasser left Moscow, Soviet officials had all but decided that they would come to his aid. As historians Dima P. Adamsky and Isabella Ginor have shown, preparations were already under way to send to Egypt air defense units from Moscow, Leningrad, Byelorussia, and Dnieperpetrovsk.[22] The tipping point for the Soviet decision to intervene massively in the War of Attrition, however, may have come on January 28, after the Israeli attack on a house that killed Soviet personnel. "We have the hardest possible intelligence that the decisions leading to the present situation were approved by Brezhnev on January 28–29, in the wake of Nasser's secret visit to Moscow," William Hyland of the NSC staff explained in a memorandum to Kissinger. "The Soviets had no choice but to support Nasser and strong moves were obviously called for."[23]

Hyland was most likely referring to the report of an intercepted telephone conversation between Brezhnev and defense minister Marshal Andrei Grechko shortly after the Israeli attack, which revealed that Brezhnev was "obviously bitter" about the accuracy of the strike. The conversation also indicated that top Soviet leaders had been meeting on the Middle East and that the general secretary had informed Grechko that he wanted to send to Egypt "a system" to provide a "means of defense" against continued Israeli attacks. Brezhnev did not specify what sort of "system" he had in mind, but the only logical choice was to provide Nasser with the low-altitude SA-3 system, the most sophisticated of Soviet surface-to-air missile systems, requested by the Egyptian president during his visit. In the meantime, the Soviet leaders settled on sending Kosygin's letter, which Brezhnev had a "personal hand" in drafting.[24]

Kosygin's letter quickly grabbed the attention of Nixon's senior foreign policy advisers. Less than forty-eight hours after being informed of the contents of the note, Secretary Rogers informed Nixon that the letter "had an element of threat" and "could signal that the Soviets have taken a decision to give more arms to Nasser." He recommended a "prompt" and "firm" reply to Kosygin to dispel the notion that the United States had "colluded" with Israel and to convey to the Kremlin the need for "positive reaction" to the Rogers Plan.[25] Kissinger, though, went even further in his assessment. In his estimate, the Kosygin letter constituted the "first Soviet threat" to the administration and warranted a reply from Nixon that would not only "come down very hard" on the Soviets but would press the Kremlin to spell out its views on what the Arabs would commit themselves to if Israel agreed to a cease-fire and withdrew from the occupied territories.[26]

For Kissinger, moreover, there seemed to be no doubt in his mind that Moscow had already decided to ratchet up tensions by sending weapons and personnel to the region. He warned Nixon that for the Soviets to provide Egypt with "effective means" to offset Israeli supremacy, they would have to insert their own people into "more exposed combat positions" and "supplement" Egyptian pilots with Soviet "volunteers." Another possibility Kissinger feared was the development of an air defense system similar to that employed by North Vietnam, which would entail saturating areas with SA-2 missile sites and the use of more conventional antiaircraft systems to protect against Israeli planes flying at lower altitudes.[27]

Even if the Politburo proceeded with the scenario Kissinger laid out, however, it still, in his mind, did not explain the "diffuse" nature of the Soviet threat. In fact, the more Kissinger reflected on the Kosygin letter, the more "inept" and, for that reason, "disturbing" he found it. In his third memo to the president analyzing the letter in less than a week, Kissinger argued that what made the Soviet warning so surprising was that there was very little upside for the Kremlin to get Israel to desist in its attacks. If the cease-fire was not restored, as seemed likely in view of Moscow's inability to deliver their clients, the Soviets were "stuck" with their threat to "provide means for a rebuff." But, he added, sending more equipment, even if it was more advanced, was unlikely to encourage the Israelis to curtail their deep-penetration bombing of Egyptian territory. "So the onus of escalation is on the Soviets and the Kosygin letter has added to its weight," he concluded. Nixon concurred with Kissinger's assessment: "I agree," he scribbled on the top of Kissinger's memo. "Confused men do the unexpected and wrong things."[28]

It was exactly because of the "unexpectedness" of the Kosygin letter that the White House gave the utmost consideration on how to respond to such a threat. On February 4, Nixon replied to Kosygin, rejecting his interpretation of the events and placing responsibility for Israel's deep-penetration raids squarely on Nasser's inability to curtail the fedayeen attacks against Israel. Any implication that the United States had been a party to or had encouraged violations of the cease-fire was "without foundation," he charged, and he warned that the United States would carefully monitor the military balance in the Middle East and would "not hesitate to provide arms to friendly states as the need arises." The president concluded the letter by rejecting the notion that Israel would have to withdraw before there was a "full agreement" between the parties on all elements of a peace settlement, and reminded the Soviet premier that the Rogers Plan met the "legitimate concerns" of both sides on all key questions, including withdrawal.[29]

The president, however, did not stop there. Despite seeking Soviet cooperation on Vietnam, arms control, and other areas of mutual concern, he wanted to make sure that the United States did not appear a paper tiger in the Middle East or that he was too preoccupied with Vietnam to deal with the events in the region. As his advisers prepared the president's first annual report to Congress on foreign policy, Nixon made sure the report included a stern warning on the Middle East that would grab the Kremlin's attention. When the report arrived on Congress's doorsteps in mid-February, the message was quite clear: "The United States would view any effort by the Soviet Union to seek predominance in the Middle East as a matter of grave concern." He added that "any effort by an outside power to exploit local conflict for its own advantage or to seek a special position of its own would be contrary to that goal."[30]

At the same time, Kissinger indicated his concern over the potential US-Soviet confrontation in the Middle East by organizing two separate meetings of the Washington Special Actions Group (WSAG)—the NSC subcommittee for contingency planning and crisis management—to develop a strategy in the event that Moscow openly assumed responsibility for Egypt's defense. During its first meeting on February 9, Kissinger indicated that he felt it was "essential we make sure our plans were in order" and that "all possible contingences" be examined. He ordered the development of a US position for responding to Soviet moves in Egypt and asked both the State Department and the Central Intelligence Agency to assess the overall power balance in the region, pointing out that the United States could not afford to stand back in the face of Soviet aggression. "This would in effect be an extension of the Brezhnev doctrine to the Mid-East," he said, "drawing the UAR symbolically into the area of Soviet predominance."[31]

When the WSAG convened again two days later, there remained widespread concern that should the Soviet Union assume responsibility for the

Egyptian defenses there was little the United States could do to counter the move other than to supply Israel with a new shipment of Phantoms. Yet even that move, the WSAG acknowledged, could "blow the place apart" and could force Moscow to respond with its naval forces in the Mediterranean. Just as important was the glaring fact that militarily the Soviets would be left in a superior position in the event that a crisis in the Middle East erupted. A CIA National Intelligence Estimate on Soviet policies in the Middle East prepared in February concluded that the Soviet military presence in the region is "likely to prove durable" and that "radical nationalist forces" will continue to receive Moscow's support.[32] "We could mount a strike," said air force lieutenant general John W. Vogt during the February 11 meeting of the WSAG, "but if the Soviets responded they could rapidly outbid us."[33]

One conclusion that certainly emerged from the two WSAG meetings was the potential arms race likely to erupt in the Middle East if a cease-fire was not quickly reached. Writing to the president on February 10, Kissinger again warned that that "substantial numbers" of Soviet "technicians" were likely to arrive in Cairo to assist Egyptian ground-to-air defense systems; that Soviet pilots could assume responsibility for Egyptian air defenses; and that new "offensive weapons systems," such as surface-to-surface missiles, could be installed to thwart continued Israeli missions inside Egypt. If any of these steps were taken, he explained, the administration had to consider seriously whether it could afford to let Moscow "openly" assume responsibility for the defenses of a Middle Eastern country without responding. "So far we have indicated our determination not to let the local arms balance shift against Israel," he wrote. "But if the Soviets enter the picture, more may be required and our response would assume a direct anti-Soviet character."[34]

Thus, hoping to avert what quickly emerged as a showdown between the superpowers, Kissinger summoned Dobrynin to the White House to discuss how to defuse the unfolding crisis in the Middle East. Kissinger assured the ambassador that the president attached the "utmost importance" to Kosygin's message and gave "special attention" to the Soviet threat to adopt measures to ensure that Arab countries had the capabilities to repel Israel. But he also made it clear that the president would be especially troubled if he were to learn that Moscow had dispatched its military personnel to Arab countries.[35] Kissinger also suggested that given the fact that the Two Power

talks between the State Department and Soviet ambassador ended unsuc-
cessfully, Moscow and Washington should "bypass the usual diplomatic
channels" and therefore should discuss the Middle East situation through
the "confidential Soviet Ambassador-Kissinger channel," not point-by-point
as Dobrynin had done with Sisco and Rogers, but in much broader terms.
"Wouldn't it still be possible to do something to alleviate the situation and
find ways to make some progress on the settlement issue?"[36]

Dobrynin would not admit it during the meeting, but Kissinger's reaction was exactly what the Soviets had wanted. As soon as he returned to the
embassy, he gleefully dashed off a telegram to the Foreign Ministry indicating that Kosygin's letter "obviously troubled" the president and had forced
the White House to depart from its "very convenient position" of using
Israeli military action to exert diplomatic pressure on the Arab countries.
Dobrynin encouraged his bosses to get tough with the administration and
"exploit" Nixon's fear of further Soviet military involvement in the Middle
East: "We can make use of Nixon's aforementioned interest especially if, in
this connection, the U.S. Government could be informed . . . of our pilots'
appearing in the UAR (for example, to defend Egypt strictly within its own
borders). Under current conditions, such a prospect could perhaps turn out
to be the most effective way to compel Nixon to look seriously at the Middle
East situation and at his own U.S. position in this regard."

Of course, Dobrynin recognized the possibility that the United States
could just as easily respond by increasing American shipments of Phantom
aircraft to Israel to offset the additional Soviet weapons and personnel. But
he firmly believed that for Nixon to take such measures at a time when
Israeli aircraft were attacking Arab countries was extremely remote. "The
Arab world, even the so-called 'moderate countries,' would never forgive
the current President, and U.S. prestige there would be completely undermined for a long time," the Soviet ambassador argued in his telegram.
Just as important, though, Dobrynin believed that without a credible threat,
the White House had no incentive to pressure the Israelis to desist in its
attacks. "One can say with almost complete certainty that another discussion with Kissinger of the main issues pertaining to a settlement is unlikely
to produce any kind of result. The Americans will adhere to their
well-known positions."[37]

Kissinger and Dobrynin in the Map Room of the White House. *(Nixon Presidential Library)*

The problem for the Nixon administration, therefore, was how to call for cessation of hostilities between Egypt and Israel without also appearing to capitulate to Soviet demands. On February 11, Jacob Beam, the US ambassador in Moscow, spent nearly two hours with Foreign Minister Andrei Gromyko attempting to reach a compromise on the escalating problem in the Middle East. Beam informed Gromyko that Washington favored "scrupulous adherence" by both sides to United Nations cease-fire resolutions but warned that if Moscow introduced "more sophisticated weaponry" or took other steps of an "extraordinary nature," the United States would have "no alternative" but to consider steps to restore the military balance favorable to Israel.[38]

Two days later, Undersecretary of State Elliot Richardson quietly summoned Rabin to the State Department to encourage his government to agree to a cease-fire. Richardson explained that the recent developments had created a "critical" and in many ways "intractable" situation not only between Egypt and Israel but also for the United States and the Soviet Union. But Rabin did not seem interested in trying to promote US-Soviet relations. He replied that his government had to consider its own position in the Middle East, not just the tensions that continued fighting would cause in US-Soviet relations, and he insisted that Kosygin's letter made it even more necessary to convince Nasser that the War of Attrition was far more costly to him than it was to Israel. Rabin added that it was important that his government "bring realities home" to the Egyptian people that Israel would not tolerate further casualties along the Suez Canal. "To stop now would be a sign of weakness," he added, "particularly in light of [the] recent Kosygin approach."[39]

Operation *Kavkaz*

Rabin's bold assertions would not last long. On March 17, just a little over a month after having so confidently encouraged his leadership to continue the deep-penetration bombing, despite calls from the United States to agree to a cease-fire, the Defense Intelligence Agency (DIA) informed the Israeli military attaché in Washington that a "substantial shipment" of Soviet arms had arrived in Egypt, including ten sites of SA-3 surface-to-air-missiles—the most advanced Soviet antiaircraft system. The missiles were accompanied, according to the DIA report, by fifteen hundred Russian "experts," quickly interpreted by American officials as merely the "first installment of a major Soviet military move" in the Middle East that would no doubt be followed up by additional Soviet troops to Egypt and possibly Syria.[40]

The Soviet intervention in the Egyptian-Israeli War of Attrition, known as Operation *Kavkaz*, proved to be one of the most significant military operations outside the Warsaw Pact the Soviet Union had ever made, and it was no doubt a clear sign of Soviet frustration over Israel's continued success over its Arab client. Before 1970, the Soviets had often threatened to send its combat forces to the Middle East in Arab-Israeli crises, but they had always showed restraint for fear of confrontation with the United States. During the 1956 Suez Crisis, for example, Moscow sent letters to the governments in Great Britain, France, and Israel insisting that the Soviets would use force to "crush the aggressors and restore peace" to the Middle East, but they did not intervene out of concern that the United States might respond by resisting the concurrent Soviet invasion of Hungary.[41] In 1967, the Soviets had plans for a naval landing on Israeli shores to support the Arab states, but the Kremlin later aborted the mission when it became evident that President Johnson would resist.[42] And following the Six-Day War, the Kremlin helped rebuild Egypt's army and continued to train its pilots but rejected repeated requests by Nasser to dispatch Soviet pilots to Egypt for fear of escalating the conflict into a superpower confrontation.[43]

What made this situation different, however, was Moscow's belief that the United States would not respond militarily to its intervention in Egypt. Kremlin leaders concluded that with Washington increasingly preoccupied by the Vietnam War and still seeking Soviet cooperation on arms control and European security, Washington would avoid taking steps that would lead to a superpower confrontation in the Middle East. It was also fair for the Kremlin to reason that since the United States failed to respond military to the 1968 invasion of Czechoslovakia, it would not make a stand in the present crisis. As Dobrynin wrote in a telegram to the Foreign Ministry, "Even if we currently have no plans to deploy our crews with Egypt's air-defense system, we should—in the Embassy's view—make use of this issue for political and diplomatic ends, to put pressure on the Nixon administration now."[44]

Preparations for Operation *Kavkaz*, we now know, had been in the works for some time. Beginning in the summer of 1969, after months of watching Egypt suffer significant losses to Israel's "flying artillery," air defense units from Moscow, Leningrad, Byelorussia, and Dnieperpetrovsk were organized to be sent to Egypt sometime later that year. The units were composed of a SA-3 brigade, along with two regiments (roughly seventy planes and one hundred pilots) of MiG-21 intercept planes, and SA-7 personnel antiaircraft missiles. By December 1969, approximately ten thousand men had been chosen for Operation *Kavkaz*, and the division's air defense units were being sent to the Ushuluk training area in Kazakhstan.[45] It was also during December that Brezhnev told an Egyptian delegation led by Vice President Anwar Sadat that the Kremlin had selected more than sixty Soviet pilots to go to Egypt within a month under the name of "experts" and promised to dispatch a large number of SA-3s, as well as an "additional batch" of missiles to defend major Egyptian cities and towns against Israeli air attacks. "Such missiles would be effective against low-flying aircraft," Brezhnev asserted, "and would be accompanied by about 1,000 Soviet military personnel to operate them in the first phase of the action."[46]

Nasser urged Brezhnev to make the operation overt, but the Soviet leader objected, fearing a reciprocal response by the United States. Accordingly, Soviet soldiers (and eventually pilots) were disguised in Egyptian uniforms and their aircraft painted with Egyptian markings to conceal the nature of the mission. In most instances, Soviet pilots did not cross over into Israeli-controlled territory. "The pilots were forbidden to cross certain boundaries," defense minister Marshal Grechko said years later of the instructions the pilots had to respect. "If you fly across the Canal or Gulf [of Suez] you're not longer ours."[47]

The Soviets attempted to conceal their new military commitment to Egypt by simultaneously beginning a new diplomatic offensive that would produce an Egyptian-Israeli cease-fire. The Kremlin hoped that it could keep the military aspects of the operation secret until its antiaircraft systems and personnel were firmly in place, leaving Egypt in a stronger position militarily vis-à-vis Israel by the time the cease-fire was reached. Egypt could then break the cease-fire at a later date if it desired, leaving Israel at a great disadvantage.

Early signs of the strategy appeared in a session of the Four Power talks at the United Nations on March 5 when the Soviets rather suddenly began to indicate their willingness to resume a "constructive dialogue" with the United States after weeks of attacking American officials in that forum. During the meeting, Yacov Malik, the Soviet permanent representative to the United Nations, set forth in detail for the first time his country's reactions to the United States peace proposal of December 18 dealing with Jordan, which contained language almost identical to that contained in the Rogers Plan. He stated explicitly that Moscow would accept "minor rectifications" of the Israeli-Jordanian border and agreed to language calling for the mutual recognition between Egypt and Israel, as well as the right to live in peace.[48] Two days later, Foreign Minister Gromyko cemented the plan with instructions to Dobrynin to bring the cease-fire proposal to the United States and conduct a series of talks with the American side on Soviet proposals for a settlement in the Middle East "based on the unfolding situation."[49]

Had American intelligence not detected the missile systems and personnel, it is quite clear that the Soviets would have succeeded in their deceptive plan. Kissinger, in fact, concluded that the cease-fire offer, which Dobrynin presented to him at the White House on March 10,[50] proved that "our policy of relative firmness has paid off" and demonstrated that the Soviets were concerned to "defuse the growing appearance of confrontation, which they themselves launched with the Kosygin letter."[51] In a meeting with Rabin on March 12, Kissinger asked Israel to cease its deep-penetration raids and immediately agree to a de facto cease-fire. To entice the Israelis to accept the Soviet offer, he informed the ambassador that the United States would agree to replace Israeli aircraft losses during the period 1969–1971 and in the longer term would supply the major part of the Israeli hardware request should there be "more significant" Soviet arms shipments into Egypt.[52] The Israelis accepted the cease-fire offer on March 17 but withdrew their agreement within hours on learning from the Pentagon of the arrival in Egypt of the SA-3s and the fifteen hundred Russian "experts."[53]

The Israelis were not the only ones, however, who felt deceived by the Soviet maneuver. Both Nixon and Kissinger were furious that the Kremlin had used the ruse of a cease-fire to conceal the fact that they were making a major military move in the Middle East. Indeed, just hours before Nixon received the news about the arrival of the Soviet forces and equipment in Egypt, he had dictated a tough memorandum to Kissinger in which he made it clear that he expected the Israelis to accept the Soviet cease-fire proposal. Obviously frustrated that Israel's continued shelling of Egyptian territory threatened the prospects for détente with the Soviets, Nixon wanted the message sent that Israel should stop relying on what he called the "peace at any price" Democrats in Congress—Mike Mansfield, William Fulbright, and Stuart Symington—who professed to support Israel almost unconditionally but who were "very weak reads" and would "cut and run" when any Middle East conflict "stares them straight in the face."[54]

Yet once the Soviet ploy became apparent, the president quickly changed his tone, worried that the US offer to resupply Israeli aircraft losses would invite continued deep-penetration raids on Egypt and could lead to a broader regional conflict. "I would be remiss in my duty if I did not tell you that our course involves the most serious dangers of a Middle East war and of a profound misunderstanding by the Soviets," Kissinger wrote to Nixon following a telephone conversation with Rabin late on March 17. "The Israelis are getting desperate. Convinced that they have nothing to lose, they may well attack."[55]

Nixon understood the dangers of a looming Middle East war and the potential it would have to draw the superpowers into a confrontation there, but he was not about to back down in the face of Soviet aggression. The following day, March 18, he invited Rabin to join him for a meeting in his private office in the Executive Office Building. He wanted the ambassador to know that he remained committed to maintaining the power balance in Israel's favor. "Within our bureaucracy, there are many who don't agree," said Nixon. "They think our real interests in the Middle East lie with the Arabs but those others don't have my power." More important, though, Nixon wanted the Israelis to know that the United States would not stand in the way should the Israelis feel the need to attack the new Soviet installations. He also left Rabin with a message to take back to Jerusalem that could profoundly alter the conflict: "I am aware of the Soviet SA-3s and I hope you knock them out. You can't let them build up."[56]

Rabin was not the type of person who displayed much emotion or was prone to passionate outbursts. Nor did Rabin ever express his gratitude for the support the United States continued to show his country. "Yitzhak Rabin had many extraordinary qualities, but the gift of human relations was not one of them," Kissinger later wrote of the ambassador. "If he had been handed the entire United States Strategic Air Command as a free gift he would have a) affected the attitude that at last Israel was getting its due, and b) found some technical shortcoming in the airplanes that made his accepting them a reluctant concession to us." Yet even Rabin could not contain his response to the president's suggestion to take out the SA-3s: "Attack the Russians?" Rabin blurted out, totally "flabbergasted" at the potential consequences such an action could invite.

The president did not reply to the ambassador's outburst, but all the better in Rabin's opinion. "I didn't want him to elaborate on the subject," he later wrote of the bizarre exchange with Nixon. "If the President said, 'No, do not attack them under any circumstances!' and developments later made it imperative for Israel to destroy the missiles, she would run the risk of defying the President of the United States and disrupting relations with her strongest ally," said Rabin.[57] It was highly doubtful that Israel would ever deliberately attack the Russians given that the Soviet Union now had the capabilities in the region to deliver a fierce response.

Kissinger, moreover, also felt the need to hit back at Soviets. In the thirteen months since he had established the back channel with the Soviet ambassador, Dobrynin had always been honest and up-front with him, which allowed the two to work on a range of topics of mutual interests unencumbered by the normal bureaucratic channels. For Dobrynin to double-cross him by offering a cease-fire proposal while at the same time Soviet military equipment and personnel were being sent to Egypt was a cheap stunt. The move, he believed, was reminiscent of the tactics employed by Moscow during the Cuban Missile Crisis and warranted a firm "dressing down."[58]

Kissinger delivered his rebuke of the Soviet tactic in a meeting with Dobrynin on March 20. He explained that the White House had taken the offer of a cease-fire from the Soviet government with "extreme seriousness" and had even encouraged the Israelis to accept the deal. But as a result of the new developments the president canceled his request to the Israelis for a cease-fire, and the matter was now off. More important, though, Kissinger believed that the Soviet stunt could have a detrimental impact on Washington's ability to negotiate with Moscow. "We are at an important turning point," he explained to Dobrynin, obviously upset about the entire episode. "We were prepared to deal with the Soviet Union precisely, correctly, unemotionally, and thoroughly in the direction of détente, if the Soviet Union would forgo its policy of attempting to squeeze us at every opportunity."[59]

Dobrynin professed to have no knowledge of any missiles being sent to Egypt, and he rejected Kissinger's accusations. "To equate this issue with the piratical raids by Israeli aircraft is like portraying burglars who systematically rob other people's homes as the injured parties when the homeowner decides to install a lock to keep the burglars out," he retorted, according to the account posted in his journal.[60] But, he inquired, if the missiles were defensive, why did the president object?

"Because it might be that the ceasefire was just being used to improve the Egyptian military position," Kissinger quickly shot back. Kissinger added that if the Soviet Union wanted to make a more equitable solution, then it should reconsider its position. Until then, he argued, the United States felt no obligation to ask Israel to accept the cease-fire proposal. "The introduction of Soviet military personnel could only lead to a Vietnam for the Soviet Union," he warned the ambassador, "since all we had to do was send in equipment which could be matched only by personnel."[61]

Although Kissinger took a tough line privately with Dobrynin, Nixon wanted to send a public message to Moscow that he was not interested in ratcheting up tensions in the Middle East. On March 23, he hastily arranged a press conference at the White House and announced that it was simply "too early" to determine whether the recent deliveries of the SA-3s to Egypt changed the military balance in the region, maintaining that one of his primary objectives for the Middle East was to "reduce the flow of arms" into the region.[62] "I hoped that since Israel was already in a strong military position, I could slow down the arms race without tipping the fragile military balance in the region," he later wrote in his memoirs about his decision to postpone the delivery of Phantom jets to Israel. "I also believed that American influence in the Middle East increasingly depended on our renewing diplomatic relationships with Egypt and Syria, and this decision would help promote that goal."[63]

Listening to Nixon's remarks from the Soviet embassy in Washington, Dobrynin was highly skeptical that Nixon's refusal to provide Israel with additional aircraft was a model of restraint. "Judging by our own observations and information from a variety of sources," he wrote in a telegram back to Moscow after the press conference, "the issue of Soviet crews for SAM-3 [SA-3] missiles . . . represents the new factor obliging Nixon to take action." As far as the US government was concerned, Dobrynin believed, the appearance of Soviet crews for these missiles would constitute a "qualitatively new factor" in the entire Middle East situation, since it would inevitably lead to the deployment of Soviet pilots in Egypt to defend against the new installations. "The prospect in itself of the appearance of Soviet missile crews brings the Nixon administration face-to-face with the difficult question of what the U.S. would do in that eventuality: to grant the Israelis additional 'Phantoms' in response or deploy American air-defense installations in Israel," he concluded. "In both cases the consequences for the U.S. in the Arab world could be catastrophic."[64]

Dobrynin had good reason to be skeptical. The president, however, was not about to let the Soviet Union off the hook. Following a meeting of the National Security Council on March 25, he met with CIA director Richard Helms and instructed him to step up covert operations against Moscow any place in the world he could find. "He was as emphatic on this as I ever heard him on anything," Helms recorded immediately after the meeting. Though it was not entirely clear as to exactly what kind of "black operations" the president had in mind, he wanted Helms to be "as imaginative as we could," including an increase of the use of Radio Free Europe, among other ideas. He also agreed with Helms's assertion that the United States "should give up nothing which constituted a pressure on the Soviet Union . . . without exacting a specific price in return," pointing out that "we had had nothing from the Russians in the recent past except assistance on the shape of the table at the Paris Peace talks." "Just go ahead," Nixon instructed. "Hit the Soviets, and hit them hard."[65]

"The More Perilous Crisis"

Nixon had other reasons for eschewing a protracted arms race with the Soviets in the Middle East. Not only did he still hold out the possibility of a major summit with the Soviet leadership in Moscow sometime during the year, but beginning in late March, the president shifted his attention almost entirely away from the simmering crisis in the Middle East to the escalating problems in Cambodia. Earlier in the month, Cambodian general and prime minister Lon Nol orchestrated a coup against the long-standing leader Prince Norodom Sihanouk, throwing the country into violent civil war. Although Lon Nol was a staunch anticommunist with ties to the South Vietnamese and American forces, and opposed the presence of North Vietnamese forces in Cambodia, the White House initially appeared reluctant to throw its weight behind the new regime. Speaking at a news conference on March 21, Nixon described the situation in Cambodia as "unpredictable" and "fluid," and insisted that although the United States had established a "temporary" relationship with the new government in Phnom Penh there could be a possibility of Sihanouk's return. "I think any speculation with regards to which way this government is going to turn, what will happen to Prince Sihanouk when he returns, would both be premature and not helpful."[66]

Privately, though, the administration took a number of steps to signal that they welcomed Lon Nol as an ally in Southeast Asia. Shortly after the coup, Nixon instructed the CIA director to develop and implement "a plan for maximum assistance to pro-US elements in Cambodia"[67] and began the initial plans for ground operations against North Vietnamese sanctuaries inside Cambodia.[68] Over the coming weeks, the White House approved ten million dollars in secret aid to Lon Nol and extended recognition to his government.[69] On April 22, just a little more than a week before the president authorized the American incursion into Cambodia, Nixon wrote Kissinger to make it clear where he stood: "I think we need a bold move in Cambodia . . . to show that we stand with Lon Nol. I do not believe he is going to survive. There is, however, some chance that he might and in any event we must do something symbolic to help him survive."[70]

That the White House appeared entirely preoccupied with the events in Southeast Asia was most evident to the Soviet ambassador in Washington. After two separate meetings with Kissinger in early April, Dobrynin informed the Kremlin that "in terms of urgency a Middle East settlement is not currently item No. 1 on the White House foreign policy agenda." For Nixon and Kissinger, he argued, "that issue continued to be Vietnam." At the same time, though, Dobrynin did point out that Kissinger's persistent questioning about Soviet military personnel inside Egypt was "noteworthy" and was "forcing the White House—perhaps for the first time—to take stock of events in the Middle East seriously and with increasing wariness." The ambassador added that during his conversations with the national security adviser he criticized the fact that the United States was not giving the "requisite priority attention" to seeking an early peace settlement in the Middle East while the Soviet government had proposed a cease-fire to quell the violence in the region.[71]

With Washington focused on the unfolding events in Laos and Cambodia and the White House showing no signs that it would challenge the latest Soviet moves inside the UAR, Moscow pressed for further strategic gains in the Middle East. On April 18, the Soviets completed the final stage of Operation *Kavkaz* by unleashing Russian pilots to participate in the air defense of Egypt. That day, two Israeli Phantom jets returning from a routine reconnaissance mission inside Egypt were chased down by eight MiG-21s all manned by "Russian-speaking pilots," according to Israeli intercepts of the mission. The Israeli planes were not shot down by the Soviets, but the encounter was stunning nonetheless. "It was a quantum leap in Soviet intervention," historian David Korn concluded in his study of the War of Attrition. The move showed that Moscow was willing to engage the Israelis and openly challenge a key American ally.[72]

It is possible that Soviet decision to make its mission inside Egypt overt could have been a preemptive move to what Moscow believed the United States was about to do to communist forces in Southeast Asia. One of the reasons the Kremlin brought Ambassador Dobrynin back to Moscow during the second week in April was to get his personal assessment of what the Americans were planning. More important, however, Moscow simply could no longer tolerate Israel's continued attacks on its ally in Cairo and on its own personnel inside Egypt. Just days before the Soviet-Israeli encounter, in fact, Brezhnev gave a speech lambasting "imperialist" designs in the Middle East and made it clear that the socialist countries were not only "loyal friends" of the Arab peoples but would provide the Arab states "all the necessary assistance to frustrate the plans of the aggressors in the Middle East."

In concluding his comments on Soviet foreign policy, the general secretary explicitly warned that Israel's "aggressive" policy "placed in jeopardy the security of its own people, whose future lies in good neighborliness and not in antagonism to the Arabs."[73]

The Israelis guarded the news that Soviet pilots had taken an active role in the Egyptian air defense for nearly a week, through the Passover holiday, but quickly saw this development as a way to extract more arms shipments from the Americans. On the evening of April 24, Rabin met with Kissinger at the White House and informed him of the recent encounter with the Russian pilots. According to Israeli estimates there were at least fifty Soviet pilots involved flying from three bases, two southwest of Cairo and one near Alexandria. Just as important, Rabin told Kissinger, was the "corollary" to the Soviet move, whereby the Egyptians had increased their air attacks on the Israeli positions in the Sinai. The ambassador concluded by stating "emphatically" and "with some emotion" that this was no longer an issue of Israeli-Egyptian military balance. "Now there is a new element," he said. "Israel wants more planes."[74]

The Israelis, too, felt that the policies adopted by the administration over the preceding months, especially President Nixon's decision not to provide Israel with additional aircraft following the discovery of the SA-3s, had encouraged Moscow to adopt such an aggressive policy in the region without fear of American retribution. Rabin told Kissinger that "the Soviets will fill a vacuum whenever they feel one exists" and asked for a prompt reaction from the administration to the latest Soviet move. He also told Joe Sisco at the State Department that the Kremlin's decision to fly combat missions over Egypt constituted a "drastic and significant" change to the power balance in the Middle East and maintained that the Nixon administration had an obligation to provide Israel with additional aircraft based on the commitments President Nixon had made to him back in March.[75] Three days later, Prime Minister Meir sent Nixon an emotional letter pleading for a "clear and vigorous public American reaction on the highest level of authority."[76]

Although Rabin had been in Washington only a brief time, he knew that these closed-door meetings with Kissinger and Sisco would not make the president focus on this issue when he clearly was preoccupied with the events in Southeast Asia. Thus, on April 29, in an effort to increase public pressure on the White House, he distributed a paper to members of Congress, the news media, and numerous private Americans and organizations detailing the Soviet Union's new "combatant" role against Israel. The report explained that Soviet pilots based on Egyptian airfields had been carrying out "combat missions" against Israeli planes, with instructions to "intercept and engage" them in battle. The Israeli paper also left little doubt that the Soviets, bent on aggrandizement, had systematically wrecked prospects for a relaxation of tensions in the Middle East: "This development is the culmination. .. of a progression of escalatory steps undertaken by the Soviet Union in which an increasing disposition is being displayed to assume direct combatant functions against Israel."[77]

Nixon was not averse to reconsidering his decision on Israeli arms requests, but he viscerally opposed receiving any pressure from the Israelis or Jewish groups while he was absorbed in planning the Cambodian operation. Kissinger made this point to Rabin the following morning, April 30, the very day the Cambodian mission was set to commence. In a brief, seven-minute meeting Kissinger made sure that the ambassador understood that despite problems in areas of the world that appeared to be very different, the "critical situation" in Cambodia was closely linked to the problems in the Middle East and made attacks against the administration's policy "most unfortunate" since they could not but have concomitant effect on the administration's attitude with respect to the Middle East. "It is inconceivable that the United States could be crushed in one place and be expected to take a firm stand with even higher risks in another," he said.[78]

If Kissinger had hoped that his conversation with the Israeli envoy would quiet the storm, he was sadly mistaken. Over the next two weeks American newspapers and weekly magazines were filled with stories and editorials detailing the "ominous escalation toward the Big Power confrontation" that had emerged in the Middle East and were openly critical of Washington's perceived weakness in the region. "It [is] doubtful that a U.S. warning, even if Washington decided to issue it, would compel the Soviets to diminish their growing involvement," *Time* magazine reported. Even in the midst of the Cambodian incursion, the *New York Times* editorialized that the continuing crisis in the Middle East remained "more perilous" than the escalating Indochina conflict. "This step toward direct intervention by the Soviet Union on the Arab side," the *Times* concluded, "has forced the United States to reconsider its restrained policy regarding additional arms aid to Israel and raises the specter of a Big Power confrontation in the Middle East."[79]

Still, Kissinger knew that even though Cambodia was the administration's top priority at the moment, the Soviets had taken a step in the overall contest for preeminence in the Middle East that the United States could not afford to bow to or ignore. During the first week of May, while domestic protests against the Cambodian invasion erupted, he instructed his staff to prepare a series of policy options to confront the growing Soviet threat in the Middle East. Specifically, he wanted to know whether the United States was prepared to join a US-USSR power contest and whether the administration should prepare to confront Moscow by military force via Israel as a proxy or by direct US military involvement.[80]

When members of the State Department, the Central Intelligence Agency, the Pentagon, and the National Security Council met on May 8 to discuss these questions, it was evident that Washington had few plausible options for directly confronting the Soviet Union while at the same time leaving the door open to continue working with Moscow on issues like arms control and ending the Vietnam War. If they made it known that President Nixon was preparing for a direct US-Soviet military confrontation, the United States would strengthen its relationship with Israel and demonstrate that the administration did not lack determination regardless of the consequences for its positions elsewhere in the area. The problem, as the wave of antiwar protests across the country demonstrated, was that it was almost inconceivable the president could convince the American people to support military action in the Middle East when they would not support it in Southeast Asia. "Without domestic support," one study concluded, "the Administration might have to back down in a crunch and therefore should avoid one. Unless the US is prepared to attack Soviet forces, it should not assume that a show of force will produce a negotiated settlement."[81]

Kissinger left the meeting obviously frustrated with the seeming lack of options, and he felt that a new strategy was needed. In a telephone conversation with Sisco on May 11, he pleaded with the assistant secretary of state, who had been the architect of much of the administration's Middle East policy, that "we are making a Middle East war" and increasing the "domestic storms" against the president.[82] The following day, he proposed to Nixon an entire reevaluation of American policy in the Middle East. In two separate memoranda, Kissinger conceded that the basic foundations of US policy in the Middle East since the beginning of the administration "had been wrong across the board." The assumption that "major power talks" would break the impasse between the parties had not brought any of the parties to modify their positions in "any significant way," he argued. The belief that the Soviets would limit its involvement in Egypt and press Nasser to adopt a "more positive attitude" had also proved incorrect. And the notion that Israel would accept a "properly guarded U.S. position," he concluded, had not just been "flatly rejected" but had brought on the administration only increasing pressure to support Israel military and economically whether or not there was progress in the negotiations. "Perhaps it is time to shift our attention from the two-power and four-power exercises to direct action vis-à-vis the principal actors—Israel, the Palestinians, and the UAR."[83]

Although Kissinger was certainly correct to point out that a new approach was needed, by the time his memo reached the president's desk it was too late. The Soviet Union had outmaneuvered the United States in the Middle East without any retribution and had left both Washington and Jerusalem searching for new strategies to combat the Soviet threat. By the end of May, the SA-3 antiaircraft missiles were firmly emplaced inside Egypt, more than 150 Soviet pilots were aggressively defending Egyptian cities, and at least ten thousand Soviet "experts" had been sent to Egypt to defend against continued Israeli attacks. The Israelis, moreover, were no longer in the strategic position to penetrate beyond the Suez Canal zone without risking direct confrontation with the Soviets, and the Egyptians no longer felt as apprehensive about Israeli air raids. Defense Minister Moshe Dayan perhaps put it best when he said that the new situation could lead to "something we did not intend—our attacking the Russians and Russians attacking our aircraft. In whatever words you may wish to define it, this means war with the Russians."[84]

For the United States, the situation was equally dangerous. NSC staffer William Hyland aptly described the dilemma the Soviets moves in the Middle East had left for the White House:

One of the dangerous consequences of their forward policy in the Middle East is that having accumulated a large vested interest, they have had to devise new ways to protect their gains. It is not only a question of Soviet willingness to accept a much higher level of risk, it is their willingness to do so in a situation over which their control is limited, and in which no one, including the Kremlin, can foresee the outcome. This is why it is a dangerous path the Soviets have embarked on, and why we must treat it with the utmost seriousness.

. . . Having scored an immense psychological gain, with apparent impunity, it has generally been the Russians tactic first of all to consolidate their gains, and then press forward, testing the ground they move. Clearly, there is no evidence from the Soviets that their bargaining position has softened. To seize on minor changes in old Soviet formulas as 'movement' is a delusion. If anything, the Soviet position is tougher now.

. . . The toughening can only spring from their estimate of what their moves have cost thus far and what the future risks and gains are. Looking at our position and the Israeli standdown from deep raids, the Soviets must conclude that we have acquiesced in their direct intervention. . . . Thus the question of whether the Soviets will in fact, begin to inch forward becomes a crucial determinant. The policy issue is: are the Soviets more likely to extend their protective umbrella if we proceed with the sale of aircraft of Israel, or if we withhold them?[85]

Combined with the massive Soviet intervention and the president's own problems stemming from the Cambodian operation, it was not even practical to think that a new policy could develop in time to thwart Moscow's recent gains. Even Kissinger, who led the charge for a new American policy in the region, understood the realities of the moment: "The surrounding circumstances prevented the mustering of energies for such a battle. The physical and psychic toll of the Cambodia incursion was too great. Not until Watergate was Nixon so consumed and shaken; he was not prepared to add to his problems."[86]

FOUR

Crisis on the Suez,
June–September 1970

By the summer of 1970, the Middle East was at its most dangerous point since just before the outbreak of the Six-Day War. In the six months since the collapse of the Rogers Plan, the number of Soviet military forces in the region had doubled, Moscow had sent its most sophisticated air defense system to Cairo, and Russian pilots had assumed responsibility for the Egyptian air defense, coming into regular contact with the Israeli Air Force and even losing planes to Israel on occasion. Although the outbreak of another full-scale Arab-Israeli war was far from certain, the War of Attrition between Egypt and Israel was also far from over. As President Nixon said in a television interview on July 1, the Middle East "is like the Balkans before World War I, where the two superpowers, the United States and the Soviet Union, could be drawn into a confrontation that neither of them wants because of the differences there."[1]

Not since Nikita Khrushchev decided to send missiles to Cuba in the summer of 1962 had the Soviet Union posed such a challenge to the United States, and never before had the Soviets put their own forces in combat jeopardy for the sake of a noncommunist government. Having committed itself to the defense of Egypt, the Kremlin also assumed a much higher level of risk of conflict with the United States, for which no one could foresee the outcome. "This is why it is a dangerous path the Soviets have embarked on," William Hyland of the NSC staff told Henry Kissinger, "and why we must treat it with the utmost seriousness." Hyland also believed that Moscow, having scored an "immense psychological gain" by moving its forces into Egypt, would no doubt "press forward," testing the ground as it went. "Clearly, there is no evidence from the Soviets that their bargaining position has softened," he concluded. "If anything, the Soviet position is tougher now than only a few weeks ago."[2]

Over the summer, continued encounters between Israeli and Soviet military forces exacerbated tensions in the region and threatened the prospects for superpower détente. On the night of June 29–30, the Israeli Air Force attacked a deployment of Soviet ground-to-air missiles that had been moved to a line twenty-five to thirty-seven miles from the Suez Canal, destroying between eight and ten, with a loss of five airplanes. On July 26, Soviet-piloted MiG-21s attempted to intercept Israeli aircraft, firing some seven air-to-air missiles, and the following day provided air-to-air cover to Egyptian strike aircraft hitting Israeli emplacements on the east bank of the Canal. And on July 30, Soviet aircraft successfully intercepted Israeli fighters along the Egyptian bank of the Gulf of Suez, while the Israelis shot down four Soviet-piloted planes during the battle.[3]

For American policymakers, few good options were available. If they chose to provide Israel with new shipments of Phantom aircraft to match what the Soviets had provided Egypt, they would risk further weakening US standing in the Arab world, escalate the arms race in the Middle East, and heighten the prospects for a superpower confrontation. If instead they chose not to support Israel demonstratively with military assistance, the Soviets could exploit the weak response by continuing to move its military forces and defense systems toward the Canal. It would also be reasonable for the Soviets to conclude that the domestic fallout after the Cambodian operation, combined with the political and economic considerations of military escalation, had deterred Nixon from taking action.

Instead, the United States opted for a weak middle ground by pushing a temporary cease-fire agreement on the Arabs and Israelis. Although the cease-fire successfully ended the War of Attrition, prevented a probable US-Soviet crisis, and held until the outbreak of the 1973 October War, it left the Soviet military presence in Egypt intact and encouraged the leaders in both Moscow and Cairo to use the cover of cease-fire to fortify their positions along the Canal.

Back in the USSR

On June 29, 1970, Egyptian president Gamal Abdel Nasser arrived in Moscow seeking medical treatment from a number of Soviet doctors. In the three years since Egypt's humiliating defeat in the Six-Day War, Nasser's health had steadily declined. Diagnosed with diabetes in the early 1960s, Nasser also suffered from arteriosclerosis, the hardening of the arteries, high blood pressure, and heart disease. These problems were exacerbated by the fact that Nasser maintained a ferocious eighteen-hour workday, rarely taking time for vacations or relaxation, and continued his chronic smoking. Visitors to his office, *Time* magazine reported, noticed that he constantly wiggled his leg and smoked a hundred US and British cigarettes a day. Nasser's physician's ordered him to cut out the smoking and follow an easier regiment, but the Egyptian leader repeatedly ignored these warnings. "I don't need rest because I feel happy," he told the *New York Times*'s C. L. Sulzberger during a lengthy interview. "I have no problems in my life, with my family. I don't worry."[4]

Nasser did his best to hide his many ailments from the Egyptian people, his closest advisers, and family members, but by the late 1960s his deteriorating health became increasingly visible. During a visit to Moscow with PLO chairman Yasser Arafat in 1968, the Egyptian leader was hospitalized with acute pain in his legs as a result of the arteriosclerosis. Soviet doctors believed that the pain could be cured through mineral water treatment at Tskaltubo, a warm-springs facility in west-central Georgia where Stalin used to vacation, but Nasser repeatedly put off treatment.[5] The following year, he suffered a massive heart attack—his second in three years—and remained in bed for six weeks. The Egyptian government and media downplayed the severity of Nasser's health by reporting his illness as a bout of influenza, but Nasser knew his time was short. In December 1969, he reestablished the post of vice president of the United Arab Republic and appointed Anwar Sadat, a faithful confidant and a senior member of the Free Officers Movement responsible for the Egyptian Revolution in 1952, to the position.[6]

Although Nasser rarely left Egypt during the War of Attrition, he came to Moscow in the summer of 1970, after the end of the Israeli deep-penetration

With the issues of war and peace very much on his mind, President Gamal Abdel Nasser (right) views a Soviet troop formation with President Nikolai V. Podgorny (center) during the Arab leader's extended stay in Moscow, July 1970. (Bettman/ Corbis)

bombings, for almost three weeks of medical treatment. According to Sadat's autobiography, Soviet physicians placed Nasser in the "Astronauts Oxygen Room" for the rejuvenation of all of his body's cells. While Sadat believed the treatment did in fact rejuvenate the Egyptian president and made him look twenty years younger, the diagnosis remained bleak. Soviet doctors pleaded with Nasser to curtail his schedule and advised complete rest.[7]

But Nasser did not stop. While in the Soviet Union for his medical treatment, Nasser set aside several days to discuss with Soviet officials the latest Middle East peace initiative launched by Secretary of State William P. Rogers on June 19, 1970. Rogers's "Stop Shooting, Start Talking" cease-fire initiative has often been treated synonymously with the Rogers Plan of 1969. But the two proposals were quite different. What Rogers had in mind for this latest effort was far different and more limited than what he had proposed in his speech before the Galaxy Conference six months earlier. Instead of focusing on a comprehensive peace agreement that called for the withdrawal of Israeli forces from Arab territory, his new initiative concentrated solely on a publicly declared cease-fire between Egypt and Israel for ninety days.[8]

Once the parties accepted the cease-fire, negotiations between the two would then begin under UN envoy Gunnar Jarring. The advantage of this limited approach was that it created the necessary framework to begin negotiations. Israel would end its deep-penetration raids, while Egypt—and by extension the Soviet Union—would have to refrain from changing the military status quo in a twenty-five-mile zone on either side of the Suez Canal cease-fire line. Rogers envisioned that the cease-fire would last from July 1 to September 15, the opening day of the UN General Assembly, during which time "major efforts" would be made to get the parties to start talks on a political solution.[9]

The cease-fire initiative did not come as a surprise to officials in either Moscow or Cairo; Rogers, in fact, had been floating the proposal for almost a month. On June 8, the secretary of state had invited Anatoly Dobrynin, the Soviet ambassador to the United States, to his home in the Washington suburbs for a "secret unofficial conversation" devoted to the topic. There he informed the ambassador that under heavy pressure from Golda Meir, who believed that the Soviet Union "has decided to go on the path of a military blow to Israel," he planned to announce a "new American initiative" calling for a temporary Egyptian-Israeli cease-fire and an immediate return to the Jarring negotiations. The United States and the Soviet Union could at the same time "continue parallel discussions, helping Jarring and the sides themselves," Rogers suggested, but he left the possibility of those future talks intentionally vague, knowing how well the previous Middle East discussions with the Soviets had turned out.[10]

From the outset, Nasser seemed inclined to accept the cease-fire proposal even without Moscow's approval. The deep-penetration raids had exacted a devastating toll on the Egyptian economy, and the military and civilian populations were in need of a respite. The cease-fire proposal also appeared to Nasser as the response to the appeal he had made to Nixon on May 1, during his annual May Day speech, in which he asked the president to restore the peace between Egypt and Israel," as well as the statement he had made during an interview broadcast by the American National Educational Television Network on June 14, in which he indicated that he would accept a cease-fire of six months, so long as it would be used to arrange for Israel's withdrawal to the 1967 borders.[11]

Nasser's seeming willingness to invite a new American diplomatic initiative may simply have been an attempt to head off a hasty US commitment to provide more aircraft to Israel in the wake of the introduction of Soviet combat pilots to Israel, but it is also true that the cease-fire fitted well with his overall strategy to finish building the missile wall around the Canal. Once completed, not only would Egyptian armed forces along the west bank of the Suez be protected from Israeli air attacks, but when the time came for Egyptian troops to cross the Canal in an offensive operation, they would have the needed cover on the east bank as well. "I think it was probably from the outset . . . that Nasser decided to accept the Rogers initiative, though nobody knew of his decision until much later," Heikal later wrote.[12] Riad echoed these sentiments to historian David Korn during an interview in 1990: "Nasser saw the U.S. proposal as a situation in which we could not lose. On the one hand, we give the Americans the chance to try for a diplomatic solution. If that doesn't work, we will have improved our military position."[13]

Although Nasser's thinking made sense from a military and strategic point of view, convincing the Soviets to accept the US peace proposal was no easy task. There could be no doubt that Soviet prestige in the region would be severely damaged if Egypt were to accept an American-led peace effort. Having in mind Brezhnev's recent election speech in which he boasted that the "defense capacity" of the Arab states had been "restored" by Soviet forces, the Kremlin would not take well to being relegated to the role of spectator while the United States emerged as the power that, by its pressure on Israel, had achieved a settlement. "The Soviet Union," said Heikal, "aims at being itself the instrument for achieving a settlement, since it is the party which has paid the price for one. . . . Hence the contradiction between Soviet and Egyptian interests. A genuine balance between the two must be sought."[14]

During the first session of talks in Moscow with Brezhnev, Kosygin, Podgorny, Marshal Grechko, and Ambassador Vinogradov on June 30, Nasser explained why he wanted to accept the cease-fire. He told the Soviet leadership that his country continued to be subjected to intensive air raids by the US-built Israeli F-4 Phantoms, the objective of which, he argued, was to prevent the Egyptian army from completing its "offensive preparations to liberate our occupied lands."[15] When the talks resumed in Moscow between the Soviets and Egyptians on July 11, after Nasser had completed his medical treatment, Nasser made it clear why he planned to accept the proposal. He explained the United States would use an Egyptian rejection of the cease-fire to justify further arms supplies to Israel, but more important, he argued, Egyptian and Soviet military forces could use the temporary reprieve from Israeli deep-penetration raids to work on their own defenses in and around the Canal. "In other words, we exploit that period to reinforce our positions?" Brezhnev asked in response to Nasser's remarks. "That is true," the Egyptian replied. "But it would also benefit us politically, and prove that Egypt and the Soviet Union were working for peace."[16]

Although Brezhnev recognized the potential gain in using the cover of the cease-fire to complete the construction of the missile wall inside the Canal zone, he still resented the idea of Egypt accepting an American-led peace effort. In an impassioned speech to Nasser toward the end of their discussions, he made it known that he believed the United States sought to "grab the initiative as if they deserved credit for resolving the problem," even though it was the Soviets, Egypt's true "friends" and "brothers," who had participated with Egypt in "huge activities" in the military, economic, and political spheres. "We should think of a way which would not allow the enemy to reap the fruits of our efforts," said Brezhnev. Concluding his remarks, the Soviet party leader acknowledged that he spoke "frankly" and perhaps "emotionally" because of the "shrewd" and "cunning" way in which the United States presented its proposal.[17]

Before his final meeting with Nasser, Brezhnev received a telegram from Dobrynin cautioning the Soviet leadership from accepting the latest, American-led initiative. Dobrynin had been closely following the cease-fire proposal since the secretary of state had discussed the idea with him in early June. At that time, he had argued that that the initiative was clearly designed to "sell" possible Israeli concessions to Nasser "as a purely American achievement" and a "direct bridge" with the Arabs.[18] Dobrynin again stressed that it would be a mistake to allow Nasser to accept the Rogers initiative without any role for the Soviet Union. "Through this proposal the U.S. hopes to serve Israeli interests in excluding the USSR from the picture; to show the Arabs that the U.S. takes their interests into account and that they should do business with the U.S. not the USSR; and to halt the growth of the Soviet military presence in the Middle East," he argued. "We should not let the U.S. escape serious negotiations with the USSR on a basic settlement document, and that Nasser should be warned of the purely tactical goals behind the U.S. initiative."[19]

Brezhnev made these arguments to Nasser one last time, but he also warned Nasser that all Soviet advisers, experts, and pilots would be immediately withdrawn once the Middle East crisis was resolved, though what Brezhnev meant by "resolved" was not entirely clear. "We do not believe in occupying the territory of others," Brezhnev remarked, ignoring much of Soviet history in the postwar period. But Nasser retorted that he was "unhappy" to hear such words, as he would have never have come to Moscow if he had the slightest suspicion of a so-called Soviet occupation. He reminded Brezhnev that he had asked for the Soviet experts and pilots, and he would ask Moscow to recall them on the completion of their mission. "Those who talk of Soviet occupation of Egypt," Nasser concluded, "are Golda Meir, Nixon and Kissinger."[20]

Despite Brezhnev's pleas, however, by the end of his three weeks in Moscow, Nasser had obtained Soviet acquiescence in, though hardly an endorsement of, the US cease-fire offer. On July 23, the anniversary of the 1952 Revolution, Nasser delivered a major speech at Cairo University in which he announced Egypt's acceptance of the cease-fire but declared that this was Israel's "last chance," warning that "while we inform the United States that we have accepted its proposals, we also tell them that our real belief is that whatever is taken by force cannot be returned except by force."[21] The same day Nasser was delivering his speech, Dobrynin, in what amounted to a complete reversal of his previous statements to Sisco that Moscow would not endorse a "unilateral" peace overture, informed Rogers that the "Soviet Government's attitude to [the cease-fire] is positive" and that Moscow "holds no objections" to the "resumption by Ambassador Jarring of his mission."[22]

Kissinger Versus Rogers

Egypt's acceptance of the cease-fire proposal did little to convince Kissinger of the merit of Rogers's latest initiative. Since the moment the secretary of state proposed the idea to the president during the second week in June,

Kissinger had aggressively led the charge against the new maneuver. It was not that he opposed an end to the fighting in the region. In fact, he strongly believed that the Middle East situation had developed into the "most difficult" problem confronting the administration, and that a superpower confrontation "was much more likely there than in Southeast Asia."[23] He also recognized that while he did not know how to break the current "impasse" between Arabs and Israelis, there would have to be a "very firm diplomatic confrontation" between Washington and Moscow to convey that there were "limits" beyond which the United States would not be pushed, and the integrity of Israel was one such limit.[24]

For Kissinger, the major flaw in the State Department's new approach was that a temporary cease-fire left the Soviet military presence inside Egypt unchecked. If history had taught him anything, it was that the "normal pattern" of Soviet activity began with a "relatively moderate step" and then that the Soviets would "inch forward testing the ground as they go." Left unchecked, he argued, Moscow would continue to solidify its position in the region with impunity. The United States, therefore, had to convince the Kremlin that its present course of maintaining a vast and assuming responsibility for the Egyptian air defense had incalculable risks. "The choice for the U.S. is not whether to try for a settlement or to confront the USSR," Kissinger argued at a meeting of the National Security Council on June 10. "The choice is how to do both in order to achieve a settlement."[25]

Kissinger was certainly correct to point out that the State Department proposal did nothing to address the vast Soviet military presence inside Egypt, but his objections to the cease-fire seemed somewhat over the top. Certainly, it was unreasonable to expect that the Soviets would withdraw their forces from Egypt while Israeli forces continued to shell Egyptian cities, nor in the wake of the uproar over the Cambodian incursion could the United States expect to confront the Soviets militarily in the region. Even Nixon conceded during the NSC meeting that Moscow knew "the likelihood of U.S. action directly against them is in doubt."[26]

Most likely, Kissinger's objections stemmed in large part from his growing personal rivalry with Rogers rather than from any serious disagreement over what essentially amounted to a ninety-day cease-fire. According to H. R. Haldeman, the president's chief of staff, Kissinger was "basically jealous of any idea not his own," and "could not swallow . . . the Middle East plan because it is Rogers's." In fact, Haldeman concluded, "he's probably actually trying to make it fail for just this reason."[27]

While Nixon took the week to consider the merits of Rogers's new initiative, Kissinger continued to push ahead with his efforts to ensure that the cease-fire never saw the light of day. In a June 10 meeting with Dobrynin aboard the presidential yacht *Sequoia*, just hours after the NSC debate on the cease-fire proposal, Kissinger stressed that despite what he may have previously heard from Rogers, the United States had "no interest at all in a settlement, which would leave the combat personnel in Egypt."[28] Kissinger went on to ask the ambassador if his government would, for the benefit of US-Soviet relations, consider it possible to convey to Washington, "in any form and on a strictly confidential basis," that it had no intention of maintaining its military presence in Egypt even after a final settlement and the withdrawal of Israeli forces.[29]

Several days later, in a last-ditch effort to sink the proposal, Kissinger sent Nixon perhaps his most important memorandum on the Middle East in the eighteen months he had been working for the president. The State Department initiative to "Stop Shooting, Start Talking" had to be judged against the "compulsive peace initiatives" of the previous year, which "emboldened the Arabs" to increase the military pressure on Israel's borders, he argued. The new proposal seemed to Kissinger to involve the same dangers. Nasser would almost certainly interpret the action as a "halfway move," while the Soviets were sure to see the cease-fire as "a weak gesture in the face of their continued expansion of influence." Even if the Soviets and Egyptians did accept the cease-fire, the formula would be of "too little military consequence" and too hesitant to convince them that Washington would match their escalation in the area. Above all, Kissinger considered a major initiative "inopportune" unless it settled the issue of the Soviet combat presence, which for him remained the "heart of the problem."[30]

Instead of authorizing Rogers to move ahead with the cease-fire, Kissinger encouraged Nixon to pursue a "a more promising course" in which the United States would call on Israel to withdraw its forces from the Arab territories in return for "substantial" American military deliveries, while at the same time insisting on Egyptian acceptance of a peace agreement with

Israel and the withdrawal of all Soviet combat personnel from Egypt. For Kissinger, it was essential to tell Nasser that *only* the United States could bring about an Israeli withdrawal. Such an approach, he argued, "would combine the sticks of diplomatic pressure and withholding aircraft deliveries with the carrot of a large number of planes as a settlement is reached."[31]

Nixon decided on June 18 to move ahead with the cease-fire over Kissinger's objections, but that did not stop Kissinger from continuing to do his best to undermine the State Department's initiative. During a June 26 background press briefing on the Middle East, Kissinger continued to pound on the theme that the Soviet presence in Egypt represented a strategic threat to the United States. "We are trying to get a settlement in such a way that the moderate regimes are strengthened, and not the radical regimes," he said. "We are trying to *expel* the Soviet military presence, not so much the advisers, but the combat pilots and the combat personnel, before they become so firmly established."[32]

Had the comments remained on background, they may not have elicited much response. But on July 3, Murrey Marder, diplomatic correspondent for the *Washington Post*, quoted administration sources from the briefing as saying that Nixon believed that Soviet air combat forces must bc "expelled" from Egypt before they can become a "springboard" for long-term Soviet domination of the Mediterranean and the Middle East.[33] According to Kissinger, "all hell broke loose" in response to Marder's article. "I was accused by the State Department and pundits in the media of trying to scuttle the peace initiative, of making vainglorious threats beyond our capacity to carry out," he later wrote in his memoirs. Kissinger spoke with Marder on July 3 and said he wished he had used a "milder term" than "expel" for public consumption and asked for a retraction.[34] By that time, though, the damage had been done.

The *Washington Post* picked up on the White House–State Department disagreement and ran a lengthy editorial stating that the use of the word "expel" understandably raised public concern as to whether Nixon intended to employ military power for that end, and was used by the administration's "top officials" to "come to grips with the tough issues posed by the Soviet combat initiative."[35] Syndicated columnist Joseph Kraft added on July 9 that the "stiffening" Near East stand by the White House revealed "still another fissure" in the Nixon team. Said Kraft: "Secretary of State William Rogers and his aides have been coming on so soft about the Near East that there began to loom the danger the Russians would feel they could move with impunity in the area. The president and his aides felt obliged to speak with special force in order to unsay and undo some of the impressions left by the secretary of state."[36]

So concerned was Kissinger with the "mischievous press campaign" that he cabled Rogers in Tokyo to emphasize that the allegations of a "sharp policy disagreement" between White House and the State Department on the Middle East initiative "are completely without basis in fact." He assured Rogers that both he and the president were "completely behind" the State Department effort, which resulted from a "thoroughly coordinated State–White House action." Kissinger also wanted him to know that despite the press efforts to exploit the "spontaneous response" that he gave during his briefing the previous week, "nothing is being said or done here at the White House to convey the impression of differing policy views between State and ourselves on the Middle East issue."[37]

The Israelis, of course, were well aware of the policy disagreements between Kissinger and Rogers and used the fissure to try to ensure that the cease-fire did not take hold. Meir was hardly inclined to accept any proposal with Secretary of State Rogers's name attached to it, given what had happened with his Middle East peace plan the previous fall. But like Kissinger, she also saw no incentive to accept a proposal that left Soviet forces in Egypt virtually unchecked and that gave the Egyptians and Soviets cover to strengthen their position along the Canal. On learning the details of the cease-fire proposal, Meir instructed Rabin to inform the White House that Israel flatly rejected the American initiative and criticized the plan as "based on the lowest common denominator of American positions ever put in writing."[38]

For Meir, moreover, there were also strong domestic considerations within her own government for rejecting the proposal. Although Deputy Prime Minister Yigal Allon and Foreign Minister Abba Eban felt that it was illogical to refuse a proposal to "stop shooting and start talking" and that doing so would cause irreparable damage to Israel's image abroad, several ministers representing Gahal, a right-wing party led by Menachem Begin, threatened to resign from the government should Meir accept Rogers's latest initiative.[39]

When Rabin met with Kissinger at the White House on June 22, he not only conveyed the prime minister's message but outlined in detail why Israel remained so critical of the present American position. To begin with, said the ambassador, the United States had formulated its position with respect to the form of negotiations in "much vaguer terms" than in the Two and Four Power talks and had "abandoned" the Rhodes formula as a way for negotiations to take place. Second, the current formulation did not call on the Arab states to agree to a "formal state of peace" with Israel. Last, the proposed American public statement would make clear that the United States had decided not to sell additional planes to Israel. "This would just encourage additional blackmail and would encourage the Soviet Union to try to escalate its military involvement in the area," he argued.[40]

Kissinger half-heartedly defended the cease-fire proposal, telling Rabin that the State Department plan reflected the president's "best judgment" of what would be in the mutual interests of the United States and Israel in bringing about the conditions for peace in the Middle East, and he assured the ambassador that Nixon intended to deliver the planes to Israel this year and did not foresee the "drastic events" in early September that Rabin predicted.[41] But there could be no doubt that Kissinger agreed with much of what Rabin had to say. In fact, he told Nixon over the telephone minutes after this meeting that the Arabs would have to be "mad" not to accept the cease-fire. "We don't give the planes; Israel must accept the '67 border and all they [the Arabs] have to do is negotiate." He added that the wording of the proposal made it such that Israel would get the planes only if the negotiations failed, and therefore had no incentive to see the cease-fire hold. Nixon agreed: "That's for sure," he replied, "so we might as well give it to them.[42]

Rogers and Sisco were mystified at the prime minister's "groundless" apprehensions and instructed Wally Barbour, the US ambassador in Israel, to meet with Meir to discuss the proposal further. But Meir would not budge. She explained to Barbour that even if Soviet and Egyptian leaders agreed not to build up Egyptian defenses in the proposed cease-fire zone, there was nothing in the agreement that prevented them from pouring in additional hardware and continuing all-important troop training west of the zone. Meir did not question the Nixon administration's "goodwill and determination" to provide for Israel's security, but she could not be dissuaded that the cease-fire would leave Israel in a worse position militarily while gaining little in return from the Egyptians. Following the meeting, Barbour regrettably reported to Rogers that "while my inimitable style may impress you back there . . . I cannot claim to have made a major impression here."[43]

In case Meir did not make her position clear enough to Barbour, the prime minister went public with her opposition to the cease-fire proposal three days later. In a major speech before the Knesset on June 29, Meir called the temporary cease-fire a "trick" that would give Nasser "the transitional period" he required to prepare for the renewal of the war "in a more intense form." From the military point of view, Meir argued, Nasser needed such an interval to strengthen his fortifications all along the Canal line, to rehabilitate his bases and installations that had been damaged by the Israeli Air Force during the deep-penetration bombing, and above all, to "facilitate the installation of Soviet missiles for the purpose of achieving an air umbrella, trying to prevent our Air Force silencing the Egyptian artillery aimed at our positions, and enabling him to make an attempt to cross the Canal."[44]

Just as important, Meir made it clear that she believed the United States had mistakenly determined that through a temporary cease-fire Nasser would somehow reverse decades of hostility and violence directed against Israel. In fact, she read to the Knesset portions of a speech Nasser had delivered to a rally in Benghazi, Libya, on June 25 in which he declared that Egypt "will under no circumstances" agree to any bargaining about withdrawal. The withdrawal of Israeli forces from the Golan, Jerusalem, and the West Bank, Nasser maintained, must come before Sinai. "How can this statement possibly be interpreted as a sign of readiness for a peace settlement?" Meir asked the Knesset. "Nasser is fanning the flames of hostility and taking pains to give the conflict a pan-Arab character."[45]

Israel Reverses Course

Almost as soon as Meir finished her speech to the Knesset explaining why Israel would not accept the cease-fire agreement, "dramatic developments" along the Suez Canal compelled the Israelis to moderate their intransigent position. On the evening of June 29–30, five Israeli Phantoms were shot down by the Soviet-Egyptian missile system that had moved within twenty miles west of the canal under the cover of darkness the previous evening.[46] According to historian David Korn, it was the "most serious loss" inflicted on the Israeli Air Force in a single day in the three years since the June 1967 war, and it sent a "shock" through the Israeli government.[47] Rabin recounted in his memoirs that the attack signaled "a new and far more perilous situation" for his government and left Israel in a "terrible bind." On the one hand, the cease-fire proposal remained unacceptable to the prime minister. At the same time, however, if Israel rejected the cease-fire proposal, its planes were "helpless" against the missile system that had moved forward toward the Suez.[48]

After a week of consultation with his government in Jerusalem, the Israeli ambassador returned to Washington with an "urgent request" to meet with Kissinger to discuss the latest military developments. The meeting took place in Kissinger's office during the early afternoon on July 8. Rabin came prepared with maps containing what Israeli intelligence considered to be known SA-2 and SA-3 sites threatening the Canal zone and emphasized that while the SA-3s were not yet in range of the Canal itself, they provided "overlapping coverage" for the SA-2 sites already protecting the Canal. He also pointed out to Kissinger a newly occupied Soviet base inside Egypt, located within twenty-five miles of the Canal, and referred to the existence of a Soviet destroyer at Port Said with electronic gear and an SA-3 missile.[49]

To cope with the newly developed Soviet-Egyptian air defense capability, Rabin made it clear that a campaign to remove the SA-2s had been initiated but informed Kissinger that Israel would need additional American military assistance to deal with the SA-3s. He requested Phantom and drone reconnaissance to locate and identify new surface-to-air missile sites, improved electronic countermeasure equipment, and new and improved ordnances to attack the SA-3s. At the advice of his military advisers, moreover, the ambassador also urged the United States to start assembling the earmarked A-4 aircraft from US Navy and National Guard units to avoid any potential delays in bringing the new planes to Israel.[50]

Rabin's meeting at the White House lasted less than twenty minutes, but the significance of the change in military situation, and Rabin's acknowledgment that the Israelis intended to deal with the new realities, even if that included attacking Soviet combat personnel inside Egypt, caught Kissinger's attention. The following day, Kissinger arranged an NSC Special Review Group Meeting on the Middle East to address the issues raised by Rabin and to develop contingency plans in the event that the Egyptians rejected the cease-fire proposal and Israel attacked Soviet installations around the canal. While the group sympathized with Israel's new predicament, it did not want to provide Israel with any additional aircraft, other than what had already been earmarked for September–December, given that withholding future shipments appeared to be the only means to convince the Israelis to change their position on the cease-fire.[51]

Another two weeks went by with Israel losing an additional three of its first-line warplanes before Foreign Minister Riad informed Rogers on July 22 that Egypt accepted his cease-fire proposal.[52] With Egypt on board, the Nixon administration began using the full weight of its powers to ensure that Israel replied with a "prompt and unconditional acceptance" of the cease-fire as well. Nixon jumped in personally, sending a message to Meir that she would be unable to ignore. He assured her that while he was "fully aware" of her "strong objections" to the proposal, he expected a "prompt affirmative reply" that would lead to an "early stop of hostilities and blood-shed" on both sides and to serious talks to begin under Jarring.[53]

To entice the prime minister to accept the initiative, Nixon gave Meir his word that when peace talks began with the Arab states, the United States would not ask Israel to accept the Arab interpretation of Security Council Resolution 242. "Our position on withdrawal is that final borders must be agreed between the parties by means of negotiations under the aegis of Jarring," he wrote. The president also made it clear that he would not press Israel to accept a solution to the Palestinian refugee problem that would "fundamentally alter the Jewish character of the State of Israel or jeopardize Israel's security." Above all, said Nixon, the United States would, under no circumstances, call for one Israeli soldier to be withdrawn from the occupied territories "until a binding contractual peace agreement satisfactory to you has been achieved."[54]

According to Rabin, some Israelis considered Nixon's letter "a latter-day Balfour Declaration" that would be insane to dismiss. In view of the "highly favorable" contents of the president's commitment to Meir, Rabin advised the prime minister that Israel must "under no circumstances reject the American initiative."[55] He also spoke with Kissinger's deputy, General Alexander Haig Jr., and indicated that while the president's letter "helped a great deal," Meir expected some "additional compensation" on the military and economic fronts if Israel decided to accept the cease-fire agreement.[56] Foreign Minister Eban for once concurred with Rabin's assessment. He, too, encouraged Meir to accept the cease-fire, even if it led to the dissolution of the Israeli government.[57]

All of the pressure levied on Meir to accept the cease-fire was helped by the escalating crisis along the Suez. On July 29 a massive dogfight of sixteen aircraft—eight Soviet-piloted Egyptian MiG-21s, four Israeli F-4 Phantoms, and four Israeli Mirages—erupted over Ain Sunka, along the Gulf of Suez. The Soviet pilots were "aggressive" and "eager to fight," the National Military Command Center in Washington reported, "but showed a lack of combat experience." Within minutes, the Israelis had downed four MiGs; three of the Soviet pilots ejected, one at a speed of over Mach 1, while the other apparently went down with his aircraft.[58] Although the Israelis had won this battle in the Egyptian skies, it was only a matter of time before the Soviet Union determined they could not allow a country the size of Israel to dominate its air force and increase its military presence inside Egypt.

Combined with the commitments from Nixon and the escalating violence against Soviet forces in Egypt, the Cabinet voted on July 31 to approve the cease-fire initiative and released an official statement to that effect.[59] As expected, Menachem Begin submitted his resignation and that of the five other Gahal ministers as soon as the Cabinet approved the initiative. Meir tried to hold the cabinet together, offering Begin the opportunity to vote against the American initiative in the Cabinet and in the Knesset, an unprecedented move as no coalition partner in Israel's history had been able to vote against a major policy adopted by the government and still retain its position in the cabinet. But all her efforts were to no avail. Begin delivered an impassioned speech to the Knesset on August 4 stressing that any acceptance of Resolution 242, especially in the Jordanian context, meant renunciation of Judea and Samaria—"not all of those territories, but undoubtedly most of them."[60]

The only remaining hurdle to overcome before the cease-fire took effect was to finalize the official text of the agreement. The Egyptians had accepted the simple three-paragraph US proposal in the form of a Jarring report to the secretary-general in which he would report the agreement of Egypt, Jordan, and Israel to the American proposal. The Israelis, however, had mistakenly assumed that the letter Rabin handed to Rogers on August 4, which agreed to the cease-fire while stating certain reservations to the Jarring report, would become the "official" document.[61] They were unwilling for Jarring to transmit the American text on the ground that they had not agreed to every word in it but rather had agreed to it within the framework of their own response. Sisco considered this a minor issue and, in effort to get the cease-fire moving before any more hostilities occurred, instructed the US mission to the United Nations to inform Secretary-General U Thant that the parties had given their consent to the original memorandum from Jarring to him.[62] The confusion caused a major uproar in US-Israeli relations and would threaten the success of the agreement.

Indeed, when Meir learned that Sisco had submitted the text of a document that Israel had not agreed to, she erupted in rage. She called Rabin in Washington and instructed him tell Sisco that she was "shocked" and "dismayed" at the behavior of the United States—placing before Israel a fait accompli. "The Prime Minister has told me to tell you that the conduct of the US government is an insult to Israel, its government, and its people," Rabin said to the assistant secretary of state on the evening of August 6. "You have taken upon yourselves to place words in the mouth of the government of Israel which we have never agreed to say." He added that such an attitude "bears the mark of dictation—not consultation," and that Sisco's decision to forward the letter to Jarring had the "gravest implications" to the relations between their two governments. "Your conduct seriously questions how we can embark on the process of negotiation."[63]

When Rabin informed the prime minister that Sisco felt her comments "unjustified," Meir personally called Sisco to make sure that he fully understood the depth of her anger. Israel, she declared, "was not some kind of banana republic that the Americans could treat as they wished."[64] As far as the prime minister was concerned, the cease-fire initiative was in no way synonymous with the Jarring letter itself, and she personally accused Sisco of forging Israel's signature on the agreement by telling the secretary-general that they had accepted its terms.[65] "What do you mean 'forged'?" he asked the prime minister, stunned at what he was hearing.

"You notified Jarring that we had accepted the initiative before we accepted it!" the prime minister barked over the telephone. "That's what I mean by 'forged.' I reached an agreement with Barbour, and the United States now denies that agreement. You can't formulate answers on our behalf. We have our reservations about the text of Jarring's letter."[66]

Sisco felt that it was absurd to think that the Jarring letter would not have been circulated when it was the centerpiece of the Rogers proposal. Why did Israel believe that their text was "official" when Egypt and Jordan had already accepted the wording, which was contained in the original proposal Rogers had sent them back in June? Even if Meir did believe that Rabin's letter remained the official document, the differences between Israel's text and the text delivered to the secretary-general were so minor that it certainly did not warrant this vitriolic reaction. Rabin tried to calm Sisco down, but even he admitted that he was "in the dark as to which portion of the text Israel agreed to and which she opposed."[67]

Before the conversation concluded, Sisco tried once more to reason with Meir. He told the prime minister that they were at a critical moment in their relationship. "This is an opportunity to bring not only an end to the shooting, but to try to launch a peace process." But, he insisted, "you must accept on the same basis as the Egyptians." When Meir still refused to move ahead with the State Department language of the agreement, Sisco lost his patience: "You received the text of our initiative weeks ago," he shouted, loud enough that the secretaries outside his office could hear him. "One page, one paper—that's the whole initiative. Did you accept it or didn't you?"[68] Sisco even suggested a variety of options all of which would leave the text of the Jarring report unchanged but would have Israel express its reservations to Jarring, orally or in writing. But Meir simply would not budge.

"It was a dialogue of the deaf," Rabin later said of the conversation, having witnessed it personally from Sisco's office at the State Department, much to Meir's displeasure. "Sisco obviously did not understand what the Israeli formulation was. Meir did not understand why Sisco was getting tough."[69]

Sisco hung up the phone convinced that Rogers would have to fire him for the way he spoke to the prime minister, but as far as Rogers was concerned, the Israeli objections were so "inexplicable" that Meir deserved a good lashing. To substitute a different text of the cease-fire agreement at this point in the discussion would reopen the entire negotiations to which Israel had already told the world it had responded affirmatively. The Soviets and the Arabs would interpret Israel's reservations as nonacceptance, which would jeopardize not only the beginning of the talks but also the start of the cease-fire. Rogers and Sisco worked through the night on options that would leave the text of the Jarring report unchanged but would permit Israel to express its reservations to Jarring in one form or another.[70]

Hoping to have better luck with the White House, Rabin approached Kissinger around 10:00 p.m. that same evening to again voice Israel's objection to the State Department's refusal to accept the substitute text that had been worked out between Prime Minister Meir and Ambassador Barbour as stated in his letter to Rogers. "We [are] approaching one of the most critical moments in United States–Israeli relations as the result of some misunderstanding," he said on behalf of the prime minister. Israel, Rabin explained, was willing to begin talks, but the Knesset would not authorize Jarring to issue the report. Kissinger, however, was no more sympathetic to Rabin than Sisco had been earlier with Meir. The national security adviser admitted that while he had not been following the tactics of the initiative closely, he could not understand why this had just now surfaced when the Israelis had more than six weeks to study and digest the contents of a single sheet of paper.[71]

"How long does the government of Israel need?" Kissinger asked Rabin. "I don't understand you people. The paper's been with you for six weeks! If you have any comments, complaints, demands—go ahead, talk! Speak! The Egyptians have accepted our initiative. Have you or haven't you? Let us know clearly!"[72]

Rabin made one last attempt to explain his government's position, which he later admitted he did not entirely agree with, but by this time even Kissinger had lost his cool with the Israelis. Instead of listening to any further complaints over what he considered to be a completely trivial issue, Kissinger told Rabin to sit down with his secretary and dictate the specific examples in which the texts differed. In the meantime, he called over to the State Department to find out exactly why the Israelis were about to withdraw from the cease-fire, for even he was at a loss at the Israeli position. "I have them in a separate room," he told Sisco's deputy Roy Atherton, who answered the telephone in the State Department's Office of Near Eastern Affairs at 10:30 p.m. "I have asked them to tell me the difference between the two versions. They claim the Jarring message wasn't to be surfaced."[73]

"That's not plausible," Atherton quickly responded. The Israeli reply "was understood in the same light as from both Egypt and Jordan."[74]

When Kissinger reached Sisco by phone a few minutes later, the assistant secretary admitted that despite his earlier conversations with Rabin and Meir, both he and Rogers still did not understand the differences in the texts. "If the President calls me tomorrow morning and asks me to explain the problem, I am not sure I can explain it easily," he said. "If two bright people like Joseph Sisco and Henry Kissinger cannot explain the problem," he added, "maybe there is no problem."[75]

Fifteen minutes later, Kissinger returned to Rabin only to find that the Israelis did not want to put the differences down on paper since it might in some way "bind" them to an agreement they were unable to accept. Rabin did, however, stress that his government would refuse to endorse the use of the words "just and lasting peace" in the original text without spelling out specifically what was meant by such a phrase. But Kissinger felt that the Israelis were simply making something out of nothing. "Letting the Jarring text go through does not preclude Israel from raising specific interpretations," he said, hoping to reason with Rabin. "If this was understood and all the parties concerned knew what to expect, I do not see what the problem is."[76]

Although Kissinger took the same position with Rabin as Sisco had done earlier with Meir, Rogers arrived at his office on the morning of August 7 infuriated that Kissinger had accepted a meeting with the ambassador, permitting the Israelis to circumvent the State Department. After reading a report of the conversation, the secretary of state told Kissinger in no uncertain terms to stay out of the discussions unless the president specifically asked him to be involved. "This meeting last night screwed it up so badly," he complained to Kissinger over the telephone. "These things are operational and I think I should take the lead." The idea that Rogers was perturbed when the two were finally on the same page was a little upsetting to Kissinger. "You are being absurd," he shot back. "The thing was totally screwed up and everything I did was checked with Sisco . . . . If you have a complaint talk to the President. I am sick and tired of this."[77]

Kissinger insisted that the only reason he saw Rabin in the first place was because the ambassador told him he had a message for the president, but Rogers believed that the Israelis were simply trying an "end run" to get from Kissinger what they were unable to get from the State Department and that Kissinger was being naive to think otherwise. "He didn't have a message for the President; he wanted to talk with you," Rogers explained. "When you have an audience with them they think they have two ways to play it . . . . You and I don't see alike on these things. They need to have the idea that when we are acting we act pursuant to the President. If they have a feeling that there are two channels to the President they will use them differently." The record of the conversation confirmed that Rabin did not have any message for the president and was only trying get from Kissinger what the State Department was unwilling to give.[78] Even so, Kissinger told Rogers that he did not take the complaint to the president.

"But they think you did," the secretary responded in exasperation. "It would be helpful to me if, when all it is carrying out orders, you would not take part in the discussions. When they have a message that's different, but when they have a complaint about something they did with us, you should refer them to me or Sisco."[79]

Nixon later sent Meir a letter apologizing for the confusion, but the whole point may have been moot anyway.[80] By the following afternoon, the prime minister finally backed down and accepted the original text of the cease-fire proposal without any formal reservations. The agreement, announced by Secretary Rogers at the State Department, was less than half a page and contained only six basic provisions. Beginning Friday, August 7, he said, Israel, Jordan, and Egypt would observe a ninety-day cease-fire along their borders and would stop all incursions and all firing, on the ground and in the air, across the cease-fire lines. Perhaps most important, though, was the "standstill" provision of the agreement, which made it clear that both sides "would refrain from changing the military status quo within zones extending 50 kilometers [about thirty miles] to the east and the west of the ceasefire line." Neither the Arabs nor the Israelis would be permitted "to introduce or construct any new military installations within these zones," and "all" activities within the cease-fire zone would be limited to the maintenance of existing installations at current sites and positions and to the rotation and supply of forces presently within the zones.[81]

For purposes of verification, the agreement allowed each side to rely on "its own national means," including reconnaissance aircraft which would be free to operate "without interference" up to ten kilometers (about six miles) from the cease-fire line on its own side of that line. On the Suez front approximately a hundred United Nations observers would assist in policing the cease-fire, and all parties would be able to avail itself as appropriate of "all U.N. machinery" in reporting alleged violations to each other of the cease-fire and of the military standstill. Finally, both sides agreed to abide by the Geneva Conventions of 1949 relative to the treatment of prisoners of war and would accept the assistance from the International Committee of the Red Cross in carrying out their obligations under those treaties.[82]

With agreement on those six points, the War of Attrition officially ended on August 7, 1970. That evening Golda Meir announced on radio and television that the cease-fire would begin at midnight in Israel and declared her government's "complete readiness to maintain the cease-fire arrangements meticulously in all their provisions, on a basis of reciprocity."[83] In Cairo, Foreign Minister Mahmoud Riad made a similar announcement but linked the agreement to Israeli acceptance of a timetable for the withdrawal from the occupied Arab territories and stressed that Egypt would void the agreement should Israel attack other Arab countries, even if they were not party to the agreement.[84]

For the United States, and especially President Nixon, the cease-fire agreement was a "major achievement," establishing the United States as "an honest broker accepted by both sides."[85] The New York Times wrote in an editorial that "the ingenious Rogers formula, which put classic diplomacy to work in a deceptively simple way, has now apparently awakened [the] required will to negotiate." But the sense of satisfaction inside the administration was tempered. Rogers, in particular, wanted no gloating from the administration over the cease-fire and kept his remarks to the press brief. For he knew that while the fighting may have stopped along the Suez

Canal and tensions may have temporarily eased between Egyptian, Israeli, and Soviet forces in the Sinai, it remained unclear whether this would truly be an end to Arab-Israeli fighting and the beginning of a process leading to a comprehensive peace settlement or just another "intermission" in the long conflict between Israel and its Arab neighbors.

The Cease-Fire Unravels

No sooner had the cease-fire agreement come together than it appeared about to fall apart. Within hours of its announcement, the secretary of state received word from Israeli sources indicating that the Egyptians and Soviets were using the cease-fire to fortify their positions along the Suez Canal, just as the Israelis had predicted. Beginning on the night of August 7–8, convoys of Soviet and Egyptian vehicles began moving toward the Canal, new missile batteries were moved into the standstill zone, and work on several new missile sites was started. "An entirely new defense configuration had developed," Rabin told Kissinger, with at least fourteen new SA-2 sites advanced within the cease-fire zone. The moves were clear-cut violations of the "standstill" provision of the agreement and threatened the success of the cease-fire if the missile sites were not restored to their pre-August 7 condition. "There was no doubt about it," an Israeli general recounted years later. "The Egyptians were moving missiles toward the canal. We asked for permission to attack . . . but were denied."[86]

The movement of the Soviet missiles into the cease-fire zone was exactly the situation US officials had tried to avoid when they drafted the initiative. Before the agreement went into effect the State Department had requested permission from the British to use their bases in the Mediterranean as a staging ground for U-2 reconnaissance flights that would patrol the cease-fire lines for the duration of the ninety-day period only to be rebuffed.[87] They had also reached out to both Israel and Egypt to take aerial photographs from U-2 planes before the cessation of hostilities to provide a basis for comparisons if the other side later complained of violations. Egypt predictably objected to the right of the United States to deploy U-2s to "spy for Israel" and insisted that it would reject any evidence developed from such missions.[88] The Israelis, however, were even more opposed to the U-2 flights.

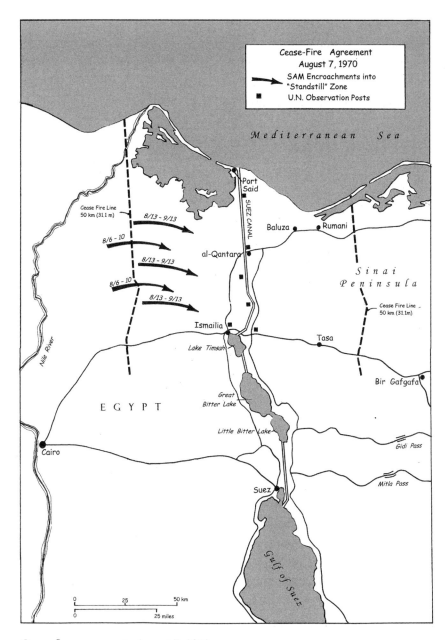

Cease-fire agreements, August 7, 1970

When officials in Washington approached the Israeli defense attaché, Brigadier General Eli Zeira, for permission to use Israeli airspace to monitor the standstill–cease-fire zone, Zeria, acting on instructions directly from Defense Minister Moshe Dayan, turned down the US request and made it clear that should US planes carry out photoreconnaissance missions without Israeli permission, Israel would intercept them.[89]

With the accusations of violations threatening to derail the cease-fire agreement and the new round of Egyptian-Israeli negotiations, Rogers had little choice but to insist on a series of American U-2 reconnaissance flights above the Suez Canal over strenuous Israeli and Egyptian objections. After convincing the British to reverse their earlier position not to allow the U-2s to use their bases,[90] on August 9, the United States launched operation Even Steven,[91] beginning U-2 flights from British military bases in the United Kingdom and Cyprus, which had the necessary landing capabilities required for the high-altitude reconnaissance planes and provided refueling and recovery capabilities. The U-2s were required because their oblique cameras provided coverage of the entire cease-fire zone without overflight of Egyptian territory. But as Rogers explained to the Spanish government, whose airspace was needed for U-2s departing from Britain, the missions would not be "covert" since the United States wanted both Moscow and Cairo to know that its activity within the cease-fire zone would be intensely scrutinized.[92]

Operation Even Steven confirmed what the Israelis had been telling the Americans for days. According to the first reports, a "substantial" forward deployment of surface-to-air missiles, including some twenty-three Egyptian-manned SA-2 sites and five Soviet-manned SA-3 sites, occurred within the Egyptian cease-fire zone between July 28 and August 10. Because the reconnaissance missions began after August 7, when the cease-fire went into effect, US intelligence officials were unable to determine precisely when the changes occurred, but they had enough evidence to "strongly suspect" that the completion of at least some of the Soviet and Egyptian activity took place after the standstill deadline. "At a minimum," the early reports concluded, "it appears that the UAR sought to beat the ceasefire deadline to improve its military position in the ceasefire zone and ran past the deadline to complete these developments."[93] British intelligence also confirmed that since August 7 there had been "some movement" of surface-to-air missiles in the standstill zone, which contravened the cease-fire agreement.[94]

As the U-2 missions continued throughout August, there could be no doubt that leaders in Moscow and Cairo had aggressively sought to circumvent the cease-fire from the start. A separate round of imagery taken later in the month detected at least seven additional SA-2 sites, three or four of which were definitely moved into the standstill zone well after the cease-fire went into effect, and found another three or four Soviet-manned SA-3 sites that had been moved within the cease-fire zone, in addition to the five SA-3 sites that were detected earlier in the month.[95] To provide the Israelis some comfort in light of the new military realities and to encourage Meir not to withdraw from the cease-fire agreement, the United States offered a new arms package to the Israelis, which would enable Israel to carry out successful attacks on a limited number of surface-to-air missile sites.[96]

The Israelis, however, hardly seemed pacified by the new arms package. When Rabin met with Kissinger at the White House on August 15, he made it clear that the Israelis were confronted by an "entirely different kind of threat" than they had faced two years earlier during the initial discussion with UN envoy Jarring. Rabin stressed that "Israel is now under the direct threat of a Soviet pistol, not merely an Egyptian military threat, but a Soviet threat— a threat which is designed to bring Israel to its knees." He added that the lack of a public response and condemnation of the violations from the White House and the State Department indicated to his government that the United States refused to understand this problem.[97]

Despite these complaints, the Israelis continued to adhere to the cease-fire agreement and maintained its commitment to participate in the peace talks scheduled to take place under Jarring. Meir, in fact, wrote a lengthy letter to Rogers on August 19 providing him with a "detailed summary" of Israel's positions with regards to Security Council Resolution 242, borders, refugees, and security. Of course, many of Meir's positions appeared incompatible with reaching the "just and lasting peace" she discussed in the letter, including her assertion that the "previous armistice lines were not 'secure and recognized boundaries,'" diplomatic speak that Israel would not withdraw to the 1967 lines. But the fact that the Israelis had yet to withdraw from the scheduled talks in light of the numerous violations of the cease-fire agreement left the State Department hopeful that the cease-fire could hold and peace talks begin if the Egyptians withdrew the defense systems to their lines of August 6.[98]

With the Israelis continuing to adhere to the cease-fire, the focus of the Nixon administration became how to respond to the Soviet-Egyptian violations without undoing the cease-fire. Kissinger stressed to Nixon the importance of adopting a much harder line against the Soviets and Nasser to prove that the United States would not acquiesce to the violations. "This has serious consequences for our current initiative in the Middle East, the longer term prospects for the area generally, and US-Soviet relations," he said.[99] The director of the United States Information Agency, Frank Shakespeare, sent a similar message to the president, warning that the Soviet violations were "creating a psychological problem of enormous world-wide dimension" and that "unless we react strongly and promptly against these violations, the credibility of the United States and your credibility will suffer almost irretrievable damage."[100]

The State Department, however, disagreed with these assessments. Although Rogers and Sisco both believed that the movement and construction of the SA-2s and SA-3s into the standstill zone constituted a clear violation of the cease-fire agreement, they argued that it did not represent a "major change" in the military situation along the Canal and felt it best therefore to focus on moving the talks forward rather than on highlighting the violations. During a meeting with the president, Kissinger, and Sisco at Nixon's private residence in San Clemente, California, on August 25, Rogers accused Kissinger of trying to "foment a crisis by being so insistent on ceasefire violations." He reminded Kissinger that the State Department had made a formal protest with the Egyptians the previous week and had even provided Nasser with map coordinates of the new surface-to-air-missile sites but did not want the violations to derail the forthcoming Egyptian-Israeli talks. Kissinger replied that "crises cannot be avoided by denying the circumstances that produce them or blaming the bearer of bad tidings."[101]

As with many of the foreign policy decisions he faced during his administration, Nixon was caught somewhere in the middle between the views of his two senior foreign policy advisers. On the one hand, he viewed the cease-fire as a "major achievement" for his administration and did not want to see it undone. On the other hand, he felt that the Soviets were "the main cause of Middle East tensions" and could not acquiesce in the violations.[102] Nixon met again with Rogers and Kissinger on September 1. At this meeting, according to the president's chief of staff, H. R. Haldeman, Kissinger "went at it pretty hard" with the president, to the point where after the meeting Nixon ordered Haldeman to "get K[issinger] off of the Middle East." He also directed that "a very strong protest" be made in both Cairo and Moscow and that Israel be asked to send a representative to the Jarring talks in New York.[103]

On September 3, at Nixon's orders, official démarches were presented in both Cairo and Moscow.[104] The Egyptians appeared caught off-guard by the stern language in the démarche and feared this could signal that the Israelis were about to launch a preemptive attack on Egypt. Foreign Minister Mahmoud Riad summoned the British ambassador in Cairo "on short notice" and expressed his belief that the American "accusations" that Egypt had "breached" the cease-fire were almost all "ill founded." With the exception of an isolated incident on August 10, said Riad, when a unit commander on his own initiative had moved a missile to an alternative site, the Egyptian command refrained in deference to the American interpretations of the cease-fire terms from alternating missiles between existing sites. More important, in Riad's estimate, was the fact that the United States had failed to mention Egyptian complaints of Israeli violations, leaving the British ambassador to conclude that the Egyptian confidence in the US government, "which with the Rogers initiative had been restored to 10% of its former strength, had now slumped once more to zero."[105]

Similar reactions to the American démarche were seen from the Soviet leadership. Deputy Foreign Minister Vinogradov launched into a "lengthy, repetitive, and largely unyielding reply" to the accusation by Jacob Beam, the US ambassador in Moscow, that the Kremlin would bear responsibility to the resumption of Arab-Israeli fighting. The Soviet Union had not been a signatory to the cease-fire, Vinogradov insisted, and therefore could not be held responsible for things with which it was not connected.[106] In Washington, Soviet chargé Yuli Vorontsov paid an urgent call on Sisco on September 5 to present a Soviet démarche. The Kremlin feared that the Israelis were planning an imminent air attack on Egyptian regions beyond

'Aw, You're Just Seein' a Mirage!'

Cartoon on cease-fire violations. (Buffalo News, *August 20, 1970*)

the cease-fire and urged the United States to "undertake the necessary steps to restrain Israel from the dangerous actions it is planning, the entire responsibility for the consequences of which . . . would fully fall on Israel and the United States."[107]

By this time, however, even Rogers conceded that the chances of the protests working and the cease-fire holding were remote. If the Egyptians and Soviets were not going to respond to American calls to abide by the cease-fire, it was only a matter of time, he reasoned, before Israel took military action against the new installations and withdrew from the cease-fire agreement altogether. The problem, he knew, was that neither Moscow nor Cairo believed that the United States had an effective political or military sanction to use. Sisco encouraged Rogers to send a protest letter to Gromyko, but the secretary did not want to launch a "major confrontation" with Moscow and saw no point in lodging another protest short of an ultimatum. "I don't want them to say that the U.S. is helpless," he told Kissinger's deputy, Alexander Haig, over the telephone during the first week in September. "If we had a follow up move, I'd be happy to do it."[108]

But no follow-up move would come. On September 6, the Israelis announced that in light of the continued violations of the cease-fire, they would not participate in the Jarring talks. The cabinet's decision, reported by an Israeli spokesman, stressed that Israel would continue to honor the ninety-day cease-fire, would remain committed to the American peacemaking efforts, and would resume the talks after Egypt had rectified the changes and adhered to the agreements it had signed in August. "If Egypt and the Soviet Union entered these talks, on the American initiative, willingly and sincerely, they must fulfill the agreement," said Prime Minister Meir in a radio address shortly following the cabinet's decision to withdraw from the talks. "If they did not, what would be the point of any agreements they would ever sign?"[109]

Black September

At virtually the same time that Meir announced Israel's intention to withdraw from the Jarring talks, events on Israel's eastern border were also working to undermine the cease-fire agreement. That day, two US airliners and one Swiss aircraft were hijacked by gunmen representing the Popular

Front for the Liberation of Palestine (PFLP), the most extreme wing of the Palestinian movement. A fourth plane, El Al flight 219 flying from Amsterdam to New York, was also hijacked by two Palestinian guerrillas, but El Al crew members shot and killed one hijacker and wounded the other. The Palestinian hijackers took one of the planes—Pan Am flight 93—to Cairo, where, after the 170 persons aboard were evacuated, they blew up the plane. The other two planes were flown to Dawson's Field, an abandoned airfield thirty miles east of Amman, Jordan, where, for the next three weeks, Palestinian commandos and the Jordanian army engaged in a standoff for the safe release of the passengers. The fedayeen announced that they would blow up both themselves and the aircraft if any attempt was made to storm the aircraft or otherwise "checkmate" the hijacking effort.[110]

The hijackings came just five days after a group of armed men opened fire on a motorcade carrying Jordan's King Hussein and his daughter to the airport in Amman. Although the king escaped unscathed, the fate of the Hashemite regime hung in the balance. Both the hijackings and the assassination attempt were moves by the Palestinian groups operating in Jordan and Lebanon to bring down Hussein and create an independent Palestinian state on the West Bank of the Jordan River. On September 7, Palestinian commandos began efforts to take over the Jordanian capital, leaving the US embassy in Amman to report a "near-anarchical" condition in most areas of the city, with instances of shooting, auto theft, and persons subjected to search at fedayeen roadblocks.[111] The fighting spread throughout Jordan and left Hussein in a brutal struggle with the Palestinians for control of his kingdom. The Jordanian Civil War had begun.

On its surface, the events of "Black September" in Jordan appeared completely unrelated to the Egyptian-Israeli cease-fire along the Suez Canal. The Marxist-inspired PFLP and the Popular Democratic Front for the Liberation of Palestine, minority factions under the umbrella of the Palestine Liberation Organization (PLO), were ideologically committed to the overthrow of the traditional Arab regimes and had been operating a de facto state-within-a-state inside Jordan for almost three years.[112] Yet there were also strong connections between the two events. First, as historian Paul Chamberlin has astutely pointed out, Nasser's decision to accept the cease-fire in July sent "shockwaves" through the Palestinian Liberation Organization and convinced elements in the fedayeen, particularly the PFLP, to conclude that the Arab regimes had turned against them. That PFLP guerrillas took one of the planes to Cairo and destroyed the plane under the watch of the Egyptian army was the clearest expression the Palestinians could make that they viewed Nasser as a traitor for having accepted an American-led peace initiative with Israel.[113]

On a broader level, though, how the parties involved in the cease-fire responded to the events in Jordan would also directly affect the future of the cease-fire agreement. If Jordanian forces could resolve the crisis without the assistance of any "outside" power, there was a strong chance that the cease-fire agreement could hold, even if the Israelis were not going to partake in the peace talks until the violations were rectified. If, however, United States sent forces to assist the king, as it had in 1957 when President Eisenhower ordered the Sixth Fleet to the eastern Mediterranean when Hussein's rule came under threat from Syrian and Egyptian meddling in Jordan,[114] or if Israeli forces moved against the fedayeen—with or without the king's blessing—then the Soviets and the Egyptians would have a difficult time standing on the sidelines and could threaten Israel by attacking its forces stationed on the east bank of the Suez Canal.

For the United States, the paramount concern in the Jordan crisis was preserving Hussein's regime, while maintaining the sanctity of the cease-fire agreement. "If the fedayeen could use Jordan as their principal base and in the process destroy the authority of the King—one of the few rulers in the region distinguished by moderation and pro-western sympathies—the entire Middle East would be revolutionized," Kissinger argued in a National Security Council meeting during the early days of the crisis. It was also crucial, argued Kissinger, not to let the "political balance" on the Jordan front be destroyed by force at the very moment the military balance along the Suez Canal had been altered by "cheating" from Egyptian and Soviet decision-making.[115]

The problem for the United States was that there were few options available that would save the King *and* preserve what slim chance still remained that the cease-fire could hold. From the beginning of the crisis Department of Defense officials were reluctant to use American forces in Jordan "except as a move of desperation" in case it became clear that planes and passengers would be blown up.[116] The reasons against using US military power were quite simple and overwhelming. First, if Hussein was too weak to deal a decisive blow to the fedayeen, outside intervention could save his regime for only a limited time. There was also concern inside the administration that by taking action in Jordan, it would provoke the Soviet Union to "take advantage of the situation by heating up the Suez front" and ignite a regional Middle East war.[117]

The larger consideration for the Pentagon had to do with American military capabilities. Not only would the United States have a difficult time supporting sustained military operations in a country that did not have easy access to the Mediterranean, but sending in the four brigades required to successfully handle the crisis would drain the entire US strategic reserve when several hundred thousand American forces were still fighting in Southeast Asia. Such a move would make the United States increasingly vulnerable to Soviet action in other areas around the world. "That scares the hell out of me," CIA Director Richard Helms said emphatically when the Admiral Thomas Moorer, chairman of the Joint Chiefs of Staff presented the bleak assessment in a meeting of WSAG on September 9.[118]

The best solution, from the American standpoint, was for the Israelis to intervene if it appeared Hussein could not handle the fedayeen on his own or if Iraq or Syria entered the conflict. The Israelis were better prepared logistically, could move faster than American troops, and were more experienced in fighting the fedayeen and the surrounding Arab armies than the United States. Some in the administration believed that King Hussein had already clandestinely reached a tacit understanding with the Israelis that if the Iraqis intervened in Jordan, Israel would attack. Yet Israeli action in Jordan also involved significant risks. An Israeli intervention would almost certainly draw a response from the Soviet Union, Nasser would resume attacks across the Canal, and the cease-fire would almost certainly collapse, leaving the area on the brink of another regional war.

The other problem with using Israeli forces was that Nixon wanted to keep them out of the conflict. Caught up in election-year politics and still hoping to receive an invitation to Moscow for a summit with Soviet leaders, he made it clear to Kissinger that he opposed "any Israeli military moves unless he specifically approved them in advance." Should outside forces be required to save the king, the president stressed they should be American.[119] For Nixon, this was an opportunity for the United States to demonstrate resolve and show some "guts" in response to the hijackings and continued Soviet meddling in the Middle East. "If they should move," Nixon told Kissinger in response to the speculation that Syria and Iraq were about to enter the conflict, "my strong feeling at this time is that we should use American air and knock the bejesus out of them . . . . It would be a show of strength on our part."[120]

Any decision, though, would depend on how King Hussein decided to respond to the Palestinian insurrection. Some analysts doubted whether the Jordanian army would be able to deal a decisive blow to the fedayeen and were encouraging the king to reach a power-sharing agreement with Yasser Arafat and the PLO. The United States pressured Jordan from a different direction. After the PFLP made a spectacle of the hijacking incident by blowing up the remaining airplanes on national television, Secretary Rogers called in the Jordanian ambassador and emphasized the importance for the king "to demonstrate to all concerned that they are able to take control of internal Jordanian situation." Rogers noted that the events of the past week caused further doubts about Hussein's ability to exercise "clear-cut authority" throughout the kingdom and raised additional questions with Israeli officials about reaching a peace settlement in the Middle East when it was unclear with whom peace could be made in Jordan. The secretary of state believed these were relevant questions and hoped that a "stronger stance" on part of the Jordanian government over the coming days would provide the answers.[121]

Although the king feared that moving on the Palestinians would prompt Syrian and Iraqi intervention, he had no choice but to crack down on the fedayeen if he wanted to preserve his kingdom. On September 16, Hussein disbanded his civilian government and appointed a temporary military cabinet of twelve generals under the premiership of Brigadier General Muhammad Daud with the charge to "insure security, restore order and impose the state's authority and protection."[122] The following day he ordered the Jordanian army to move into Amman and begin shelling the Wahdat and Al-Hussein refugee camps, where the fedayeen maintained their head-quarters. Heavy fighting ensued in the Jordanian capital over the next ten days, with heavy Palestinian casualties.[123]

The Jordanian army appeared on the verge of a quick victory. Troops and tanks under the orders from Hussein's new military government swept into Amman in the early hours of September 17, expanding their control of the city and disrupting Palestinian communications. By the end of the first day of fighting, Hussein felt confident enough in the progress of his army over the fedayeen that he reported to Washington: "The situation is under control and Amman will be in Jordanian hands by tomorrow afternoon." The king offered a cease-fire to the fedayeen under the condition that the fedayeen evacuate all towns and leave Jordan and agreed to provide buses to take the fedayeen to the frontier. Israeli reports confirmed the king's optimistic assessment. "Things look good," Rabin told Sisco, and he promised that "if Hussein can pull it off, we will announce within 24 hours that will resume participation in the talks with Jarring."[124]

So encouraging were the early reports out of Jordan, in fact, that when Prime Minister Meir visited Washington for prescheduled meetings with Nixon and Rogers on September 18, there was little discussion of the crisis in Jordan. At one point during Meir's meeting with the secretary of state, Rogers stressed that the American peace initiative had "no chance" if Hussein did not remain in control of his kingdom. "If there is chaos, you cannot work out an agreement, and you cannot make peace with chaos," said Rogers. But the bulk of their conversations focused on the cease-fire violations, an indication that after the king had the crisis in his country resolved, attention would once again return to the cease-fire in the Sinai. Meir brought with her several maps detailing the movements of Soviet SA-2 and SA-3 sites between August 6 and September 13, which left little doubt why Israel refused to partake in peace talks under Jarring. "What disturbs us immensely is the preparation for future shooting," Meir stressed. "When this starts, it may be much more serious than before."[125]

Before the prime minister completed her visit in the United States, however, events in Jordan took a dramatic turn. On September 19, two armored Syrian brigades crossed into northern Jordan and began shelling Jordanian forces near Dar'a. By nightfall on Sunday, September 20, the Syrians reportedly had about 150 tanks and artillery in the area, had occupied the town of Irbid, and had a "spearhead" of 40 tanks moving south toward Amman.[126] The situation in Amman had also deteriorated. Although the army continued to have the "upper hand," King Hussein was reluctant to apply the "maximum force available to him" out of concern for causing numerous civilian casualties and reducing the city to shambles.[127] Fearing his kingdom about to collapse, Hussein sent a "most urgent" message to Nixon, informing him that the Syrian invasion was having a "disastrous effect on tired troops in the capital and surrounding areas" and pleading for "immediate physical intervention both air and land . . . from *any quarter*" to safeguard the sovereignty, territorial integrity, and independence of Jordan.[128]

Nixon and Kissinger viewed the Syrian invasion as a "Soviet-inspired insurrection" that had to be met with force. If it succeeded, Nixon later wrote, "the entire Middle East might erupt in war . . . . It was like a ghastly game of dominoes, with a nuclear war waiting at the end."[129] Every senior official inside the administration agreed with Nixon's position. After receiving the king's request, Kissinger and Rogers discussed the need for the United States to lend its support to the king's request for an Israeli strike. "My view is that we should favor it because if the King goes down the drain than the [goddamn] thing is a total mess," said Rogers. "This way it will be a mess, but if they can save the King there is some advantage." Kissinger agreed: "If there isn't an air strike the whole thing may come apart. I don't think we have any choice."[130]

After securing Nixon's approval for the Israeli strike,[131] Kissinger called Yitzhak Rabin, who was with Meir in New York attending a dinner of the United Jewish Appeal. He informed the ambassador that the king had approached the United States with a message describing the plight of the Jordanian army and requesting an Israeli air strike on Syrian forces in northern Jordan. "We can now assure you under these circumstances that we would look favorably on your actions and the President has asked me to tell you if you undertake such action we would of course make good any material problems that might arise as a result of these actions and we are cognizant of the fact we would have to hold the situation under control vis-à-vis the Soviets."[132]

Rabin transmitted the king's request to the prime minister, who quickly called Deputy Prime Minister Yigal Allon and Defense Minister Moshe Dayan in Israel for their assessments. Not surprisingly, Allon and Dayan were split down the middle; Allon wanted to help the king while Dayan was reluctant to get involved.[133] Most important, they did not agree with the facts and the implications as Hussein laid them out. According to their latest intelligence reports, the situation was "quite unpleasant," with more tanks and armored forces than the Jordanians and the Americans reported. Israeli defense officials were not sure if airpower alone would be sufficient to repel the Syrian advance and needed to undertake further reconnaissance missions before responding to the king's request.[134]

The Israeli reconnaissance missions conducted in the early hours of September 21 confirmed their earlier predictions. A "massive Syrian force" of almost three hundred tanks had dug in to the Ramtha-Irbid area, while the Syrian army took control of the town of Irbid. There were also indications, according to the Israelis, of Iraqi involvement in the conflict on the side of the fedayeen.[135] With the new reports in hand, Allon chaired a meeting of the cabinet to discuss whether Israel should meet the king's request. One group, led by Allon and Foreign Minister Eban, with support from Meir and Rabin, favored preserving the king's regime because Hussein had proven to be the friendliest Arab leader to Israel. Yet others in the Israeli leadership, including Ezer Weizman, and Generals Ariel Sharon and Rehavam Ze'evi, argued forcefully that this was an opportunity to turn the Hashemite Kingdom into a Palestinian state, which would solve Israel's Palestinian problem once and for all.[136] As Eban made clear to American officials in New York shortly after the cabinet discussion, "while Israel, on balance, favored Husayn as of this time, the world would not come to an end if he departed the scene." The Palestinians, Eban maintained, would become more responsible when "saddled with the day-to-day burdens of government, and the long-term trend in Jordan was toward greater recognition of the fact that Jordan was 70 percent Palestinian."[137]

If there was an area where almost all the Israelis agreed, however, it was that air action alone would not be sufficient to move the Syrians out of Jordan. Before agreeing to send in ground forces, though, the Israelis wanted a number of questions answered by both the United States and Jordan. Would King Hussein agree to request Israeli assistance directly, to avoid the appearance of an "invasion," and undertake methods of communication and coordination? How would the United States prevent Soviet intervention when Israeli ground forces moved into Jordan? Would the United States veto any action from the Security Council condemning Israel or

King Hussein's victory over Palestinian guerrilla fighters helped restore his
monarchy's control over Jordan. Hussein, seen here with his troops in 1968,
maintained a close relationship with his military and relied on it as a key pillar
for his regime's stability. (*Ookaboo*)

calling for Israel's withdrawal from Jordan? And would Israel be held
responsible for the fate of the hostages if the fedayeen took action when
the Israelis moved?[138]

After receiving the report from Rabin around 5:30 a.m. on September 21,
Kissinger awoke Nixon to convey the Israeli response to the king's request:
"They believe air alone won't do it and that if it's done, ground action will be
necessary either at the beginning or shortly thereafter."[139] The Israelis were
considering three courses of action for a ground assault. The best route, according to Rabin, would be straight across the Jordan River south of Lake Tiberias,
making a direct thrust at Irbid. A second scenario involved a strike to the north
from the Golan Heights, which would allow the Israeli Defense Forces to cut
Syrian supply lines and force Syrian units to withdraw from Jordan. And the
third option was to adopt a combination of the two approaches.[140]

Nixon, though, still opposed an Israeli "invasion" of Jordan, unless under
dire circumstances. He understood that many of Israel's military leaders

would want to "go in and fuck a little of the ground," but he instructed Kissinger to call Rabin back with a message that he found it "imperative" that the Israelis "must lean in the direction of accomplishing a true air action alone," having in mind such action could provide the "psychological impact" needed to convince the Syrians to withdraw its forces. If, however, air action proved to be militarily inadequate, than Nixon supported the use of Israeli ground forces as long as that activity was "strictly limited" to Jordan. "It cannot expand to Syria or, even less, into other countries. However, air action in Syria would be understood."[141]

In support of the Israeli intervention but, more important, to shore up morale of the Jordanian regime, Nixon made a number of decisions to "heighten the perception" of imminent American or Israeli action. He ordered the 82nd Airborne Division on full alert; heightened the alert status of the airborne brigade in Germany; flew a reconnaissance plane to Lod Airport in Tel Aviv to pick up targeting information and signal that American military action might be approaching; and sent a warning to leaders in Damascus and Moscow.[142] "It's obvious from the latest reports that the King remains very upset and psychologically shaken," Nixon stated during a meeting of the National Security Council on September 21, "and what matters at this point is whether he will continue to resist, whether or not he as an individual can hang on."[143]

By the following morning, the tide appeared to turn in favor of the Jordanian army. Emboldened by the show of strength from the American military, the king's forces moved aggressively against the Syrian armored brigades in the north, turning back the southern Syrian thrust and inflicting significant losses on its forces near Irbid.[144] Although an Israeli ground assault no longer appeared needed, the Jordanians were aided by the Israeli Air Force, which flew a squadron of Phantoms low over Syrian tanks in the north, creating a sonic boom designed to warn the forces below of what might face them should they continue their advance.[145] Sporadic fighting continued in Amman, with one "major pocket" of resistance left in the city, but overall the military situation had stabilized. Zaid Rifai, the king's confidant, reported to American officials in Jordan that if Syria did not move up reinforcements and if Iraq continued to stay out of the conflict, the Jordanians could handle the situation.[146]

Of course, the Jordanians had made these same predictions before, but this time their confidence seemed validated. On September 23, the Syrians withdrew their three armored brigades from Jordan. The same day, King Hussein and a representative from the PLO announced an agreement providing for the movement of the fedayeen out of the cities and back to the borders with Israel.[147] Three days later, Hussein flew to Cairo where, under heavy pressure from Nasser and other Arab leaders, he signed a new agreement with Yasser Arafat and the PLO. Besides calling for a cease-fire between the Jordanian army and the Palestinian resistance, the Cairo Accord provided for the withdrawal of the Jordanian army and the Palestinian guerrillas from all cities, the appointment of a three-man committee to restore order in the country and oversee military and civilian affairs, and the immediate release of all those arrested or detained during the crisis.[148]

Although the Palestinians lost the battle militarily, many analysts considered the Cairo Accord an important victory for the PLO. The director of the Research Department of the Israeli foreign minister informed US officials that the Cairo agreement merely brought the situation back to what it was prior to the outbreak of fighting, and that the fedayeen had a "clear advantage" since they will re-enter the city clandestinely and rebuild their bases. CIA analyst also argued that the Cairo Agreement would be nothing more than a "stopgap," allowing the Palestinian resistance.[149]

In reality, though, Hussein had won a decisive victory. In addition to retaining control of his kingdom, the king reorganized his government under new prime minister Wasfi Tall, widely considered much "stronger" and "uncompromising" than Hussein and very popular in the army. Within a year, Tall had consolidated control of Jordanian cities and forced the last remnants of the fedayeen out of Jordan. As historian Avi Shlaim has written, "The PLO state within a state was snuffed out and exclusive Jordanian sovereignty was re-established over the country."[150]

The United States also scored a major victory out of the Jordan crisis. By helping Hussein retain control of his kingdom without having to send in American or Israeli forces, the United States not only saved a moderate Arab regime friendly to the west but preserved the cease-fire along the Suez Canal. True, the Egyptians and Soviets had yet to withdraw the missile systems they had moved into the cease-fire zone in clear violation of the agreement, and the peace negotiations that were scheduled to take place under Jarring were on hold as a result. Still, with the fighting stopped along the Canal, it significantly reduced the growing possibility that the United States and the Soviet Union would end up in a major clash in the Middle East.

This is not to say that the autumn crises in the Middle East did not leave some casualties. Indeed, while Hussein held on to his kingdom and the War of Attrition came to an end, significant strains developed in US-Soviet relations as a result of the two events. Nixon and Kissinger remained convinced that Moscow had pushed the Syrians into invading Jordan and that Soviet leaders had intentionally deceived the United States by indicating support for the cease-fire when they intended only to use it to protect and strengthen Egyptian and Soviet forces along the Canal. For its part, the Kremlin adamantly objected to the "ongoing anti-Soviet campaign" in the United States, which blamed the Soviet Union for the "current impasse" on the peace settlement and the Jarring mission. Dobrynin complained to Kissinger that the whole "fabricated" issue over "violations" had been "blown out of proportion" to such an extent that it had already taken a toll on relations between their two governments. "Isn't it time for the U.S. Government to think about the possible serious consequences of all this?" he asked Kissinger during the first week of October.[151]

Perhaps the main casualty of the crises, however, was Gamal Abdel Nasser. On September 28, 1970, at the conclusion of the Cairo summit that had produced the cease-fire agreement between Hussein and Arafat, Nasser suffered a fatal heart attack. With Nasser's death came an end to an era of Arab politics. Although his successor, Anwar Sadat, promised to follow Nasser's path, he moved Egypt in an entirely new direction. Over the following year, he would gradually distance Egypt from grip of the Soviet sphere, establish new contacts with the United States, and take steps to explore improving relations with Israel. Each of these moves eased tensions in the Middle East, repaired relations with Washington, and allowed the United States and the Soviet Union to pursue détente in the absence of heightened Arab-Israeli tensions.

Fighting for Sadat,
October 1970–August 1971

No single event changed the landscape of the Arab-Israeli conflict more than the death of Gamal Abdel Nasser and the accession to power of his successor, Anwar el-Sadat, in September 1970. For nearly two decades Nasser had been the strongest figure of leadership among the Arabs. By nationalizing the Suez Canal in 1956 and resisting the Western powers during the ensuing war, he had developed a following throughout the Arab world and continued to increase his influence across the region by using his powerful personality and considerable charm to appeal to Arab nationalism. In 1958, Nasser formed the United Arab Republic with Syria in the hope that all Arab nations would soon join, and during the 1960s he helped the Palestinians organize its resistance groups under one umbrella, which became known as the Palestine Liberation Organization. Though many believed he was largely to blame for the humiliating defeat to Israel in the 1967 Six-Day War, most Arabs rallied behind Nasser as he rebuilt Egypt's shattered army and continued to resist Israel's occupation of Arab land through his war of attrition with the Jewish state.[1]

Nasser's sudden death, therefore, opened the door for Egypt to move in an entirely new direction. Although his successor was very much a product of Nasser's pan-Arab movement and had served Nasser loyally for more than twenty years, Sadat had a far different vision of Egypt's role in the world. An ardent nationalist, Sadat detested the vast Soviet military presence inside Egypt that Nasser had cultivated, and he saw no reason for his country to maintain a hostile attitude toward the United States. "There's no reason why the Arabs should be closely aligned to the Soviet Union," he would later tell Secretary of State William P. Rogers. "My people like the West better."[2] Sadat also differed strongly as to how best recover the land lost to Israel in the 1967 war. Instead of relying solely on Moscow, as Nasser had done, Sadat believed he could reach out to the United States in the hope that the Americans could squeeze Israel into returning the occupied territories. As he explained in his first letter to President Nixon in December 1970, Egyptians take "our own decisions freely and independently, so that if you prove friendly to us, we shall be ten times as friendly."[3]

At fifty-one, Sadat was little known to anyone outside the Arab world. Born in 1918 in the Nile Delta village of Mit Abu al-Kom, forty miles north of Cairo, he was one of thirteen children of Mohammed el-Sadat, a government clerk, and a Sudanese mother. Throughout much of his childhood his family lived below the poverty line, but Sadat believed that these years were the happiest of his life. "I could never tear myself away from life in the village," he wrote in his autobiography. "It was a series of uninterrupted pleasures. There was something to look forward to every day."[4] Sadat also believed that his early experience of village life, with its fraternity, cooperation, and love, gave him the self-confidence to make his way in the big city. "It deepened my feeling of inner superiority, a feeling which has never left me and which I came to realize, is an inner power independent of all material resources," he said. In 1925, Sadat moved to Cairo when his father returned from the Sudan. It was there he later developed deep sentiments against the British, who had maintained troops in Egypt from their occupation of Egypt in 1882. As he wrote in his autobiography, he had "a hatred for all aggressors" and a love and admiration for anyone trying to liberate his land.[5]

Sadat's life took a dramatic turn in 1936 when he was admitted to the Royal Military Academy. Although once reserved for men of the aristocracy, the academy began taking cadets from the middle and lower classes in accordance with the Anglo-Egyptian Treaty of 1936, which allowed the Egyptian army to expand.[6] While there, Sadat studied the history of the British occupation of Egypt, as well as the Turkish Revolution and his hero Atatürk, and became convinced that the British would not leave Egypt "except by the force of arms." Following his graduation from the academy two years later, he entered the army as a second lieutenant and was posted in the Sudan. There he met Gamal Abdel Nasser, and together, along with several other junior officers, they formed the secret, anti-British Free Officers Movement. "We were young men full of hope," Sadat wrote in *Revolt on the Nile*. "We were brothers in arms, united in friendship, and common detestation of the existing order of things. Egypt was a sick country."[7]

When World War II broke out, Sadat saw an opportunity to collaborate with the Nazis against the British. He took part in a clandestine attempt to fly an Egyptian officer to Iraq to work against the British interest there and later was arrested for treason. After his release from prison, he rejoined the army and the Free Officers organization and, along with Nasser, began plotting the uprising against King Farouk. On the morning of July 23, 1952, Sadat took control of Cairo Radio to announce the birth of the revolution to the Egyptian people. "As I came out of the broadcasting station and drove up to our headquarters in the North of Cairo, I saw the streets of the metropolis crowded with people as I had never seen them before," he recalled. "It was clear that what mattered to them was to wait together for the one thing for which they had waited so many years separately, individually, and perhaps sometimes quite hopelessly."[8]

During the 1950s and 1960s, Sadat served in a number of highly visible positions throughout the Egyptian leadership. In 1954, he was appointed Minister of State, and the following year became editor of *Al-Jumhuriyah*, the official newspaper of the Egyptian government. He also served as a member of the Revolutionary Command Council, as secretary-general of an Islamic Congress, and as deputy chairman, chairman, and speaker of the National Assembly. In 1964, at the age of forty-five, Nasser named Sadat vice president, a position widely thought inside Egypt to be largely ceremonial and possessing no real power.

When Nasser reappointed Sadat vice president in 1969, Nasser's intentions remained unclear. One early study of Sadat concluded that his nomination as vice president was almost certainly a "tactical move of the moment" rather than the anointing of an heir-apparent.[9] A more recent biography of the Egyptian president similarly found that there was "no way that Nasser would have ever wanted Sadat to assume the Presidential reins" even though he was a "natural choice."[10] But according to Sadat, Nasser made it clear to him on his appointment that he did not want to leave behind a "vacuum" in the event that he fall victim to the perpetual "intrigues" hatched against him and therefore wanted Sadat as his successor.[11]

Egyptian President Anwar Sadat. (NARA)

To most outside observers, however, Sadat was seen merely as a transitional figure that would last no more than a few months. Within hours of Nasser's death, in fact, Harold H. Saunders, Henry Kissinger's Middle East expert on the NSC staff, concluded that while the constitutional successor was Vice President Sadat, "it seems likely that some sort of collective leadership would take over while potential leaders jockey for control." Even more likely, Saunders added, was that "some other military leader would eventually assume the real power since it seems unlikely that a purely civilian leader alone could consolidate control."[12] When two weeks later the Egyptian National Assembly officially nominated Sadat to become its next president, Kissinger told President Nixon that it was still "impossible to determine ... who will ultimately hold the reins of power in Egypt," believing that although Sadat could turn out to be more than a front man, "the men around him will undoubtedly be more influential than those Nasser kept around."[13]

Inside the Kremlin, Sadat's ascension to the Egyptian presidency caused Soviet officials considerable consternation. On the one hand, there were KGB analysts who believed that Soviet political, military, and economic support to Egypt made it almost impossible for Sadat to "withdraw" from the Soviet Union. Sadat, these analysts believed, would at first "balance" a little between Washington and Moscow, hoping to obtain "privileges" from each, but in the end would resume the "Nasserist course."[14] Yet others were far more skeptical about Sadat. According to Foreign Minister Andrei Gromyko, the Soviet leadership had plenty of information on Sadat of a "distinctly negative kind," and many knew that Nasser had not kept Sadat informed of his most important plans, even when Sadat was vice president.[15] There was also concern in Moscow that Sadat, a strong nationalist, would be less inclined to have an open relationship with the Soviet Union and that Moscow would quickly find itself on the outside looking in. At Nasser's funeral, Premier Alexi Kosygin arranged three separate meetings with Nasser's potential successors to stress how "essential" it was that the new Egyptian regime communicate with the Kremlin. "Each side must be able to understand what the other is thinking," Kosygin said. "We don't want to interfere in your plans, but don't forget that our troops are here in Egypt. We have a community of blood, as well as a community of interests.

This is very important, and something that you must always take into consideration."[16]

Still, despite all the misgivings the United States and the Soviet Union had about Nasser's successor, both countries fought aggressively to win Sadat's backing. For Washington, this was the first real opportunity since 1956, when Secretary of State John Foster Dulles had withdrawn American financial support for the construction of the Aswan Dam, that it had to make inroads inside Egypt.[17] It was also a chance to prove to the Arab world that the United States could adopt a more even-handed approach to the Arab-Israeli conflict or, in Nixon's words, "tilt" American policy, if it was to be tilted at all, "on the side of 100 million Arabs rather than on the side of two million Israelis."[18]

For Moscow, Sadat's ascension to the Egyptian presidency was also an important moment. Having staked so much economic and military assistance for the sake of a noncommunist government during the preceding three years, the Soviet Union had a vested interest in seeing that its strategic gains were protected. Although the Soviets would have much preferred a leader who was less nationalistic and while they no doubt wanted an Egyptian president more sympathetic to the Soviet Union, they needed Sadat's support not only to maintain their strategic position in the Middle East vis-à-vis the United States but also to prove to their allies—both in the communist bloc and out—that Soviet power and influence was still valued.

The Decline of Soviet Influence in Egypt

It was not at first obvious that Sadat would bring dramatic changes to Egypt. His very selection by the National Assembly after having served alongside Nasser for almost twenty years indicated that continuity in policy should be maintained. During his opening remarks to the Egyptian National Assembly immediately following his nomination, he pledged to follow Nasser's objectives to liberate all Arab lands occupied by Israel during the 1967 war, to defend the socialist gains of Egypt, and to maintain Nasser's policy of nonalignment between the major power world blocs. "I have come to you along the path of Gamal Abdel Nasser," Sadat said, "and I believe that your nomination of me to assume the responsibilities of the presidency is a nomination for us to continue on the path of Nasser."[19] After hearing these remarks, one *New York Times* columnist was quick to characterize Sadat's selection as simply "Nasserism without Nasser," and suggested there was bound to be a behind-the-scenes struggle for the apparent succession in terms of real power.[20]

From a strategic standpoint, too, there was also no reason to expect that Sadat would loosen Egypt's ties with Moscow. At the time he assumed power, Egypt remained almost exclusively dependent upon Soviet military and economic assistance. In the previous year alone, more than ten thousand Soviet military "advisers" had arrived in Egypt, and Russian pilots had assumed responsibility for much of the Egyptian air defense. The most sophisticated of the Russian-made surface-to-air missiles, the SA-3, had also been installed inside Egypt, protecting the country from continued Israeli deep-penetration bombing.[21] For Sadat even to think of cutting ties with the Soviet Union would not only place Egypt's security, and that of his own political future, at considerable risk but would deny Egypt the necessary capabilities to launch another war with Israel in the event that the Sinai was not returned through diplomacy.

As a public signal that Sadat intended to maintain Egypt's close relationship with the Soviet Union, he appointed Ali Sabry, the head of the Arab Socialist Union (ASU), as his vice president. A former prime minister and deputy prime minister under Nasser, Sabry had long been identified with Soviet interests in Egypt, and many expected him, not Sadat, to succeed Nasser. At the time of Nasser's death, according to Mohamed Heikal, the group around Sabry controlled the National Assembly, the Central Committee of the ASU, and elite Vanguard Movement of the ASU, as well as the intelligence apparatus and the Ministries of Presidential Affairs and Information.[22] The Central Intelligence Agency regarded Sabry as a "capable" leader and an "intelligent and able administrator with an impressive knowledge of Middle East problems,"[23] and leaders inside the Kremlin were hopeful that Sabry would keep a close watch on the new Egyptian president. In early 1971, as a sign of how much faith he placed in Sabry's relationship with the Kremlin, Sadat asked Sabry to lead a delegation to Moscow to demand more arms from the Soviet Union in the wake of President Nixon's decision to increase US military aid to Israel.[24]

Yet for all of Sadat's public pronouncements about carrying on Nasser's legacy and maintaining the Soviet-Egyptian partnership, privately the new Egyptian president began to distance his country from the grips of Soviet control. During Nasser's funeral Sadat quietly summoned Elliot Richardson, the highest-ranking American official in attendance, and left him an assurance to take back to Washington that under his direction Egypt planned to become much closer aligned to the West.[25] He also made it clear during his first conversations with Donald Bergus, the American chargé d'affaires in Cairo, that he wanted a friendly relationship with Washington. Following a meeting with Sadat on October 3, Bergus reported to the State Department that he "found it hard to believe that this was the same man who had indulged in so much plain anti-American rabble-rousing in public meetings throughout Egypt during the first six months of this year," adding that Sadat stressed his and Egypt's "feeling of friendship" for the United States.[26]

In his first letter to President Nixon in December 1970, Sadat again went to great lengths to point out that Egypt was not a puppet of the Soviet government even though his country continued to rely heavily on Soviet military and economic assistance. "You would be mistaken to think that we were in the sphere of Soviet influence," he said. "We are not within the Soviet sphere of influence, nor, for that matter, anybody's sphere of influence." He also made it clear that although he was prepared to begin a dialogue with Washington, he did not want the United States communicating its messages to him through the Soviet Union. "If you wish to talk about anything concerning Egypt, the venue will be in Cairo and the talks will be with me, not with any other party."[27]

For the most part, Sadat did his best to keep these early contacts with Washington extremely quiet. We now know, however, that many Egyptian officials were well aware of the direction Sadat was moving Egypt. In an interview with historian Kirk Beattie, Sadat's former minister of war, General Muhammad Fawzi, alleged that by early 1971 Egyptian intelligence services had detected a direct line to Washington from Sadat's house. When confronted by Fawzi to remove the line, Sadat complied, but according to Fawzi, the damage was already done. "He was working behind everybody's back, making his own foreign policy," said Sadat's former aide. "Why did he want to do this privately?"[28]

Sadat may have removed the direct line to Washington from his home, but he continued to signal to Washington that he wanted to move Egypt in a new direction. On February 4, just hours before the expiration of the Egyptian-Israeli cease-fire, he declared in a forty-five-minute speech to the National Assembly that not only would he extend the cease-fire for another thirty days but that he was also prepared to open the Suez Canal as the first step of an interim peace initiative designed to obtain Israel's withdrawal from the Canal area.[29] Although Sadat was largely picking up on a proposal by Israel's defense minister, Moshe Dayan,[30] it was a positive step nonetheless, as Egyptian officials had maintained since 1967 that they would reopen the hundred-mile-long waterway to international navigation only if Israel withdrew from the entire Sinai Peninsula.

But Sadat did not stop there. Less than two weeks later, in a response to a request by Gunnar Jarring, the UN special representative assigned to the Arab-Israeli conflict, to clarify the current Egyptian and Israeli positions with respect to Security Council Resolution 242,[31] Sadat indicated that Egypt would terminate all states of claims of belligerency with Israel, as well as respect Israel's "right to live within secure and recognized boundaries."[32] Sadat's reply to Jarring made no mention of the United Sates or the Soviet Union per se, but his message was clearly a signal to Washington that Egypt was moving on a new course. In fact, after hearing no immediate reaction from Washington to his response to Jarring, Sadat dispatched his special adviser, Mohamed Heikal, to meet with Bergus to ensure that the message did not get lost. According to Heikal, Sadat wanted it conveyed to President Nixon that his proposal was not in any sense a "cold war exercise" and that there had been "no Soviet pressure on him to make this proposal." Sadat asked Washington to "exercise influence" on Israel to secure a "most careful" consideration of his proposal, and he wanted to be sure that his initiative did not turn into an "academic exercise." Heikal concluded by saying that if Sadat's proposal were accepted and a partial withdrawal of Israeli forces from the Canal area were to take place, Egypt could resume diplomatic relations with the United States and "bring to an end the 'artificial situation' existing between Washington and Cairo."[33]

While all of these steps were impressive enough, perhaps Sadat's most overt signal that he wanted to cut ties with Moscow came in the early spring, when he initiated a move to consolidate his power and purge the Soviet influences from his government. On May 2, in response to accusations from members of the Arab Socialist Union that he was being "diddled by the Americans," and right on the heels of a visit by Secretary of State Rogers to Cairo, Sadat removed Ali Sabry from his post of vice president. In taking the decision, Sadat maintained that he wanted to prove that "Moscow has no man in Egypt" and that the Soviet Union was "dealing with a government, not with individuals."[34] Two weeks later Sadat announced that he had arrested several pro-Soviet members of his cabinet, including the minister of the interior, Shaarawi Gomaa, and the minister of war. Although the crisis largely involved domestic politics, the fact that the men opposed Sadat's efforts to secure American rather than Soviet support for his foreign policy obviously influenced his decision.[35]

If Sadat believed that his February 4 peace initiative had gone unnoticed in Washington, his efforts to change the leadership in Egypt no doubt caught the attention of US officials. Following Sabry's dismissal, Bergus commented in a cable to Washington that Sadat's move was a "victory for the good guys in Egypt" and increased Sadat's need for some kind of "tangible movement" toward a peaceful settlement with Israel.[36] In a similar memorandum to President Nixon on May 7, the deputy national security adviser, Alexander Haig, reported that Sadat's "decisive move" against his most "prominent critic" suggests "an increasing confidence in his ability to manipulate the instruments of power." But even more important, Haig believed that Sabry's dismissal would no doubt be an "embarrassment" for Moscow, particularly in view of the coincidence of his dismissal with Secretary Rogers's visit. "In short," he concluded, "if Sadat gets away with this, and the chances are he will, he will have strengthened his claim within Egypt as Nasser's successor."[37]

Reaching for Sadat

For Secretary of State William Rogers, Sadat's rise on the Egyptian scene could not have come at a better time. At just the moment he began to lose what little control he still held over American foreign policy, Rogers received a boost from Sadat's willingness to move forward on another peace agreement with Israel and his strong desire to open a new dialogue with Washington. On November 17, just weeks after Sadat officially assumed the Egyptian presidency, Rogers proposed to Nixon a number of steps the United States could take to improve its relationship with the new leadership in Cairo. Reactivation of the Fulbright exchange program to enable Egyptian graduate students and professionals to study in the United States was considered as a means to improve cultural exchanges; debt rescheduling and export-import financing were contemplated to assist Egypt economically; and even a high-level visit to Cairo by the secretary of state, or visits by "high ranking" Egyptians to the United States, to bolster political relations between the two countries was considered. "We do not, of course, know whether the present leadership in the UAR will be able to maintain itself," Rogers explained, but in his view "any such initiatives," as modest as they might be, would not go unnoticed in other Arab states and would strengthen the confidence of these governments in maintaining ties with the United States.[38]

Rogers also began reaching out to the Soviets in the hope that Moscow could persuade Sadat to extend the cease-fire with Israel another three months to allow negotiations to resume between Egypt and Israel without the fear of a looming deadline or the resumption of hostilities. On the afternoon of December 24, he invited the Soviet ambassador, Anatoly Dobrynin, to his office for a private discussion on the prospects for a new round of negotiations. Rogers appeared convinced that the change in leadership in Cairo, along with the recent events of Black September, which had significantly weakened the Palestinian organizations in Jordan, made the prospects for peace in 1971 more likely.[39]

For the United States to improve its relationship with the Egypt, however, Rogers understood that he had to actively help Sadat get his land back, even if it included pressing the Israelis into a peace agreement. In response to Sadat's pledge in early February to open the Suez Canal to international navigation and sign a peace agreement with Israel, Rogers and Assistant Secretary of State Joseph Sisco held numerous meetings with Yitzhak Rabin, the Israeli ambassador in Washington, and made it clear that future US arms sales would be held in abeyance unless Israel demonstrated some flexibility with the Egyptians. Rabin complained to Sisco on February 12 that cutting off arms supplies would force Israel to cope with Russian pilots and crews without adequate military supplies, subjecting the United States to criticism for abandoning an ally, but both Sisco and Rogers felt that the best way to avoid a confrontation with the Soviets was for the Israelis to work with Sadat in reaching an agreement.[40]

Thus, when word reached Rogers that the Israeli leadership had decided to respond negatively to Gunnar Jarring's February 8 aide memoire, asking Israel to withdraw to the international boundary in return from commitments from Sadat to terminate all states of claims of belligerency with Israel and open the Suez Canal and Straits of Tiran to international shipping,[41] the normally affable Rogers became extremely upset with Israel. He invited Rabin for a "talk" at the State Department on February 24 to tell the ambassador that "the United States government is concerned that the Israeli answer will be interpreted as evasive." Rabin attempted to defend his government's position, saying that Israel had communicated its stance on various occasions to the United States, at which point the conversation quickly turned heated. Rogers rejected Rabin's implication that their reply to Jarring was not a new position and insisted that Israel's position would both create "major problems" in US-Israeli relations and lead the United States to take a position against Israel in the United Nations Security Council. "It is just an evasion," Rogers bellowed at Rabin. "It's only a matter of time before your hand will be disclosed. Sooner or later you will have to face up to it."[42]

Two days later, at a meeting of the National Security Council, Rogers again stressed the importance of Sadat's recent moves and the necessity of getting Israel to respond favorably to Jarring's message. "If, in 1967, we could have gotten from Egypt what they are now willing to give, Israel would have been delighted with it," Rogers stated. "Now, Israel is . . . unwilling to make a decision of any kind. . . . And if that is their response," he said very clearly, "then the United States is in one hell of a position."[43]

Like Rogers, Nixon appeared to be equally frustrated by Israel's reluctance to respond favorably to Sadat's new overtures, and he began to question America's continued commitment to Israel when the Israelis would not live up to their obligations. "Why do we provide the arms," he asked, if Israel refuses to negotiate? The president had grown tired of Israel's games and believed it was time to increase the pressure on Israeli leaders. "We cannot be in a position where we [continue to provide aid] and Israel says we won't talk," he said in response to Rogers's comments. "That's what it gets down to."[44]

Nixon's frustration with Israel, however, did not mean that he was completely behind Sadat. In fact, he made it quite clear during the NSC meeting that he "had no confidence at all about the Egyptians," and was highly skeptical about whether the Egyptians could be trusted after breaking similar promises to the United States just six months earlier.[45] In addition, he affirmed that for the time being the United States would "maintain the [military] balance in [Israel's] favor," in light of Soviet arms shipments to the Middle East, as well as support Israel's claim of "secure and defensible borders." Still, both Nixon and Rogers believed that with Nasser out of the picture and with Sadat's recent statements there was a reasonable possibility of getting Egypt and Israel to agree to an interim settlement. At the very least, Nixon knew that with the chances of a summit with the Soviet Union still about a year away, and with little progress being made in Vietnam, he had some time to maneuver on the Middle East. Yet any agreement, the president maintained, must address the Soviet military presence in Egypt. "They've got to quit messing around over there," he said firmly to Rogers and Sisco. "That has to be part of the deal."[46]

Over the next six weeks, both Nixon and Rogers took aggressive measures to demonstrate to Sadat that the United States planned to take a more direct role in the Middle East to ensure Israel's commitment to a peace agreement. On March 9, Rogers held what in effect amounted to a rump meeting of the National Security Council in his office with defense secretary Melvin Laird, CIA director Richard Helms, chairman of the Joint Chiefs Admiral Thomas Moorer, Kissinger, and Sisco. During the meeting, Rogers made it known that he intended to push the Israelis hard over the coming weeks so that they would be more forthcoming in working with Sadat. He told the group that in exchange for long-term arrangements to satisfy Israeli arms requirements and a "major U.S. financial contribution" to the resettlement of refugees, among other things, the United States would ask Israel to accept the 1969 US position on boundaries, which, in Kissinger's estimate, meant a "total confrontation" with Israel.[47] The same evening, moreover, Rogers gave an interview to the Public Broadcasting Service in which he declared that the United States was willing to send military forces to the region as part of an international peacekeeping force under United Nations auspices. Though he admitted that such a force would in no way substitute for an agreement, he argued that the presence of US forces would be a "very adequate guarantee for peace" and would demonstrate that the Nixon administration was "willing to play our part."[48]

The following month, as a clear indication of where the White House was leaning, Nixon agreed to send Rogers to Cairo for direct talks with President Sadat with the hope that the two might be able to reach an interim agreement much in line with what Sadat had proposed back in February. In discussing his decision with Rogers over the telephone on April 19, Nixon told the secretary of state that he felt it was a good time to "put the spotlight of attention out there and if something can come out of it, that would be great."[49] At the same time, the president also told his chief his staff that the purpose of Rogers's trip is to "keep the momentum going—to keep the ceasefire going," and instructed him to tell the press that the White House was "very glad" that the secretary was going to Egypt. "This is the first time in history that a Secretary of State has visited a country which denies it diplomatic relations," he said. "The president urged this. His goals—his long-range goal is to reestablish diplomatic relations with Egypt."[50]

From Cairo to Jerusalem

In strictly Cold War terms, Rogers's very arrival in Cairo on the afternoon of May 5, 1971 was a major achievement. Not only was it the first time an American secretary of state had been to Egypt since John Foster Dulles's official visit in 1953, but to come to Cairo at a time when the United States maintained no official relations with Egypt, and when the Soviet Union had firmly entrenched itself as Egypt's prime economic and military supplier, demonstrated the extent to which the United States wanted to reverse the Soviet gains in the Arab world.[51] Rogers, too, made sure that his visit would be seen in marked contrast to that of official Soviet visits. During his two days in the Egyptian capital, Rogers and his wife made stops at Nasser's tomb; visited Egypt's famous museum preserving Tutankhamen's artifacts; met with leaders of an orphanage caring for children whose parents suffered from tuberculosis; toured the Pyramids; and perhaps most important paid a visit on Nasser's widow and children as a gesture of friendship to the Egyptian people.[52]

Of course, all of this "public diplomacy" would mean very little if the private diplomacy with Sadat went poorly. But Rogers felt confident that he would leave Egypt with a commitment from the Egyptian President to open the Suez Canal to international navigation as part of an interim peace agreement with Israel. Before his departure from Washington, he had received a message from Sadat, through Bergus, in which he said he wanted to spend at least three hours with the secretary of state to discuss the Suez proposal. "He's got a big map drawn and he wants to talk to me about how he sees it," Rogers told Nixon in the Oval Office on April 22.[53] Rogers was also hopeful that the Suez proposal would lead to a "full agreement" down the road, much in line with the plan he had publicly launched in December 1969.[54] "That's the long-term proposition," he told Nixon. "It would be impractical to think that we could do it in less than a year," he added, "but that should be our goal."[55]

The meeting between Rogers and Sadat took place at the presidential palace on the morning of May 6. Rogers had expected Sadat to open the discussion with a history of grievances perpetuated on the Egyptians by the Israelis, as most conversations with Arab leaders often began, but Sadat quickly shifted the discussion, indicating that removing the Soviet military presence from his country had become central to his strategy. "I know what's uppermost in your mind and I want to talk about it at once . . . and that's the Soviet Union," Rogers quoted Sadat as telling him. "I don't like the fact that we have to depend on the Soviet Union as much as we do. I am a nationalist. I want to remain a nationalist. . . . I don't want to have to depend on anyone else. The only reason I have is because we were humiliated and I had no place to turn."[56]

According to Rogers's account of the conversation, the financial burden of maintaining the Soviet presence in Egypt weighed heavily on Sadat. In the three years following the Six-Day War, Egypt's military expenditures, including the costs of the Soviet advisers, almost doubled.[57] "I'll tell you,"

President Sadat (left) and Secretary of State Rogers discuss the Middle East political situation in Cairo, May 6, 1971. (*Getty Images*)

Sadat told Rogers, "you may not believe this but it is the truth: I have to pay for everything. . . . I can't afford it. It's a drain on me. We should be spending money for other [things]. I pay for it all in hard currency. . . . I pay for the salaries and expenses of the Russians who are here. . . . I need the money for other things."[58]

Although these statements in some ways echoed what Sadat had been telling American officials during the preceding months, Rogers seemed genuinely surprised by Sadat's discontent. Sadat believed that the Soviets had no interest in seeing the immediate return of the occupied territories to the Arab states. So long as Israel controlled these areas, he reasoned, the Soviets would continue to justify the expansion of their military presence in the region. He pleaded for the United States to be more evenhanded, and he left Rogers with a clear message to take back to Washington that he believed would not only end the impasse but would change the direction of American policy in the region for years to come: "I want to give you this promise," Sadat said unambiguously to Rogers. "If we can work out an interim settlement . . . I promise you, I give you my personal assurance that all the Russian ground troops will be out of my country at the end of six months. I will keep Russian pilots to train my pilots because that's the only way my pilots can learn how to fly. But in so far as the bulk of the Russians—the ten or twelve thousand—they will all be out of Egypt within six months if we can make a deal."[59]

The significance of Sadat's proposal was not lost on Rogers. Since the earliest days of the Nixon administration, he had been trying to negotiate an Arab-Israeli peace agreement only to see his efforts come up short. The idea that Sadat would now include the removal of the Soviet military presence in addition to agreeing to sign a peace agreement with Israel was something the United States could not ignore. "For as much as we would like to be friendly as hell with you, we can't as long as you have this number of Russians here," he told Sadat in response to the Egyptian's new promises. Rogers acknowledged that he too was frustrated with Israel's refusal to respond favorably to the proposals put forth during the preceding months, and he understood that Sadat desperately needed a deal to maintain his power. But Rogers made it clear that Israel would continue with their pattern of behavior, and the United States would continue to support Israel so long as the large number of Russian troops remained in Egypt. "On the other hand," Rogers told Sadat, "once that is not the case, once they've left, or most of them, it's a different ballgame."[60]

What seems even more evident from Rogers's conversations with Sadat, however, is that Sadat's later decision to expel the Soviet presence from Egypt had little to do with preparing Egypt for another war with Israel. For Sadat the Soviet removal was the most overt way he could tell the United States that he was serious in wanting to change their existing relationship. He assured Rogers that his position regarding to Jarring's memorandum in February—the decision to live in peace with Israel, to sign a peace agreement with Israel, and to stay out of Israeli internal affairs—resulted from a desire to align Egypt more closely with the West. To be sure, Sadat was even willing to accept an American military presence in the region as part of a peacekeeping force so long as Israel would agree to return Egypt's land. "I have no interest in violating the security interests in anything you want to do, in anything the United Nations wants to do, or anyone else wants to do," he pleaded with Rogers. "I don't want to bother Israel. . . . I'll sign an agreement. . . . I just want my land back."[61]

Before the meeting concluded, Sadat expressed to Rogers that he hoped the time had come where the United States would change its relationship with Egypt, believing that with the Soviet presence removed from his country, there could be a much more evenhanded approach to the Middle East conflict. "I realize too that you can't change overnight," he said. "You've sort of built a monument in your relationship with Israel that can't be affected quickly, but can be changed over a period of time. And if you can do that, I'm prepared to change our relationship with you." He said, "If we can work out some interim settlements on the Suez, we'll renew diplomatic relations with you . . . and I think others will too."[62]

Rogers and Sisco were absolutely stunned by their two-and-a half hour meeting with the Egyptian president. Sisco in particular found Sadat "full of understanding for Israel's problems" and had "never heard an Arab leader express himself in such a manner." For the first time, he believed, a leader in the Arab world had acknowledged that he wanted to reduce his dependence on the Soviet Union and was willing to place himself in Israel's shoes and consider Israel's security concerns—including borders—as part of any future agreement.[63] Rogers, too, found Sadat to be a "realist" and "anxious for peace"[64] and left Cairo convinced Sadat had decided to "change his position" with regard to the Soviet Union and was "determined to become closer to the West." He was also impressed by Sadat's determination to improve his relations with Jerusalem. As he later told President Nixon, Sadat "is willing to go much farther than any other Arab leader has ever gone in stating what he'll do with Israel."[65]

From Cairo, Rogers and Sisco flew immediately to Israel to relay Sadat's message to the leaders in Jerusalem. The secretary tried to impress on Prime Minister Meir that the Egyptian president had made a firm commitment to remove the Soviet military presence from his country and wanted to be the first Arab leader to make peace with Israel. "He does everything he can to convince you that he is prepared to sign a peace agreement," he told Meir during a meeting at her office in Jerusalem. "He says that is what Egypt wants. He thought that is what the U.S. wanted and he thinks that any kind of guarantees that anybody wants is satisfactory to him." Any doubts, moreover, that Sadat would not stay in power long enough to see these commitments through should also be put to rest, Rogers insisted. "If you were making a prediction you'd have to say . . . that he is going to take Nasser's place. He is it. We had serious doubts about it when he came into office," Rogers added, but "the impression that you get in Egypt that would surprise you some is that Sadat seems to be totally confident of his own position. He doesn't seem to have any doubt about it, nor do the people around him."[66]

The prime minister, however, was hardly impressed with what Rogers had to say. In response to his opening statement, she insisted that Sadat did not want peace, maintaining instead that "all he wants is his land back," and questioned why her government would make such a deal after a history of Egyptian aggression against Israel. She reminded Rogers that Egypt had violated its peace agreements after 1949 and stressed that the Israeli government was "happy" with the United Nations force in the Sinai before the Egyptians threw it out in 1967, not to mention the fact that less than a year ago, after Israel had agreed to a temporary cease-fire with Nasser, Egypt violated the spirit of the agreement by allowing the Soviets to move their defensive weapon systems into the Canal area. "I can only say this," said Meir. "We have to learn from our experiences."[67]

It was also clear that Meir did not share Rogers's rosy picture of Sadat. Meir reminded Rogers of the numerous statements Sadat had said about Israel since becoming president. These statements included Sadat's threat that Israel "will not escape punishment, no matter how long it takes," and his talk about the expected "total war," which would not only encompass the armies deployed opposite one another but spread to every factory, plow, village, and homeland.[68] "These things have not been said in secret to anybody. This is on the radio; this is at the conference of the so-called [Arab] Socialist Union; this is at the conference that was held of Fatah in Cairo by the same Sadat."[69] So, Meir asked Rogers, "Which Sadat are we to believe?"[70]

To Rogers's dismay, moreover, Meir appeared unwilling to cooperate with Sadat on working out an agreement to reopen the Suez Canal, even though Israel had made an offer to do so less than two weeks earlier. She insisted that while Israel would negotiate with Egypt on the withdrawal of Israeli forces from Egyptian territory, she did not want to drag out the withdrawal in stages, as the Canal initiative would entail. More important for Israel, Meir maintained, was a commitment from Sadat that "this is an end of *all* shooting," not just for three months or six months. As far as opening the Suez Canal was concerned, Meir simply did not see why such a proposal would benefit Israel without a full commitment to peace from Sadat. "We have lived without shipping through the Suez Canal for quite a few years," she explained. "That isn't the greatest tragedy that happened to Israel. We can go on."[71]

The two-and-a-half-hour session with the Israeli prime minister left Rogers completely dejected.[72] He had come to Jerusalem confident, if not hopeful, that a compromise could be achieved for opening the Suez Canal as part of an interim peace agreement, especially in light of the guarantees Sadat had left him with in Cairo. But when he returned to his room at the King David Hotel later that evening, Rogers drafted a message to President Nixon expressing clear doubts that Israel had a leader capable of making a deal. "Mrs. Meir has great strengths, but also great weaknesses," he explained in a carefully worded telegram. "She is showing understandable strain, irritation, signs of weariness, and age, but more important," he concluded, "she suffers psychologically from the 'trauma of 1957' when as Foreign Minister she announced Israeli withdrawal [from the Sinai]. She strongly prefers arguing the past, has difficulty talking specifics, and has to be pushed forward rather than lead her platoon of ministers."[73]

Sisco called Dayan later that evening and expressed extreme "unhappiness" with the prime minister, requesting a meeting with the defense minister the following morning to iron out their differences before Meir's second meeting with Rogers.[74] The two met in Tel Aviv on the morning of May 7, along with Simcha Dinitz, the director general of the prime minister's office, and Roy Atherton, Sisco's deputy. Dayan began the meeting adopting much the same line that Meir had with Rogers. That Sadat now wanted to make peace, he maintained, was a direct result of the fact that Israeli forces had been sitting for four years on the Canal and four years on the Jordan River. "It has never happened before," said Dayan. "So I am not sure the Egyptians changed, but I think they learned a lesson." As the meeting progressed, however, Dayan's tone began to moderate; he not only indicated that he supported an interim Suez Canal agreement with Egypt but went further than any Israeli leader had up to that point in detailing Israel's positions on a Canal agreement, the demilitarization of forces, and a territorial settlement with Egypt.[75]

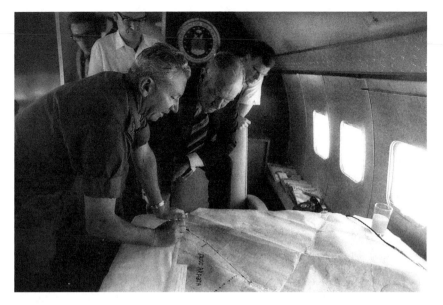

Secretary of State Rogers (center) with Israeli chief of staff Chaim Bar-Lev during their flight in Air Force Two over Sharm el-Sheikh, May 7, 1971. *(Moshe Milner, Israel Government Press Office)*

Dayan said he envisioned a Suez Canal agreement under two separate concepts. The first concept, based on an extension of the cease-fire for a limited time, held that Israel must be left in a position to "shoot its way back to the Canal," the Bar-Lev Line must be maintained, and Israel must have the Suez under direct observation. Such a formula would leave the Israeli Defense Forces in the necessary positions, and its fortifications along the Canal intact, in the event that Sadat resumed fighting on the termination of the cease-fire. The second plan, according to the defense minister, to be considered only following an unlimited extension of the cease-fire, was based on the assumption that Israel would not return to the Canal. Under this concept, Israel would withdraw a greater distance, beyond six miles, but there would have to be assurances that the Soviets would not cross the Canal and a US peacekeeping force would need to be stationed in the Sinai between the Egyptian and Israeli lines. Egypt would also have to limit its "offensive forces" west of the Canal, though it would be permitted "administrative and police personnel" east of the Canal.[76] "I want you to know that I am the only one who is speaking of a larger distance than just off the Canal," Dayan told Sisco. "But if we could get from the Egyptians something with unlimited cease-fire, then we could have our concept reviewed."[77]

Dayan reported on his conversation with Sisco to the broader ministerial group before Meir's meeting with Rogers. The defense minister came under criticism from what some of his colleagues regarded as "excessive flexibility." Eban sent Dayan a note asking whether he would put this idea to a vote to the cabinet, in which case not only would Eban support him, but he believed ministers from the Mapam and Independent Liberal groups would also lend their support. Dayan replied that if Meir did not accept the proposal, he would not even put it up for discussion and would deny that the proposal had any "official" status.[78]

No consensus emerged from the ministerial group for a twenty-mile withdrawal, but Dayan's conversation with Sisco and the meeting among the Israeli leadership presumably made an impact on the prime minister. When the talks between Meir and Rogers in Tel Aviv resumed that afternoon, Meir made almost a complete turnaround from the position she had taken with Rogers the previous day. For the first time, she grudgingly indicated Israel's willingness to withdraw its forces along the Suez Canal in exchange for an interim peace agreement with Egypt and was prepared to begin discussions with Sadat. The prime minister wanted to ensure, however, that as part of any settlement, the Suez Canal would be open to Israeli shipping, there would be an *indefinite* extension of the cease-fire with Egypt, and absolutely no Egyptian military forces would be permitted on the east side of the Canal.[79]

Meir also remained concerned that Sadat would envisage a Suez agreement as *part* of a final agreement on borders and recognition rather than an end in itself. She feared that "one fine morning" Sadat would tire of the interim agreement and would issue an ultimatum that would lead to war. For Rogers, though, these were points that could be worked out directly with Sadat, and he hoped that Meir's concerns would not be used to thwart a prospective deal. Meir, however, appeared committed to the agreement: "We are prepared to move from the Canal, we do not want any more shooting, we do not want military personnel to cross the Canal.

If we have to face the Egyptian army we would rather face them across the Canal."[80]

Although Meir's comments were by no means a guarantee that Israel would sign an agreement, they elicited enough progress that Rogers sent a message back to the White House informing Nixon that "we hit pay dirt" in his long, detailed, and point-by-point discussion of the interim settlement in which the United States was able to get some "helpful Israeli flexibility" on certain key points.[81] He also sent Sisco back to Cairo to convey to the Egyptian president the details of the discussions in Israel and to see how far Sadat would go in dealing with the Israelis.[82]

The one issue where Rogers foresaw difficulty was in Israel's "hard-rock insistence" that no Egyptian military forces be permitted to move into evacuated territories. In Cairo, Sadat had insisted that some Egyptian forces be permitted to cross the Suez, if only for symbolic purposes. "After all," he told Rogers, "that's part of sovereignty."[83] But Meir was adamant that absolutely no Egyptian military forces be permitted to cross the Canal, even for a symbolic gesture. She was willing to accept a "civilian presence," and Dayan helped by keeping open the possibility of an Egyptian police force in "symbolic numbers." But, Rogers admitted, "this point will be tough."[84]

Rogers left Israel not knowing what would come of his visit to the region, but he seemed convinced that despite the two days in "worried, suspicious, querulous Israel," significant progress had been made during his visits to Cairo and Jerusalem. As he later explained to Nixon, he felt strongly that the United States added a "measure of confidence" in its relations with Sadat, and that it had "reaffirmed our continuing interest in Israel's security, while leaving them with no doubt that our direct interests in the area can be affected adversely unless they adopt a more flexible position on an overall interim peace settlement." More important, though, the secretary of state returned to Washington convinced that the United States had finally begun to "take the play away from the Russians," and both sides—Arabs and Israelis—now saw the United States as the "key" to peace. "So long as we maintain our strength to bulwark this kind of active U.S. diplomacy," he added, "we ought to be able in time to move from neutralizing Soviet influence to reversing that trend and at least keep pace with them in the Persian Gulf and the Indian Ocean."[85]

Rogers knew all this would mean nothing if he failed to deliver the interim agreement Sadat desperately wanted. As soon as he returned to Washington he pressed Nixon on the necessity of getting the Israelis to cooperate with Sadat. Rogers believed that in Sadat they had found a leader capable of reshaping the political landscape of the Middle East. Not only was he prepared to sign a peace agreement with Israel, but his agreement to remove the Soviet military presence from his country was a concession of enormous magnitude. "The thing I want to emphasize," Rogers told Nixon in the Oval Office on May 19, "if [Sadat] stays in power, we can make a breakthrough here that will have tremendous importance. . . . If we can pull this off, it will be a step toward peace that no one thought was possible."[86]

For his part, Nixon was highly intrigued by what he learned of the new Egyptian president. While it was unclear whether Sadat would remain in power long enough to see these promises through, he also understood that Sadat had been far more forthcoming than the Israeli leaders had been during the preceding months and recognized that this was by far his best chance to advance American objectives in the region. True, there were risks that colluding with the Egyptians could affect the relationship Nixon had built with Moscow during the preceding years. Would the Soviet Union, for example, increase its military aid to North Vietnam if it learned that the United States was secretly seeking Soviet expulsion from Egypt? Or would Moscow withdraw its most recent offer of an antiballistic missile agreement if the president's efforts to remove the Soviet military presence came to light?[87] Still, Nixon recognized that this was his chance to get the Soviets out of Egypt, and he seemed prepared to accept the risks that expelling them might entail.

In fact, less than an hour after receiving Rogers's first briefing of his conversation with Sadat, Nixon met with his chief of staff, H. R. Haldeman, and left little doubt that Sadat's attitude had convinced him that the United States had to begin titling its policy in favor of the Egyptians. He complained that the Israelis were just "sitting tight" and "not doing a damn thing" on Sadat's offer to reopen the Suez Canal and insisted that "we cannot just continue to go down the line" with such policy. "We've got to pressure them," he said, "and we're going to do it." The president also informed Haldeman that he did not "buy" Kissinger's idea of "taking the

Jewish line." He believed Kissinger was "blinded" by his desire to bring the Russians into the discussions and felt that whenever Kissinger involved himself in the Middle East, "he is totally irrational about anything else." Nixon instructed his chief of staff to "keep Henry out of it" and make sure that the message got passed through the system that the administration would not endorse Israel's intransigence: "The United States just cannot continue to sit in there supporting Israel alone against 100 million Arabs," he said. "They expect us to give them [economic and military aid] and not do a goddamn thing about moving from the Suez or anything else. They're not going to get it."[88]

The president, however, did not stop there. On May 26, in what is perhaps the most clear expression of his thinking on the Middle East during his entire presidency, Nixon sent Rogers an "eyes only" memorandum in which he clearly authorized the secretary of state to press the Israelis into an agreement so as to ensure the expulsion of the Soviet forces from Egypt. "Under these circumstances," Nixon said referring to Sadat's recent revelations, "it is essential that no more aid programs for Israel be approved until they agree to some kind of interim action on the Suez or some other issue." The president strongly believed that Meir had "diddled us along" during the previous two years and that it was now time for the Israeli government to make the hard decisions. "In the month of June or July," he told Rogers, "[they] must bite the bullet as to whether they want more U.S. aid at the price of being reasonable on an interim agreement or whether they want to go at it alone."[89]

The president acknowledged that there were certainly times when the national security interests of the United States were better served by siding with Israel. "Where the Soviet Union is obviously siding with Israel's neighbors," he wrote, "it serves our interests to see that Israel is able to not only defend itself but to deter further Soviet encroachments in the area." This, he said, is what had influenced him in coming down hard on the side of Israel in maintaining the balance of power in the area at a time when Soviet influence in Egypt and other countries surrounding Israel had been particularly strong. But in this instance, Nixon believed, with the possibility of moving the Soviet military presence out of Egypt, and with the likelihood of getting Egypt to enter a peace agreement with Israel, he strongly felt that "the interests of the United States will be served . . . by tilting the policy . . . on the side of 100 million Arabs rather than on the side of two million Israelis."[90]

Nixon, though, fully understood that his window of opportunity to "tilt" American policy toward the Arabs was extremely narrow. In fact, he made it clear to Rogers that "unless [he] was able to get some kind of a settlement now with the Israelis on the Suez or some other issue, there was not going to be any kind of settlement until after the 1972 elections." By that time, he knew, "the Soviets will have had no other choice but to build up the armed strength of Israel's neighbors to the point that another Mideast war will be inevitable." As far as Sadat was concerned, the president acknowledged that "he obviously does not want to have a Soviet presence in Egypt." On the other hand, he told Rogers, "If his policy of conciliation fails, he will either have to go along with a new program of accepting Soviet aid or lose his head, either politically or physically."[91]

The Egyptian-Soviet Treaty of Friendship

Sadat's obvious intention to move closer to the West had placed the Soviets in an uncomfortable position. On the one hand, the Kremlin's principle foreign policy objective was to seek détente with United States in an effort to avoid an arms race that would bleed the Soviet Union's economic resources. Negotiations were nearing fruition with Washington on an antiballistic missile agreement, on a treaty to end the long-standing difference over the final status of Berlin, and on convening a high-level summit between Nixon and Brezhnev the following year. Upsetting progress on these issues to prevent the United States from making inroads with Sadat was not in the Soviet interest.[92] At the same time, however, Moscow had invested millions of dollars in Egypt, helping to finance the construction of the Aswan High Dam, and had sent thousands of its military personnel, along with its most advanced technology, to Cairo in an effort to prevent Israeli deep-penetration bombing of the Egyptian hinterland. Allowing Sadat simply to cut ties with Moscow after years of economic and military support, and the loss of Soviet lives in defense of Egypt, did not sit well with many Soviet officials.

The US effort to keep the Soviet Union out of the Middle East dialogue, moreover, was a source of growing frustration and irritation for the Soviets.

In January and February 1971, Dobrynin sent numerous reports to Moscow commenting on the direction of the Nixon administration's Middle East policy and its implications for the Soviet Union. Dobrynin acknowledged that the White House showed "great interest" in continuing talks on the issue of strategic weaponry and the prospect of a summit meeting with Soviet leaders but displayed a "marked disinclination to have concrete talks on the Middle East."[93] During three meetings with Kissinger in January, the Soviet ambassador made numerous requests to move the Middle East discussions into the "confidential channel," rather than through the State Department, stressing that Washington could not "settle this without us or, even less, that you can settle it against us," but failed to get Kissinger to go beyond general phrases and assurances.[94] "Judging by all the evidence," Dobrynin wrote in a telegram to Moscow, "neither Nixon nor Kissinger wants at all to get into the specific substance of formulations for a peace settlement on their own initiative, just as they are not rushing to reply to the proposals that we made more than a year and a half ago on bilateral talks."[95]

Given Washington's efforts to exclude the Soviets from the Middle East talks and weaken their influence in the region, Dobrynin recommended to officials inside the Kremlin several steps to undermine US efforts to pursue individual agreements with Egypt and Jordan. He encouraged Moscow to systematically bring to Arab attention the "obstructionist" US role on issues of core importance to Arabs, especially Israeli withdrawal from occupied territories, and encouraged the Soviet leadership to send several messages to Nixon on the withdrawal issue, to be publicized if necessary, and convene a meeting of the United Nations Security Council to consider the issue. Another possibility might be to warn the White House that the Soviets were considering supplying modern offensive weapons to Egypt in the event that peace talks foundered.[96]

Brezhnev did not ignore Dobrynin's warnings, but he feared that making threats to Washington would be counterproductive. Instead, Brezhnev believed the Soviets needed to place added pressure on Sadat to ensure that he would not take action against Israel that would draw the Soviet Union into a possible confrontation in the Middle East with the United States. He invited the Egyptian president to Moscow in early March, at which point he criticized Sadat for failing to renew the cease-fire with Israel, set to expire on March 7, and implied that the Egyptians had no long-term strategy to effectively deal with the Israelis. "What is going to happen on March 8th—or on the 9th, or on the 10th?" Brezhnev wanted to know. "Do you know what Israel's reaction will be? Are they going to attack you in depth? Are they going to attack your missile sites? If they do, what will you do?" The general secretary also refused to send Sadat the new shipment of MiG fighters he had requested, although Sadat later insisted that it was he who turned down the supply of aircraft because of the "strings attached"—namely, that he should seek Moscow's approval before using the equipment.[97]

The Rogers visit to Cairo and the internal purge of the pro-Soviet personalities from the Egyptian leadership, which could only be seen by the Russians as a swing to the West dangerous to Soviet interests, forced the Kremlin into more aggressive action to prevent further deterioration of its position in Egypt. On April 30, just days before the secretary of state's arrival in Cairo, the Politburo met to reassess the status of Soviet-Egyptian relations. The Soviet ambassador to Egypt, Vladimir Vinogradov, along with Vadim Kirpichenko, the KGB resident in Cairo, and General Vasili Vasilyevich Okunev, the senior military adviser, were summoned back to Moscow to offer assessments of the new Egyptian president and the status of the Soviet position in Egypt. According to accounts of the meeting by Kirpichenko and Victor Israelyan, a foreign ministry official, Vinogradov and Okunev presented a rather "optimistic" view of the current state of view of relations between the two countries—namely, that "we are forever tied to Egypt through commerce"—although they conceded that Sadat did exhibit "certain dangerous tendencies." Kirpichenko's presentation, by contrast, was more direct. He argued that Sadat planned a break with the Soviet Union and was deliberately deceiving the Kremlin. The KGB officer also reported on the instability of the Egyptian leadership and the possible "break" in the ruling top in the near future.[98]

Following their presentations, there was a "lively" and "stormy" debate regarding the future of the Soviet-Egyptian relationship. Both Foreign Minister Gromyko and Defense Minister Grechko shared Kirpichenko's "apprehension" over the direction of Moscow's relations with Cairo. Grechko argued that continued military assistance to Egypt only complicated matters between the two nations and felt there should be serious consideration by the Politburo about whether additional armaments and military personnel should be sent to Egypt in light of Sadat's recent behavior.[99]

Although many details of the Politburo meeting remain unclear, the actions from the Kremlin in the days following the meeting suggest that the Soviet leadership reached a firm decision to challenge US efforts to strengthen ties with Sadat by solidifying its position inside Egypt. On May 3, in fact, the Soviet troika—Brezhnev, Kosygin, and Podgorny—sent a letter to Sadat stating that they now believed a treaty of friendship was of "great importance" to the Kremlin and would be a "significant means of pressure on Israel and the US, who now confront the UAR struggle to achieve its legitimate rights and to liquidate the consequences of aggression."[100] Three weeks later, on May 24, Soviet president Nikolai Podgorny arrived in Cairo with a treaty of friendship in hand and every expectation that Sadat would agree to its terms.

Signed on May 27, and citing an objective of "struggle against imperialism and colonialism," the Treaty of Friendship and Cooperation reaffirmed the Egyptian-Soviet relationship and provided for continued Soviet military, economic, and cultural aid, as well as an Egyptian commitment to pursue a socialist course regardless of who was in power. There was also a provision in the treaty, much to the displeasure of the United States and Israel, stipulating the continued assistance from the Soviet Union in "the training of the U.A.R. military personnel, in mastering the armaments and equipment supplied to the United Arab Republic with a view to strengthening its capacity to eliminate the consequences of aggression as well as increasing its ability to stand up to aggression in general."[101]

Perhaps the most important aspect of the treaty from the Soviet perspective, however, was the echo to the "Brezhnev Doctrine" contained in article 2.[102] Stating that "the USSR as Socialist state and the UAR, which has set the Socialist transformation of society as its aim, will co-operate closely and in all ways to secure conditions for the safeguarding and further development of the socio-economic gains of their people," the treaty implied that the Soviet Union had a right to watch over Egypt's internal policies and to interfere if they developed in a way that the Soviet Union regarded as a threat to the "gains" made hitherto. Brezhnev had made a similar point when explaining the Soviet Union's 1968 intervention in Czechoslovakia, and now it appeared that he sought to apply a similar formula to the "third world."[103]

The Treaty of Friendship and Cooperation was viewed in Moscow as a major foreign policy accomplishment. In a matter of days, an apparent Egyptian rapprochement with the United States had been replaced by a fifteen-year commitment to "friendship" with the Soviet Union and demonstrated that Moscow would accept the risks of polarizing the Middle East at the possible expense of détente with the United States. *Pravda* hailed the treaty as a "qualitatively new phase" in Soviet-Egyptian relations, opening up "new horizons" between the two nations,[104] and when the Presidium of the USSR Supreme Soviet met on June 28, the treaty was unanimously endorsed and praised by Foreign Minister Gromyko as "an outstanding event in the life of the peoples of the two countries." Gromyko added that the "international significance" of the treaty would create a "good, long-term basis for the future development of relations between the two states and their peoples."[105]

In the West, the treaty was met with mixed reactions. Certain circles appeared to accept the Soviet line that the treaty dealt a significant blow to the hopes of the United States for a reduction of Soviet influence, and particularly the Soviet military presence in Egypt. Shortly after the new agreement was signed, the *New York Times* editorialized that "except for religion, it is difficult to think of a major area of Egyptian life which Mr. Sadat has not now promised to bring closely under Moscow's guidance."[106] The *Washington Post* similarly argued that the treaty by Russia and Egypt "destroys the widespread notion that Sadat . . . had managed to diminish the Soviet influence [in Egypt]."[107] And Henry Kissinger was so convinced the treaty was a new foundation in the Soviet-Egyptian relationship that he quickly sent a memo to President Nixon asserting that "the treaty would give the Soviet Union a veto over [any] future negotiations."[108]

The British, however, disagreed with those assessments. Sir Richard Beaumont, the British ambassador in Cairo, argued that the treaty should be seen as nothing more than a "salvaging operation," believing that Sadat was to some extent "bounced" into signing it, having had little time to think through the implications of the language proposed by the Russians.[109] The British ambassador in Moscow, A. D. Wilson, had a similar reaction. In a lengthy cable to London on June 7, he argued that while the treaty "at first sight" appeared as a "major diplomatic success" for the Russians and provided Moscow "major opportunities in the long run," it should also have been seen as a "fairly improvised reaction" to the Rogers visit and exposed the Soviets' deteriorating position in Egypt. According to Wilson, the Russians were "genuinely frightened by the danger of Mr. Rogers bringing off a diplomatic *coup* which might end in a marked increase of American and NATO influence in the area" and were afraid that, following the heavy political and economic investment in Egypt since the Six-Day War, Egypt "would now swing decisively towards the West and away from the Soviet sphere of influence."[110]

Secretary of State Rogers agreed with the British assessment. On learning of the Egyptian-Soviet treaty, Rogers informed Nixon that the treaty in no way reversed the assurances Sadat had made to him in early May. In Rogers's view, the treaty was simply a diversion from the Egyptian side and a move from the Russians to solidify the relationship that they knew they were losing. "I think what [the Soviets] are trying to do is make it appear that they have not lost their position with Egypt," Rogers told the president over the telephone on May 28. "They don't want to threaten anything because that would really make Sadat mad as hell. So what they are doing is trying to figure out other ways to make it appear that there has been no change in their relationship."[111]

From the Egyptian perspective, moreover, Rogers almost blatantly dismissed the treaty as a smokescreen. Not only did he believe that Sadat planned to use the treaty to continue the flow of arms in the event that an agreement was not reached, but after carefully studying the treaty's provisions, Rogers knew that the document changed nothing in the existing Egyptian-Soviet relationship. "I think he's trying to play both ends against the middle," he told Nixon. "It didn't say a hell of a lot that they didn't already have in informal treaties. So this is just window dressing, I'm quite convinced of that."[112]

Sadat, too, tried to downplay the significance of the new Egyptian-Soviet treaty. Just two days after he completed the agreement with the Soviet Union, he told American officials in Cairo not to exaggerate its importance[113] and later reiterated that his recent agreement with the Kremlin in no way implied that he did not want an interim agreement or the reopening of the Suez Canal. Nor, Sadat made clear, should Washington deduce from the treaty that it should discontinue its diplomatic role in helping the two sides achieve an agreement. "Tell Secretary Rogers, tell President Nixon, that everything I said when Secretary Rogers was here in May and when I saw Sisco later still stands."[114]

Indeed, so convinced was Rogers that the new treaty was nothing but a smokescreen, that instead of reassuring the Israelis of a continued flow of US military supplies, or making a similar friendship treaty with Israeli, the secretary of state informed the Israeli government that the shipment of aircraft (Phantoms) would be suspended at the end of June unless they agreed to concessions on an interim agreement with Egypt.[115] On May 31, Nixon told Rogers over the telephone that if asked by the press about the change in US policy, he would say only that "we're still trying to persuade the parties involved to continue the cease-fire and also to make progress toward a settlement either on an interim or other basis." But Nixon was clearly behind the new direction Rogers was moving, believing that it was critical "to keep that bargaining position because you have to be in a position . . . to hold it [financial and military assistance] over their heads."[116]

Henry Kissinger, on the other hand, appeared disillusioned about the new path that Nixon and Rogers were going down in the Middle East. He feared that if the United States negotiated an agreement between Israel and Egypt without the assistance of the Soviet Union, it would severely undermine his efforts to negotiate a summit in Moscow the following year and would tell the Kremlin that the White House was not serious about détente. On several occasions, he complained to Nixon that the State Department wanted to take credit for an idea conceived within the White House and that he believed Rogers was usurping his authority. "He hasn't told us a goddamn thing of what he has done in the Middle East, and he is not your equivalent," Kissinger said to the president in the Oval Office on May 19. He also believed that Rogers's recent trip to Egypt and Israel was the "only time that a Secretary of State has ever shot around the world without telling us ahead of time what he was going to do" and "without writing any meaningful report."[117]

The Soviet Union, meanwhile, seemed equally concerned about the direction of American policy in the Middle East. In a meeting with Kissinger at Camp David on June 8, Dobrynin professed to be baffled by what Nixon and Rogers were trying to accomplish in Egypt. "Did you really think you can push the Soviet Union out of the Middle East?" he asked Kissinger. According to Dobrynin, Rogers's trip to Cairo was taken very badly in the Soviet Union; as he told Kissinger, "it didn't make any sense from any other point either."[118]

Whether Dobrynin truly believed that Sadat would not remove the Soviet presence from Egypt or whether he was just trying to make it appear that the Soviets had not lost ground with Sadat is difficult to say. At the same time, though, the Soviet ambassador made it known that regardless of what progress the United States had made with Egypt there would be no interim agreement without Soviet approval. "We can always prevent a settlement if you push us to it," he promised Kissinger. "We got a 15-year treaty out of the Rogers visit and we have taken adequate precautions, you can be sure."[119]

Less than a week after his discussion with Dobrynin, Kissinger brought these concerns to the president. In fact, on the morning of June 12, as President Nixon was getting ready for his daughter's wedding later that afternoon, Kissinger can be heard in the Oval Office questioning Nixon about the State Department's handling of Middle East policy. "I know you don't want to discuss it now, [but] the Middle East camp is really getting screwed up," he said to Nixon. "I think they [the State Department] have done too many things that, in my view, have produced an explosion. And they've cut off now—the airplanes have been cut off to Israel at the end of this month, which is going to produce an explosion amongst the Jewish leaders here. And all of this for no discernible objective."[120]

To be sure, Kissinger believed that guarantees he had made to the Israeli ambassador regarding future arms shipments were severely undercut by the recent steps taken by Nixon and Rogers. He had assured Rabin that the United States would continue supplying the Israelis with weapons, and he felt that the best way of getting a peace agreement in the region was not to go over to the Egyptians but to so increase the strength of the Israelis that the Arabs would have no choice but to make concessions on their own.[121] Moreover, he simply could not understand why Nixon permitted Rogers to be so aggressive in the Middle East when there were more important things—the rapprochement with China, détente with the Soviet Union, and the ending of the Vietnam War—to worry about. "The thing we need for the next two months is quiet," he explained to Nixon. "We don't want to get the Russians lining up with the Egyptians and get everybody steaming up with a big Mid-East crisis. I think we should just slow that process down a little bit for the next two or three months."[122]

Despite Kissinger's warnings, Nixon remained convinced that he had to get the Israelis to accept the provisions of the interim agreement. During a meeting of the National Security Council held at the Western White House in San Clemente on July 16, 1971, Nixon gave clear instructions to Rogers to continue pressing for the interim agreement and instructed Sisco to go back to Israel to "narrow the gap" between the Egyptian and Israeli positions on an interim settlement. The president wanted to be careful that Sisco's trip to Israel would in no way overshadow his recent announcement that he (Nixon) was planning to visit the People's Republic of China in early 1972, and he made it clear to Sisco that he did not want the United States to "get into a position where we would trigger a confrontation for which we do not have an answer." Still, there was no doubt that Nixon wanted Sisco to play it very tough with the Israeli government. "Don't promise a damned thing," he told Sisco. "This is not going to be a free ride this time. From now on it is *quid pro quo*."[123]

Kissinger once more objected that the United States was continuing to withhold military supplies to Israel. He told the president that the military balance in the region was now shifting toward the Arabs, as Israel was no longer in a position to win a war quickly and could now be engaged in another prolonged war of attrition. But Rogers assured Nixon that both the State and Defense Departments had just gone through another extensive review of the military balance in the Middle East and concluded that the balance remained in Israel's favor. Sisco, too, reiterated that with the addition of Soviet weapons into the region over the preceding four years, it was next to impossible to re-create the conditions of 1967 in which the Israelis were able to win an overwhelming victory.[124] As the meeting concluded, Nixon gave the assistant secretary a clear mandate to take with him to Israel. "Joe, I want you to press Golda on this because I think there is an opportunity," Sisco recalled of the instructions President Nixon gave

Assistant Secretary of State Joseph Sisco (right) with Ambassador Rabin at Lod Airport in Tel Aviv, July 28, 1971. *(Moshe Milner, Israel Government Press Office)*

him in San Clemente.[125] "Don't cause a major donnybrook between Israel and the United States," he said. But "press Golda. Press her hard."[126]

The records of Sisco's conversations with Prime Minister Meir indicate that the Israeli government had no intentions of making an agreement with the Egyptians. Although Meir assured Sisco that the Suez Canal initiative was not "dead,"[127] she gave little indication during the assistant secretary's five days in Israel that she would sit down with Sadat, nor did she seem eager to accept the very limited disengagement agreement on the Suez that Sisco had brought with him.[128] "The cabinet showed no inclination to alter its [position] . . . nor was there any give on the other fundamental issues bound up with the partial agreement," Rabin admitted years later of their meeting with Sisco.[129]

What is surprising from Sisco's conversations with Israel's leaders, however, is the extent to which they were unwilling to take advantage of Sadat's pledge to remove the Soviets in exchange for an interim agreement. At one point during his July 30 conversation with the prime minister, Sisco reminded Meir that Sadat "would like to use an interim settlement as a way to alter the Soviet presence" but acknowledged he had no way to "tell [her] whether he means it . . . and whether he can produce it." At the same time, Sisco made it clear to the cabinet what the cost of not reaching an agreement with Cairo would entail. "In the Vietnam climate of our country," he explained, "the situation is such that if we ever get to that point . . . [where] hostilities have broken out, Egyptians have called in help from the Russians and the Russians are helping them, the US may be confronted with an awful decision: does it intervene or not intervene in order to protect the situation? Nobody can predict what that decision would be."[130]

This is not to say that the Israelis would have altered their position had Sadat taken the decision unilaterally to expel the Soviets from his country. Although the Israelis remained extremely concerned about the Soviet presence in Egypt, they felt the continued shipments of Phantom aircraft from the United States would provide the necessary deterrent on Soviets military action, and maintained that the absence of future guarantees of Phantoms would actually exacerbate tensions in the region. "If I were Sadat," Meir tried to reason with Sisco, "I would say to myself, I am now in a position where Israel is not getting planes. What am I waiting for? Until the US will begin to deliver planes? This is the time."[131] Moreover, the prime minister refused to believe that Sadat would cut ties with the Soviet Union, especially after the signing of the Soviet-Egyptian Treaty of Friendship and Cooperation. She referred Sisco to Mahmoud Riad's recent trip to Moscow in which the Egyptian foreign minister affirmed the treaty as well as received further guarantees of Soviet arms. "At any rate," she said, "there is talk about August being a month of many activities . . . of [Soviet defense minister Marshal Andrei] Grechko coming to Egypt, of Egyptians going to Moscow. What is Grechko going to talk about? A cultural agreement? Pushkin translated to Arabic?"[132]

Still, there can be no doubt that Prime Minister Meir's refusal to work with Egypt during the summer of 1971 effectively quashed the idea of the interim agreement. That Sadat decided to expel the Soviets less than a year later without any formal settlement from Israel or any indication that the Israeli government would return Egypt's land only lends credence to Sadat's assertions that the Soviets had become an increasing burden to his country and that he wanted to become much closer to the West. Those who insist, therefore, that the expulsion of the Soviets was simply a result of the improving relations between the United States and the Soviet Union or somehow believe that this was his first step on the road to another confrontation with Israel have failed to see the broader implications of Sadat's strategy from the earliest days of his presidency: removing the Soviet military presence was not only the most direct way he could avoid another Arab-Israeli war but the surest way to align Egypt with the United States and change the balance of power in the Middle East for years to come.

SIX

The Race to the Summit, September 1971–May 1972

R ichard Nixon had a flair for the dramatic. Although he made most of his decisions in solitude on the basis of memoranda or with a few intimate aides, he liked to unveil his biggest decisions in major, prime-time television speeches that moved audiences without being subjected to questions and demonstrated decisiveness and courage of action. It was an art that he first learned in 1952 when, as the embattled Republican vice presidential candidate, he delivered a half-hour-long television address to defend himself against accusations of misusing a political fund. Nearly sixty million Americans witnessed Nixon's speech and his now infamous pledge to keep his black-and-white cocker spaniel, named Checkers by the Nixon children, that had been given to him by a Texas supporter. The speech led to an outpouring of public support for him and the decision by General Dwight D. Eisenhower to retain Nixon on the ticket.[1]

Nixon never forgot the lessons of the Checkers speech. As president, he frequently took his case directly to the American people through dramatic television and radio appearances and highly publicized press conferences. In a November 3, 1969, prime-time television address, for example, Nixon theatrically called on the "silent majority" of Americans to join him in his plans for diplomatic negotiations and Vietnamization to end the Vietnam War. Six months later, he stunned the nation with the news that he had ordered American combat forces into Cambodia for the first time, triggering a wave of antiwar demonstrations and student protest across the country.

President Nixon announces to the White House Press Corps that he has accepted an invitation from the Soviet leadership to visit Moscow, October 12, 1971. *(National Presidential Library)*

And in the summer of 1971, Nixon "shocked" the world with two revelations that had profound international implications: On July 15, he disclosed that after months of secret negotiations he would travel to the People's Republic of China for unprecedented meetings with Chairman Mao Zedong and Premier Zhou Enlai, breaking more than twenty years of diplomatic isolation with the mainland. And on August 15, the president "rocked" the internal economy and political structure by gutting the Bretton Woods dollar-for-gold system that had existed for decades without consulting members of the international monetary system.[2]

Nearly three months after the "Nixon Shocks," the president pulled another rabbit out of his hat. Stepping in front of the White House press corps without notice on October 12, he announced that he had accepted an invitation from the Soviet leadership to visit Moscow in May 1972, "with a view towards further improving [our] bilateral relations and enhancing the prospects for world peace." The president would not reveal what items would be on the agenda during the summit, but he left little doubt that he expected to return from Moscow with significant agreements on strategic arms limitation, trade, a European security conference, and cooperation on Vietnam. "I do not believe in having summit meetings simply for the purpose of having a meeting," he declared. "I think that tends to create euphoria. It raises high hopes that are then dashed, as was the case with Glassboro. We are not making that mistake."[3]

Nixon's invitation to Moscow had been almost three years in the making. He had first broached the idea at a press conference in February 1969, at which time he said he would not have such a meeting unless something concrete came out of it; otherwise it would be merely "cosmetic" and there would be a great letdown.[4] In April 1970, the Soviets explored the possibility of a summit at lower levels, but the president did not think then that a meeting at the highest level could serve a "useful purpose," and major disagreements between the superpowers on the Middle East, Cuba, and Vietnam ensured that a summit meeting remained a distant prospect.[5] Indeed, the chances of a summit were so dim at the end of 1970 that Soviet Foreign Minister Andrei Gromyko and Yuri Andropov, head of the KGB, concluded in a report to the Politburo that "the confrontation between the United States and the Soviet Union will apparently last for a historically long period."[6]

But in early 1971 things began to change. Prompted by a major reexamination of US-Soviet relations inside the Kremlin, in which the Politburo made a "major decision" to become more actively involved with Nixon, the Soviet leadership informed the White House on January 23 that they were prepared to host a summit during the second half of the summer.[7] It was certainly wishful thinking to believe that a meeting of this level could come together so quickly, but Soviet eagerness, and American receptiveness, triggered a wave of US-Soviet agreements on arms control, biological warfare, sea beds, the hot line, and accidental war. By the end of the summer, it was clear to leaders in both capitals that there had been enough improvements in their bilateral relationship to warrant a meeting at the highest levels.

On its surface, Nixon's announcement that he would be the first president to visit the Soviet Union in more than twenty-five years appeared to have little impact on events in the Middle East. The president's goals in Moscow were to secure Soviet cooperation on Vietnam, finalize the agreement on Berlin, conclude new agreements on trade, scientific, and cultural exchanges, and, most important, return to Washington with a treaty on strategic arms that would limit the size of their nuclear arsenals and mitigate the chances of an unnecessary and costly arms race. "The overwhelming fact was that if there ever was a superpower conflict there would be no victors, only losers," the president said to congressional leaders minutes after his press conference. "The Soviets know this as well as we do. . . . Therefore, we should explore areas where we can limit or even perhaps reduce arms."[8]

But for Egyptian president Anwar Sadat the news came as a devastating blow. He feared that if he did not secure an agreement with Israel before Nixon arrived in Moscow, the United States and the Soviet Union would "sell him out" at the summit by placing their differences in the Middle East on ice and leaving Israel in firm possession of the occupied Arab territories.[9] Short of another humiliating military defeat, nothing could set back his efforts to reclaim the Sinai Peninsula more than a Soviet-American accord that accepted the status quo in the region. Still recovering from the 1967 debacle, Egypt lacked the offensive capabilities to launch a successful military attack on Israel in 1972, and the only hope it had to recover its lost territory was for leaders in Washington and Moscow to compel Israel to withdraw.

Sadat was not the only one with concerns, however. Inside the Kremlin, there were growing fears that the Egyptian president would launch an attack on Israel before the summit with the intention of drawing the superpowers into a regional conflict. Egypt would surely lose the war, the Soviets reasoned, but it would force President Nixon to call off the summit and set back Soviet-American relations for years. For General Secretary Leonid Brezhnev, who viewed his meetings with Nixon as a long-sought personal and political goal, the outbreak of a Middle East war was anathema. He resisted Sadat's calls for more offensive weapons, refused to endorse the Egyptian's military objectives, and was prepared to do whatever it took to avoid the outbreak of another Arab-Israeli war before the summit, including withdrawing all the Soviet military advisers in Egypt to limit's Sadat's military capabilities.

Thus, in the months leading up to the summit both the Soviet Union and Egypt were rushing to get a Middle East peace agreement, but for completely different reasons. Brezhnev wanted an Arab-Israeli settlement so that he could pursue détente with the United States. Sadat, for his part, sought an agreement to prevent détente from leaving him in a perpetual stalemate with Israel. Neither trusted the other, and both appeared willing to force an agreement on the other despite their history of friendship and cooperation. The race to the summit had begun.

Gromyko's Gambit

The Soviets were the first out of the box. Just before 3:00 p.m. on Wednesday, September 29, 1971, two weeks before the superpowers announced their intentions to hold the summit, Soviet foreign minister Andrei Gromyko arrived at the White House for his annual meeting with President Nixon. Gromyko wanted that this year's meeting to be far more productive than his last. At that time, Moscow's relations with Washington had become "beclouded" and "uncertain," as Henry Kissinger put it in his memoirs. The United States was angry over what it believed were Soviet-inspired violations of the Egyptian-Israeli cease-fire agreement; there had been a flare-up over Moscow's attempt to create a nuclear submarine base in Cuba, which had the potential of leading to a direct superpower confrontation; and bilateral relations had been aggravated by "small irritating matters."[10]

This year's meeting was quite different, however. For more than ninety minutes, Gromyko emphasized to Nixon, Rogers, and Kissinger that his government desired ways to overcome difficulties in their relationship and wanted to move forward with the United States on the principle of "peaceful coexistence." He said that a "collision" with Washington was "alien" to Moscow's short-term and long-term interests and "incompatible" with the basic principles on which the Soviet system was founded. And he stressed the "great importance" the Soviet Union attached to the negotiations on the limitation of both offensive and defensive armaments, to cooperation on defusing the looming crisis between India and Pakistan, and to the reduction of tensions between the East and West throughout Europe. "Our relations should be conducted in such a way that the absence of agreement on certain issues not create obstacles for agreement on those issues which could be resolved between us," said Gromyko.[11]

Had the meeting ended there, it would have been a success. Both countries remained committed to the summit, and the possibility lingered that the two superpowers could reach an agreement on strategic arms limitations before Nixon went to Moscow. At the end of the meeting, however, Gromyko indicated that he had a "personal message" from Chairman Brezhnev that he would like to convey to the president in private—without Rogers, Kissinger, and Dobrynin, or any note takers and translators. As soon as the Oval Office emptied, Gromyko unveiled to Nixon a secret Middle East peace plan that had long been in the works inside the Kremlin and that he hoped would form the basis of US-Soviet dialogue leading up to the summit.

The plan called for moving the Middle East discussions out of the State Department's control, where they had been since the beginning of the Nixon administration, and into the special channel between Kissinger and Dobrynin. Once that happened, he said, the Kremlin would offer the following deal: (1) in exchange for the "complete withdrawal" of Israeli troops from all occupied Arab territories, the Soviet Union would agree to withdraw *all* of its "organized military units" from the Middle East; (2) the Kremlin would ban future arm shipments to the Arab states once the conflict had been "fully resolved"; and (3) Moscow would participate in political and security guarantees of any future settlement between Arabs and Israelis. All of these measures would go into effect as part of an interim settlement provided that the interim settlement contained provisions for how to get to a final settlement. Gromyko stipulated that some military "advisers" would have to remain in "relevant countries" for "purely advisory functions," much like the military advisers the United States had in Iran, but insofar as the bulk of the Soviet military forces in the Arab states was concerned, "we will remove them all."

To stress the importance the Kremlin attached to this initiative, the foreign minister added that this proposal came directly from Brezhnev. "He is a man of . . . strong will, and when he says that something must be done, he [moves] in the direction like a [straight] line," Gromyko insisted. But Brezhnev wanted to complete the deal in time for the summit and before another Middle East war could draw in the superpowers and threaten détente. "Is it possible . . . that the Soviet Union and the United States must tolerate a situation where the risk of a clash between them in the Middle East region would arise because of third countries?" Gromyko asked Nixon. "It would seem that the two powers have an opportunity to prevent all this if

Soviet foreign minister Andrei Gromyko (left) and President Nixon confer in the Oval Office, October 22, 1970. *(Nixon Presidential Library)*

they wish to do so. Isn't it time to put an end to the current situation and agree to a radical solution on the basis I have tried to present to the President on behalf of the Soviet Union?"[12]

Nixon replied to Gromyko's generous offer with platitudes, insisting in "a thoughtful, non-polemical tone" that he, too, believed that Arab–Israeli differences should "not have the effect of keeping Soviet-U.S. relations in a constant state of tension."[13] But there can be little doubt that he was impressed by the Soviet proposal. "Nixon returned, beaming, from the private meeting," Kissinger recalled.[14] The following day, the president added that the offer was a "hell of a concession" and wanted a message sent to the Israelis explaining that this was a "hell of a deal."[15] Kissinger, too, found Gromyko's offer to be "a tantalizing modification of the standard Soviet position" and believed that the Kremlin's offer to withdraw the Soviet military presence from the Middle East was a "major concession," and no doubt the "biggest step forward" in Arab-Israeli diplomacy since the beginning of the Nixon administration.[16]

Indeed, Kissinger was so astounded at the proposal that he met with Gromyko the following evening at the Soviet embassy in Washington to ensure that the president had understood his offer correctly. Gromyko indicated that he had, and even suggested a number of options for reaching an interim settlement, including a "fixed obligation" that Israeli ships would have the right to traverse the Suez Canal as soon as a settlement was reached. "Quite frankly, we will have to sell the settlement to our allies," he explained. "The withdrawal of our air forces and other organized units will not be happily greeted by our allies, and therefore we have to show them that we are doing it for a greater cause."[17]

Gromyko may have been correct in stating that the Soviet proposal would be difficult to sell to its allies, but there can be no doubt that his conversations with Nixon and Kissinger left him confident that a deal could be worked out. After Kissinger left the embassy, the Foreign Minister sent a cable back to Moscow indicating that Nixon seemed eager to conduct a "strictly confidential" and "exploratory exchange" of views on this issue with the Soviet leadership through the Kissinger-Dobrynin channel with a view to identifying possibilities for agreement to be "nailed down during the personal meeting between Nixon and the Soviet leaders in Moscow in May 1972."[18]

Despite the willingness on both sides to pursue an agreement based on Gromyko's private conversation with Nixon, the larger question remained as to why the Soviet Union would make such a concession when the Kremlin had recently signed a treaty of friendship with Sadat[19] and had spent the previous two years augmenting its military presence inside Egypt. Did Moscow truly believe the United States could pressure Israel into withdrawing from all occupied territories, as Gromyko's proposal stipulated? Was Gromyko's offer a signal that the Soviet Union had overextended itself in Egypt, leaving itself vulnerable to a possible attack from the People's Republic of China? Was Moscow aware that Sadat was planning on expelling the Soviet military presence in the near future? Or was this a sign that Soviet leaders knew Sadat was prepared to launch a war with Israel and did not want to end up in the middle of the conflict and invite a confrontation with the United States?

The obvious explanation is that Moscow's proposal to withdraw its forces from the region was a direct result of the deteriorating patron-client relationship between the Soviet Union and Egypt. Sadat's decision to remove vice president and Soviet supporter Ali Sabry from his government in May, his willingness to negotiate directly with Secretary of State Rogers over the interim peace agreement with Israel, and his continued refusal to keep the Kremlin informed of his intentions was reason enough for many Soviet officials to forgo their heavy military commitment to Egypt. Others inside the Kremlin believed that it was only a matter of time before Sadat made the decision to remove the Soviet military presence from his country and that it was better for the Soviet Union to withdraw their forces unilaterally rather than being left in the embarrassing position of having their forces expelled from Egypt. That view is not entirely without foundation and certainly contributed to the Soviet plan.

What really lay behind the Kremlin's peace proposal, however, was its shift in strategy of placing détente with the United States above its treaty commitments with its Arab client states. Once the Soviets had secured agreements with Washington on Berlin and on strategic arms limitation and had invited Nixon to Moscow for a summit with the Soviet leadership, it became imperative to prevent the outbreak of Arab-Israeli hostilities, which could place the superpowers on opposing sides. Brezhnev was particularly worried that the absence of an Arab-Israeli peace agreement and Israel's continued occupation of Egyptian territory would compel Sadat to act on his "Year of Decision" by initiating hostilities on the eve of the summit for dramatic effect.

On August 5, the same day Nixon received his invitation from Brezhnev to visit Moscow, the Politburo agreed to send Yevgeny Primakov, a former Middle East correspondent for *Pravda* with ties to the KGB, to Israel for confidential discussions with Israeli officials regarding a possible Middle East peace settlement.[20] Primakov's talks took place over several days at the end of August and were attended by Prime Minister Meir, Defense Minister Moshe Dayan, Foreign Minister Abba Eban, and Simcha Dinitz, Meir's political secretary. "What I got from our exchanges was a sense that the Israel government might, at the very most, be interested in a partial withdrawal of troops from Sinai," Primakov later wrote. Indeed, the Israelis made it clear that while they wanted to improve their relationship with the Soviet Union, they had no intention of altering the status quo and would prefer the situation in the Middle East to remain unchanged long term.[21]

In Moscow, Primakov's detailed report on the trip got an "encouraging response" and convinced the Soviet leaders that if they wanted to reach a Middle East settlement before the summit, they were going to have to offer something substantive to convince both parties. The withdrawal of Soviet forces would be welcomed in Cairo, Jerusalem, and Washington and could form the basis of an agreement.[22] True, Gromyko's offer failed to call for Egyptian recognition of the Jewish state, an Israeli precondition for almost any agreement, and conditioned the withdrawal of Soviet forces from the Middle East at the *end* of the entire process, leaving Israel to execute its withdrawal before the Soviet had to do anything any in return. At the same time, however, the Soviet proposal went much further than its 1969 proposals during the Two Power talks and demonstrated that Moscow was serious about getting something done before the summit.

Kissinger Becomes Involved

Gromyko's plan may have been far from perfect, but it contained enough substance to get Henry Kissinger directly involved in the negotiating process. Since 1969, Nixon had largely sidelined his national security adviser the day-to-day negotiations on the Middle East. In part, this reflected the fact that an Arab-Israeli peace agreement was not high on the list of Nixon's foreign policy objectives when he entered office. But the president also knew that with Kissinger deeply involved in talks with Dobrynin regarding arms control, trade, the upcoming summit, and the future status of Berlin, not to mention his ongoing secret negotiations with the Chinese and the efforts to bring the Vietnam War to an end, it was not practical for Kissinger to invest himself in the timely and often tedious Middle East discussions. In September 1970, Kissinger successfully orchestrated the White House response to the civil war in Jordan, but he returned to his limited role in the Arab-Israeli discussions after the crisis subsided.

The State Department's predominance in the Middle East had been a constant source of irritation for Kissinger during his tenure in the Nixon

White House and the cause of much of the friction in his relationship with William Rogers. The two butted heads in August 1970 over sharp disagreements regarding the Egyptian-Israeli cease-fire agreement in which Rogers ultimately prevailed.[23] Tensions between the secretary of state and the national security adviser again escalated in January 1971 after the *New York Times* published a series of articles on the decline of the State Department's influence in foreign policy that Rogers believed Kissinger had deviously inspired.[24] And in March 1971, after Rogers had circumvented the NSC system by holding a senior-level meeting on the Middle East at the State Department rather than through the normal NSC channels, Kissinger threatened to return to Harvard rather than constantly battle the State Department. "If a presidential assistant, for whatever reason, becomes himself such a controversial figure, and if the bureaucracy continually challenges him even if he's totally right, I think one should seriously consider leaving," he told Nixon. "I might as well draw the line now."[25]

Gromyko's proposal to bring the Middle East negotiations entirely within Kissinger's private channel with Dobrynin, therefore, afforded the national security adviser the opportunity to supplant the State Department role in the Middle East, much like he had already done with negotiations pertaining to the Soviet Union, China, and Vietnam. He welcomed the opportunity. As he explained to Dobrynin, further State Department negotiations with Arabs and Israelis were "useless," especially since Rogers had no "serious new proposal" to his name and clung to the "secret hope of somehow maneuvering and forcing the two sides to make mutual concessions" that could lead to a compromise on an interim Suez agreement. "Kissinger is trying to leave the impression that he personally would not mind at all if Rogers's and Sisco's new attempts—which are interfering somewhat with the nascent US-Soviet dialogue—came to a dead end sooner rather than later, thus leaving the way completely clear for his own, more 'global' approach," Dobrynin recorded in his diary days after Gromyko unveiled the Soviet peace proposal.[26]

The problem for Kissinger, however, was that by the time he took control of the Middle East negotiations, the White House saw little incentive for altering the status quo in the region. During his meeting with Gromyko on September 30, he made it clear that "certain domestic political complications"—namely, an intensive presidential election campaign in 1972—made it difficult for

Nixon to agree to any measures that would "seriously displease" Jewish groups and hurt the president's chances for reelection. Exacerbating the difficulties of reaching a Middle East settlement by the summit was White House preoccupation with its February visit to China and trying to bring the Vietnam War to an end before the November elections. In view of these considerations, Kissinger argued that a comprehensive Middle East settlement along the lines of Gromyko's proposal could not be implemented until at least 1973, after Nixon no longer had to worry about the pressures of domestic politics.[27]

Thus, preoccupied with more pressing concerns, Kissinger waited more than a month before bringing Gromyko's Middle East proposal to the Israelis. On November 5, after returning from a brief trip to Beijing, he met with Yitzhak Rabin under what the Israeli ambassador later described as "cloak-and-dagger" conditions to present the details of Gromyko's plan. He asked Rabin to come alone to the White House, said that he, too, would be alone and had him admitted through a side entrance in the West Wing to avoid any press attention or questions from Foggy Bottom over why Kissinger was meeting with the Israeli ambassador without informing the State Department. "What I am about to say is on behalf of the President and you must promise that you will report it to no one other than Prime Minister Meir," he began in a "conspiratorial" manner, "and even to her privately and personally."

He then revealed to Rabin the offer Gromyko had made to Nixon back in September, explaining that it was a "secret proposal from Leonid Brezhnev" that the Soviets wanted to finalize during Nixon's summit in Moscow. The settlement would take place in two stages: first a limited agreement for reopening the canal; then, after the 1972 American presidential elections, a comprehensive settlement that included Israel's withdrawal to roughly the June 4, 1967, lines. Kissinger doubted that the Israelis would accept any agreement that called for a return to the borders before the Six-Day War, but he emphasized that once the parties reached an "overall" agreement, the Soviet Union would eliminate its "operational military presence" in Egypt, leaving "no more than a small number of advisers," and join the United States both in an embargo on weapons shipments to the region and in measures to safeguard the agreement in whatever form the United States found necessary.[28]

Kissinger paused to gauge Rabin's initial reaction. He could tell from the ambassador's silence that Rabin had his doubts about the plan from the beginning. The Israelis clearly saw this as another ploy for the Soviets to renew "intensive talks" between the two powers, which had ceased since the rejection of the Rogers Plan in 1969, and to "impose" a solution on Israel. During the past few months, the State Department had clearly expressed its impatience with Israel, and now, Rabin concluded, "Kissinger was signaling me that our time had run out." The ambassador also had his doubts that the plan came directly from Brezhnev. "I could not shake free of the vision of Kissinger and Dobrynin closeted away cooking up deals, with Kissinger subsequently announcing the results to us a *fait accompli*—much as Sisco had during his earlier talks with the Soviet ambassador," he admitted in his memoirs. As if reading Rabin's mind, Kissinger tried to reassure the ambassador that this was not the case.

"I do not intend to negotiate with the Soviet Union, not even at the top level without close coordination with Israel," he said. "I don't think that the United States should negotiate on a matter of fateful importance to Israel without taking her into our confidence at all stages of the negotiations. That is why I want an answer from Prime Minister Meir: Does Israel agree to the United States entering into such negotiations—on the assumption that the future borders will not basically be different from the June 4, 1967 lines and that the boundary between Egypt and Israel must be the international border?" Hearing Kissinger even mention the pre–Six-Day War borders left Rabin with a "black" expression on his face, which prompted Kissinger to interject: "I understand your difficulties, and if Israel replies to the Soviet proposal in the negative, I wouldn't blame her. I would seek ways of preventing American-Soviet negotiations on Brezhnev's proposal."[29]

Rabin undoubtedly did not like the proposal. The Soviets were asking Israel to agree to complete withdrawal of Israeli forces before a final peace agreement with the Arabs. They had made the mistake in 1957 and were not about to repeat it again, even if this offer included removing the Soviet forces from the region. Following the meeting, Rabin returned to Israel, where he submitted a detailed report of his conversation with Kissinger to the prime minister. After short deliberations both agreed that it was "vital" to reject the initiative. The problem was that the Israelis simply did not believe the Kremlin wanted a peace agreement, despite what Gromyko may have conveyed to Nixon and Kissinger. A recent Israeli intelligence report confirmed that only two weeks earlier Moscow agreed to provide Sadat with a major new arms deal, thereby increasing the likelihood that Egypt "will opt for a resumption of hostilities with Soviet understanding bordering on explicit approval."[30] How could the Soviets claim to want peace while at the same time providing Egypt with the weapons needed to attack Israel?

Rabin informed Kissinger of the Israeli position when he returned to Washington on November 16, but Meir wanted to deliver the message personally to Nixon to ensure that there was no misunderstanding between their two governments as so often happened while Rogers was conducting the negotiations over the interim agreement. She arrived in United States on November 30 and spent several days with American officials trying to convince them not to be lulled into the new Soviet peace initiative while Sadat prepared for war. "Our assessment based on intelligence is that he is getting arms and that there was never a stoppage of the flow of Russian arms," she told Rogers on December 2. She reminded the Americans that Sadat had just returned from visiting his troops in the Sinai, where he promised that "we will meet [the Israelis] in the Sinai" to thunderous applause. "With every speech he becomes more vicious and a slave of his own words and he may strike," said Meir. "We don't believe that he thinks that he can win, but we must be prepared because he can start at any time."[31]

Although Nixon sympathized with the prime minister, he also believed Meir failed to see the larger geopolitical picture. After accepting Brezhnev's invitation to visit the Soviet Union, there was no way he could go to the Moscow summit and not discuss the Middle East. How could he ask for Soviet cooperation on Vietnam and not expect the Soviets in return to ask for American cooperation on the Middle East? During a meeting with the prime minister at the White House on December 2, he pressed Meir to "show some flexibility" and to give further consideration to Gromyko's proposal, even if it did not fulfill all their security requirements. "Let's face it," Nixon began, "[I am] the last to trust the Russians, and they're the last to trust me." But Gromyko "didn't say this in front of the others" and "this [proposal] has not gone to the bureaucracy. . . . That's what made it so meaningful."[32]

But Meir simply would not budge. "I'll tell you how I understand the situation," she responded. "There will be no American-Soviet deal contrary to Israel's wishes, and the United States will not exert pressure on Israel to concede to positions reached in any such discussions. . . . Israel will convey to the United States her views regarding both a partial agreement and an overall settlement; and delivery of arms—including planes—will continue unimpeded."[33]

According to Kissinger, moreover, Meir also convinced the president to agree to abandon the Soviet demand for a "comprehensive" settlement, focusing instead on an effort to reach an interim agreement with Egypt, and a commitment that the "real negotiations" would be carried out between Rabin and Kissinger, not with the State Department. "In other words," Kissinger later wrote, "we had finally established in the Middle East the same dual-track approach that characterized our other negotiations. Only the Egyptians were as yet missing."[34]

Kissinger's Secret Trip to Moscow

After three months without a formal response to Gromyko's proposal, Brezhnev's patience began to wear thin. The Soviet leader wrote Nixon in late January to stress the importance of moving ahead quickly on finding a solution to the conflict. He believed that Middle East "tension" was "not diminishing" and argued that "many elements in Israel's behavior cause apprehension." He also reminded the president of the detailed proposal for a settlement Gromyko had presented him back in September and pushed once again for talks to begin between Kissinger and Dobrynin immediately on that basis. "We are prepared, as before, to work in real earnest to find concrete solutions on the basis of the principles set forth in that conversation, and to bring what has been started to successful conclusion," he wrote unambiguously. "And here it is important to act without delay."[35]

Dobrynin, too, tried to press the Middle East settlement from Washington but to no avail. "For now the White House is not exhibiting great interest in active and concrete discussion of this issue," he wrote in a report to the Kremlin on February 20, after three unsuccessful meetings with Kissinger. In Dobrynin's opinion, the White House was entirely preoccupied with preparing for Nixon's trip to China, and took "special caution" to avoid giving Golda Meir grounds to appeal to Jewish circles in the United States, especially during the election campaign. After the president returned from Beijing, however, the Soviet ambassador encouraged Brezhnev to "draw Nixon himself into a preliminary discussion with us of the basic terms of a settlement instead of leaving this entire issue to Kissinger's sole discretion."[36]

To this end, he suggested sending the president a separate message "devoted entirely and specifically to the problem of a settlement in the Middle East" that would set forth the main issues which would form the basis of settlement at the summit. "Otherwise," Dobrynin concluded, "at the Moscow meeting the U.S. side could basically confine discussions on a Middle East settlement to a rather general colloquy."[37] Brezhnev, though, decided to wait until Kissinger arrived in Moscow in April for preparatory summit talks to press the issue. By that time, he knew, the China visit would have been well behind the White House, and he felt that the United States would be far more desperate for cooperation on Vietnam, that Kissinger would have no choice but to compromise on the Middle East.

Brezhnev arranged for Kissinger's visit to take place in mid-April, a month before Nixon's scheduled arrival. Most of the summit arrangements could have been handled by Dobrynin, but given that Chinese officials received a secret visit from Kissinger in advance of Nixon's trip, Brezhnev expected equal treatment. In accordance with Kissinger's request for total secrecy, the meetings took place at the Guest House in the Lenin Hills, on the outskirts of Moscow, and attended only by Soviet staff. Neither the American embassy nor the ambassador, Jacob Beam, knew about Kissinger's stay until the final day, when Kissinger chose to speak to Beam about the purpose of his visit.[38] For Kissinger, it was a major accomplishment and a testament to his rising public stature that within the span of two months he had come face to face with the powerful heads of both communist giants.

In his discussions with Dobrynin leading up to the "secret trip" it was clear that Washington and Moscow remained at odds as to what items should be placed on the Summit agenda. The Soviets were primarily interested in discussing SALT, the Middle East, and European Security. The United States, on the other hand, wanted to finish SALT but remained almost entirely preoccupied with securing Soviet cooperation on Vietnam.

Everything else was secondary. In fact, the only reference to the Middle East in the hefty briefing books Kissinger's staff prepared for his trip came in the final sentence of the last paper that read: "*Nothing included on the Middle East.*"[39] Nixon, too, instructed Kissinger that the "primary" and "indispensable" purpose of his visit was to "force a massive shift in Soviet Vietnam policy" by the threat of bringing summit preparations to an end. "Be tough as nails and insist on talking about Vietnam *first* and not let [Brezhnev] get away with discussions of philosophy, personalities or other summit agenda items until you have reached some sort of understanding on Vietnam."[40]

Kissinger did his best to adhere to Nixon's instructions. His first two days of talks with Brezhnev, Gromyko, and Dobrynin were spent largely on Vietnam, with some preliminary discussions on SALT, US-Soviet bilateral relations, and European security. But Kissinger could only hold off the Soviet leader for so long. Near the end of his second day of talks on April 22, Brezhnev handed Kissinger a paper outlining the Soviet principles of a Middle East settlement and said that he expected to discuss the issue in detail on April 24, Kissinger's final day in Moscow.[41] The paper reflected the standard Soviet position, stating that a final settlement in the Middle East should contain an obligation by Israel for a complete withdrawal of its troops from all Arab territories occupied in 1967, as well as the establishment of demilitarized zones, possibly manned by troops and military observers from the United Nations, on both sides of the Israeli border. Surprisingly absent from the proposal was any mention of the Soviet offer to withdraw its forces from Egypt, as Gromyko had promised Nixon. But the foreign minister reaffirmed to Kissinger that the offer was still on the table. "We are proceeding from the assumption that this is a continuation of that scheme we discussed when I visited Washington and talked with the President," he maintained. "It goes without saying that what we said then remains in force."[42]

Despite the Kremlin's fierce insistence to place the Middle East on the agenda for the Nixon-Brezhnev talks, Kissinger remained determined to put this issue off until the fall. He had enough discussions with Rabin and Meir to know that the Israelis would never agree to borders along the 1967 lines, did not accept the idea of establishing demilitarized zones, and insisted on having a military presence at Sharm el-Sheikh. None of those provisions were included in the Soviet proposal, and trying to work them out at the summit, when there were far more important issues to deal with, seemed to Kissinger to be a fool's errand. "We cannot . . . go to war with Israel in an attempt to reach a settlement," Kissinger told Gromyko on April 23, hoping to reason with the foreign minister before his meeting with Brezhnev. "It may turn out to be an insoluble problem. Within that framework, we are prepared to have discussions."[43]

Having lowered the bar for his meeting with Brezhnev, Kissinger arrived at the ornate Guest House on Vorobyevskii Road on the morning of April 24 accompanied only by his aide Peter Rodman to take notes. There, he was met by Brezhnev, Gromyko, Dobrynin, A. Alexandrov, Brezhnev's assistant, and Viktor Sukhodrev, the skilled Soviet interpreter. Brezhnev opened the meeting with a "long emotional statement" about Vietnam, stressing that Moscow was not behind the recent North Vietnamese offensive, before moving the discussion to the Middle East. "As we understand it," he began, "the agreement reached between the President and Gromyko in Washington last fall remains fully valid, and now the question is how to formalize that understanding without making public the main substance."

"As an objective reality, it will be impossible to complete any agreement before mid-1973," Kissinger insisted, immediately trying to lower the general secretary's expectations. "We cannot do it before the elections, and cannot do it immediately after the elections. November and December will be taken up with constituting a new government. And the agreement can be done only by the new government." The president had to be able to come back from the summit and say truthfully that no "secret agreements" were made in Moscow, and the only way to make that happen was to relegate the Middle East talks at the summit to "preliminary" discussions. "Then, when I come back in September, we can talk about completing an agreement. We will keep our word."

Kissinger also let Brezhnev know that he was under the false impression that Nixon had agreed to Gromyko's formula back in September. "Minister Gromyko made a proposition, we agreed to consider the proposition, but we did not say we accepted it," he maintained. This was not to suggest that discussion of Gromyko's proposal could not continue in the "confidential channel" with Dobrynin. But insofar as concluding at the summit a "comprehensive" or "global" agreement on the scale the Soviets envisioned, that was out of the question. "For two years there were theoretical discussions which were divorced from reality," said Kissinger. "We do not want to promise more than we can deliver, but what we promise, we will do. . . . If we approach the Middle East problem with the same flexibility and subtlety as we approached the West Berlin problem, we will be able to achieve a great deal at the Summit. But something will also be left for September."

Brezhnev agonizingly waited for Sukhodrev to finish his translation before pouncing on Kissinger's remarks. "I'll tell you honestly. I certainly cannot say that satisfies me," he said. "As Gromyko told me clearly . . . concrete things were discussed in Washington in September. Implementation could not begin until after the elections, but a principled agreement could be achieved at the Summit. That is what I understood." In "very tough" terms, the general secretary described the US position on the Middle East of failing to pressure the Israelis and refusing to work out principles of a settlement before the summit as "totally incomprehensible," emphasizing that a summit agreement remained the only leverage he had to prevent the Arabs from resorting to military action. "As things stand now, I do not know how to talk to Sadat, in particular. If I'm deprived of this weapon, that is the agreement with you, I don't know how we can approach the Arab leaders without causing an explosion."

What Kissinger failed to understand, Brezhnev averred, was that the Arabs' military inferiority would not prevent them from taking action against the Israelis to break the stalemate. Sadat had almost a hundred thousand forces mobilized for action near the Sinai, which the Soviet Union would have no other choice but to support if the superpowers failed to deliver an agreement at the summit. "An Army as big as that cannot stay tranquil all the time, especially in these conditions," he darkly warned Kissinger. Before departing for a Politburo meeting, Brezhnev returned to the fundamental question: "If the issue hasn't been agreed on at all, then what are we supposed to tell Sadat and the other Arab leaders?"[44]

Kissinger did not supply an answer. He merely replied with comments "long on good will, sparse on specifics." But for Kissinger, there remained little advantage for the United States to delve any further into this matter when he knew that the Israelis were never going to agree to anything more than a limited withdrawal of its forces, and Nixon did not want to spend any time on the matter when he knew there was no chance of reaching an Arab-Israeli agreement at the summit. "A Middle East condominium was a card that we had no interest in playing at all," Kissinger confessed. "My objectives here were modest: to gain time and use the prospect of future US-Soviet consultations for whatever effect it might have as an incentive for Soviet restraint."[45]

In the weeks leading up to the summit, Brezhnev again appealed to the United States for cooperation on the Middle East, asking Nixon in a letter on May 1 to use the days leading up to the summit to find a "mutually acceptable approach" toward *completion* of an Arab-Israeli settlement. "Preservation of those uncertain moments and dangers is hardly in the interests of our countries," he said.[46] Yet Brezhnev was not alone in this belief. The same day Nixon received Brezhnev's letter, Secretary of State Rogers, who had all but disappeared from the negotiations, cautioned Nixon about the dangers of avoiding discussion of the Middle East at the summit.

"We must face the fact that a standoff on the Middle East in Moscow will leave a very unpredictable situation in the post-Summit period when all concerned will be reassessing their positions in the light of what does or does not happen there," he said. The Soviets, he argued, cannot guarantee Sadat would remain patient in the absence of negotiating progress. While this was sure to be part of a Soviet "pressure tactic," it could very well prove true. Egypt remained the most "unpredictable factor" in the Middle East equation and would become increasingly so as time went by. Sadat, he maintained, was frustrated at the lack of stronger Soviet military and political support, at the US failure to produce any softening of Israel's positions while strengthening Israel militarily, at his own military weakness, and at his inability to mobilize the Arab world against Israel and the United States. "He could strike out, directly or indirectly (for example, through Libya) at American interests; he could initiate at least limited military action; or he could be overthrown, with consequences in Egypt and the Arab world that are difficult to foresee."[47]

Sadat's Malaise

As the summit approached, Sadat grew desperate. He knew that if he did not get a Middle East settlement prior to Nixon's arrival in Moscow, the chances of recovering the Sinai Peninsula before 1973 would be lost. He had contemplated taking limited military action against Israeli forces in early December to appease his restless armed forces thirsting for any movement to break the stalemate but opted against it after the Soviets deliberately let him down by not sending the weapons he had requested in October. On December 12, he complained bitterly to Vladimir Vinogradov, the Soviet ambassador in Cairo, for the Kremlin's refusal to send the weapons and demanded a meeting with the Soviet leadership to ask why they were not living up to their commitments. Brezhnev, however, refused to see Sadat for at least two months. "The Soviets . . . made a laughing stock of the year of decision, while I had to suppress my agony and conceal my wounds," he recalled. "I knew then that as a result of having previously declared that 1971 would be the year of decision, I would now have to face a vicious campaign of denigration."[48]

Sadat's problems were exacerbated by growing unrest inside Egypt for his failure to deliver on his Year of Decision. In January 1972, more than six thousand angry undergraduates at Cairo University staged a wave of protests in opposition to the Egyptian leadership's apparent acceptance of the "no war, no peace," situation. Most of the students had been orderly and well organized, and they admitted that their aims and that of the government were basically the same: the liberation of the occupied territories. The difference between the students and the government was more one of methods than one of aims; the students were far more impatient than their elders.[49] By themselves, the students were no threat to the regime. But Sadat recognized that they were "symptomatic of national frustration" after nearly five years of diplomatic deadlock and that other Egyptians had similar doubts about his rule.[50] "I began to suffer from the disillusionment of the outside world," Sadat confessed in his autobiography. "The year [of decision] was already behind and no decisive action had been taken."[51]

Anxious to break the stalemate, Sadat traveled to Moscow in the first week of February 1972 for meetings with Brezhnev and Kosygin. The talks were "difficult" and "sharp," Sadat recounted, and demonstrated that the Soviet-Egyptian relationship was considerably more reserved than it was before Nasser's death. Disagreements arose over the Kremlin's repeated failure to send promised armaments to Egypt, including the Tupolev TU-22 supersonic bomber, as well as pontoon bridges for the crossing of the Suez Canal. Brezhnev admitted that he had intentionally stopped the deliveries because he did not want anything to happen in the Middle East before Nixon's visit to the Soviet Union. But he promised Sadat that if he remained patient and did not resort to hostilities before the Moscow summit, he would "exert pressure" on the Americans for a Middle East settlement when they arrived in May.[52]

To appease the Egyptian leader in the interim, the Soviets promised to send to Cairo one hundred MiG-21s, two hundred tanks, and twenty TU-22s by the end of the year, but Sadat saw this as just another attempt to hold him at arm's length before the summit.[53] "I was beside myself with rage," he recalled of his testy meeting.[54] Stopping in Yugoslavia on his return to Cairo, he told President Tito that the talks in Moscow left him "bitter" over the Kremlin's decision to place détente with the United States above its commitments with its allies. "They are being passive and handing over all initiatives to the Americans," he complained. "In such a situation, there are not real expectations for a political solution that would be acceptable to Egypt. . . . The only thing that remains then is the military solution."[55]

Without Soviet assistance, Sadat was forced to seek alternative outlets for military and diplomatic support. In March, he sent the seasoned diplomat and former minister of foreign affairs Mahmoud Riad to Beijing to explore "new possibilities" of securing Chinese military aid. Although China was in no position to supply Egypt with modern aircraft, it could provide ammunition and other kinds of arms that China manufactured locally."[56] The following month, Sadat asked Romanian president Nicolae Ceausescu, the only Eastern European leader not to sever diplomatic relations with Israel after the Six-Day War, to deliver a message to Meir that he remained committed to be the first Arab leader to recognize Israel and its borders. "I am ready to make any daring decision on the condition that it benefits the country," Sadat told Ceausescu. "But I do not want to end up as King Hussein, completely cut off from the Arab world."[57]

Prime Minister Meir speaks to reporters as she leaves the presidential palace in Bucharest, Romania, after a two-hour meeting with President Nicolae Ceaucescu on May 5, 1972. *(Moshe Milner, Israel Government Press Office)*

After initially refusing Sadat's request, Ceausescu agreed to deliver the message to the Israelis.[58] He met with Prime Minister Meir in Bucharest during the first week of May, where he made it clear that the Egyptian leader "seriously wants to reach a peaceful resolution as quickly as possible." Sadat, said Ceausescu, "is prepared to recognize the borders of Israel, ready to recognize Israel's frontiers, its sovereignty and to this effect to sign a peace treaty." He was also willing to admit international forces in the Sinai to "supervise the fulfillment of the agreement" and to provide guarantees.[59] "There was no question in his mind that he was delivering a historic and absolutely genuine message," Meir later wrote of her conversations with the Romanian dictator. "After so many years it really looked as though the ice were about to break."[60]

Meir spent more than four hours, in two long sessions, with Ceausescu, insisting that Israel "sincerely" wanted peace and that he could tell Sadat she would be glad to meet with him at a time and place of his choosing. She returned to Israel expecting to hear from the Romanian leader within two weeks of the confirmation from Sadat. "I am sure Ceausescu delivered the message, but nothing," Meir insisted.[61] Meir speculated in her autobiography that the reason she never heard anything more from Ceausescu about the meeting with Sadat was that "he couldn't bring himself to confess, even to me, that Sadat had fooled him." Without full access to Egyptian archives, it is difficult to discern why Sadat did not follow up on what appeared to be a genuine and historic initiative with the Israeli prime minister. It is unlikely that Sadat tried to "fool" Ceausescu, as Meir suggests. Nor was it possible that Sadat suddenly became disinterested in a meeting with the Israelis, given his desire to reach a settlement before the summit.

The most likely explanation was that Sadat simply got cold feet about meeting with Meir while the Israelis occupied Egyptian territory. If the news that he was even contemplating a meeting with the prime minister surfaced, it would clearly be seen by his people as a major capitulation to Israeli aggression. Domestic protests would certainly erupt on a scale far larger than what had occurred in January, and the army could move against his regime. Other Arab leaders, particularly in Syria and Jordan, whose land the Israelis still occupied, would also see a meeting with the Israeli prime minister as an attempt to make a separate peace agreement with Israel and sell out the Arab cause. Sadat could perhaps live with the Arabs if his efforts succeeded. But should he fail, this would make it extremely difficult to later ask for Syrian and Jordanian participation in launching a joint attack on Israel if he felt compelled to military action.

Sadat's refusal to meet with Meir, however, did not mean that he did not continue to worry about the results of the forthcoming summit. While Sadat waited to hear from Ceausescu, he continued to press the Soviets not to make an agreement at the Moscow summit that prolonged the stalemate in the Middle East. On April 12, he sent a letter to Brezhnev warning the Soviet leader of what might be expected from Nixon's forthcoming visit to Moscow. "Any new American policy will certainly be against our interests," he argued. He accused the Soviets of not having been as active in support of their friends as America had been in support of Israel, and for the first time he brought up the question of the flow of Soviet immigrants to Israel: "Some of them are young men, intellectuals and scientists, who are going to be of great material assistance to Israel."[62]

Two weeks later, Sadat made another trip to Moscow—his third in six months—where he spent several days consulting with the Soviet leadership over how to address the Middle East crisis with Nixon. Sadat still maintained that the best solution was the interim agreement Rogers had worked for the previous summer, which included the opening of the Suez Canal and leading to the partial Israeli withdrawal from the Sinai Peninsula. But if that was not obtainable at the summit, he stressed that it was imperative that the Soviets make no concessions either to the June 4, 1967, boundaries or, most important, to the nonacceptability of the "no war, no peace" condition. Brezhnev said that he would strive to reach such an agreement but believed that Nixon would not exert pressure on Israel during an election year and felt it better to put off discussions of a settlement until 1973, after Nixon had been reelected.

In the joint communiqué issued at the conclusion of their meetings, the Soviets and Egyptians attempted to paper over their differences by asserting their "profound satisfaction" with the results of the visit and pledging "to conduct a further consistent struggle against the perfidious intrigues of the enemies of peace and progress in the Middle East."[63] But this was clearly a transparent gesture. In fact, after receiving a report of the Moscow meetings, Kissinger informed Nixon that "the overall theme of the late April talks reflects Sadat's fears that the Soviets would sell him out at the summit." Sadat, added Kissinger, remained "insistent" that the Middle East situation called for "more explicit Soviet diplomatic support of the Egyptian position and for delivery of new types of arms to give Egypt a convincing offensive capability, especially in the air. The protocols do not suggest that Sadat received much real satisfaction."[64]

Returning from Moscow empty-handed once again, Sadat and his advisers remained highly concerned over the Nixon-Brezhnev talks. The summit, in fact, became the focus of a high-powered seminar organized by the Center for Political and Strategic Studies at *Al-Ahram*, Egypt's leading newspaper, on May 18. Mohamed Heikal, Nasser's and Sadat's former confidant, chaired the proceedings, and representatives of the Ministry of Foreign Affairs, including Undersecretary Ismail Fahmy, attended. On the Middle East, a consensus emerged that the subject would be a "low priority" on the summit agenda because the Arab countries had failed to make

President Anwar Sadat is greeted by Soviet Premier Alexei Kosygin at Vnukovo airport on April 27, 1972. (*ITAR-TASS*)

an impact on the superpowers in the way that Vietnam had done. It was therefore unlikely that the Nixon-Brezhnev talks would have any effect on the Arab-Israeli dispute, except insofar as it altered the general international climate in which the parties were pursing their policies.

The *Ahram* seminar was also unanimous in considering that the "no war, no peace" situation in the Middle East served the interests of both superpowers. Why, asked Tahsin Bashir, until recently the official Egyptian government spokesman, should the Soviet Union change its stand and expose itself to danger in the Middle East for the sake of the Arabs? Despite massive Soviet investment in arms and development projects, the position of the United States remained stronger than that of the Russians. Several at the seminar believed the answer lay in achieving some sort of "linkage" between Vietnam and the Middle East in Moscow, presumably that a concession by one on Vietnam would produce a quid pro quo by the other over the Middle East.[65] But Egyptian officials, including Ismail Fahmy, insisted that Egypt did not want the Arab-Israeli discussion to become part of some international game.

"I suggested that the superpowers were contributing to the maintenance of the 'no peace, no war,' because permanent settlement in the Middle East had low priority for them," Fahmy recalled. "Détente was likely to make this priority even lower, as the two superpowers would now be preoccupied with safeguarding their new rapprochement. As a consequence, the Soviets would become even more reluctant to provide Egypt with the arms it needed for a new confrontation with Israel."[66]

How then could Egypt solve this seemingly intractable problem and exert effective power on the superpowers? Short of starting a war with Israel before the summit, most at the seminar conceded that there was little the Arabs could do to move Washington and Moscow off their frozen positions. Fahmy stated firmly that action against American oil interests in the Middle East was "unthinkable, at least for the time being," but he also knew that the present stalemate could not last. "The state of 'no peace, no war' was causing a gradual hemorrhage of Egypt's resources," he said. Egypt, therefore, had to take "military initiative to revitalize the crisis."[67] Others, however, seemed resigned that the progress on a Middle East settlement could not be made unless the United States and the Soviet Union decided that it was in their interests, and there was little the Arab states could do to hasten matters. "This is pretty gloomy stuff," British officials in Cairo concluded in their analysis of the seminar, "but it seems to us to reflect fairly accurately the mood and thinking of prominent Egyptians involved in formulating Egyptian foreign policy and presenting it to the public."[68]

In his own regular Friday columns preceding the Moscow Summit, moreover, Heikal took a sharp line against leaders in the Arab world for failing to exert pressure on the superpowers to move off their current position. On May 12, for example, he complained at length in Al-Ahram about the failure of the Egyptian army to take action and the lack of commando operations against Israel as effective measures to exert pressure on Soviet and American officials. Paradoxically, however, even pressure of the kind the North Vietnamese had managed to exert with the launching of their Easter Offensive was not sufficient to deflect Washington and Moscow from the course dictated by their own interests. Indeed, the fact that Nixon and Brezhnev decided to proceed with the summit while attacking each other's clients in Southeast Asia proved that the superpowers would not allow regional conflicts to stand in the way of a rapprochement between them and that their bilateral relations were of far greater importance. Said Heikal: "This might not make welcome reading."[69]

Whether Sadat read Heikal's columns is difficult to say. But according to Fahmy, Sadat paid close attention to the transcripts of the seminar published in *Al-Ahram* on May 19 and believed that the views expressed there and in Heikal's columns fairly reflected Sadat's pessimistic attitude on the eve of the summit.[70] In fact, just days after the seminar, Murad Ghaleb, Egypt's minister of foreign affairs, confessed to Marshal Tito during a meeting in Belgrade that Sadat feared the United States and the Soviet Union would reach agreements in Moscow "at the expense of the Egyptians" or, at the very least, the Middle East problem would be dismissed by the superpowers "as a question of secondary importance." According to Ghaleb, the Soviets favored the current "dead-end" situation in the Middle East as more convenient to the realization of their goals vis-à-vis the United States, creating a general "malaise" and "nervousness" in Egypt. "Such situation cannot last much longer," he insisted, "because it would be useful only to the enemy and the Americans."[71]

Sadat made these concerns explicit in a final, written appeal to Brezhnev on May 22, the very day Nixon arrived in Moscow. Once again, he asked the Soviet leader not to accept any agreement that would reinforce the status quo in the region and leave him with what he called "a border dispute" that would lead to "defeat." He also asserted that if the Soviets failed to change the terms of the power between Egypt and Israel, Soviet objectives and even the existence of the "progressive" Arab regimes may be threatened. Although Sadat did not refer directly to the possibility of a superpower agreement to limit the quality or quantity of arms supplies to Egypt and Israel, the letter implicitly reflected Egypt's concern that the balance of power between the Arabs and Israel could be shifted only if the Kremlin provided Egypt with the means to develop an offensive capability in the air. Failing this, he argued, the Israelis and the United States could freeze the present situation indefinitely.[72]

"The letter is another reflection of Sadat's frustration with a situation in which the openings for movement seem virtually nil," Kissinger wrote in a memorandum to Nixon after receiving a copy through intelligence channels. "It is also an expression of his concern that the Soviet leaders at the summit talks may tacitly or otherwise agree to leave the Arab-Israeli situation as it now stands. . . . It is defensive in tone and very much the plea of a worried client to his patron rather than an argument presented by one partner to another in whom he has real confidence."[73]

Sadat's letter made little impact on Brezhnev, however. The Soviets were not about to run the risks of giving Egypt the kind of offensive power Sadat needed to regain his territory by force, nor did Kremlin officials believe that Egypt's desire to reclaim the Sinai Peninsula warranted risking progress in US-Soviet relations. At any rate, by the time Brezhnev had the opportunity to read Sadat's letter, he and Nixon were exchanging toasts in the Granovit Hall of the Grand Kremlin Palace, driving home the message to Sadat that US and Soviet pursuit of détente was about to surpass their concerns for their clients in the Middle East.

The Moscow Summit

The Moscow that Richard Nixon arrived in on Monday, May 22, 1972, was a far different place than it was during his first official visit as vice president in 1959, when he held his famous finger-waving "kitchen debate" with Nikita Khrushchev at an American exhibition in Moscow. Gone from Moscow was the oppressive atmosphere brought about by the 1956 Hungarian invasion, the Berlin crisis, and the fear of a Nazi revival that had dominated Soviet propaganda. In the twelve years since his encounter with Khrushchev, the Soviet standard of living had increased, and the Russians had surpassed the United States in coal and steel production, uncovered new oil and gas resources, and achieved parity with the United States in weaponry, something clearly reflected in psyche of the Soviet people and its leadership. "There is no question that the Russian leaders do not have as much of an inferiority complex as was the case in Khrushchev's period," Nixon wrote in his diary.[74]

Greeting Nixon in the light rain at Moscow's Vnukovo Airport were President Nikolai Podgorny, Premier Alexei Kosygin, and Foreign Minister Andrei Gromyko. Brezhnev, as party secretary, stuck to protocol and did not attend the arrival ceremonies. Much like his arrival in China in February, which was understated and austere, the Soviets intentionally kept Nixon's reception in Moscow subdued. Uniformed police officers and civilian auxiliaries wearing red armbands prevented most onlookers from getting within twenty-five yards of the president's motorcade speeding down broad Lenin Avenue, while many Muscovites gathering in Red Square were shuttered into the narrower streets in the center of the city.[75] But all that hardly mattered to Nixon. As the first American president to step foot inside the Kremlin, he knew that this summit would cement his legacy as a statesman and boost his chances for reelection in the fall.

That the summit occurred at all was one of Nixon's great diplomatic coups. Only three weeks earlier, the president had seriously contemplated canceling the meetings as a result of the beginning of the North Vietnamese Easter Offensive. "How can you possibly go to the Soviet Union and toast to Brezhnev and Kosygin and sign a SALT agreement in the Great Hall of St. Peter when Russian tanks and guns are kicking the hell out of your allies in Vietnam?" he repeatedly asked his senior advisers.[76] To prove that he would not be held hostage to the summit, Nixon responded to the offensive with a massive bombardment of Hanoi and the mining of Haiphong Harbor, forcing a wave of discussions in the Politburo about withdrawing their invitation to the president, who had ordered attacks on a de facto Soviet ally. "The summit literally hung in the balance," Dobrynin recalled. But the Politburo decided to proceed with the summit, fearing that the alternative would amount to handing Hanoi a veto over its relations with the United States.[77]

By welcoming Nixon in Moscow in spite of the mines and bombs, Soviet leaders signaled that the summit was perhaps more important for them than it was for Nixon. For Brezhnev, in particular, the meeting with the president was a "long-sought goal," both politically and psychologically. Since Stalin's meetings with Franklin Delano Roosevelt and Harry Truman during World War II, Soviet leaders had seen encounters with American presidents as a boost to their authority and recognition of their stature. Khrushchev reveled in his summits with Presidents Eisenhower and Kennedy, while Premier Alexei Kosygin's position in the Soviet leadership improved after his after his 1967 meeting with President Johnson in Glassboro, New Jersey. "Brezhnev, like Khrushchev, finds this [summit] useful in terms of the never-ending power struggle within the leadership," Kissinger told Nixon before departing for Moscow. "And whether he admits it to himself or not, to be seen in Nixon's company fills a deep-seated personal need to be accepted as an equal."[78]

Nixon's state visit in Moscow lasted eight days and turned out to be the most significant event in Soviet-American relations since the Yalta conference in the waning months of World War II. It demonstrated the desire of leaders on both sides to "start a process of détente" and conveyed to people and nations throughout the world that the superpowers wanted to move the Cold War in an entirely different direction. The talks covered arms control and political, economic, strategic, and technical ties and culminated with the signing of the Basic Principles of Mutual Relations, the SALT treaty, and the joint communiqué.[79] "What we have agreed upon are principles that acknowledge differences, but express a code of conduct which, if observed, can only contribute to world peace and to an international system based on mutual respect and self-restraint," Nixon said in a report to the Congress after the summit. "These principles are a guide for future action."[80]

Still, despite the success the summit brought about in Soviet-American relations, Sadat's fears that the Middle East would be a low priority for Nixon and Brezhnev turned out to be entirely justified. Nixon, in fact, approached the summit with the intention of "keeping the Middle East on ice until the Soviets were willing to talk compromise."[81] According to the briefing books Kissinger's staff prepared for the summit, there was little chance to duplicate the success on the Middle East that officials in Washington and Moscow had achieved on the Berlin and antiballistic missile agreements. "The parties involved are more volatile," and "the root conflict is much more bitter." The task for Nixon at the summit, therefore, was to "find ways to be forthcoming and positive to the Soviets but without committing ourselves to anything which we cannot accomplish or which is in fact dangerous."[82]

The only significant discussion on the Middle East between Nixon and Brezhnev took place on May 26, during the afternoon that preceded the signing of the SALT treaty, thereby guaranteeing that the Soviets would not "rock the boat" and thereby delay progress for months. "Putting it cold turkey," Nixon told the Soviet troika of Brezhnev, Kosygin, and Podgorny,

Nixon and Kissinger in Moscow, May 1972. *(Nixon Presidential Library)*

"we can't settle it before the [presidential] election, but after that we can make progress, in a fair way." The president acknowledged that the Middle East, though not as "urgent" a problem as Vietnam, had far more serious "long term" repercussions to Soviet and American "vital interests" in the Mediterranean region. "If you continue to help the UAR and we continue to help Israel, there won't be a settlement; there will be a war," he said.

"I simply want to assure all concerned that I feel very strongly that the issue has to be settled," Nixon added. "We are not in a position to settle it today because frankly we're not in a position to deliver the Israelis on anything so far proposed. But we simply cannot allow that festering sore to continue. It is dangerous to both of us."

"We are not saying something has to be done today, or tomorrow, or the day after," Brezhnev replied. "But as important major powers, we can make an effort so that both sides can reach tranquility on the basis of guaranteeing the interests of all states."[83]

No serious effort to resolve the outstanding differences between Arabs and Israelis would be made at the summit, however. In an attempt to appease the Soviets and make it appear that the United States had not dismissed the issue altogether, the president presented Brezhnev with an eight-page paper entitled "Basic Provisions for a Final Settlement in the Middle East," which outlined the American positions of what could eventually constitute a formal Arab-Israeli agreement.[84] But by refusing to have the text translated into Russian before the meeting and by avoiding discussing the specifics outlined in the proposal, Nixon conveyed to the Soviets that the meeting was nothing more than a "holding action."[85] "The gist of your comments, Mr. President, comes down to uncertainty and hopelessness," Brezhnev said in frustration. "We can hardly abandon our active efforts to promote a peaceful solution to the Middle East problem, because otherwise it could lead to an explosion that will be difficult for us to manage."[86]

Yet as much as Brezhnev complained about Nixon's rigid adherence to the status quo, the Soviets refused to press the issue while they had some leverage with the United States. Had Brezhnev really wanted to help Sadat and deliver an agreement for the Arabs, he could have withheld cooperation on Vietnam, SALT, or trade. The Soviet leader also had the option to issue a separate communiqué at the end of the summit, instead of a joint statement, which would have given the Soviets greater latitude to express their views and would have place the onus for thwarting Middle East progress on the United States.[87] Instead, Brezhnev let Nixon and Kissinger off the hook and accepted the "no war, no peace" situation in the Middle East for the benefit of détente.

On May 28, the last full day of negotiations in Moscow, Kissinger met with Gromyko and Dobrynin for several hours at the foreign minister's office to discuss the Middle East, but both sides knew the meeting was a charade. "So far as we were concerned," Kissinger confessed, "our objectives were served if the status quo was maintained until either the Soviets modified their stand or moderate Arab states turned to us for a solution."[88] Kissinger, admittedly, conceived of ways throughout the discussion to waste as much time as possible, including asking Gromyko to repeat some of his formulations over and over again so he could "understand them better" and having his aides hand him numerous notes regarding Gromyko's various formulations to the point that even he admitted it was excessive.[89]

At one point during the conversation, Gromyko appealed to Kissinger to sign a minor agreement committing the superpowers to the limited principles on which they agreed, including the withdrawal of Israeli forces from Arab territories occupied in 1967 and mutual arrangements for Israel's security and the Arabs' sovereignty. But Kissinger would accept only a "tentative agreement" that did not go beyond the existing United Nations resolutions or were so vague as to leave wide scope for negotiation in implementation.[90] He suggested putting off discussion of the Middle East until September, when Gromyko would visit the United States, with a timetable of completing an agreement in late 1973.

"Let me ask you this," Kissinger said. "Suppose we do not agree. What do you imagine will happen?"

"I don't know," Gromyko admitted. But "our leaders will go to bed not knowing what the next day will bring. All good things produced from the President's visit will be weakened to a great extent by the course of events, and our relations may be thrown back if war results."[91]

Once it became clear that there would be no agreement, Kissinger sought the "blandest" possible Middle East formulation to include in the joint communiqué. And he succeeded. On the final day of the summit, Nixon and Brezhnev agreed to a "meaningless paragraph" on the Middle East, which merely reaffirmed their support for Security Council Resolution 242 and called for "further steps to bring about a military relaxation in that area."[92] Without stating so specifically, the communiqué effectively accepted de facto Israeli control of the occupied territories and ensured that there would be no serious effort to bring about a political settlement between the Arabs and Israelis until the spring of 1973. "The practical consequence [of the communiqué] was to confirm the deadlock," Kissinger happily admitted in his memoirs. "It was practically an implicit acceptance of the status quo and was bound to be taken ill not only in Cairo but elsewhere in the Arab world."[93]

To say that the overall summit was somehow a failure because the Middle East portion of the communiqué did not adequately address the ongoing conflict between the Israelis and Arabs would be missing the point. By most accounts, the negotiations in Moscow were an unparalleled success and arguably a high point in Cold War Soviet-American relations. As Raymond Garthoff later wrote, the "remarkable" summit would be the "base for future development of American-Soviet relations," would reinforce America's position as the "fulcrum" in triangular diplomacy with the Soviet Union and China, and, especially for President Nixon, "was a symbol at home and abroad of his achievements at building a structure of peace."[94] Even the *New York Times* editorial page, a frequent critic of Nixon's foreign policy, conceded that "one need not be utopian to believe that an important first step has been made toward a safer future for the Soviet and American peoples and for the world."[95]

Still, there can be no mistaking the fact that the Middle East agreements at the summit "proved the last straw" for Sadat.[96] By telling the Egyptian president, who had promised his people 1971 would be the year of decision, that 1972 would also pass without a decision of any kind, and by calling for a "military relaxation" in the area for the benefit of détente, Soviet and American leaders left Sadat in an untenable position. "It was a violent shock to us," Sadat said of the results of the summit, because "we lagged at least twenty steps behind Israel and so 'military relaxation' in this context could mean nothing but giving into Israel."[97]

Sadat, therefore, was left with three choices. He could make a separate peace agreement with Israel on unfavorable terms. This could possibly mean the return of the Sinai Peninsula to Egyptian hands, but Sadat would be castigated by the Syrians, Jordanians, and the Palestinians for weakening their bargaining positions, and Egypt would sacrifice its leadership of the of the Arab League by capitulating to Israel. He could deliver on his countless promises to take his country to war to recover the Sinai through a military conquest, in which case his army would almost certainly be destroyed and more Egyptian territory lost. Or he could continue to place his faith in the superpowers with the distant hope that they would understand his plight and help deliver an agreement. Given what they had just accepted at the Moscow summit and that Nixon was entering an election campaign, this must have seemed to Sadat a worse prospect than military action.

One thing was certain, however: Sadat could not afford to do nothing. His people were agitating for action, military or political. They were tired of the stalemate. And they felt humiliated by the continued foreign occupation—both Israeli and Soviet—of Egyptian land. Sadat, therefore, decided that his best option was to make a highly symbolic, though not necessarily political, break with the Soviet Union by terminating the Soviet military mission in Egypt. Although this would certainly weaken Egypt militarily in the short term, it would send the message to his people, as well as to leaders in Moscow and Washington, that the results of the Moscow summit were unacceptable. Sadat hoped that the move would set off alarm bells that Egypt might be on the verge of a major military move and demonstrate that that he was not afraid to take bold action. If the Soviets were not going to help Egypt recover the Arab territories through political means, and if their forces inside Egypt had no intentions of assisting the Arabs in a military mission to reclaim the occupied territories, then it was time to send the Russians packing.

SEVEN

Bombshells and Back Channels,
June 1972–February 1973

"GET OUT! EGYPT TELLS RUSSIANS."

So read the headline emblazoned across the front page of the *Los Angeles Times* on July 18, 1972, announcing the momentous decision by President Anwar Sadat to expel the nearly fifteen thousand Soviet military advisers and experts inside Egypt.[1] Across the country, America's leading newspapers and periodicals heralded Sadat's grandiose move to terminate the Soviet military mission: "Russians Go Home!" declared the *New York Times* and *Time* magazine. "An Astonishing Turn in Cairo," said the *Washington Post.* "Friction along the Nile," read another headline.[2]

Not since Nikita Khrushchev withdrew Russian missiles from Cuba in 1962 had the Soviet Union suffered such a humiliating setback to its foreign policy. "President's Sadat's move . . . is clearly a blow to Soviet prestige and a favorable development from our point of view," Secretary of State William Rogers told Nixon shortly after learning the news.[3] British officials in Cairo similarly concluded that the elimination of Soviet "exclusivity" would lead to "somewhat cooler relations between Egypt and the U.S.S.R. and will thus provide a greater opening for others."[4] And Israeli prime minister Golda Meir, never one to celebrate an Egyptian overture, viewed Sadat's grand gesture as a possible strategic opening. "It would seem that this hour in the history of Egypt can, nay, should be the appropriate hour for change," she said in a major speech before the Knesset on July 26. "And if it truly is the hour for change, let it not be missed."[5]

Brezhnev tried to put the best spin he could on the hasty termination of the Soviet military mission in Egypt, telling Nixon in a letter on July 20 that this was a "unilateral move" in partial fulfillment of Gromyko's proposal the previous year, when he offered to remove the Soviet military units from Egypt in exchange for Israel's withdrawal from the Arab territories seized in 1967, with the implication that it was now up to the United States and Israel to take reciprocal action.[6] But the letter fooled no one. Kissinger later wrote that it was written with "amazing Chutzpah" and told Nixon that it was a "stupid thing for them to say because it's so transparent."[7]

In the days following Sadat's bombshell announcement, speculation ran rampant about what compelled the Egyptian leader to break with the Soviet Union at a time when Egypt remained virtually dependent on Soviet military and economic aid. Had the Egyptians decided to embark on another war with Israel that they felt could not be launched so long as Soviet forces remained deeply entrenched inside their country and acted as a brake on their offensive movements?[8] Was it possible that, in an effort to win American support, Sadat felt this move would compel the United States to pressure Israel to modify its frozen position?[9] Had internal frustrations become so unbearable that the president needed to demonstrate Egyptian independence at a time when there was growing frustration and anger in Egypt over the country's client status?[10] Was the move, as one European observer claimed, a "clear-cut call for peace"?[11] Or was this simply a "bluff" to obtain more Soviet offensive weapons that would be needed to neutralize Israel's military superiority?[12]

Explaining his decision to a closed session of the Central Committee of the Arab Socialist Union, Egypt's only political party, on July 18, Sadat maintained that the Soviets' refusal to supply Egypt with more and better offensive weapons, Soviet criticism of Egyptian discipline, and the abortive communist coup in Sudan in 1971, in which the Soviets were involved, all contributed to his declaration that a "pause" in the Soviet-Egyptian "friendship" was needed. Years later, reflecting on the move in his autobiography, the Egyptian president argued somewhat disingenuously that removing the Soviet advisers was part of his larger military strategy to reclaim the Sinai Peninsula. "No war could be fought while Soviet experts worked in Egypt," he said. "The Soviet Union, the West, and Israel misinterpreted my decision . . . and reached an erroneous conclusion which in fact served my strategy, as I had expected—that it was an indication that I had finally decided not to fight my own battle. That interpretation made me happy; it was precisely what I wanted them to think."[13]

Although the removal of the bulk of Soviet military advisers and technicians certainly freed Sadat's hand in launching an attack on Israel in 1973, and while no one could deny that the Kremlin's refusal to live up to its treaty obligations and personal commitments in arms supplies to the Egyptian president exacerbated tensions between Moscow and Cairo, Sadat's decision must ultimately be viewed as a direct consequence of détente. Frustrated that the Soviets had solidified the status quo in the region at the 1972 Moscow summit, rather than pressure Israel to evacuate the territories it had seized in 1967, Sadat correctly determined that Moscow's pursuit of détente with the United States had far surpassed its friendship with Egypt in terms of global interests. "Perhaps to [the Soviets] the Middle East problem is not the number one problem," he proclaimed in a July 24 speech commemorating the Egyptian Revolution, "but to me, the problem of the occupation of the land and the Middle East problem is not only the number one problem but is sleep, life, food, waking hours, and water. It is my problem. It is the problem of my occupied land."[14]

At the same time, Sadat's decision to terminate the Soviet military mission inside Egypt also had little to do with preparing Egypt for another war with Israel, as the Egyptian leader later claimed. For Sadat, the decision to remove the Soviets was clearly one he had made from the earliest days of his presidency not only to become much closer to the West but also to avoid another war with Israel, which he knew Egypt would lose. Instead of taking immediate steps to prepare his country for war, Sadat sought new back channels with the White House and launched a "diplomatic offensive" to draw Nixon and Kissinger into a serious negotiating process that would force Israel to withdraw from the occupied Arab territories and avoid another Middle East war that would have profound regional and global consequences.

The Russians Are Going

On June 7, 1972, one week after Nixon and Brezhnev concluded their historic summit, Sadat sent Egyptian prime minister Aziz Sidqi to Moscow with an ultimatum: either the Soviets would honor their agreements on arms supplies made in April and at the same time agree to the rescheduling of Egypt's loan repayments or the Egyptians would request the withdrawal of Soviet military advisers. "It [is] unreasonable for Soviet units to be stationed in Egypt without being under our command," Sadat wrote to Brezhnev, signaling a looming break in their relations. The Soviets, not unexpectedly, refused both demands, believing that Sadat would "swallow" the rejection of his ultimatum in the way that he had taken back remarks about the Soviet Union before his visit to the Kremlin in February. But the Egyptians did not back down. Sidqi immediately adjourned the talks with the Soviets and returned to Cairo a day earlier than planned.[15]

Sadat's decision to terminate the Soviet military mission had been building for a year. He had first broached the idea with Secretary of State William Rogers in May 1971, when he had used the removal of the Russians as a bargaining card that he would have played in return for the territory occupied by Israel.[16] The deal failed to materialize, but Sadat never gave up his desire to free his country from the grips of Soviet military control. Indeed, as one of the Free Officers who participated in the 1952 Egyptian Revolution, which helped rid Egypt of the vestiges of British rule, Sadat knew that Egypt would never have its sovereignty and the ability to control its future so long as Soviet troops remained entrenched inside his country and Egyptians remained dependent on Soviet weapons to reclaim the Sinai Peninsula. "Freedom, for a country that has been coveted by almost every would-be empire-builder, means first ridding itself of foreign military rule," he wrote in the journal *Foreign Affairs* in 1972.[17]

Relations between Moscow and Cairo continued to sour in the six months before the Moscow summit, as the Soviet leadership repeatedly withheld offensive arms shipments to Egypt. In that time the Egyptian president made three trips to Moscow, pleading with Brezhnev to release the offensive weapons, including surface-to-surface missiles, fighter-bombers, and longer-range artillery. Sadat did not want to go to war with Israel, but he argued that Egypt needed the offensive capacity either to recover its lost territory should diplomacy fail or to force the Israelis to the negotiating table in order to prevent another war.[18] The Soviets refused to budge. Moscow decided that whatever Egyptian retaliation might entail, the need to avoid a confrontation with the United States before the summit and the risk of being involved in a repetition of the 1967 "debacle" made it imperative to reject Egyptian demands.[19]

But it was the results of the Moscow summit that ultimately compelled Sadat to request the withdrawal of the Soviet military advisers from Egypt. The lack of urgency of the superpowers to reach a political settlement and their acceptance in the joint communiqué of the "no war, no peace" situation, proved to him that the crisis with Israel remained "frozen" and that no means of breaking the present deadlock were available.[20] "By God, after the Moscow meeting I said there must be a pause with the [Soviets] to speak and to be frank because we have been in disagreement since March 1971," Sadat confessed.[21] The Kremlin, he added, felt that it enjoyed a "privileged position" in Egypt, similar to that of the British during their occupation of Egypt, and he therefore needed to put the Soviets in its "natural position" of a friendly country, no more, no less. "I wanted to tell the Russians that the will of Egypt was entirely Egyptian," he said. "I wanted to tell the whole world that we are always our own masters."[22]

Following the summit, Sadat came under increasing domestic pressure to take action against the Soviets. Student demonstrations erupted throughout Egypt, protesting Sadat's inaction and the unreliability of his Soviet allies, and rumors began to circulate that "certain circles" in the Egyptian army had been preparing a coup to coincide with the twentieth anniversary of the Egyptian Revolution on July 23.[23] The Lebanese newspaper An-Nahar, moreover, printed the text of a secret memo from several of Sadat's old army colleagues criticizing him for "over-dependence on the Soviet Union" and for permitting Moscow to augment its position in Egypt without helping the country recover the occupied territory.[24] And Mohamed Heikal, editor of Al-Ahram and one of Egypt's most influential political figures, wrote a series of articles on the state of "No Peace and No War in the Middle East," concluding that Egypt's friendship with the Soviet Union had outlived its usefulness. "The Soviet Union has given us a lot," he said, "but the United States has always been one or two steps ahead."[25]

More alarming still was that high-ranking army officers were demanding an end to the Soviet military mission. At a meeting of the inner circle of the Armed Forces Supreme Council on June 6, General Mohamed Abdel Gamasy, the army chief of staff, read out a report prepared by Egypt's director of the National Intelligence Service. Its conclusion held that despite three years of Soviet military assistance, and the presence of almost twenty thousand Russian advisers, Israel's superiority, especially in the air, was such that Egypt's armed forces "were in no position to mount a successful assault" to reclaim its lost territory.[26] The implication was clear: relying heavily on the Soviet Union had done nothing to improve Egypt's military position, and there was therefore little point in continuing to endure the humiliating treatment from the Soviets.

The pressure of events left Sadat with a daunting decision. Although he knew that expelling the Soviets would be popular in Egypt in the short run, the decision entailed significant long-term risks. Not only would the army struggle to maintain and operate much of their Soviet-built equipment without Russian help, but by endangering Soviet military and political support Sadat also weakened his hand in either a military confrontation or in any future negotiation with Israel. More radical elements within the Egyptian army, including many younger officers, moreover, would likely see the removal of the Soviet advisers as a tacit abandonment of any hope of recovering the occupied territories by force, leaving Egypt in the humiliating position of having to accept Israel's continued occupation of its land. When he first learned that Sadat had ended the Soviet military mission, General Saad el Shazly warned the Egyptian president how "dangerous" the decision was, a sentiment echoed by Ahmad Ismail, Egypt's intelligence director.[27] But Sadat accepted the risks.

"I have decided to dispense with the services of all Soviet military experts and that they must go back to the Soviet Union within one week from today," Sadat "very irritably" told Soviet ambassador Vladimir Vinogradov during a meeting at the presidential palace on July 8. All remaining Soviet equipment, including MiG-25s and Soviet-manned stations for electronic warfare, should either be sold to or immediately removed from Egypt. Vinogradov was stunned; he thought it was an attempt at blackmail and tried to persuade Sadat to reconsider the decision.[28] But the matter was not open to debate. "After studying the situation in all its aspects and in full appreciation of the tremendous aid the Soviet Union has extended to us, and while fully anxious for the friendship of the Soviet Union," Sadat said, the time had come for "objective pause" in that friendship.[29]

Sadat did not explain to Vinogradov exactly what compelled him to make this decision, but in a letter to Brezhnev weeks later he left little doubt that he found the results of the Moscow summit "disappointing," declaring that the Soviets had "completely ignored" his repeated requests for weapons on par with what the United States continued to send to the Israelis. In the Egyptian view, said Sadat, the summit proved that the "crisis" between the Arabs and Israelis was "frozen." The American claim that the United States "alone" could resolve Egypt's problem had been "increasingly vindicated," even after the Moscow meeting, he charged. "It confirmed to me . . . the fact that such a method as you adopted in dealing with us—of ignoring our position and the battle we have ahead—followed from a certain mentality from which we have been suffering year after year since the aggression."[30]

Sadat kept his decision secret for more than a week, allowing the Soviets to plan their departure in an orderly way, but on July 18 he launched into a heated attack on the Soviet Union for its lukewarm support for Egypt since he became president and announced to the world that the mission of the Soviet military advisers and experts in Egypt had ended. All the military equipment and installations built on Egyptian soil after June 1967 would become Egypt's "exclusive property" and would fall under the administration of the armed forces. "Our sons in the armed forces will replace them in everything they did," he declared in a ninety-minute speech to Egypt's highest political body. "All decisions taken must emanate from our own free will and the Egyptian personality and in service to the people of Egypt who never accepted to enter into spheres of influence."[31]

The following week, at an event commemorating the twentieth anniversary of the Egyptian Revolution, Sadat devoted more than half of his four-hour speech to explaining his decision to demand the departure of the Soviet military personnel. Tracing the evolution of the deteriorating relationship with Moscow back to his first trip to the Kremlin in 1971, when the Soviet leadership failed to discuss a joint political and military strategy for reclaiming Egypt's lost territory,[32] Sadat said that Moscow's "excessively cautious stand" in the Middle East left him no alternative but to order the bulk of Russian advisers and experts out of Egypt. "The point of difference between me and the Soviet Union is that in its pledge to Israel, the United States not only fulfills its pledges but even goes farther than that." He had signed the Egyptian-Soviet treaty last May but had done so in the expectation that this would induce the Soviets to give Egypt the military equipment it desired. "I prefer that pure blood should flow from us on the battlefield rather than continue to live under delusions in the grip of the state of no peace, no war which daily exhausts our blood drop by drop," he said to thunderous applause from the delegates in attendance. "I will not accept, our people will not accept, our Arab nation will not accept, our history will not accept, and our future will not accept this."[33]

Sadat's words electrified the ASU Central Committee and "shocked" the world. "Everyone was astounded," said Yitzhak Rabin, Israel's ambassador to the United States, "especially when it turned out that what at first appeared to be a move coordinated with the United States was actually a completely independent step."[34] Henry Kissinger, similarly, recalled that Sadat's decision to expel the Soviet military advisers came as a "complete

THE HOUR HAS COME — LET IT NOT BE MISSED

Although many viewed Sadat's decision to expel the Soviet military advisers from Egypt as the first step towards war with Israel, others saw the move as a genuine opening for peace that should not be missed. (LOC)

surprise in Washington," and he quickly met with the Soviet ambassador to dispel any notion that the United States had colluded with the Egyptians in reaching this end.[35] "We have given the strictest orders to our diplomats to stay the hell out of that discussion and not to make any approaches or anything else," he told Dobrynin.[36] And President Nixon hurried a letter to Leonid Brezhnev, asserting that the United States had "no advanced knowledge of the recent events in Egypt" and assuring the Soviet leader that the United States would "take no unilateral actions in the Middle East" as a result of the recent developments.[37]

The news certainly came as a surprise to US officials, but most were pleased that Soviet troops would be leaving Egypt and believed that this was the "first sign" that Nixon's strategy of détente was beginning to pay off in the Middle East.[38] Kissinger reported to Nixon on July 20 that "the US-USSR Summit confirmed the sense that nothing was going to happen this year and brought to a head criticism of the Soviet role that had been going on in Cairo even before the summit."[39] Rogers agreed: "The Egyptian feeling that the US-Soviet summit did not advance their cause has heightened their unhappiness. Just as [Sadat] sought to blame the US for failure of last year's peace efforts, he now seems to be trying to lay responsibility for Egyptian failure to regain Sinai by war on alleged lack of Soviet military support."[40]

The Kremlin tried to put a positive spin on the brusque manner in which Sadat dismissed its forces, insisting in a TASS news agency statement on July 19 that the return of military personnel stationed "temporarily" in Egypt on "completion" of their functions, as agreed by Egypt and the Soviet Union, in no way affected the foundations of Egyptian-Soviet friendship.[41] But these statements were utterly transparent and were not even accepted by many of the Soviet advisers in Egypt. Rear Admiral Nikolai Ivliev, the senior Soviet defense attaché in Cairo, confirmed to British officials that the Soviets had "definitely" been told to go and that the TASS report suggesting that the departure of the Soviet advisers had been "arranged" with the Egyptians was not true. "The Egyptians asked us to come and now they have asked us to leave," he said.[42]

The termination of the Soviet military mission in Egypt did not signal a complete break in Soviet-Egyptian relations, nor did military cooperation between the two countries cease. Indeed, several thousand Soviet "specialists" (technicians, instructors, and anyone in a supporting role) remained in Egypt, and the Soviet navy still had the freedom to use the facilities at Port Said and Alexandria for "replenishment, recreation, and self-maintenance," as well as the Mediterranean seaport of Marsa Matrouh to shelter and rest small ships, such as minesweepers.[43] Sadat, moreover, left room for the Soviets to repair the damage should they quickly come through and provide Egypt with the weapons it had requested. He gave Brezhnev a deadline of October 31 as "the decisive factor in our relationship," in which he meant to reverse the "partial embargo" he believed the Soviets had imposed on Egypt in regard to "retaliation weapons." At that point, he believed, the US presidential campaign would be over and Egypt would find itself in a situation marked by joint US-Israeli efforts to "impose" a solution favorable to Israel.[44]

Still, enough Soviet personnel did leave Egypt and in such an abrupt manner as to leave little doubt that the Soviet Union not only had suffered a strategic setback with its most important client state in the Middle East but also had lost some of its influence and position in the Arab world in general. In view of all these considerations, Sadat told Brezhnev, "my decision to terminate the mission of the advisers has been designed to give us a pause — to mark the inevitable end of a certain era and the beginning of another based on fresh concepts, recalculations and redefinition of our stands."[45]

Back-Channel Possibilities

Sadat's decision to terminate the Soviet mission in Egypt stemmed in part from his desire to open a fresh dialogue directly with Richard Nixon and Henry Kissinger with the hope that the White House would convince Israel to return the Sinai Peninsula to Egyptian hands. Like many other leaders around the world, Sadat realized following the revelation in 1971 of Kissinger's secret trip to China that the State Department was being used only for "routine diplomatic business" and that the "really big issues" of foreign policy were being handled by Kissinger in the White House.[46] The Egyptians believed Rogers to be a "fair-minded man" but felt he misled them in 1971 and had proved unable to deliver what he had promised. Joe Sisco, moreover, aroused "a degree of mistrust" that they believed could prove a "serious obstacle" if the State Department continued to handle any renewed attempt to achieve a Middle East settlement.[47]

Sadat began to distance himself from the State Department in February 1972 during a major speech to the People's Assembly. Using a venue sure to grab headlines, he deliberately attacked the United States, and Rogers in particular, in the harshest of terms.[48] Later that spring, Sadat entertained a proposal from Donald Kendall, chairman of the Pepsi-Cola Company, and a personal friend of Nixon, who suggested that Heikal meet with Kissinger as a means of opening a direct line to the White House. But Heikal resisted the proposal. "I thought we should strengthen our internal and external positions before we got into serious talks with anyone, even if they were only called 'exploratory,'" he later wrote. After conferring with Sadat, Heikal sent a telegram to Kendall calling off the meeting and apologizing, but the meeting, he admitted, helped "whet the appetites in Cairo for a top level meeting."[49]

Although he agreed to close the Kendall door, Sadat continued to seek outlets to open up a direct line of communication with the White House. Before the Moscow summit, he had a "high ranking Egyptian officer" tell Eugene Trone, the CIA station chief in Cairo, that Egypt remained "dissatisfied" with the existing diplomatic conduits to the United States and felt that it was essential to communicate instead at the "Presidential level," bypassing both foreign ministries. The official suggested that either Kissinger or CIA director Helms visit Cairo as one possibility, or that Hafez Ismail, Sadat's national security adviser, be sent to Washington for private talks. "I cannot say that I was shocked or offended by the proposition that both sides bypass the foreign ministers," Kissinger later admitted. "I considered it the precondition for success." When the Egyptian report reached Kissinger on April 8, he sent a note to his deputy, General Alexander Haig Jr., that he felt it best to bring Ismail to Washington after the elections.[50]

The delay from Kissinger forced Sadat to seek alternative means for reaching both the Americans and the Israelis. In May, senior Egyptian officials approached Dr. Neville Marzwell (aka Nabil I. Marzouk), a professor at the California Institute of Technology in Pasadena, seeking his mediation with the United States and Israel. The son of Egyptian Jews, Marzwell was born in France during World War II and was educated at the American University in Cairo, where he studied chemistry. He was known to Egyptian authorities because his father, who retired in 1969 as the director of projects for the electrification of Egypt, had reached the highest position of any Jew in Egypt and because his family had been friendly with Gamal Abdel Nasser. At one point, Nasser introduced Marzwell's father to Nikita Khrushchev in connection with the High Dam Project, and he often presented Marzwell and his father to foreign dignitaries (such as the Polish ambassador, who was Jewish) to prove that Egyptian Jews were respected and not harassed.[51]

Marzwell's family also had the unique distinction of having connections with Israeli officials. A cousin, whose family name was also Marzouk, was hanged for his involvement in the 1954 Lavon Affair, and the brother of that cousin remained a "high official" in Israeli intelligence. Although the Israelis had never contacted Marzwell in the United States, he had met Moshe Dayan and David Ben-Gurion's son on occasion. Thus, for the Egyptians, Marzwell seemed appealing to all parties involved: as a Jew and a US citizen, but also as someone who understood the Middle East and "Egyptian mentality," he could act as an "unofficial go-between" because he would enjoy the confidence of all parties concerned.

Marzwell's initial reaction was not to get involved. He knew little of the issues and had no prior experience in dealing in secret negotiations at extremely high levels. But he determined that this could be his only opportunity to obtain an exit permit for his father, who was very ill, and bring him to the United States for medical treatment. Marzwell, therefore, grudgingly accepted the invitation and traveled to Egypt on May 27 to begin his new duties.

On arriving in Cairo, a uniformed Egyptian guard escorted Marzwell to the airport exit, avoiding the "customary formalities," and told him that Mohamed Heikal, editor of the influential Al-Ahram daily, would be contacting him shortly to set up a meeting. The meeting took place at the newspaper's building two days later and lasted almost five hours. There, Heikal explained that Sadat had authorized the meeting to see whether he would be able to get something moving on a peace settlement with Israel. Sadat was "fed up" with dealing with Rogers and Sisco, who always expressed "good intentions in words" but had failed in three and half years to "deliver the goods," and believed Gunnar Jarring to be a "cold fish" who did not understand the feelings of the peoples of the Middle East. As for the US and Soviet positions on the Middle East, Heikal opined that the recent summit between Washington and Moscow demonstrated that the two powers were only concerned that a war not break out in the area and were "indifferent" to the "burdens," human and otherwise, that the prolonged conflict imposed on the peoples involved.[52]

Between June 4 and June 10, Heikal, with Sadat's blessing, arranged for Marzwell to meet with former foreign minister Mahmoud Riad, Vice President Mahmoud Fawzi, and National Security Adviser Hafez Ismail. Each meeting lasted about three and a half hours and illustrated the degree to which the Egyptians feared the publicity of undertaking direct negotiations with Israel. Both Riad and Ismail informed Marzwell that the mounting pressures on the regime from "pro-war elements"—namely, Libya and Syria—made it "impossible" to enter "person-to-person negotiations" for a settlement with Israel. "The entire Arab world would find it difficult to understand why Egypt is acting alone in such a case," said Riad. Ismail also explained that if possible he wanted it conveyed to the Israelis that Egypt would like a "map of three colors" that would outline Israeli demands. The first color would show what Israel would give up; the second would show the territory over which they would be willing to negotiate; and the third would illustrate what Israel would never relinquish. According to Ismail, "everything"—all three color areas—would be up for negotiations. At one point during their conversation, Ismail said that even an "oral map" would be sufficient to determine, but that could only be a "first step."[53]

Marzwell's conversations with the Egyptian leadership left him perplexed about the exact nature of his role in the discussions. On the one hand, the Egyptians believed that he "understands [the] psychology of both Israelis and Arabs" and appeared to want him to convey to the "highest levels" of the US government, including Kissinger and/or Nixon, unofficially and secretly, that Egypt would welcome a "discreet approach" from Washington that would help get their land back. On the other hand, however, the Egyptians seemed to have "mixed feelings" about the extent to which the United States should be involved in open negotiations with Egypt. Each of the Egyptians he spoke with conveyed to him that they were "distrustful" of the State Department and resented the continued US support of Israel.

American intelligence officials were "dubious" that Marzwell's contacts would achieve any concrete results, but they believed that Marzwell had told the truth in his conversations with them. Following their debriefing of Marzwell, they telegrammed back to Washington a report of his contacts with the Egyptians, and indicated that they believed that based on these conversations the Egyptians were either "very desperate" or had "a surprisingly naive view of the conduct of the international negotiations." They also argued the conversations illustrated that the Egyptians felt "hurt" and "frustrated" because no initiatives were being undertaken on their behalf, and proved that Sadat remained fearful of attacks from pro-war Arabs who would attack him if he got involved in another negotiation process.[54]

Marzwell returned to the United States on June 19. What happened after that regarding his role as an intermediary remains unclear. In his memoirs, Kissinger wrote that during the summer "an Egyptian who claimed to be a friend of Sadat" made an appearance as a "prospective" intermediary.[55] He may have been referring to Marzwell, though it is difficult to confirm, given that Marzwell produced no account of his own of his contacts with the Egyptians and would not respond to interview requests.

The most likely reason that the Marzwell channel never materialized, however, was that Kissinger officially opened his own channel with Ismail at the end of July, thereby rendering Marzwell's involvement with the United States and the Israelis useless. Responding to a July 19 request by the chief of Egyptian intelligence to "take seriously" Cairo's invitation to develop new ideas as a prelude to "a secret high-level" meeting, Kissinger replied on July 29 affirming his willingness to conduct "confidential talks," even though he still did not want to get involved in offering "new" ideas that could only disappoint Sadat. In a message back to Cairo, Kissinger made it clear that in all the previous successful negotiations conducted at the White House level, the parties had first achieved in preliminary discussion an understanding on the principles of an agreement before engaging in concrete negotiations. "New proposals that led only to a new stalemate would serve neither side's purpose," he cautioned. He therefore proposed that initial contacts concentrate instead on what is "realistically achievable."[56]

Nearly six weeks went by before the next contact between Cairo and Washington in the secret channel. Then, on September 7, Kissinger received a back-channel message from Sadat reiterating his desire for private discussions between Kissinger and Ismail and informing him that the expulsion of the Soviet advisers was a "purely national decision" and had not been done "to please or displease anyone." Kissinger later admitted that at the time he did not fully understand Sadat's "insight" then, but he replied the following day, accepting the invitation for a secret meeting with Ismail. Ten days later, Kissinger again wrote the Egyptian president, assuring him of the Americans' "firm determination" to end the cycle of violence in the Middle East and stressing that he and Nixon placed the "greatest importance" on discussions with Ismail.[57]

Unfortunately, it would be another five months before Ismail would sit down with Kissinger. As Nixon focused on his reelection bid, Kissinger thrust himself virtually full-time into lengthy negotiations with the North Vietnamese to bring the Vietnam War to an end, and thus precluding any chance to meet with Ismail. Said Kissinger, "The seminal opportunity to bring about a reversal of alliance in the Arab world would have to wait until we had finally put the Vietnam War behind us."[58]

Mr. Ismail Goes to Washington

When Hafez Ismail arrived in Washington on February 22, 1973, the Middle East was like a volcano waiting to erupt. In the six months since Ismail and Kissinger had agreed to set up their private negotiations, Arab-Israeli fighting had erupted on a number of fronts, placing in jeopardy the Egyptian's opportunity to resolve the dispute with Israel and open new ties with the United States. Problems began in September 1972 when eight Palestinian gunmen, linked with the PLO and calling themselves Black September in commemoration of the events of 1970, kidnapped eleven Israeli athletes at the Olympic games in Munich, Germany. Two athletes were killed in the initial attacks on the Israeli quarters in the Olympic village; the remaining nine and five of the eight terrorists died during the botched rescue attempt by West German authorities.[59]

The Israeli cabinet vowed that the Munich massacre could not go unanswered and responded forcefully by immediately launching Operation Wrath of God. On September 8, in the largest operation of its kind since the

Six-Day War, the Israeli Air Force bombed PLO bases in Lebanon and Syria, killing or wounding about two hundred Palestinians. Rail links between Syria and Beirut were cut, and targets near the Mediterranean port of Latakia were attacked. Another score of Arabs were killed in October when Israeli letter bombs began arriving on the desks of Palestinian leaders throughout the Middle East. Prime Minister Meir also authorized the Mossad, the national intelligence agency of Israel, to target and assassinate Black September and PFLP officers wherever they could be found and in a manner "to sow fear within Palestinian ranks."[60]

Arab-Israeli hostilities escalated into 1973. On February 21, two days before Ismail's scheduled meeting with President Nixon, Israeli troops raided two training bases for Arab guerrillas near the Lebanese border with Syria, one of which, the Israeli military said, contained a Palestinian responsible for the Munich events.[61] The following day, the Israelis mistakenly shot down a civilian Libyan passenger jet that had strayed over the Sinai Peninsula, killing seventy passengers aboard and wounding another thirteen. Kissinger described the incident to Rabin as a "bore" and "the sort of problem that will go away in a few days,"[62] but Nixon feared that Israel's actions would force Ismail to cancel his visit. He directed Kissinger to get a message to Meir expressing his outrage over their actions and demanded that Israel compensate the victims of the attack.[63]

Although fairly well known throughout the Arab world, Ismail was a largely unknown quantity in the United States. Born in 1919 and educated at the Royal Military Academy in London in 1937, Ismail had served through the years in a number of midlevel posts in the Egyptian leadership, including director of the office of the commander-in-chief (1953–1960), where he took part in the negotiations for the Czech arms deal in 1955, and in the talks with the Soviet Union for the Aswan High Dam in 1958. In September 1960, he accepted an appointment as undersecretary in the Ministry of Foreign Affairs, but he demonstrated a poor grasp of foreign policy in discussions and took refuge in platitudes and "obscurity."[64]

In April 1970, after serving a decade in the Ministry of Foreign Affairs, Ismail was appointed director of the General Intelligence Services by Nasser. Although he served in this capacity for less than a year, his strong performance paved the way to his appointment in September 1971 as adviser to the president for national security affairs with the rank of deputy prime minister. In this post, the most powerful in the Egyptian leadership behind Sadat, he oversaw the intelligence arrangements and kept watch of the activities of individual ministries. Sometimes referred to as "Sadat's Henry Kissinger," Ismail was not an ideas man like Kissinger, but he no doubt shared the same influence with Sadat that Kissinger had with Nixon. "Hafez Ismail is a heavyweight," concluded a British foreign ministry report. "He has Sadat's ear and confidence and is probably the second most powerful man in Egypt."[65]

Ismail came to Washington with one purpose: to secure Henry Kissinger's involvement in a negotiating process that would lead to the return of the Sinai Peninsula to Egyptian hands. Sadat felt spurned by the State Department's failure to deliver the Israelis after he went out on a limb in 1971 to propose the idea of an interim agreement providing for partial withdrawal from the Suez Canal. He believed that Israel turned aside this initiative and that, when Israel objected, Rogers and Sisco backed down.[66] In 1972, his efforts at achieving a Middle East settlement were again rejected when both the United States and the Soviet Union agreed at the Moscow summit to maintain the status quo in the Middle East for the benefit of détente. But now that the Vietnam War had ended and that US-Soviet détente continued to advance, Sadat hoped the United States would "throw its weight" into finding a solution to the Middle East conflict. "The situation in our region has deteriorated almost to the point of explosion," he wrote in a letter to Nixon on the heels of Ismail's visit. "And our intense awareness of our responsibilities urges us to exert a new and intensified effort to achieve peace based on justice guaranteeing the freedom and independence of our peoples."[67]

Sadat's appeal came at the right time. With his election behind him, Nixon was ready to turn his attention to finding a settlement in the Middle East, the one area of the world where he believed "war was always imminent" and where the danger of a "great-power nuclear confrontation remained extremely high."[68] In the past, Nixon confessed, he had been "inhibited" from taking action in the Middle East by either US or Israeli election cycles.[69] Now freed from political constraints and worried that a Middle East war would threaten détente, the president made it clear to his staff that further delay of an Arab-Israeli settlement was not an option. "Henry, the time has now come that we've got to squeeze the old woman [Golda Meir]," he told Kissinger shortly after the election.[70] "I am determined to bite this bullet and do it now because we just can't let the thing ride and have a hundred million Arabs hating us and providing a fishing ground not only for radicals but, of course, for the Soviets."[71]

Nixon's sweeping victory in the 1972 election also afforded him the opportunity to reverse what he believed was an unsettling trend in American politics of leaning too heavily toward Israel at the expense of the Arabs. Although he had supported the state of Israel throughout his political career, he strongly believed that as a result of the "enormous influence" of the Jewish lobby, the United States had often subordinated its security interests to the interests of Israel. In May 1971, he told Secretary of State Rogers that with the one exception of the 1956 Suez Crisis, when President Eisenhower strongly condemned Israel's participation in the "comic opera war" with Great Britain and France, US policy had consistently "gone overboard in support of the state of Israel against their neighbors." Some of the decisions by previous administrations had been justified on humanitarian grounds, he conceded, but the majority resulted from political expediency.[72] All of this had to change in his second administration, the president argued.

Nixon's desire to "squeeze" the Israelis into a settlement met stiff resistance from Henry Kissinger, however. In Kissinger's estimate, it was best to delay US involvement in any negotiating process until after the Israeli elections in October, when the Israelis would have more flexibility to negotiate and the Arabs would feel increasingly desperate for a settlement. "Mrs. Meir will argue vigorously for this course, so as not to encourage Sadat to think the US will relieve him of responsibility to make the hard decisions that will be required if Egypt is to come to terms with Israel," he told Nixon.[73] Delaying the Middle East negotiations until the end of the year also had the advantage of putting it past the US-Soviet summit in June, which would prevent their differences in the region from tying up the summit and keep Brezhnev from claiming credit for any potential agreement. But Nixon refused to put off negotiations any further, fearing that if they did not take advantage in 1973, "we wouldn't get it done at all in the four year term."[74]

When Kissinger suggested to Nixon in February that he could not see how another few months' delay in moving toward a negotiation would be disastrous for US interests, and argued that it may be best to "stand back and let the two sides reflect further on their position," the president erupted. "*Absolutely not,*" he scribbled in the margins on Kissinger's memorandum. "I have delayed through two elections and this year I am determined to move off dead center. . . . I totally disagree. This thing is getting ready to blow."[75]

With this in mind, Nixon welcomed Ismail to the White House just past 11:20 a.m. on Friday, February 23. As a throng of photographers snapped pictures of the Egyptian envoy seated next to the president in the Oval Office, Nixon recounted his previous visits to Egypt and his "great affection" for the Egyptian people. He then yielded the floor to Ismail, who seized it dramatically: "Before starting [my] recent journeys, the Egyptian leadership had felt that [we] were in a dangerous stage of confrontation with Israel." The stalemate had become a "burden" and a "strain" on the Egyptian people and it was necessary either to break it through military action or to establish peace. Sadat wanted peace, but he would not accept an agreement at the expense of Egypt's sovereignty, territory, or pride. "Egypt will not be humiliated and the Egyptian leadership would take no action for which its children would blame it in the future," said Ismail. "Peace . . . must be as just as it is stable. Otherwise, it simply sows the seeds of another war."

Ismail then moved on to the thorniest issue of all: US support for Israel. He argued that Egypt simply did not understand why the United States permitted Israel to hold on to Egyptian land, in violation of its sovereignty and United Nations resolutions, and complained about the development of long-range missiles and atomic weapon research going on in Israel, with the implication being that this could not happen without American assistance. "At one time, the Soviet Union was in Egypt, but the Soviet Union has now left and Egypt saw no further genuine motive for [US] support of Israel," he said. Ismail did not suggest that the United States could stop that support tomorrow, but he did believe that the president could move toward an "even-handed" policy in the Middle East to define long-term objectives and to tell Israel that it was in the interest of all parties in the region to get along. "The time has come when the United States and Egypt should start

Hafez Ismail meets with President Nixon in the Oval Office on February 23, 1973, surrounded by dozens of reporters and photographers eager to get a glimpse of the Egyptian envoy. (NARA)

improved relations," Ismail said. "Egypt is not hostile to the United States, and it hopes that the U.S. is not hostile to Egypt."

Nixon patiently let Ismail vent about Egypt's frustrations with the United States and Israel for almost half an hour. At that point the president interjected to say he wanted to speak on "very sensitive matters" and that notes should not be taken. He said that while he wanted to begin serious talks with Egypt, discussions would have to move on two tracks: a public track with the State Department and a private track with Dr. Kissinger. If the private track was to produce any benefits, it would be absolutely essential to keep it secret. The State Department, he knew, wanted to bring the Egyptians and Israelis together in a summit to bridge their differences over sovereignty and security. But Nixon cautioned against adopting this approach. "I have a very great skepticism about summitry," he said. "The reason the one in Peking and Moscow succeed is that we did not go there until we knew what was going to come out. I think it's very important that at this particular time that we not start a process which will raise the hopes . . . and then fall apart."

Instead, Nixon encouraged Ismail to discuss the Egyptian position secretly with Kissinger in New York over the weekend, with the objective of setting some long-term goals that would lead to a "phased" settlement with Israel. "Let us see whether in that format whether we can find some way to help," he said. "I don't want to indicate that I have a solution . . . but the only way to find out is to have a frank discussion." What was important, the president argued, was for the Egyptians to be open-minded about various solutions to the conflict that could bridge the differences between Egyptian sovereignty and Israeli security. "I know that you're concerned about interim agreement because you feel that interim would be final," said Nixon. "I understand. If I were in your position, representing your government, I would feel exactly the same way. On the other hand, my feeling is that if we say that the only thing that can work here, the only thing that we will consider, is for the parties to sit down and to work out a final agreement that settles everything there will never be a settlement."

The president gave his word that his goal was a permanent settlement, but he stressed that he did not think it was possible, in view of the gulf between the parties, to reach such a settlement all at once. "We must do some walking before we run," he maintained. It might, therefore, be necessary to consider interim steps. He understood that the Egyptians might reject such an approach, but he urged Ismail to discuss it with Kissinger, and he stressed that "as long as he was in this office," he was committed to a long-range solution to the problem. "No possibility should be overlooked in our search for a way to move toward our goal," he said. The president concluded by emphasizing that he hoped this would be only the first, and not the last, meeting. "Let this be the beginning of a process," he said, and if nothing concrete emerged, he hoped Ismail would not report back to Sadat that the effort had failed.[76]

Ismail's meeting in the Oval Office lasted just over an hour. By his own description to Lord Balniel, Britain's minister of state for foreign and commonwealth affairs, Ismail found Nixon to be "relaxed, cordial, and warm," and he was encouraged that the president himself had picked out the most important aspect of the whole problem in asking whether it would be possible to find some formula reconciling the requirements of sovereignty and security. In light of the president's remarks, Ismail knew he had to give further thought to the linkage between the two before he met with Kissinger, but he was left with the impression that a continuation of the dialogue might lead to something.[77]

From the White House, Ismail and his aides hurried down to Foggy Bottom, where he had a rather fruitless two-hour meeting at the State Department with Rogers and Sisco, who were still advocating an interim agreement along the lines that they had pushed in 1971 without any idea of how to connect it to a final settlement. The whole experience was somewhat comical for it exposed the Egyptian envoy to the "many layers" of the American government. As Kissinger recalled, in less than six hours, he had a meeting with the president, who refused to discuss specifics of Middle East settlement; a conversation with the secretary of state, who supported an interim agreement without White House backing; and then a secret rendezvous with the national security adviser, who wanted to talk details so long as Ismail agreed to keep the State Department out of the loop.[78]

Of course, Ismail knew that his meetings with Nixon and Rogers were just shadowboxing. The real discussion would take place with Kissinger in two days, at which point the Egyptians would determine if the United States was serious about negotiating. After his meetings in Washington, which were long on talk but short on substance, Ismail had doubts. But Nixon believed that there was a real opportunity to get something done. Before Kissinger left for New York, the president gave him clear instructions for his secret negotiations: "The time has come to quit pandering to Israel's intransigent position," he said unambiguously. "Our actions over the past have led [the Israelis] to think we will stand with them *regardless* of how unreasonable they are. . . . You know my position of standing firmly with Israel has been based on broader issues than just Israel's survival. Those issues now strongly argued for movement toward a settlement. . . . This is the time to get moving."[79]

Kissinger and Ismail

Despite Nixon's repeated instructions to "get going" on the Middle East, Kissinger arrived for his secret meetings with Ismail with "no great proposals" and determined to slow down the process until after the Israeli elections.[80] "My strategy with Ismail will be to say next to nothing, or to speak at such a level of generality that it doesn't mean anything," he told Yitzhak Rabin, the Israeli ambassador to the United States, on February 22. In part, Kissinger believed that he had to distinguish his approach from that of Rogers and Sisco, who were willing to dive into the heart of Arab-Israeli negotiations at the first opportunity. But he also felt that his newfound celebrity stature, produced by the successful negotiations with China, the Soviet Union, and Vietnam, made it such that he should "sell" his involvement in an Arab-Israeli negotiating process only for something concrete in return. "I will make no proposals to them, no promises," he insisted. "Nothing will come out of this meeting unless they come in with a new proposal. And if they do that, I will tell them I will study it. My guess . . . is that they will not have a new proposal."[81]

Yet it was also true that Kissinger did not have the same flexibility as a Middle East interlocutor, acting more as a middleman than as a direct participant, as he had in his other secret negotiations. In contrast to his private conversations with Anatoly Dobrynin, Zhou Enlai, and Le Duc Tho, where he always had something to offer and knew what he wanted back in return, Kissinger could not "speak" for the Israelis, nor could he guarantee Israeli withdrawal from the territories seized in 1967. The only leverage he had with Israel was to threaten the delivery of future arms shipments and economic aid, but even then the president and Congress would have the final say. "On Vietnam, I knew what I wanted," he explained to Rabin. "Here I would not know how to speed up the process even if I wanted to. I do not want to speed it up, so you need not worry about something coming out of this meeting."[82]

The meetings between the two national security advisers took place in an "elegant house" in Armonk, a quiet suburb of New York City, on February 25 and 26. It was a perfect venue: close enough for the Egyptians to maintain contact with their interests section in the city, yet far enough away, and shrouded in the sylvan setting, where nobody — especially State Department officials — would pay them any attention. Formal meetings were held across the dining room table, while Kissinger, Ismail, and their aides chatted informally during breaks in front of the fireplace in the drawing room, sharing a lunch on the second day of talks.[83] After a lengthy opening statement by Kissinger on the importance of the "private channel" and the need for both sides to maintain a "great deal of discipline" in these secret meetings, Ismail made it clear why Sadat had gone to such lengths and secret channels to secure this private meeting.

"We in Egypt have a problem that we would like to see solved in the coming months, before the end of the coming year," he told Kissinger, hoping to convey the urgency of the problem. By the end of September, if not earlier, Sadat wanted to reach an agreement with Israel on fundamental principles ("heads of agreement") that would establish a "state of peace" and end the state of war. This agreement would provide a situation different from the Egypt-Israel relationship before 1967 in that it would allow Israel free passage through the Straits of Tiran and the Suez Canal, end hostile propaganda and the boycott of foreign companies trading with Israel, and give Israel a commitment to prevent guerrilla operations from Egyptian soil. Egypt was also prepared to let King Hussein negotiate his own agreement with Israel, including border changes, and would relinquish claims to Gaza, allowing the territory to pass to full Palestinian sovereignty, which could be worked out under United Nations auspices.[84]

As a sign of how far Sadat was prepared to go, Ismail now indicated that Egypt would sign a *separate* peace agreement with Israel that would take into account the "legitimate concerns" of Israel's security, including demilitarized zones on both sides of the international border and the stationing of an international force at "areas of special importance" like Sharm el-Sheikh.[85] This sounded far-fetched to Kissinger, but according to Ismail, the time had come for an "independent" Middle East, freed from "external influences," with a number of "political units," including Israel, cooperating between themselves in peace and security. "Egypt wants a full settlement, a final one, an immediate one," he stressed.[86] "The Middle East cannot stand waiting for 15 years while new relationships evolve, as some Israeli leaders recommend."[87] Ismail's aide, Dr. Muhammad Hafiz Ghanim, who attended the meeting as a member of the Central Committee of the Arab Socialist Union, concurred with Ismail's assessment: "Peace is what we want," he said. "We want real normalization of relations in the area. We can achieve a peace agreement, and we believe you can help us, Dr. Kissinger."[88]

Kissinger listened intently to the Egyptian presentation, poking and prodding his interlocutor throughout the discussion, but he was not convinced that Ismail's offer was anything other than the familiar Egyptian position.[89] Although Egypt's willingness to sign a separate agreement was a major concession and its commitment to peace appeared genuine, masked beneath the proposal was the glaring omission that Egypt still refused to recognize the existence of the State of Israel. Short of this commitment, Kissinger knew, the Israelis would never accept the offer. "If we do all this," he asked, "how will the state of [your] relations differ from 1966? Supposing we present your thinking to Israel at some point. . . . If they say, 'This only gets us back to the state of 1966. Then we had an armistice that theoretically ended a state of war.' What should we say? How would you answer that question?"

"The difference would be passage in the Suez Canal; there would be non-intervention which means the end of the boycott on third-party goods," Ismail replied. "At the present time . . . you are developing goods inside Israel and we cannot deal with you. That kind of thing would come to an end. For example, on international agreements we put a reservation. So that kind of recognition." Ghanim agreed: "It would be wholly different,

Dr. Kissinger," he said, "because since 1948 up to now we have been in a state of war. Now the state of war will end with a peace agreement."

Kissinger still had his doubts. "Would that imply that you then recognized the existence of the State of Israel?" he said. "That does not mean that you have diplomatic relations. You and we don't have diplomatic relations but you don't challenge the existence of the United States as a political entity."

"Sometimes we do," Ismail quipped, breaking the tension amongst the two delegations as the room burst into laughter.

Ismail joked, of course, but the question of what the Egyptians meant by "normalization" of relations with Israel remained at the heart of any future agreement. For Egypt, normalization simply meant an "end of the state of war," including Israel's withdrawal from the Sinai Peninsula, security commitments, free passage of international waterways, an end to hostile propaganda, and the boycott of foreign companies trading with Israel—nothing more. Full diplomatic relations, including the exchange of ambassadors, the establishment of liaison offices in each other's countries, trade agreements, and formal recognition of Israel as a state would be "excluded" from any agreement until Israel withdrew from all the Arab territories seized in 1967 and there was "full peace" in the region. "It will be some time before Madame Meir can come to Egypt to shop," Ismail acknowledged. But that should not prevent their two countries from ending the state of war that had existed between them for twenty-five years.

Besides, extending formal recognition was unnecessary, according to Ismail, since Egypt had acknowledged the existence of Israel as part of Resolution 242. Reading directly from the text of the resolution, the Egyptians argued that in 1967 they had agreed to the establishment of a "just and lasting peace" in the Middle East, which should include "acknowledgement of the sovereignty, territorial integrity and political independence of *every state* in the area and their right to live in peace within secure and recognized boundaries." "By this Security Council Resolution we meet [Israel's] concern about recognition," Ghanim said. "We acknowledge its existence, independence and sovereignty, and recognition."

"But you are not recognizing Israel as a state," Kissinger countered. "If we are candid with each other—the genius and the disaster of [the]

Resolution is its vagueness. It is too general. By 'secure and recognized borders' you mean the 1967 borders; by 'secure and recognized borders' Israel means the borders it can get. By 'states' you mean 'states' you recognize. Each side can take the resolution to mean what it wants."[90]

The two sides continued to haggle over the meaning of "normalization" and "recognition," with little give on either side. At one point, Kissinger made it clear that Egypt, as the "defeated side," should not "make demands acceptable only from victors" and encouraged the Egyptians to make additional concessions if they expected to keep the private channel moving forward.[91] But Ismail did not back down. "The first point that must be presented to the Israelis is, are they willing to have a final, complete settlement," he said. "If they say no, then we expect you to convince them. You personally, Dr. Kissinger!"[92]

The meetings between Kissinger and Ismail lasted nearly twelve hours over two days, with the Egyptians making little headway in convincing Kissinger to become actively engaged in a serious negotiating process. "In its essential points this was the familiar Egyptian position unchanged," Kissinger later commented.[93] Ismail, he believed, "had come less to discuss mediation—and therefore compromise—than to put forward a polite ultimatum for terms beyond our capacity to fulfill." Even if he accepted that the Egyptians had made major concessions by agreeing to sign a separate peace agreement with Israel and the establishment of an international security force at Sharm el-Sheikh, at the tip of the Sinai, the Egyptian offer was "so heavily qualified with unacceptable conditions" that there was little chance that the Israelis would accept the offer.[94]

More important, Kissinger believed that the hasty timetable Sadat had in mind for completing the peace agreement with Israel was based on "fancies and wishful thinking."[95] "I must say candidly that just because a private channel has been established does not necessarily mean rapid progress," he told Ismail. It took eighteen months to get the China initiative off the ground; SALT took about a year; with Vietnam it was three and a half years; and in the case of Berlin, it took six months just to educate the Russians about the two channels, and then an additional six months to settle it. "There is no sense of doing anything—drawing maps, and so on, unless we know exactly what we want to accomplish, unless we have some idea of what is doable," he said. "Otherwise, we will just be buying ourselves three months of good will, and great distrust afterwards. You must have a sense that when you deal with the White House our word counts. I would rather tell you honestly that we can't do something than to tell you something we can do and later we would not deliver."⁹⁶

On the second day of talks, Kissinger spent much of his time trying to curb Egyptian expectations as to how quickly a settlement could be reached. Just as the Soviet Union could not tell Egypt what to do, Kissinger made it clear that Ismail had the false impression that the United States could do "anything" with the Israelis. "That really is not true," he maintained. The type of settlement that Egypt wanted would take time to develop, and the Israelis, who did not want to negotiate until after their elections in October and who were in the comfortable position of sitting tight until there was a better offer on the table, had no incentive to negotiate. "So please don't underestimate the difficulties we will confront when we talk with the Israelis," he stressed. "I don't see any basis for assuming that anything will happen quickly."

The only way to speed up the process was for the Egyptians to offer full recognition as a quid pro quo for Israeli withdrawal from the Sinai Peninsula. Short of that, Prime Minister Meir would refuse to negotiate seriously with the Egyptians and the United States would have little incentive to convince the Israelis to do otherwise. "If we are suddenly in the position that we must deliver the maximum Egyptian program, then we are playing into the hands of those with the incentive for delaying tactics," Kissinger said. "I am not asking you now, but it is essential that we be able to answer the question, what is Israel getting out of this? I know the question has for you an unjust implication; I can understand your view that they shouldn't get anything out of occupied territory. But your problem will be to answer that question. Our problem is to show that not to use this opportunity would be to miss perhaps the final opportunity for peace."⁹⁷

Kissinger and Ismail parted on good terms, with plans to meet again in May, but the message the Egyptians took away from the secret talks was unmistakable: "The theory in Washington's mind about concessions was so astonishing that I think if Hafiz Ismail had conducted these talks with Golda Meir the results would have been less ridiculous," Sadat told *Newsweek's*

Arnaud de Borchgrave in March, breaking Nixon's instructions to keep the meetings with Kissinger private.[98] "We couldn't pin any hopes on the Americans, as Israel evidently had them completely in her grip. . . . We clearly couldn't hope to achieve peace through U.S. efforts so long as Israel herself didn't want it."[99] Ismail, too, found his two meetings with Kissinger "less encouraging" than his talks with Nixon and Rogers, and he returned to Cairo "depressed," as "Dr. Kissinger saw no hope of an American initiative until 1974," well beyond what the Egyptians were prepared to accept.[100]

British officials in Cairo, who met with Ismail shortly after he returned from his US meetings, painted an equally grim picture as to the results of the secret talks. Sir Philip Adams, the British ambassador, concluded that "the positions of the two sides are essentially the same as they have been for some time, with the Egyptians obsessed by the weakness of their position and not daring to seek at the negotiating table the peace they so desperately need." The State Department was "barking up the wrong tree" by pushing the interim peace agreement, and Nixon and Kissinger had little incentive to negotiate seriously, given that the improvement in Soviet-American relations and the withdrawal of the Soviet military presence from Egypt had dampened the potential of great power confrontation in the area. "It therefore seems from here that unless the Americans are willing to try a new approach, detaching themselves from the Israelis and adopting a middle position somewhere between those of the two parties, there is little or no hope for progress," said Adams.[101]

For Kissinger, however, his two days of meetings with Ismail went exactly according to plan. The Egyptians showed enough flexibility to continue discussions in the private channel, but the procedures they outlined, if followed through to their "logical conclusions," would take well beyond 1973 to complete. "In short, [Ismail] did not change Egypt's position on any basic issue, but he seemed quite open-minded in considering fresh approaches," Kissinger told Nixon when he returned to Washington.[102] The "most important thing" to come out of the talks, he believed, was Egypt's willingness to make a separate peace agreement with Israel, because up to now the Egyptians and the Soviets had always insisted on a comprehensive settlement that also included Syria, Jordan, and the Palestinians. Ismail was "not emotional and he didn't give us the old Arab procedures," Kissinger added. If the United States could push the Egyptians "over the hills," there was a "glimmer" of hope to reach an agreement down the road, which "gets the Russians off our back" leading into the summit with Brezhnev in June.[103]

The problem, as Kissinger knew, was that the Israelis were not going to be easy to budge. He informed Prime Minister Meir during a breakfast meeting in Washington on February 28 that while he had made no proposals of his own to Ismail, he saw "some flexibility" in the Egyptian position, especially in the field of the time limit between the ending of the state of war and the beginning of "normal relations." Ismail offered an agreement that would meet Israel's "legitimate" security concerns, with the purpose of achieving a *state of peace* that would allow Israel free passage through the Straits of Tiran and the Suez Canal, prevent guerrilla operations from Egyptian soil, and end the boycott of third-party goods. This would not be "full peace," he acknowledged, but there could be the beginning of some "practical normal contacts" between Egyptians and Israelis developing out of day-to-day situations.[104]

Meir rejected the proposal out of hand, however. "It is simply incredible — the Egyptians behave as if they had won the war and as if their troops were staying in Petah Tikvah for the last six years," she said. "There is no realism. Do we really have to take all this?"

"I told you that I believe they would be flexible," said Kissinger, trying to calm the prime minister.

"I can see no flexibility whatsoever," she shot back. For the Israelis, the Egyptian offer of a "state of peace" was just another ploy to "win a war that they had lost in 1967." Meir confessed that her government in the past had made a "very serious mistake" by failing to spell out precise conditions that Israel would accept for terms of a peace agreement, which had led to years of confusion, military stalemate, and diplomatic deadlock. "We erred because we thought we could talk sense with the Arabs, but the trouble is that they do not want us there," she said. Besides, there was little point in negotiating with Arabs so long as it did not hurt either Israeli or American interests to maintain control of the occupied territories, and the Soviets were not beating down.

"Has the US lost on any level because of its policy on the Middle East in the last year?" she asked.

"You will not get the President to accept a policy of do-nothing," Kissinger replied. He told Meir that while he favored letting the Arabs' frustration continue to the point where they would have to make further concessions and he had no intention of beginning any serious negotiating process for several months, the Israelis were eventually going to have to decide if they wanted to let the State Department move ahead with the interim agreement, whether they were prepared to have Kissinger continue the private discussions with the Egyptians, or whether the United States should pursue a Middle East settlement with the Soviets when Brezhnev met with Nixon in June.

None of the options sat well with the prime minister. "Golda was so dispirited that I felt genuinely alarmed," Rabin recalled. The Israelis did not object to further contacts between the United States and the Soviet Union or Egypt, but they insisted that the United States not make any commitments on Israel's behalf.[105] Meir offered to begin discussion with the Egyptians on an interim peace agreement, along the lines that the State Department had proposed in 1971, but made it clear that she would never accept a full peace agreement with Egypt unless it included terms that would lead to recognition. "Why should only Israel be forced to negotiate a 'state of peace' which is not really peace?" she wanted to know. "We will just not go along with this."[106]

The following day Nixon had his turn with Meir, telling her during brief meeting at White House that the time had come to "get off dead center" in the negotiations. "I have talked to Hafez Ismail," he said. "They are hard, but I think there is a window." But the prime minister considered Israel militarily impregnable and felt there was no need for change. "We never had it so good," she proclaimed. "The planes are coming in and we are okay through '73." For Meir, Ismail's conversations with Kissinger was further confirmation that the Egyptians simply wanted "a repeat of the '57 performance," when the Israelis were forced to withdraw from the Sinai Peninsula without receiving any assurances from the Arabs to Israel's security or legitimacy in return. "The trouble with Egypt is they want to end before they begin."[107]

Conclusion: The Failure of Sadat's Diplomatic Initiative

Seven months after he expelled the Soviet military presence from Egypt and opened the secret back channel with Henry Kissinger, Sadat's "diplomatic offensive" came to a crashing halt, leaving the Egyptian president in a state of disillusion and despair. "Everything was discouraging," he said after the failure of Ismail's mission. "Every door I have opened has been slammed in my face." Having exhausted his political options and confident that Egypt had made all the concessions that could be expected of it, Sadat concluded that military action against Israel remained the only way to change the dynamics in the region and force the United States and the Soviet Union to abandon the "no war, no peace" situation. "If we don't take our case in our own hands there will be no movement, especially given Washington's ridiculous ideas evidenced by Hafiz Ismail's trip," he said.[108] "It was impossible . . . for the United States to make a move if we ourselves didn't take military action to break the deadlock."[109]

Adding insult to injury, the latest US-Israeli arms deal, which leaked after Ismail's visit to Washington, dashed any hope Sadat had that the United States would place pressure on Israel to enter a serious negotiation. The agreement called on the United States to assist Israel in the production of at least a hundred Super Mirage aircraft, with a continuation of the supply pipeline for A-4 and F-4 aircraft through 1975. Further Israeli requests for additional planes in 1973 would be considered "sympathetically," Kissinger told Secretary of Defense Elliot Richardson, leaving Israel as the preponderant military power in the region and giving Meir every reason to perpetuate the stalemate.[110] "[The Israelis] have convinced themselves that they are quite happy where they are," Sadat said an interview. "Everything we have offered hasn't made the slightest difference in their outlook. . . . The situation is hopeless, and make no mistake, highly explosive."[111]

Beginning in March, Sadat started active preparations for launching a military strike against Israel: surface-to-air missiles were moved closer to the Suez Canal; Libya transferred thirty Mirage V jet fighters to Egypt; and the Egyptian air force was placed on a high state of alert. American intelligence also detected the arrival of about sixteen Hawker Hunter jet fighters in Egypt from Iraq, and believed that another ten Lightning jet fighters were expected from Saudi Arabia. There were even "reliable reports" that hundreds of Russian "technicians" had come back to Egypt to help restore sensitive radar equipment and mobile missile units and that Sadat had ordered the Egyptian staff to prepare a detailed plan for an attack across the Suez Canal.[112] Speaking to a joint meeting of the People's Assembly, Parliament, and the Central Committee of the Arab Socialist Union on March 26, the Egyptian president declared that he took these steps after reaching a "prominent landmark" in his foreign policy and announced that he had assumed the position of premier, in addition to the presidency, to lead Egypt through a crucial period of military pressure against Israel. "The stage of total confrontation has become inevitable," he said, "and we are entering it whether we like it or not."[113]

Most American and Israeli intelligence assessments dismissed the Egyptian maneuvers as a "bluff," concluding that Sadat was simply trying to "increase pressure on the Israel, or the United States, to be more responsive to Egyptian wishes."[114] Nor did these events do anything to compel Washington to speed up the peace process. "We are pushing nothing, we are wasting time," Kissinger told Simcha Dinitz, Israel's new ambassador to the United States, on March 30. "I will take no initiatives. I will react in a slow-moving way to their proposals. If it moves slowly and drags through the summit, that is their problem. I am not aiming at a Nobel Prize on the Middle East."[115]

But after Ismail's meetings with Kissinger, Sadat fully expected this response from Washington and warned that the United States would be committing "the gravest error in its history" if it continued to think that Egypt was "crippled" and could not take action. "For the first time we see total and complete agreement between the United States and Israel on Middle East policy," he said. "The time has come for a shock. . . . Everyone has fallen asleep over the Mideast crisis. But they will soon wake up to the fact that Americans have left us no other way out."[116]

EIGHT

The Contradictions of Leonid Brezhnev, March–October 1973

By the beginning of 1973, Soviet general secretary Leonid Brezhnev had reached the pinnacle of his power. When he seized control from Nikita Khrushchev as part of a bloodless coup in 1964, he appeared little more than an "apparatchik," a Communist party man, who was an able administrator and bureaucrat but who lacked a strong personality that would make possible effective and dynamic leadership. "He seemed somber and dull," wrote a Western journalist about Brezhnev in 1963, a year before he took power, and few outside observers believed that he would emerge as Khrushchev's successor.[1] Days after Khrushchev's ouster, in fact, both CIA director John McCone and Llewellyn E. Thompson, a former US ambassador to the Soviet Union and noted Kremlinologist, told President Johnson that Brezhnev would remain in power only a few months and that some other individual would likely evolve as the leader of both the Presidium and the party.[2]

For most of his first years in power, Brezhnev worked quietly behind the walls of the Kremlin supervising the military industrial complex and outer space projects in an effort to achieve strategic arms parity with the United States, while the role of leading Soviet statesman fell to Premier Alexei Kosygin. It was Kosygin who helped broker the cease-fire between India and Pakistan in 1965, avoiding a major war on the subcontinent, and two years later met with President Johnson at Glassboro, New Jersey, in the wake of the 1967 Arab-Israeli war.[3] When Richard Nixon entered office in January

1969, communications from the Soviet leadership were sent in Kosygin's name, a sign that he remained the "dominant figure" on foreign policy in the Politburo, and the Kremlin repeatedly delayed its decision to invite Nixon to Moscow because it was not clear whether Brezhnev or Kosygin would represent the Soviet leadership.[4]

By the early 1970s, however, Brezhnev skillfully broke out of the confines of "collective leadership" and secured his position as the dominant figure inside the Kremlin. The decisive moment came at the Twenty-Fourth Soviet Party Congress in March 1971. Although the event was forecast as a "rather dull affair,"[5] Brezhnev used the occasion to deliver a six-hour key-note address in which he not only declared that there would be no return to Stalinism in the Soviet Union but set forth a six-point program of "peace" to relax tensions with the West. It was the only speech broadcast on national television during the entire event, and it was met with thunderous applause by the nearly five thousand Soviet delegates in attendance. By the time the congress ended, Brezhnev had solidified his preeminence among the Central Committee and the fifteen-man Politburo, while Kosygin was demoted to the number-three position, after aging President Nikolai Podgorny, whose post was seen as largely ceremonial.[6]

Brezhnev was no doubt a talented politician and an effective bureaucrat. But he was also a man full of contradictions. Although he was neither a cold-blooded tyrant like Stalin nor an impulsive reactionary like Khrushchev, at times he appeared to follow some of his predecessors' ruthless policies. Under his leadership, the Soviet Union remained a rigidly authoritarian society in which dissidence was stifled, expression remained tightly controlled, and the KGB security police thrived. "Stalin would have his opponents shot," a Soviet historian observed after Alexander Shelepin, once considered a rival for power to Brezhnev, was dropped from the Politburo. "Khrushchev liked to humiliate them. Brezhnev is more subtle. He just neutralizes them. It takes longer but the effect is the same."[7]

Brezhnev also demonstrated that he was not afraid to use force when necessary. In 1968, taking a page out of Khrushchev's playbook, he sent the Red Army into Czechoslovakia to crush the liberalization of the Prague Spring and then lent his name to a doctrine that supported aggression. "When forces that are hostile to socialism try to turn the development of

General Secretary Leonid Brezhnev *(ITAR-TASS)*

some socialist country towards capitalism, it becomes not only a problem of the country concerned, but a common problem and concern of all socialist countries," declared Brezhnev, justifying Soviet intervention while stomping on the sovereignty of countries in the Eastern bloc. In 1969, Soviet troops clashed with Chinese forces along the Ussuri River, raising the prospect of a nuclear war between China and the Soviet Union. And in 1970, Brezhnev sent more than ten thousand Soviet forces to Egypt, the first time the Kremlin put its own forces in combat jeopardy for the sake of a noncommunist government.

At other times, however, Brezhnev appeared as a champion of peace who wanted to avoid war at all costs. Like many Russians of his generation, World War II was the defining experience of his life. Having served as a political commissar in the Red Army, advancing in rank until he became a major general in 1943, Brezhnev witnessed firsthand the human disaster of war and vowed to never lead the Soviet Union into such destruction. Part of his motivation for orchestrating a coup against Khrushchev, the man largely responsible for his meteoric rise in the Communist party, was that he abhorred the constant saber rattling that defined the Khrushchev years and led to crises with the United States over Berlin, Cuba, and the U-2 spy aircraft. Indeed, twenty years after the Cuban Missile Crisis he still remained bitter at Khrushchev for having led the Soviets down a dangerous path: "We almost slipped into a nuclear war! And what effort did it cost us to pull ourselves out of this, to make the world believe that we really want peace!"[8]

These words may seem surprising coming from the man responsible for ordering troops into Czechoslovakia and later into Afghanistan. But Brezhnev did not see the contradictions. During meetings with foreign leaders, he was fond of recounting a conversation with his father about what should be done to those who wage wars. "What is the world's highest mountain?" his father asked. "Everest," said Brezhnev. How high is the Eiffel Tower? "About 300 meters," Brezhnev answered. Then his father suggested that a steel tower of this height should be built on top of Everest and Hitler and his closest associates should be hanged for the world to see. Brezhnev told the story so many times that his longtime interpreter, Viktor Sukhodrev, referred to it as the "Sermon on the Mount" and could recite it by heart. "This story left an indelible impression on Brezhnev," said the historian Vladislav Zubok, "his international worldview, and his policies — indeed, on his whole work and life."[9]

The contradictions in Brezhnev's personality — one of the gentle, gregarious, peace-loving advocate, the other of the brutal, gruff, dictator — was something American officials came to accept when dealing with the burly communist leader. President Nixon recalled that during the 1972 Moscow summit, he was stunned at how Brezhnev could almost simultaneously display a mixture of crudeness and warmth. "I momentarily thought of Dr. Jekyll and Mr. Hyde when Brezhnev, who had just been laughing and slapping me on the back, started shouting angrily that instead of honestly working to end the war [in Vietnam], I was trying to use the Chinese as a means of bringing pressure on the Soviets," said Nixon.[10] Kissinger, too, observed Brezhnev's "split personality" on several occasions. Brezhnev, he said, was full of "conflicting impulses" that made Soviet policy toward the United States ambivalent. "On the one hand, he no doubt wants to go down in history as the leader who brought peace and a better life to Russia. This requires conciliatory and cooperative policies toward us," said Kissinger. "Yet, he remains a convinced Communist who sees politics as a struggle with an ultimate winner; he intends the Soviet Union to be that winner."[11]

Brezhnev certainly had conflicting impulses, as Kissinger suggested, but rarely did his commitment to détente waver. For Brezhnev, improving relations with the United States was the surest way to avoid a needless superpower confrontation that could lead to a nuclear war. Détente also helped him achieve his grand design of consolidating the Russian victory in World War II by securing European and American acceptance of the territorial borders at the end of the war. It offered the Soviets much-needed economic rewards in trade, agriculture, and technology and prevented a costly arms race with the United States. And it elevated Brezhnev's status inside the Kremlin by shedding his image of a "brutal, unrefined person" who lacked the intellect to direct foreign affairs.[12]

Indeed, it was this commitment to détente and the reduction of Cold War tensions that made Brezhnev fear the outbreak of another Arab-Israeli war that could place United States and Soviet forces on opposing sides. By the spring of 1973, all signs pointed the Arabs' intention to strike Israel in order to break the diplomatic deadlock. On May 7, the KGB informed Brezhnev that the Egyptian army had taken steps to improve its combat readiness and that an "operational plan" had been approved for crossing the Suez Canal. Similar signs were also seen in Syria, the KGB concluded, whose leadership had decided to prepare for "offensive military actions" against Israel with the Egyptian army. "Analysis of available data indicates that the actions of Sadat [and] Asad . . . can lead to uncontrolled development of events in the Middle East."[13]

On the heels of his summit with Nixon, scheduled in the United States near the end of June, a Middle East war remained Brezhnev's nightmare scenario. It would confront him with a "painful" question: If Israeli forces began to defeat the Arabs, as they had in 1967, would the Soviet Union intervene militarily to prevent the destruction of the Arab armies? If so, what were the risks of confrontation with the United States and the potential collapse of détente?[14] Hoping to avoid this ominous situation, Brezhnev used the full force of his personality to demand from Washington some tangible signs of progress toward a Middle East peace settlement. Although

Nixon and Kissinger may have underestimated the dangers of a Middle East war, Brezhnev understood that it would test his conflicting impulses. Would he remain the "convinced Communist" who would not hesitate to use military force to come to the defense of his Arab allies? Or would he be the champion of peace who would avoid war at any cost and preserve his legacy as an architect of détente?

Hunting with Brezhnev

The contradictions of Brezhnev's personality were on full display when Henry Kissinger arrived in Moscow for discussions with the Soviet leader in May 1973. Kissinger had expected the visit to be strictly official, to prepare for Brezhnev's US summit with Nixon, which was scheduled for the end of June. Brezhnev had different objectives in mind, however. Instead of meeting in the formal setting of Kremlin and in the ponderous guest houses in the Lenin Hills, as they had the previous year during the preparations for the Moscow summit, Kissinger and his staff were whisked away to Zavidovo, the Politburo hunting preserve—the Soviet equivalent of Camp David—about ninety miles northeast of Moscow.[15]

Brezhnev intended the invitation to be a great honor and hoped to convey through it the warm atmosphere that had developed in US-Soviet relations. No Western leader had ever been invited to Zavidovo, and the only other foreign leaders to visit were Yugoslavia's Josip Broz Tito and Finland's president Urho Kekkonen. There, Kissinger received treatment generally reserved for heads of state: dinners at Brezhnev's private villa, cruising with the general secretary on his high-speed boat, drives with the Soviet leader through the picturesque Russian countryside. "Our Soviet hosts . . . certainly did their best to convey that good relations with the United States meant a great deal to them," Kissinger recalled. "They went out of their way to be hospitable, on occasion stiflingly so."

One afternoon, Brezhnev took Kissinger boar hunting, a favorite pastime of the Soviet leader. Before departing, he provided Kissinger with a rifle and what was perhaps his first–and only—hunting attire. "It was an elegant, military-looking olive drab, with high boots, for which I am unlikely to have any future use," said Kissinger, who hated the killing of animals for sport.

General Secretary Brezhnev (center) escorts Kissinger to the hunting preserve at Zavidovo, May 1973. *(ITAR-TASS)*

Yet deep within the Russian forest, as the two waited hours for the wild boar to be lured by the bait that had been spread on the ground and passed the time eating cold cuts and drinking beer, Kissinger got a glimpse of the Soviet leader that he would not soon forget.

Halfway up a tree on a makeshift stand with a small bench and an aperture for shooting, Brezhnev's "split personality" came into full view. On the one hand, he spoke aggressively, even militantly, of the Chinese and hinted at the possibility of having to take military action against them. Recalling the experiences of his brother, who had worked as an engineer in China before Khrushchev recalled all the Soviets advisers, Brezhnev described the Chinese as "treacherous, arrogant, beyond the human pale," and "cannibalistic" in the way they destroyed their top leaders. He also emphasized his concern about Chinese efforts to acquire nuclear weapons and the growing menace of its military might. "The Soviet Union could not accept this passively," Brezhnev ominously told Kissinger. "Something would have to be done."[16]

Yet as easily as the truculence appeared in his discussion of China, Brezhnev conveyed sentimentality and a devotion to peace unexpected from the leader Kissinger once characterized as "tough and shrewd labor leader" whose "ruthless intelligence" was "earned from brawls on the docks."[17] He revealed to Kissinger stories about his youth in the Ukraine, his rise through the Communist party hierarchy, and his father's experience in World War I. His father had learned from the carnage that peace was the noblest goal; he had never stopped insisting on this theme. Brezhnev agreed: "We had reached the point of history where we should stop building monuments for military heroes," he told Kissinger. "Public memorials should be reserved for peacemakers and not generals." Brezhnev made it clear that he wanted to "dedicate his tenure to bring about a condition in which war between the United States and the Soviet Union was unthinkable."[18]

But Brezhnev reserved his most forceful presentation in Zavidovo for the Middle East. Having in mind the recent KGB report that warned that Sadat and Syrian president Hafiz al-Asad planned to "resume limited military operations" on the eve of Nixon-Brezhnev summit, leading to "uncontrolled chain of events in the Near East,"[19] Brezhnev pressed Kissinger for more flexibility on the Middle East than he and Nixon had demonstrated during the Moscow summit. "It will certainly be very strange indeed and incomprehensible if two big states as the US and the Soviet Union should prove to be so impotent as to be unable to solve this problem," he told Kissinger. The Kremlin, he added, had restrained the Arab states from taking military action for years, and the Soviets would continue to urge restraint provided the Arab states saw prospects for a peaceful solution. But it was a mistake for the United States to count on its influence being effective if the Arab states failed to see such prospects.

"I want to be quite frank," said a "very apprehensive" Brezhnev, "all good things done by us in the direction at the Summit of achieving détente and avoiding a confrontation will all be scrapped, and no one will believe us any more. No one can say what practical nature such a war will assume. . . . That is how we view the general situation. It's our feeling that you and we can prevent such a course of events only if we can work out some principles and measures aimed at putting both sides on the right track."[20]

"It is hard to convince Israel why they should give up the territory in exchange for something they already have [a cease-fire], in order to avoid a war they can win—only to have to negotiate with the most intransigent element of the Arabs [that is, the Palestinians]," Kissinger countered. He also dismissed the talk of war as a bluff because in his estimate a war would lead only to an Arab defeat. "The general assessment of our people is that it is unlikely that the Egyptians and the Syrians will start military operations in the next six weeks," he said in an effort to push Brezhnev off the topic. "The trouble is, the Arabs cannot win a war, and the Israelis cannot achieve a peace by their own efforts and on their present course. Now, in this situation, it is clear that unless some new element is introduced into the situation, the stalemate will continue."[21]

Kissinger assured Brezhnev that the United States planned a "major diplomatic initiative" after Israel's election in late October, at which time the president would attempt to squeeze the Israelis into the necessary concessions. But the general secretary had heard these promises from Kissinger many times before. He hinted at the "increasing difficulty" of holding back his Arab allies, accused Kissinger of taking a "tranquil" attitude toward this problem, and "growled" that the United States was counting on a state of affairs that might not last: "It is impossible not to take some steps or President Nixon and I might find ourselves in an impossible situation," he insisted. "After all, nothing in this world is eternal—similarly the present military advantage enjoyed by Israel is not eternal either."

For Kissinger, however, the general secretary's "veiled threat" of war was just the standard Soviet operating procedure. "Brezhnev's idea of diplomacy was to beat the other party into submission or cajole it with heavy-handed humor," he recalled.[22] Kissinger recognized that the stalemate in the region could not last and that the Arab states were getting desperate, but he did not want this issue to become the focus of the Washington summit since it was unlikely to produce any results. "We have to be realistic in recognizing the scope of effective action," Kissinger told the Soviet leader. "You have referred to the fact that some people overestimate what you can do with the Arabs, and this is probably true. But some people also overestimate what we can do with the Israelis, especially in a short period of time. The present situation is intractable because both sides would rather go to war than accept the program of the other."

The discussion between Brezhnev and Kissinger on the Middle East ended inconclusively and left the general secretary bitter over Nixon and

Kissinger's failure to live up to their commitments at the Moscow summit. On the evening of May 8, during Kissinger's final hours with the Soviet leaders, Foreign Minister Andrei Gromyko chided Kissinger for "underestimating the danger of the situation" in the Middle East and asked why a "taboo" had been imposed by the United States on the Middle East problem. "If the United States thinks that the Soviet Union will be a partner to agreements promoting the Israeli occupation of lands, it is a profound mistake," declared Gromyko. "It shows that we are talking in two different languages. . . . We can't accept the proposition that the U.S. is impotent. We see this as the unwillingness of the U.S. for reasons of its own."

"The foreign minister knows that we can't settle the Middle East," Kissinger answered, refusing to budge from the position he took with Brezhnev. "We are not underestimating the danger; we don't know how to handle it."[23]

Kissinger left Zavidovo on May 9, having once again successfully put off discussion of a Middle East settlement that would require Israel to withdraw from the Arab territories seized in June 1967. But he knew that the Kremlin would not drop the issue. "We're under massive pressure from the Soviets . . . to have some Middle East result at the summit," Kissinger warned Nixon as soon as returned to Washington.[24] This was no easy task. The problem, as Kissinger maintained, was that Brezhnev had no practical ideas how to solve the issue. The Soviet "principles" for an Arab-Israeli settlement were a "stale repetition" of what they had offered since the end of the Six-Day War and a clear "retrogression" from what they had offered during the Moscow summit. "[Brezhnev] has a simple concept that we can simply deliver the Israelis," Kissinger added. "In his talks in Washington he will press you for some action, on the grounds that the Arabs are so frustrated that they must now be shown that there is some hope. The alternative, he believes, is a war."[25]

The other issue thwarting progress with the Soviets on a Middle East settlement during the summit was that it was going to be next to impossible to sell the Israelis on accepting a deal based on the principles Brezhnev outlined. Days before the summit, Israel's new ambassador to the United States, Simcha Dinitz, made it clear to Kissinger that his government had "serious doubts whether there is any document the U.S. could reach with the USSR that we could live with." The joint US-USSR paper discussed at the 1972 Moscow summit could not serve as the basis for an Egyptian-Israeli peace agreement, argued Dinitz, since it failed to address Israel's "right to live within secure and recognized boundaries" and permitted international forces at Sharm el-Sheikh. "We don't understand why the United States at any point should agree to a document that is worse than 242," Dinitz said. "We don't accept it at all."[26]

As his summit with the president neared, the Politburo instructed Brezhnev to "draw the president's attention to the mounting threat of a new Arab-Israeli war." The Soviet Union found it "increasingly difficult" to keep its Arab allies in check, said Dobrynin, and in Moscow's view this should lead to closer cooperation between the United States and the Soviet Union to find a solution to prevent the war.[27] Having had little success getting through to Kissinger, Brezhnev wrote to Nixon before the Summit warning that "Great dangers are in wait of us in the Middle East" should their talks pass without a Middle East settlement. "The developments there can take such a turn which neither we, nor—I believe—you would like to happen." He admitted that his "blunt" statements to Kissinger in Zavidovo were dictated by the "explosiveness" of the situation itself and appealed to Nixon not to make the mistake of letting this summit pass without reaching an agreement as they had done the previous year.

"We, on our part, are prepared to work on the Middle East problem, sparing neither time nor efforts, before my visit to the US," said Brezhnev. "There may not be any doubt that the fixation at our meeting of exact and clear understanding between ourselves regarding the ways of the Middle East settlement on a just and solid basis would be another major milestone both in the relations between our countries and in the normalization of the world situation as a whole. I believe that this is a feasible task and the achievement of such mutual understanding would undoubtedly give a due impetus to the peaceful settlement in the Middle East and to the working out by the parties concerned of concrete measures of its implementation."[28]

Brezhnev Comes Courting

For Richard Nixon, Brezhnev's arrival in Washington on June 17, 1973, came at an inauspicious time. His staff was undergoing a major transition following the resignations of two of his most influential aides, H. R. Haldeman and John Ehrlichman, and the Senate was conducting hearings on the circumstances surrounding the break-in of the Watergate Hotel, headquarters of the Democratic National Committee in 1972. On June 14, Jeb Stuart Magruder, deputy director of the Committee to Re-Elect the President, testified before the Senate that senior officials in Nixon's inner circle, including former attorney general John Mitchell and former White House counsel John W. Dean, among others, had planned and approved the Watergate wiretapping and burglary, and he accused Haldeman of taking part in the conspiracy to obstruct justice with a fanciful cover-up story. Dean, moreover, was scheduled to provide explosive testimony before the Senate Watergate committee during the very week of Brezhnev's visit, alleging Nixon's deep involvement in the cover-up, including authorizing payments used to buy the silence of the Watergate conspirators.[29]

Although he would never admit it publicly, the investigation into Watergate and the Senate hearings took an immense toll on Nixon's ability to conduct foreign affairs. In his memoirs, Kissinger recounted that during this period the president's mind was "troubled and distracted," as he often conducted meetings and policy discussions without the sense of direction and self-assurance characteristic of his first years in office. "In the past, even in calm periods, Nixon had immersed himself in foreign policy to enliven the job of managing the government, which ultimately bored him," said Kissinger. "Now it was difficult to get him to address memoranda. They came back without the plethora of marginal comments that indicated they had been carefully read. On at least one occasion Nixon checked every box of an options paper, defeating its purpose."[30]

The Soviets were well aware of Watergate but admittedly did not understand it. Several times during the spring, Dobrynin confessed to Kissinger that he was "utterly dismayed" by the way Americans were acting over the whole affair, and he later wrote in his memoirs that Moscow's inclination was to think that Watergate was "some kind of intrigue organized by his political enemies to overthrow him."[31] Brezhnev even told West German chancellor Willy Brandt that he viewed Watergate as "a plot of certain circles in America working against détente."[32] For the Soviets, Nixon's use of the Central Intelligence Agency, the Federal Bureau of Investigation, and the "considerable powers" of his own office to remain in the White House was considered at that time "a fairly natural thing" for the chief of state to do. "Who cared if it was a breach of the Constitution?" said Dobrynin.[33]

With all the drama surrounding the Senate hearings and the changes in Nixon's staff, the summit provided the president a welcome respite from Watergate and the opportunity to show the country that despite his domestic troubles he could continue to govern effectively. Both Nixon and Brezhnev had high hopes that the summit would further the advancement of détente and strengthen the US-Soviet bilateral relationship. Before departing for Washington, Brezhnev wrote Nixon a letter saying that he looked forward to the signing of a treaty on the nonuse of nuclear weapons; to the completion of a further SALT agreement; to the signing of trade and economic agreements; and to "fruitful" discussions on the Middle East, the "second most important unfinished problem" outside of the Agreement on the Prevention of Nuclear War.[34]

For Brezhnev, the first Soviet leader to be hosted by an American president since Khrushchev's meetings with President Eisenhower in 1959,[35] the summit afforded him the opportunity to demonstrate that he was the equal of Richard Nixon. The summit was also considered by many Russians as the moment of his highest triumph. "What could be greater than his being placed on equal footing to the American president, with the Soviet Union equal to the United States . . . in its nuclear might, its missiles, and its warheads?" Dobrynin later wrote. "The leader of the Soviet Communist Party standing side by side with the American president for the whole world to see — all this was for the Soviet leadership the supreme act of recognition by the international community of their power and influence."[36]

The summit lasted eight days, taking place at the White House, Camp David, and Nixon's private residence in San Clemente, California. It produced nine separate agreements, including one outlining "fundamental principles" for limitations on strategic weapons, and a pact on further scientific and cultural exchanges. There were agreements in the fields of oceanography, transportation, and peaceful use of atomic energy, as well as a tax treaty.[37] The most important agreement for the Soviets, however, was the Agreement on the Prevention of Nuclear War, which was signed in a formal ceremony in the East Room of the White House on June 22. The treaty committed the superpowers to a code of conduct that would remove the danger of nuclear war and the use of nuclear weapons and compelled officials in Washington and Moscow not to worsen relations with any country so as to avoid a nuclear war.[38]

The summit also spurred talks between NATO and Warsaw Pact members on mutual reductions of forces in Europe and ignited preparations for the Conference on Security and Cooperation in Europe, which was convened in Geneva. "Thus, by mutual concessions, the Soviet Union and its allies obtained a European conference they had sought, while the United States and its allies obtained negotiations on troop reductions in Central Europe," said the Soviet ambassador. The summit was capped by the signing of a joint communiqué promising to seek new arms curbs, encourage peace in Cambodia, expand trade, and promote an early East-West European settlement. Voicing agreement, Brezhnev said the summit confirmed that "political détente is being backed up by military détente."[39]

The only bit of acrimony between Nixon and Brezhnev during their marathon negotiations came over issues regarding China. Brezhnev feared that the Americans and the Chinese were colluding against the Soviets in some form of "secret military arrangement," possibly a mutual defense treaty. This was a mistake, he argued, because Mao was a "treacherous character" and his aides were "exceptionally sly" and "perfidious" people. "What sort of leaders are they who so oppress their people while making propaganda all around the world," asked Brezhnev, oblivious to the fact that the same questions could have been asked about several of his predecessors. But Nixon assured the general secretary that he would never make any arrangement with China that was directed against the Soviet Union, or violated the spirit of the Agreement on the Prevention of Nuclear War that they had just signed in Washington.[40]

Surprisingly absent from the summit was any discussion between Nixon and Brezhnev over the Middle East. Although Brezhnev had practically begged Kissinger in Zavidovo to make the issue a central topic of his meetings with Nixon and had appealed personally to Nixon on numerous occasions not to let the summit pass without a Middle East settlement, he showed astonishingly little interest in the subject once he arrived in the United States. In fact, the subject did not come up for discussion until June 23, the last full day of the summit held at the Western White House in

California, and even then the talk was relegated to what Kissinger described as a "conventional haggle" between him and Gromyko over the Middle East portion of the joint communiqué. Gromyko said that the Soviet side found it difficult to agree on any "substantial" text for the communiqué. "It could be stated that both parties expressed their positions and added that they would continue to exercise efforts to promote a just settlement of the problem which is in accord with the interests of independence and sovereignty of all the states in the area."

"Such a statement would be less than last year's," Kissinger said, somewhat surprised that the foreign minister did not ask for additional concessions.

"In one sense less; in another sense more," Gromyko replied. "It would not mention Resolution 242." This was an important component for the Soviets; they believed that the different interpretations of Resolution 242 were the heart of the liturgy of Middle East negotiations, because the United States refused to go along with the Soviets' pro-Arab interpretation of the resolution. Last year, the foreign minister said, the two sides had "hidden the differences" between them and "accentuated the matters on which there was agreement." But since the areas of agreement were "thin" and the Arabs did not particularly like last year's communiqué, he felt that the two sides should simply indicate that they had "expressed their views"—nothing more.[41]

Kissinger responded that he did not see how the United States could separate itself from Resolution 242, believing that the Arab commitment to Israel's sovereignty and "secure and recognized" matter was essential to any future agreement and something that had already been agreed to by the parties. "It would be a pity after a week of substantial harmony if the press were to report disagreement on the issue of the Middle East," he said. But Gromyko acknowledged that the reality was that substantial disagreement remained on "fundamental" points. "The US side in Moscow in 1972 had said it would show flexibility on the issue of withdrawal of Israeli troops, but that flexibility has not materialized," Gromyko added. "The crucial point is withdrawal. Nothing has happened in the past year."[42]

The meeting lasted less than two hours, with Gromyko and Kissinger rather easily agreeing on language in the communiqué calling for a settlement "in accordance with all states in the area, be consistent with their independence and sovereignty and should take into due account the legiti-mate interests of the Palestinian people." To Gromyko's surprise, Kissinger agreed to avoid any reference to Resolution 242, as they had the previous year, which allowed the Soviets to tell the Arabs that this was the best way they could express their differences on the Middle East. "It was only a brief sentence," said Kissinger, "but it would prevent the debacle of the preced-ing year, when a vague anodyne formulation had been interpreted by Sadat as a Soviet sellout of Arab interests."[43]

With the formal negotiations out of the way, Nixon and Brezhnev spent the remaining hours of the summit unwinding in a poolside cocktail party attended by some of Hollywood's elite. In the early evening, Nixon hosted an intimate dinner for Brezhnev and gave a "sensitive toast" about the responsi-bility of both leaders for the well-being of the children of the world.[44] "I only hope that Russians and American in future generations may meet as we are meeting in our home as friends because of our personal affection for each other, and not just as officials meetings because of the necessity of settling differences that may exist between our two countries," declared Nixon. As Nixon's words were translated, Brezhnev eyes filled with tears. He walked around the table, embraced the president in a bear hug, and presented Nixon's wife, Pat, with a handwoven scarf made by artisans in his hometown.

"It is a modest gift," Brezhnev said, "but every stitch in this piece of fabric represents the affection and friendship which all the people of the Soviet Union have for the people of the United States and which Mrs. Brezhnev and I have for you and President Nixon."[45]

On that sentimental note, Nixon and Brezhnev parted around 7:15 p.m. Brezhnev claimed he needed to be in bed early to get all the rest he could before another "debilitating" time change on his return to Moscow. Nixon, too, exhausted from the negotiations and emotionally drained from the strain of Watergate, also decided to have an early night.[46] It was an odd way to end the summit. Not because the meetings did not conclude on a high note—they did. And not because Nixon and Brezhnev had not advanced détente through their negotiations; as the nine agreements signed between the two leaders demonstrated, the summit was a success in improving US-Soviet relations and reducing Cold War tensions. But for Brezhnev suddenly to drop the Middle East as a subject of discussion when all signs were pointing toward a major Arab-Israeli war that would involve the superpowers simply defied reason.

Of course, Nixon had no idea that he would soon learn that the general secretary's efforts to avoid a Middle East discussion was merely a long-planned ruse. Just past ten o'clock, a secret service agent telephoned Kissinger informing him that Brezhnev was awake and demanding a meeting with the president, who was already asleep. "It was a gross breach of protocol," Kissinger later said of the incident. "For a foreign guest late at night to ask for an unscheduled meeting with the President on an unspecified subject on the last evening of a state visit was then, as has remained, unparalleled." Still, Kissinger could not ignore the request, and he awoke Nixon with the news.[47]

Brezhnev's Last Warning

"What are they up to?" the president asked, sitting in bed in his pajamas.

"Who knows?" Kissinger shrugged, "but I fear we are not going to get through a summit without a dacha session." The reference was to Nixon's meeting at Brezhnev's dacha during the Moscow summit, when the Soviet leadership "pounded" the president "bitterly" and "emotionally" about Vietnam.[48] Nixon wanted to avoid a repeat of that experience, but he also wanted to ensure that he and Brezhnev parted on good terms and therefore agreed to see the Soviet leader.

The meeting took place in Nixon's private study overlooking the Pacific Ocean just past 10:30 p.m., with Kissinger, Gromyko, and Dobrynin also in attendance. After Nixon's valet, Manolo Sanchez, started a fire and fixed drinks for the president and his guests, Brezhnev wasted little time explaining why he had called a meeting on such short notice: "I would be glad to hear your views on the Middle East problem," he said even-handedly, obviously trying to gauge Nixon and Kissinger's reaction to having this dropped on them in the final hours of the summit.

Although he did not show it outwardly, Kissinger was furious when he heard Brezhnev's opening remarks. Dobrynin had provided no advanced warning that the Soviets wanted to discuss the Middle East, nor had Nixon adequate time to prepare for such a meeting. As Kissinger saw it, this was a "transparent ploy" to catch Nixon off guard and demonstrated that while the Soviets repeatedly professed to be ignorant of Watergate, they felt they could exploit Nixon at one of his weaker moments by using the flare of an unscheduled meeting to extract from the president a private commitment on a Middle East settlement.[49] Nixon, however, hardly seemed rattled by Brezhnev's ploy.

"The main problem in our view is to get talks started," the president answered calmly. "Once we get them started, we would use our influence with the Israelis and you with the Arabs. But if we just talk about principles, we'll never get them. . . . We can do nothing about it in the abstract; we need a concrete negotiation."[50]

Nixon's opening remarks did not impress Brezhnev. He did not pull the president out of bed to listen to vague commitments to start negotiations. Rather, he expected the United States and the Soviet Union then and there to agree on a set of principles for a Middle East settlement based on total Israeli withdrawal to the 1967 borders. In return, he said, the Soviet Union and the Arabs would offer security guarantees for Israel, no confrontation from the occupied territories, and unobstructed passage to Israeli shipping through the Straits of Tiran and the Suez Canal. The agreement could be kept secret, Brezhnev insisted, known only to the people in the room, and could be implemented later through the Kissinger-Dobrynin channel once the Arabs and Israelis had the chance to study the details. But it was critical that he not return to Moscow empty-handed. "I fully understand that we cannot write into the communiqué all the details," he added, "but we must put this warlike situation to an end."[51]

Nixon would not rise to the bait, however. "On a subject as difficult as this, we cannot say anything definitive," he said. He promised to look at all of Brezhnev's suggestions and incorporate them into the paper that could later be discussed between Kissinger and Dobrynin and presented to Arab and Israeli leaders. "I am not trying to put you off," Nixon added. "It is easy to put down principles in such a way that parties will not agree to talk. If we do it this way, then we can use our influence and you can use yours, to get a resolution of the differences. I can assure you I want a settlement—but we don't get it just by talking principles."[52]

Brezhnev became increasingly frustrated as Nixon dug in his heels. The president, he believed, simply did not appreciate the dire situation the Arabs

President Nixon meets with General Secretary Brezhnev in the library of the Nixon home at San Clemente, California, June 23, 1973. *(Nixon Presidential Library)*

were in, and had apparently dismissed his previous warnings that another Arab-Israeli war would erupt without progress on a political settlement. As soon as Nixon finished his remarks, Brezhnev launched into a long and passionate speech, at times raising his voice and pounding the table: "If we agree, the result will be a stronger peace in the area, but if the state of vagueness continues, the situation will deteriorate."[53] Without clarity about the principles, he stressed, the Soviets would have difficulty keeping the military situation from flaring up, and he warned that if the two superpowers could not find common ground on basic principles they had no basis for using their influence.

"If we can't reach agreement, it will undermine confidence in us," said Brezhnev. "Peace must be worldwide. Our actions should be aimed at an enduring and lasting peace. I am trying to see things realistically. But to influence things we must know the principles on the basis of which we can do good work together." Only then, he averred, could they convince their clients that it was in their interest to work toward a political settlement rather than resort to military action. "This is not a demand," he added, "but it is something we should do. It is necessary not only for the Arabs but for others too. As soon as there is a lasting peace, our diplomatic relations will be restored with Israel. We could agree on Vietnam. Why can't we do it here?"[54]

The meeting went on for nearly three and a half hours, with no give on either side. Nixon later described it as "a session that in emotional intensity almost rivaled the one on Vietnam at the dacha during Summit I" and that was as constant reminder of the "unchanging and unrelenting Communist motivations beneath the diplomatic veneer of détente."[55] At one point during the conversation things got so unpleasant that Kissinger took Dobrynin aside and told him that the Soviets were losing far more than they were gaining.[56] "Concessions achieved by subterfuge may embarrass," he argued, but "they are never the basis for continuing action between sovereign nations because they will simply not be maintained."[57]

Dobrynin could not disagree with Kissinger. Even he was amazed at Brezhnev's behavior and especially his use of "shock tactics" to attempt to impose a Middle East settlement on Arab terms. Dobrynin recalled that on several occasions during the session he instructed Viktor Sukhodrev, the Soviet interpreter, to refrain from translating some of the general secretary's "more pointed remarks," and he feared that Brezhnev's perseverance may have backfired by creating the impression that the Soviet leadership wanted to reach a secret agreement with Nixon on the Middle East, which only put the president on guard. Nixon, in Dobrynin's opinion, appeared disinterested in the entire subject, and it was clear that no Middle East settlement would be reached in the final hours of the summit.[58]

But Brezhnev did not back down. He remained convinced that there needed to be a Middle East agreement to demonstrate the success of détente and tried to "browbeat" Nixon into making the necessary concessions.[59] He repeated that a settlement could be accomplished in "confidential exchanges," much like antiballistic missiles talks, SALT, and the Agreement on the Prevention of Nuclear War, and assured the president he would renew official relations with Israel as soon as there was an agreement. "Perhaps I am tiring you out," Brezhnev added late in the conversation, after Nixon had propped up his head with pillows, "but we must reach an understanding. We must be careful that is the case. We must act in order to achieve the desired results."[60]

Brezhnev's dramatic presentation should have alerted Nixon and Kissinger that events in the Middle East would soon spiral out of control, but neither took the Soviet warning seriously. This is all the more surprising when considering that in the weeks leading up to the summit, the White House received numerous intelligence reports suggesting that Egypt and Syria were in active preparation for war and that the danger of hostilities would rise if the Nixon-Brezhnev talks passed without any results Sadat considered useful. Jordan's King Hussein twice warned Washington that Egyptian and Syrian troop moments should not be dismissed as routine military maneuvers, and the State Department's Bureau of Intelligence and Research, on May 31, went so far as to conclude that there was a "better than even bet" on the resumption of hostilities by the fall if there remained no "convincing movement" in the Egyptian-Israeli impasse. "Although [Sadat] has no illusions that Egypt could defeat Israel militarily," said INR director Ray Cline, "he seems on the verge of concluding that only limited hostilities against Israel stand any real chance of breaking the negotiating stalemate by forcing the big powers to intervene with an imposed solution. . . . From Sadat's point of view, the overriding desideratum is some form of military action which can . . . activate Washington and Moscow and to galvanize the other Arab states . . . into anti-American moves."[61]

Why, then, did Nixon and Kissinger not take Brezhnev's warning to heart and work with the Soviet leader to produce a set of principles for a Middle East settlement that may have prevented Egypt and Syria from resorting to war? Perhaps they believed that Brezhnev's grandstanding on the Middle East was merely an attempt to reclaim Soviet prestige in the Arab world that had largely eroded during the previous year. It was also fair to conclude that there was no chance of launching a serious peace effort before the Israeli elections in October, and certainly not under the principles Brezhnev wanted Nixon to accept.

But the most likely explanation is that they simply did not believe Sadat would take his country into a war that he knew he would lose. Since succeeding Nasser in 1970, Sadat had repeatedly threatened military action against Israel to break the diplomatic deadlock, but he had never followed through on any of his threats, understanding that his army would suffer another humiliating defeat. The Israelis, moreover, who were the best judges of Arab military capabilities, remained convinced that Egypt and Syria would not attack, and neither Nixon nor Kissinger saw any reason to doubt the Israeli estimates.[62]

This, however, was a gross miscalculation of both Soviet and Arab intentions. What Nixon and Kissinger did not know was that Brezhnev was acting on specific instructions from the Politburo to draw the president's attention to the mounting threat of a new Arab-Israeli war during the summit.[63] The Soviets were absolutely convinced that Sadat would launch a war in the absence of diplomatic progress, drawing the superpowers into a Middle East conflict and forcing the collapse of détente. Brezhnev saw no other way of conveying that to Nixon other than the use of a highly dramatic presentation.

Of course, Nixon assured Brezhnev that he considered the Arab-Israeli dispute a matter of the "highest urgency" and would devote his "best efforts" to bring about a settlement. He promised to look at all of the general secretary's suggestions and attempt to incorporate them into the communiqué to be issued at the conclusion of the summit.[64] If that did not satisfy the Soviet leader, the president committed to revise the set of principles Brezhnev had presented to Kissinger at Zavidovo and deliver the text to him before he returned to Moscow on June 25. But in the back of his mind, Nixon later admitted, he did not believe that Brezhnev seriously expected him to "rise to the meager bait he held out in return for what would amount to our abandoning Israel."[65]

"We can't settle this tonight," an exasperated Nixon said after an hour and a half of Brezhnev's monologue, hoping to conclude the meeting as it approached 2:00 a.m. in California. "I will say to General Secretary I agree with him and the Foreign Minister as to the urgency of this; we disagree only on tactics. We will try to find a formula that can work. We must avoid the issue—we must find words with subtlety that will bring both sides together. We have got to find a solution. I will devote my best efforts to bring it about. . . . We are not prepared to go any further. We can't abstractly beat the issue to death."[66]

For the Soviets, the message that the Americans conveyed during their nearly four hour meeting was unmistakable: "Neither [Nixon] nor Kissinger, evidently tired of the whole conversation, took it seriously," said Dobrynin.[67]

Nixon, in fact, later conceded that "we were stringing them along and they [knew] it."[68] Kissinger agreed: "There was no chance whatever of implementing such a proposal or of reaching any such agreement in the remaining few hours [of the summit]." He still held firm to his belief that the chances of launching a "serious peace process" before the Israeli elections in October were remote and saw no possibility of achieving an agreement along the lines that Brezhnev had proposed. It was also a mistake, in Kissinger's estimate, for the Soviets to believe that at the height of the Watergate hearings Nixon would "force the issue" and add to the allegations that he had engaged in a "diversionary maneuver" at the expense of an ally. "In any event," Kissinger concluded, "the program put forward by Brezhnev was unacceptable on its merits."[69]

In the joint communiqué signed by Nixon and Brezhnev the following morning, there was no effort to conceal the significant disagreements that remained on the Middle East. The two leaders merely agreed to the banal language that Kissinger and Gromyko had discussed the day before, which reflected their "deep concern" with the situation in the Middle East, and agreed to "exert their efforts" to promote the "quickest possible settlement." But nothing more. Significantly absent was any mention of their continued support for Security Council Resolution 242, nor, in contrast to the previous year's communiqué, did they express their wishes that the parties continue with the Jarring mission, designed to carry out the resolution.[70]

Brezhnev later professed that he left the United States with "a good feeling," but he knew he would have difficulty convincing the Arab states, and the Egyptians in particular, that he made his best effort to find a solution that would lead to Israel's withdrawal from the occupied territories.[71] The seasoned diplomat Ismail Fahmy told Sadat that "the superpowers were contributing to the maintenance of the 'no peace, no war' because a permanent settlement in the Middle East had low priority for them. Détente was likely to make this priority even lower, as the two superpowers would now be preoccupied with safeguarding their rapprochement."[72] Mohamed Heikal, the former confidant to Nasser and Sadat who remained an important voice in Egyptian politics, held a similar view.[73] "I'm afraid it looks as though détente is going to become a reality and impose itself on us before we can impose ourselves on it," he told Sadat after the summit. "Détente will set conditions for the Middle East problem instead of the Middle East problem setting conditions for détente."[74]

The Kremlin tried in vain to defend against charges that Soviet officials had once again sold out their Arab clients for the benefit of détente. In early July, the Soviet press agency, TASS, almost certainly at Brezhnev's behest, printed a statement in its Arabic service accusing some "reactionary press organs" and "anti-communistically minded figures in the Arab world" of distorting the results of the summit and circulating "lies" about the Soviet Union retreating from support of Arab efforts and agreeing to some kind of superpower "collusion" in relation to the Middle East. The Arab states would continue to receive "complete" and "unswerving Soviet support" for liquidating the Israeli occupation, and the Soviet leadership reaffirmed its continued support for Egypt and the "countries who suffered aggression" by offering to provide "broad assistance in other fields, including the military field."[75]

Brezhnev also met with Hafez Ismail, Sadat's national security adviser, unabashedly blaming Nixon and Kissinger for failing to put forward "concrete considerations aimed at achieving a mutually acceptable solution" and for refusing to make a "firm statement" supporting the withdrawal of Israeli forces from the occupied Arab territories. Just as important, in his opinion, Nixon and Kissinger envisaged that an Arab-Israeli peace agreement would be composed of "separate solutions" instead of a "comprehensive settlement" and were inclined to favor direct negotiations over other "indirect forms of contact," such as the Rhodes formula. In contrast, Brezhnev described the Soviet position as based on the principle of total Israeli withdrawal, insisting that the solution to the problem "would facilitate reaching agreement on all other aspects of the settlement."[76]

Sadat Prepares for War

Even had Brezhnev returned from the summit with a Middle East agreement in hand, it was highly unlikely that it would have prevented Sadat from taking his country to war. The Egyptians and Syrians were so far along with their preparations that to break off the plan with anything short of an immediate Israeli withdrawal from the occupied territories would have been seen as a major retreat by the Arabs. Sadat revealed in his autobiography that by June 5, four months from "Zero Hour," and well before the Nixon-Brezhnev summit, he had given the "final orders" to the Egyptian command and "created a definite sense of the war soon to be fought."[77]

Preparations for the attack began in October 1972 with the appointment of General Ahmed Ismail as minister of war. At that time, Ismail approved a plan, codenamed "High Minarets," drafted by the army's chief of staff, Lieutenant General Saad El Shazly. Recognizing Egypt's limited military capabilities, the plan called for armed forces to cross the Suez Canal to a distance of six to eight miles into the Sinai, within range of its surface-to-air missile batteries, destroy the Israeli fortification along the Bar-Lev Line, and then take up a defensive posture on the east bank of the Suez. Any contemplation of a "more aggressive" plan that included a large-scale offensive to force Israel's withdrawal from the Sinai and Gaza Strip was ruled out from the beginning because it was simply beyond Egypt's powers.[78]

The plan was also based on the assumption that a limited attack in the Sinai was all that was needed to achieve Egypt's political objectives. Sadat repeatedly told his generals that if he could win "only ten millimeters of ground" on the east bank of the Suez Canal, this would immeasurably strengthen his position in subsequent political and diplomatic negotiations.[79] Many of his generals were skeptical of this approach, but it made sense. Attacking Israeli forces along the Suez and gaining a foothold in the Sinai would be sufficient to trigger superpower intervention and compel Moscow and Washington to move off their frozen positions. The attack could also force the United States and the Soviet Union to send military forces to the region on behalf of their clients, drawing the superpowers further into the conflict and directly threatening détente.

Of course, Sadat deliberately withheld these objectives from Syrian president Hafiz al-Asad when the two coordinated their war strategy. Asad later told his biographer that when he met with the Egyptian president during a secret visit to Burj al-'Arab, the presidential rest house outside Cairo, in April 1973, Sadat's objectives in the first stage were to reach the strategic Mitla and Giddi Passes, about forty miles into the Sinai, before regrouping for the reconquest of the whole peninsula. Syrian forces would facilitate by attacking Israeli forces along the Golan Heights, forcing the Israelis to fight a multifront war. "This is what Sadat and I decided and it was on this principle that we went to war," claimed Asad.[80] Had the Syrian leader known that Sadat planned to halt his advance a short distance into the Sinai, it was unlikely Syria would have joined the assault, knowing that Israel would be able to concentrate its forces along the Golan Heights.

Sadat held out the possibility that a political settlement could be achieved and war avoided, but when Ismail returned from his unsuccessful meetings with Kissinger in February 1973, there was no turning back. In March, Sadat moved SA-6 surface-to-air missiles to firing sites within twenty miles of the Suez Canal, transferred almost thirty Mirage V jet fighters, possessing ground attack capabilities from Libya to Egypt, and imposed a high state of alert on the Egyptian air force.[81] He also took the post of premier, in addition to the presidency, to prepare Egypt for "total confrontation" with Israel and declared himself military governor of Egypt, which granted him vast emergency powers, including complete control over both internal and external security. With these new titles, Sadat assumed a level of power in Egypt that not even Gamal Abdel Nasser had possessed. As Henry Tanner, a *New York Times* foreign correspondent, wrote from Cairo, Sadat looked for the entire world like "a ship's captain clearing the deck and battening down the hatches for a storm—or a battle."[82]

The failure of the United States and the Soviet Union to achieve a Middle East settlement during the Washington summit only confirmed to Sadat the need to move forward with his strategy. Although Sadat made no public break with Moscow following the second round of Nixon-Brezhnev talks, as he had the previous year after the Moscow summit, he concluded that the improvement in US-Soviet relations continued to undermine his efforts to reclaim the Sinai from Israel and compelled Egypt to adopt a different strategy to deal with détente. Portions of this approach emerged in a "Working Paper on International Changes" discussed at a joint meeting of the ASU Central Committee and the People's Assembly on August 4. The sections in the paper on détente were perhaps most revealing.

First, the Egyptians believed that as a consequence of détente the Soviets had permitted the United States to become "more daring in consolidating

Israel politically, economically, and militarily without the least need to use the pretext of military balance in the Middle East," and stressed that Washington had become "more hostile" to the legitimate rights of the Palestinian people. Second, the report suggested that that the Middle East problem had become part of the strategy of the two major powers. In accordance with détente, the Soviet Union appeared committed to revisiting many of its attitudes, including the restrictions imposed on the emigration of Soviet Jews.[83]

Perhaps most important, the Egyptians believed that as a direct result of détente its dependence on foreign powers had "become less effective and more restricted." The paper, therefore, stressed that while Egypt must always be keen on its friendships, especially with the Soviet Union, it was important to place such friendships in their true perspectives. "We must strengthen our new friendships and adopt a liberal policy towards all world powers which support peace and justice," the report declared. "We must consolidate the policy of non-alignment because it is not true that this policy has disappeared as a result of détente. . . . It has become a way of confronting the rapprochement between the two major powers so that détente may not be achieved at the expense of the non-aligned of the small countries nor at the expense of the UN."[84]

No mention was made that Sadat would have to take Egypt to war to disrupt détente and draw the superpowers away from the comfortable position they had adopted in the region. But for Sadat, that was precisely his intent. As he later confessed, his war objectives were to engage in a "limited action" to "break the deadlock in the crisis" that had been created by the fact that leaders in Washington and Moscow had agreed to a stalemate in the region that allowed Israel to retain possession of the Arab territories.[85] His chief of staff of the armed forces, Lieutenant General Abdel Ghani Al-Gamasy, similarly confirmed that Egypt's motivations for war were almost entirely political. "[The] objective was to break the Middle East deadlock . . . and overthrow the balance of military and political force in the region," said Gamassy. "In other words, the October War was not a war of liberation and the political objective conceived for it imposed restrictions on military movement and prevented the armed forces from realizing greater triumphs."[86]

Jordan's King Hussein tried to convince the United States that Sadat wanted to break the "no war, no peace," situation by attacking Israel, but to no avail. Following a summit in Cairo with the Egyptian and Syrian leaders on September 10–12, 1973, in which he held a "private conversation" with Sadat devoted entirely to the subject of US-Soviet relations, Hussein reported to Dean Brown, the US ambassador in Jordan, that Sadat felt compelled to action because Washington and Moscow had agreed on "the status quo with no solution to the basic Middle East problem." Hussein asked Brown for permission to "authoritatively" tell Sadat that there is no US-Soviet "collusion" involving the perpetuation of the Middle East stalemate and warned that Sadat believed that Egypt's relationship with the United States would deteriorate in the near future.[87]

When Hussein heard no response from the United States regarding this request, he made a secret trip to Israel to inform Prime Minister Meir of Egyptian and Syrian intentions to launch a war to break the deadlock. The meeting took place at Midrasha, the Mossad headquarters in Herzliya, just north of Tel Aviv, on September 25. Based on his meetings in Cairo, said Hussein, it was clear that Egypt and Syria could no longer tolerate the stalemate that had solidified during the past three years, and he emphasized that in the continued absence of a political settlement, Sadat and Asad would attempt to "liberate" their territories by military means.[88]

Lest there be any doubt that this would happen, Hussein provided the prime minister with the details of a Jordanian intelligence report from a "very sensitive source" in Syria indicating that Syrian troops that were meant to be in training were now in the position of "pre-attack" along the Golan. Preparations were also under way to respond to an Israeli counterattack through Jordan, including forward aircraft and missile movement and "everything else that is out on the front at this stage." The king offered no dates when such an attack might occur, and neither Sadat nor Asad, he admitted, asked for Jordanian participation in the war, but there was little doubt in his mind that an attack would come. When Meir asked if the Syrians would go to war on their own, Hussein made it clear that this would be another multifront war for the Israelis: "I don't think so," he replied. "I think they would cooperate."[89]

Meir doubted Hussein's claims, given that he had made such proclamations before. But she also knew she could not dismiss the warning either. As soon as the meeting ended, she reported the warning to Defense Minister Moshe Dayan, who paid a visit to the Syrian border the following day to inspect the front-line positions on the Golan Heights. There he found that Syria had massed hundreds of tanks and artillery pieces just beyond the Israeli lines in the area, as Hussein suggested.[90] If Syria wanted to retake the Golan, Dayan knew that there was little the Israelis could do prevent it from happening. He warned settlers in the area to strengthen their defenses along the Syrian front in the face of the military buildup and authorized further preparations in the north in expectation of a Syrian attack.[91]

Yet even as Dayan readied Israeli forces near the Golan, the consensus among Israeli military and intelligence officials remained that an attack by either Egypt or Syria would not occur. According to one IDF intelligence report, the Syrian and Egyptian buildups were viewed as merely "a coincidental juxtaposition of two actions motivated by entirely different reasons." Egypt's large-scale exercises could serve as a "cover" for offensive preparations, the report added, but since no "collateral indications" supported this, the IDF considered the Arab troop movements "to be merely an exercise." The IDF determined that Syria did not have the capabilities to reoccupy and hold the Golan Heights; Syrian deployments should therefore be viewed as "purely defensive."[92]

With all signs increasingly pointing in the direction of a military confrontation, Brezhnev sent Foreign Minister Andrei Gromyko to Washington to ask the White House once again to make a "serious effort" at finding a solution to the conflict. He reminded Nixon of the promises he had made to Brezhnev during their late-night meeting in San Clemente to take up the Middle East problem as soon as he returned to Washington. The Soviets were obviously aware of Nixon's preoccupation with Watergate, but that could not be a reason for further delay. "A solution will not just fall down from the sky," said the foreign minister, pleading for the president to induce some flexibility out of the Israelis. Nixon assured Gromyko that he considered the Middle East a "very important priority" and that Kissinger had a "direct assignment" to "push" the issue, most likely after the Israeli elections in October. But Gromyko was not satisfied.

"Your assessment and ours do not fully coincide, even if at first sight it seems that we do since both sides feel the situation is complicated and dangerous," said Gromyko. "We have a different assessment of the danger because we feel the possibility could not be excluded that we could all wake up one day and find there is a real conflagration in that area. That has to be kept in mind. Is it worth the risk?"[93]

Conclusion

Gromyko's ominous prediction was not far off. On October 3, less than a week after warning Nixon and Kissinger not to treat the Middle East as quiescent, the foreign minister received reports from the Soviet embassies in Cairo and Damascus that Egypt and Syria would launch an attack on Israel at a "fixed" date, most likely October 6, the Jewish holy day of Yom Kippur. "I'd like to inform you officially that I and Syria have decided to start military operations against Israel so as to break the present deadlock," Sadat told Vladimir Vinogradov, the Soviet ambassador in Egypt. "I would like the Soviet leaders to give me an urgent answer to this question: What will the Soviet attitude be?"[94]

Brezhnev, naturally, opposed the operation, fearing that either his Arab clients would face a humiliating defeat, leaving Moscow to pick up the pieces again, or the Soviets would have to intervene against Israeli forces, which could lead to a superpower confrontation and the collapse of détente. He sent a message to Sadat the following day emphasizing that while the decision regarding such a "vital issue" as starting a war against Israel would be left completely to the Egyptian leadership, the Soviet government believed that the solution to the present Middle East impasse would be better settled through "political means," and he warned that any failure in such an important venture would set back a Middle East settlement "indefinitely."[95]

The larger question for Brezhnev, however, was whether he should alert the United States to the pending attack. In the spirit of détente, and in light of the improvements made in US-Soviet relations during the past two years, he knew he should inform Nixon about a crisis that could conceivably lead to global war. But he also recognized that alerting Washington to Arab intentions would prompt an Israeli preemptive strike on Egyptian and Syrian forces. If this happened, the Arab states would hold Moscow responsible, undermining Soviet credibility not only in the Middle East but also with its clients throughout the world. He did not relish the thought.

Brezhnev, therefore, opted for the best middle ground he could find. On October 4, he ordered the evacuation of the families and dependents of all the Soviet diplomats and advisers in Egypt and Syria. Although this was far short of directly informing Nixon and Kissinger that a Middle East war would soon erupt and did not live up to the spirit of the 1972 agreement on the Basic Principles of Mutual Relations Between the United States and the U.S.S.R. and the Agreement on the Prevention of Nuclear War, which set forth a code of conduct for the superpowers to reduce tension and conflict in their relations with other areas of the world, the Kremlin reasoned that the sight of thousands of Soviet citizens seen boarding passenger planes in Syria and Egypt would be easily detected by US and Israeli intelligence agencies, who would draw the proper conclusions.

"If the Americans approach the Foreign Ministry, how should we explain the evacuation of Soviet personnel?" a member of Gromyko's staff asked after the instructions went out to the embassies in Damascus and Cairo ordering the massive evacuation. But Gromyko dismissed the question, with the implicit reference that the Politburo had considered the implications. "The lives of Soviet people are dearer to us."[96]

The United States detected the Soviet evacuation, as the Kremlin had anticipated, but improper conclusions were drawn from the event. Kissinger recalled that on the morning of October 5, he woke up to the "astonishing news," based on a report from the American defense attaché in Tel Aviv, that the Soviet Union had been airlifting all its dependents out of Egypt and Syria. He requested a "fresh" political and military assessment in light of the new evidence, but the Central Intelligence Agency adhered to its position that "the military preparations that have occurred do not indicate that any party intends to initiate hostilities."[97] "It is now inexplicable how that development was misinterpreted," Kissinger admitted. "If the Soviets evacuated dependents because they feared a war, they must have had a very good idea that it would be started by the Arabs. . . . We should have known that big events were impending."[98]

The United States was not alone in missing the Soviet signal, however. Several hours after receiving the CIA report, the Israelis informed Brent

Scowcroft, Kissinger's deputy on the NSC staff, that the evacuation of Soviet dependents was not a sign that the Arab states were on the verge of military action. "Our assessment is that the alert measures being taken by Egypt and Syria are in part connected with maneuvers (as regards Egypt) and in part due to fears of offensive actions by Israel," their report concluded. "We consider the opening of military operations against Israel by the two armies as of low probability." So convinced were the Israelis that the Egyptian and Syrian moves were defensive that Meir asked Kissinger to convey to the Arabs and the Soviets that Israel had "no intention whatever to initiate offensive military operations" with the "aim of restoring calm to the area."[99]

Kissinger later forgave the Soviets for failing to alert the United States more concretely, suggesting that this sort of "big-power cooperation" was too much to expect during the infant stages of détente.[100] But it was clear that he expected more from the Brezhnev in light of all the United States and the Soviet Union had accomplished in the pursuit of détente. "Brezhnev must have decided that his warning to us in May and June fulfilled his obligation to us," Kissinger insisted. "The likelihood also is that the Kremlin believed that its interests were served whatever happened. If the Arabs did well, the credit would go to Soviet arms and Soviet support. If they did poorly, Moscow thought it could emerge, as in 1967, the champion of the Arab cause."[101]

But as he misread the Soviet signal to evacuate its citizens from Egypt and Syria, Kissinger also misread Brezhnev's motivations for "failing" to alert the United States to the pending attack. The Soviets were not engaging in "a mischievous case of collusion" with the Arabs, as he implied to Alexander Haig, Nixon's chief of staff, the following day.[102] Nor was Brezhnev trying to curry favor with the Arabs by keeping Egyptian and Syrian intentions hidden from the United States. Rather, Brezhnev's decision simply reflected the conflicting impulses in his personality. Although he desperately wanted to avoid a superpower confrontation in the Middle East and move forward with détente, in the end his desire to remain the "convinced Communist," willing to take whatever actions necessary to defend Soviet political and military interests, won the day.

Brezhnev wrote to Nixon and Kissinger on October 6 with assurances that the Kremlin had not been alerted to the beginning of military actions in the Middle East.[103] This hardly seemed credible given that thousands of Soviet citizens had been detected evacuating Egypt and Syria. But at that point it no longer mattered. The nightmare scenario that he fought so hard to avoid had befallen him. Just past 2:00 p.m. on October 6, Egyptian and Syrian armies launched coordinated attacks on Israeli forces in the Sinai Peninsula and the Golan Heights. For the fourth time in twenty-five years, the Arabs were at war with Israel.

NINE

The Crisis of Détente,
October 1973

The air raid sirens began to wail while most Israelis were still in syna-
gogue on Saturday, October 6, 1973. It was Yom Kippur, the Day of
Atonement, the holiest day of the Jewish year. As scores of worshipers
emerged from their afternoon services draped in prayer shawls and skull-
caps, they witnessed a flurry of activity all around. Streets were filled with
speeding trucks and military vehicles rushing the thousands of soldiers on
leave for the holiday back to their units. Tourists hurried into nearby bomb
shelters. Shopkeepers quickly boarded up their windows and shut down
their electricity. Radio broadcasts, normally suspended on Yom Kippur,
returned to the airwaves announcing the news of simultaneous Egyptian
and Syrian attacks and putting out the calls of "sea wolf," "meat pie," and
"wool string," military codes summoning reservists to duty. Within minutes
it was clear to all Israelis that the war its nation's intelligence leaders had
only recently dismissed as a "low probability" had begun.[1]

The fighting erupted just past 2:00 p.m., Israel time, when thousands of
Egyptian forces swarmed across the Suez Canal and Syrian tanks and troops
struck in great force on the Golan Heights, but the Israelis had known about
the attack for more than twelve hours. Earlier in the day, Prime Minister
Golda Meir received an alarming report from Zvi Zamir, head of Israel's
intelligence service, the Mossad, indicating a near certainty that Egypt
and Syria would launch a combined attack on Israel that evening. Meir
gathered her "war cabinet" at her office in Tel Aviv to discuss launching a

preemptive strike, as Israel had done in 1967, but decided against it, fearing the political and international dangers that the nation would face by initiating another Arab-Israeli war.[2]

The decision proved costly. Within hours, more than a hundred thousand Egyptian troops and a thousand tanks engulfed Israeli forces on the east bank of the Suez Canal, shattering the fortifications along the Bar-Lev Line that had taken years to construct and scoring a major psychological and symbolic victory.[3] In the north, Syrian forces also made significant advances. United Nations observers reported seeing the Syrian army moving into Israel over the central section of the Golan Heights cease-fire line and nearly breaking through the plains of Galilee. Although the Arabs insisted the Israelis had started the war by attacking naval facilities near Sukhna and Zafarana on Egypt's Red Sea coast, the evidence clearly indicated that the war had been launched by a massive Arab invasion.[4]

Heavy fighting continued throughout the night and well into the following morning with major losses on both sides. The Israelis, still not fully mobilized, concentrated on containing the Egyptian and Syrian thrusts but continued to lose ground in both sectors, as many Israeli tanks broke down in a mad rush to get to the battlefields and dozens of their best planes were lost to Soviet-made surface-to-air missiles.[5] "I did not sufficiently appreciate the enemy's strength, his fighting force and I overestimated our forces and their ability to stand fast," Defense Minister Moshe Dayan admitted during a meeting of the war cabinet on October 7. "The Arabs are fighting much better than before."[6]

After two days of hostilities, the Israelis estimated that an additional five hundred Egyptian tanks had crossed into the Sinai Peninsula, while the Syrians had massed a thousand tanks and six hundred artillery pieces in the Golan. Israeli losses in terms of casualties and equipment were also extremely high. Early reports indicated that the IDF lost thirty-five aircraft in suppressing surface-to-air missile sites in Syria, an unexpectedly large number, while several of its pilots had been captured by Syrian forces.[7] With its vast arsenals Israel still had "sufficient equipment" for a week of fighting, but if the war went on beyond that, defense officials warned the prime minister, there would be problems.[8]

Yet despite the Arabs' early success on the battlefield, Egyptian president Anwar Sadat had no intention of securing a military victory and fully expected that his forces would be overmatched as soon as Israel mobilized its reserves and recovered from the shock of the early hours of the war. During a meeting on October 7 with Vladimir Vinogradov, the Soviet ambassador to Egypt, he acknowledged that while the crossing of the Canal went "much easier" than his military experts had anticipated, his army was not prepared for further attacks across the Suez.[9] Sadat sent a similar message the same day to Secretary of State Kissinger, making it clear that his military objectives were limited: "We do not intend to deepen the engagements or widen the confrontation," he stated unambiguously. "Our basic objectives remain as always, the achievement of peace in the Middle East and not to achieve partial settlements."[10]

If Sadat did not aim for a military victory against Israel, why did he take his country into a war that he knew he would lose? Why would he endanger the lives of thousands of Egyptian soldiers and risk Egypt's standing as leader of the Arab world, not to mention his own political future, if he knew he could not regain Arab territory by military conquest?

Many historians and political scientists have speculated through the years that Sadat's aim had been primarily strategic in that he wanted to retake the Sinai by force, a view strongly supported at the time by the Israelis.[11] Others have argued that domestic political reasons—namely, Egypt's deepening economic troubles, caused by the continued closure of the Suez Canal—prompted Sadat into action. In recent years, however, a consensus has emerged that Sadat's objectives were largely political in that he wanted to give the peace process a "jolt," not embark on large-scale reconquest.[12] Sadat's objectives were certainly political, but even these explanations do not address why he chose to go to war in 1973 when he could have initiated hostilities for strictly political objectives in 1971 or 1972.

Part of the difficulty in ascertaining Sadat's motivations is that he often made contradictory statements as to why he started the war. At the beginning of the conflict, he told one Western European ambassador that his objectives were primarily strategic; he would not agree to a cease-fire until Egypt secured Israel's withdrawal from "all" occupied Arab territory.[13] Yet when Kissinger arrived in Cairo a month later, the Egyptian leader claimed

President Sadat (center) with war minister General Ahmed Ismail (right) and Chief of Staff Saad el-Shazly (left) reviewing the developments of the Sinai battle in the army headquarters in Cairo, October 1973. (AP *Images*)

that he went to war in order "to restore Egypt's self-respect," a task no foreigner could accomplish. "It was impossible for Egypt to bargain from a posture of humiliation," he claimed.[14] Later, in his autobiography, Sadat again asserted that his objectives were largely psychological. Egypt needed the war to shatter "the myth of Israel's long arm, of her superior, even invincible, air force, armory, and soldiers."[15] Of course, there is little reason to doubt that Sadat had multiple reasons for *needing* a war with Israel. Still, all of these factors were present from the day he ascended to the Egyptian presidency and do not adequately address why he waited until late 1973 to launch the war.

Sadat's decision to take his country to war in October 1973 was, in fact, a direct consequence of détente. Only after the United States and the Soviet Union had agreed to set aside their differences in the Middle East for the benefit of détente, demonstrated in the agreements signed at the Moscow summit in May 1972, and Nixon and Kissinger's repeated dismissal of Brezhnev's call for an Arab-Israeli peace agreement during the spring and summer of 1973, did Sadat feel compelled to attack Israel. Thus, in starting the war, Sadat's primary objective was not to defeat Israel militarily, which he knew he could not do, but rather to reignite the stalled political process by creating a crisis of détente—drawing the superpowers into a regional conflict and forcing leaders in Washington and Moscow to forego the "no war, no peace" situation that had been produced in the Middle East as a result of their burgeoning détente.

What Sadat understood, perhaps even better than Soviet and American officials, was that only by threatening US-Soviet relations through a Middle East crisis would leaders in Washington and Moscow move Arab-Israeli negotiations to the forefront of their foreign policy agendas. Even Kissinger later conceded that he had misread Sadat's motivations from the very beginning. "What literally no one understood beforehand was the mind of the man: Sadat aimed not for territorial gain but for a crisis that would alter the attitudes in which the parties were then frozen—and thereby open the way for negotiations. . . . His purpose, in short, was psychological and diplomatic, much more than military."[16]

His instincts proved shrewd. Within days of launching the attack on Israel, the October War became just as much a contest between the United States and the Soviet Union as it did between Arabs and Israelis.

Saving Détente

Sadat's strategy of drawing the superpowers into a confrontation was readily apparent to Henry Kissinger from the moment he learned that Egyptian and Syrian leaders planned to take their countries into a war that, militarily, they could not win. Within minutes of being informed of the pending strike, Kissinger had Soviet ambassador Anatoly Dobrynin on the telephone trying to get matters under control before the shooting began and pleading with him to not let the outbreak of another Arab-Israeli war damage détente.[17] He invited Dobrynin to use the "Hot Line" at the White House, to speed up communication with Moscow, and throughout the day on October 6 he spoke with the ambassador almost hourly to ensure that Washington and

Moscow coordinated their strategies to bring the war to an end. "If you and we could find a way of settling this now," he stressed, "then it would be an overwhelming argument . . . as to what the practical consequences have been of our relationship."[18]

Part of Kissinger's desire to see a quick end to the war stemmed from his belief that the Soviets would not tolerate another Arab humiliation. An overwhelming Israeli victory, which he fully expected in a matter of days, was fraught with consequences. "We had to keep the Soviet Union from emerging as the Arabs' savior, which it could do either by pretending that its bluster stopped the Israeli advance or by involving itself directly in the war," he insisted.[19] There was also a strong possibility that the Kremlin would exploit the crisis by reinserting its forces into the region, reversing the strategic gains that the Nixon administration had made through four years of diplomacy. Kissinger did not relish the thought. As he explained to Huang Chen, the chief of the People's Republic of China's Liaison Office late on October 6, the US strategic objectives for the war were simple: "to prevent the Soviet Union from getting a dominant position in the Middle East . . . [and] to demonstrate that whoever gets help from the Soviet Union cannot achieve his objective, whatever it is." Israel, said Kissinger, was merely "a secondary, emotional problem having to do with domestic politics."[20]

From the outset, therefore, Kissinger sought to draw the Soviets into a joint approach in the United Nations Security Council by offering a resolution calling for an end of the fighting and a return to the cease-fire lines established in 1967. The chances of the Soviets accepting the offer were dim, given that it asked the Arabs to relinquish its early success on the battlefield and left Israel occupying Arab territory. Nevertheless, he put the proposition to Dobrynin, warning that if the Soviet government acted irresponsibly by defending the Arabs, the United States would have no other choice but to "let nature take its course" and wait for the inevitable Israeli victory. "That," Kissinger said ominously, "will affect a lot of our relationships."[21]

The cease-fire proposal was welcome news inside the Kremlin. Proponents of détente, including General Secretary Leonid Brezhnev and Premier Alexi Kosygin, saw the American offer as an "omen" of Soviet-American cooperation during the crisis and an indication of the US desire to maintain détente. Like officials in Washington, Soviet leaders fully expected a "certain and speedy defeat" of the Arabs, and did not want to be forced to intervene to prevent the fall of the Egyptian and Syrian governments.[22] "It should be clear," Brezhnev told his colleagues at a Politburo meeting, "that Soviet involvement on behalf of the Arabs would mean a world war."[23] He instructed his aides to cooperate with the United States in the United Nations and at a bilateral level, and authorized Vinogradov to pressure Sadat into accepting an early cease-fire agreement.[24]

The Soviet plea for an early cease-fire fell on deaf ears, however. Sadat fully understood that his army would be unable to withstand the eventual Israeli counterattack and that militarily it was better to end the war while his forces remained on the east bank of the Suez Canal and had a foothold in the Sinai. Still, he had no intentions of stopping the fighting until Washington and Moscow were more deeply involved in the war. During a brief meeting with Vinogradov at the General Command Headquarters in Cairo, he "strongly rejected" the cease-fire proposal, insisting that "the time is still early to think about this matter" and made it clear that he would encourage President Asad to reject the offer as well.[25]

Without Sadat's agreement to go to the Security Council, there was little the Kremlin could do to end the war. Many Soviet military leaders, still upset with the Egyptian leader for having evicted their forces from Egypt the previous year, felt that Sadat deserved what was coming to him and should let Egypt fall to the Israelis. But Brezhnev knew that the Soviet Union could not just abandon its "Arab brothers" when it had commitments and obligations affixed in several treaties and agreements with Egypt and Syria. Another defeat of the Arabs, who were armed with Soviet weapons, moreover, could be viewed as a challenge to Soviet military might.[26]

Brezhnev, therefore, agreed to resupply the Arabs with an airlift of small arms and ammunition, but from his perspective this was the surest way to prevent a larger crisis with the United States. As Richard Ned Lebow and Janice Gross Stein have argued, the airlift was a "substitute" for the Soviet forces that might otherwise be needed to prevent an Arab defeat. "If Arab armies could hold their positions on the battlefield, they were less likely to require and request Soviet military intervention."[27] Over the next two days, Brezhnev bent over backward to make it clear to Nixon and Kissinger that the Soviets did not want to get involved in the war, even withdrawing the Russian fleet in the Mediterranean from the action. "We firmly proceed from the premise that the current events in the Middle East should not cast a shadow on all the good things which have developed recently in the Soviet-American relations," Brezhnev told Nixon. "We do not allow a thought to the contrary."[28]

Brezhnev's conciliatory gestures were certainly welcomed in Washington. Kissinger, in fact, described the Soviet behavior during the first days of the war as a "major triumph" of détente and could be used as leverage with the Congress for extending to the Soviet Union most favored nation trade status. Indeed, he was so confident that the Israelis would prevail in a matter of days and the war would not damage US-Soviet relations, that on the evening of October 8, Kissinger delivered a major foreign policy address to the Pacem in Terres (Peace on Earth) conference in Washington, at which he extolled the accomplishments of détente and challenged critics of the administration's foreign policy who appeared determined to return to an era of confrontation with Moscow.

"We meet . . . at a time when renewed conflict in the Middle East reminds us that international stability is always precarious and never to be taken for granted," Kissinger declared. What was needed in the midst of such crises, he argued, was not the degeneration of the Cold War into a hot war but instead "global cooperation" and "the confidence to discuss issues without bitter strife, the wisdom to define together the nature of the world, and the vision to chart together a more just future." Nothing, he added, "demonstrates this need more urgently than our relationship with the Soviet Union."[29]

By the time Kissinger left the conference and returned to his home at the end of the third day of the war, he fully expected the tide to turn quickly in Israel's favor, leading to a repeat of the events of 1967. The United Nations would agree to a cease-fire by the end of the week and détente would have passed perhaps its most significant test. But, as he later wrote in his memoirs, "the gods are offended by hubris. They resent the presumption that great events can be taken for granted. Historic changes such as we sought cannot be brought off by virtuoso performances; they must reflect an underlying reality."[30]

The Airlifts: Testing Détente

"I hope I didn't wake you," the Israeli ambassador to the United States, Simcha Dinitz, said to Kissinger over the telephone at 1:45 a.m. on October 9, but "the situation really is placing us [in] a number of difficult situations." Dinitz wanted to know what the United States could do to resupply Israeli arsenals, insisting that the quantity of weapons and ammunition the Israelis received would determine how its forces would respond for the remainder of the war."[31]

Dinitz's call came on instructions from the Israeli leadership, which had been meeting through the night at the prime minister's bureau in Tel Aviv. The Israeli counterattack in the Suez Canal sector, which began on October 8, had been a total failure, as the Egyptian army inflicted heavy losses in both arms and men and forced the Israelis to abandon its efforts to reach the Canal. During a somber meeting of the war cabinet on the morning of October 9, Dayan confessed that the quick victory anticipated by the military had been based on false assumptions and that Israel now had to face the reality of an extended war, which would require additional reinforcements, the return of retired officers to active service, and even the recruitment of Jews from abroad. The chief of staff, Lieutenant General David Elazar, presented an equally grim picture: "We prepare for 5 days of war," he said. "We are not built for a war that lasts months."[32]

The plight of the Israeli army was the subject of Kissinger's meeting with Dinitz when the ambassador arrived at the White House accompanied by his military attaché, General Mordachai Gur, just past 8:00 a.m. in Washington. Israel's losses in just three days of fighting, Dinitz and Gur explained, were much higher than anticipated. A total of forty-nine planes—fourteen Phantoms, twenty-eight Skyhawks, three Mirages, and four Super Mysteres—had been lost in less than seventy-two hours. But that was not the most alarming figure. Dinitz added that the IDF had also lost five hundred tanks, nearly a third of its stock. Many of those losses occurred as they rushed to bring the tanks to the front lines, and many tanks were forced out of commission by moving too fast. Others were lost to artillery fire along the Suez Canal.[33]

The quantity of the Israeli losses stunned the secretary of state. He had been assured by Meir that with the "full activation" of its air force and the

Minister of Defense Moshe Dayan (holding telephone) confers with his generals in the "war room," October 8, 1973. *(Shlomo Arad, Israel Government Press Office)*

mobilization of reserves and equipment Israeli forces would rapidly "turn" the situation in Israel's favor.[34] Dinitz, similarly, had promised Kissinger on the first day of hostilities that the Israelis would have the war over within seventy-two to ninety-six hours.[35]

"I don't understand how it could happen," Kissinger said. "Our strategy was to give you until Wednesday evening, by which time I thought the whole Egyptian army would be wrecked."

"Obviously something went wrong," Dinitz admitted. "It comes down to their ability to cross the Canal with armor, and the success of their anti-aircraft missiles which weakened our air effort."

This was hardly an encouraging answer, given that the Israelis were experts in judging Arab military capabilities. But what was equally alarming was the rate at which the Arabs were being resupplied. According to Dinitz, Iraq had already provided Syria with sixteen MiG-21s and thirty-two Sukhoi-7s, all with pilots, and had moved an armored division into Syria, with more tanks on the way. Egypt, similarly, had received eighteen

MiG-21s from Algeria, hundreds of Strella missiles and French antiaircraft missiles from Libya, and a squadron of Hunter jets and Me-6 helicopters from Iraq. "So that is why the Egyptians are so cocky?" Kissinger quipped.[36]

The major issue for the Israelis, and the reason why Dinitz had requested the meeting, was to secure an agreement from Kissinger to begin a massive resupply of weapons and ammunition. The Israelis wanted the United States to advance future shipments of F-4 Phantom aircraft to replace the dozens that they had lost. Tanks were also in "urgent" need, as were ancillary equipment and intelligence information. Gur informed Kissinger that Israeli El Al commercial aircraft had been mobilized, with its insignia removed, to pick up as much equipment as possible from American arsenals, but Kissinger replied that the Israelis could not get tanks from United States and that aircraft deliveries during the war would also be difficult to procure. "You have to realize that to take planes from combat units will be in every newspaper in the world," the secretary of state warned the Israelis. Kissinger agreed that the El Al planes could pick up consumables and electronic equipment immediately, but the larger items—tanks and planes—would have to be approved by the president.[37]

What the Israelis were asking of the United States was no small request. Resupplying Israel on the size and scale necessary to deliver a victory risked a Soviet military intervention to prevent an Arab humiliation at the hands of American-made weapons. This would certainly lead to détente's collapse. But an airlift would also have considerable regional implications. If the United States turned around a battle that the Arabs were winning, the Arab states would almost certainly respond with an oil embargo against the West, and it could force the moderate regimes of Jordan and Lebanon, which had abstained from participating in the Arab coalition, to join the fighting. The airlift could also have significant consequences for the postwar negotiations, which Kissinger intended to dominate.

To consider these questions, therefore, the secretary of state convened a special "Principals Only" meeting of the Washington Special Actions Group in the Situation Room of the White House immediately following his meeting with Dinitz. "They are desperate and they want help," said Kissinger, after informing the group of his discussion with the Israelis. Kissinger appeared inclined to fulfill the Israeli request, but he met stiff resistance from his colleagues. Secretary of Defense James Schlesinger, in particular, opposed sending arms to Israel in the middle of the war. Although he wanted to see Syria and Egypt "get their knuckles rapped" as much as anyone, the Israelis still possessed a "decisive edge" in aircraft, even with their heavy losses, and he stressed that providing the Israelis with new arms shipments to push back Egyptian forces from the east bank of the Suez Canal was not worth risking "our new stature with the Arabs."[38]

Others in the group sided largely with Schlesinger. According to CIA director William Colby, the military situation on both Syrian and Egyptian fronts was not as dire as the Israelis conveyed to Kissinger. The Israelis, Colby said, were beginning to push back Syrian forces on the northern front, while the Egyptians had made only minor gains in the Sinai and still posed no "immediate threat" to Israel. Deputy Secretary of State Kenneth Rush agreed. For him, the Israeli arms request was clearly a ploy to get the United States to guarantee future military appropriations. "I think they are trying to lock us in," he argued. "Golda wouldn't leave if the situation was desperate. This would be the worst thing for them to do."[39]

Surprisingly absent from the discussion was any concern about an Arab oil boycott should the United States fulfill the Israeli arms requests. After the meeting, William B. Quandt, a member of the NSC staff, warned Kissinger that acting too early or "too visibly" on the resupply would "insure attacks on US citizens [in the Middle East] and an oil embargo in key Arab states."[40] But an oil embargo was clearly not a major concern for the principals. Indeed, when Kissinger later discussed the arms request with Nixon, who was preoccupied with the pending resignation of Vice President Spiro Agnew,[41] the concern focused not on the reaction from the Arab states, or even the Soviet Union for that matter, but rather on domestic politics. "Let's give them some M-60 tanks . . . [and] go ahead on the consumables," Nixon instructed Kissinger. "But the quid pro quo is to tell Golda to call off the Jewish community in this country."[42]

Politics certainly factored into Nixon's decision to proceed with the airlift, given his mounting problems with Agnew's resignation and Watergate. But the decision to proceed with the airlift ultimately came down to a simple decision not to let an American ally be defeated by countries supported militarily by the Soviet Union. "It was unthinkable that Israel should lose the war for lack of weapons while we were spraying paint over Stars of David," he wrote in his memoirs. Nixon wanted the airlift carried out in such a way that would not "gratuitously" offend the Arabs and damage US efforts to lead the diplomatic efforts after the war, and he made it clear that in replacing Israel's aircraft and tank losses, this was not a commitment to maintain US arms shipments to the Jewish state.[43]

Nixon's decision to move ahead with the airlift was all the more dangerous given that the first reports arrived in Washington that the Soviets had a made a similar decision to resupply their Arab clients.[44] After receiving the reports of the Soviet planes on their way to Cairo and Damascus, Kissinger called Dobrynin to voice his displeasure about the maneuver. "We really don't think that is very helpful, because that's going to force us to do at least the same," he said disingenuously, knowing that Nixon had already authorized the US airlift to Israel to begin. But Dobrynin knew when he was being played. "Henry, I know you too well," he said. "When I read about our resupply, I know you're doing it too."[45]

Thus, at a time when Washington and Moscow should have been making decisions that would have brought the war to a quick end, both governments initiated airlifts to their respective clients that only prolonged the war and exacerbated problems for détente. *"You are watching the collapse of U.S. foreign policy,"* Schlesinger said in disgust to Admiral Thomas Moorer, chairman of the Joint Chiefs of Staff, after being instructed to begin the American airlift. Moorer strongly concurred: "It's just disastrous and we are getting painted right into a corner."[46] All the talk about détente and US-Soviet cooperation infuriated Moorer when the two governments could not restrain themselves in a crisis. He later complained to Admiral Elmo "Bud" Zumwalt, chief of naval operations, that Brezhnev "is purring about détente on the one hand and saying 'lets you and us fight' on the other."[47]

Brezhnev was hardly alone in deserving blame, however. In Kissinger's desire to rescue the Israelis, the secretary of state risked a superpower confrontation in the Middle East. The Soviet capabilities to resupply Egypt and Syria far surpassed what the United States could send to Israel, and it made little sense to engage in an arms race with Moscow when it was in both countries' interest stop the war. "We wondered if [Kissinger] is really

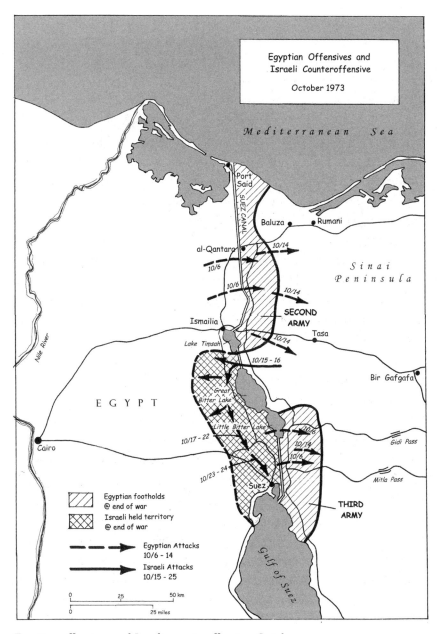

Egyptian offensives and Israeli counteroffensive, October 1973

focusing in on the fact that we are about to lose our ass in the Mideast," Moorer confessed to Zumwalt after getting the news that the airlift was about to commence. "It is at best a disaster and at worst a catastrophe. We can not win this one no matter what."[48]

Kissinger obviously understood these concerns, which is why he asked the British on October 12 to introduce a cease-fire resolution in the Security Council, before developments drove Washington and Moscow toward a confrontation.[49] The British, however, did not want to get involved. Their conversations with the Egyptians had made it clear that Sadat would invoke the Chinese veto if such a resolution were introduced, and they feared the Arab states would retaliate with the oil weapon if they offered the resolution over Sadat's objections.[50] Prime Minister Edward Heath shared Kissinger's concern that détente could possibly collapse if the war continued on its current path, but as he told his senior advisers during a meeting at Chequers on October 13, "if both the superpowers took détente so seriously, it was up to them to get on with it. . . . It would be ridiculous for us all to be exposed to a third World War because they could not control themselves."[51]

Kissinger tried to prevail on the British to reverse their position, insisting to the British ambassador in Washington, Lord Cromer, that Whitehall had misread Sadat's intentions.[52] The Israelis, he argued, had already suffered a "strategic defeat," and it was in Sadat's interest to end the war before the Israelis had the opportunity to deliver a major blow on the Egyptian army. To emphasize his point, he gave the ambassador an intelligence report of instructions issued by Hafez Ismail to Mohammed el-Zayyat, the Egyptian foreign minister, not to oppose a cease-fire resolution if it were introduced in the United Nations Security Council. Dobrynin had also assured him that the Egyptians would accept a resolution proposing an in situ cease-fire.[53] If that was not enough to compel British cooperation, the secretary of state informed Cromer of the US airlift to Israel and warned him that in the absence of a cease-fire, "we were now on a course which would be dictated by military events."[54]

Cromer, however, would not take the bait. While he, too, hoped to avoid a deterioration of the military situation, he found the mention of the resupply of Israel utterly objectionable and even further reason not to back Kissinger's gambit. "Europe would not be content to go without Middle

East oil because of American actions," he told Kissinger. He asked that the resupply be delayed, given that such a move would face his government with a "major crisis" on the oil front, but Kissinger made it clear that a postponement was out of the question. "The Israelis were out of ammunition," he replied. "The Egyptians were at this very moment starting a major offensive in the Sinai . . . and [the United States] could not now take the responsibility of leaving the Israelis to face a major Egyptian onslaught with insufficient arms and ammunition."[55]

Without a British-sponsored cease-fire resolution in the Security Council, and with the Soviet and American airlifts under way, there was little chance of the war ending any time soon. Beginning on October 14, after several days of foot-dragging inside the Pentagon,[56] the Defense Department put on a remarkable display of American power. Although "logistically insane," according to Schlesinger, psychologically and symbolically it was critical to the Israeli war effort for the United States to demonstrate its ability to fly tanks to Israel.[57] The first US Air Force C-5A, carrying four M-60 tanks, arrived at 8:01 p.m. at Lod Airport in Tel Aviv, and was followed by four C5-As and twelve C-141 every twenty-four hours. The total of all aircraft— C5-As, C-130s, and C-141s—was twenty flights a day carrying an average of one thousand tons of equipment daily. Fourteen F-4 Phantoms were sent to Israel to replace lost aircraft, and another eight sat in the Azores waiting for authorization to be sent.[58]

As expected, the Arabs responded to the airlift by initiating a massive oil boycott against the United States. Eleven members of the Organization of the Petroleum Exporting Countries (OPEC) announced an immediate cutback of oil production by 5 percent, to be followed by successive monthly cutbacks of 5 percent until Israel withdrew to the 1967 frontiers and the "legal rights" of the Palestinians were restored. The six Persian Gulf members of OPEC also increased the price of oil by 70 percent, from $3.01 to $5.12 a barrel.[59] But given that the United States did not use much Arab oil, the Nixon administration dismissed the maneuver as "a symbolic gesture of limited practical importance" and continued with the airlift over fierce opposition from the British and Japanese, both largely dependent on Middle East oil.[60] These objections mattered little to Kissinger, however. "If the Soviets see that we can get material in to Israel, which can still fight," he stressed, "they will see that it will be better for them to get the thing wrapped up."[61]

The US airlift greatly altered the course of the war. Emboldened by the show of American power and having the confidence that their arsenals would not be depleted, the Israelis, on October 15, launched a major counterattack in the Sinai. Led by General Ariel Sharon, IDF forces decisively repelled the Egyptian offensive and approached the Suez Canal. On October 16, an Israeli column slipped through a gap between the Egyptian Second and Third Armies and crossed the canal at Deversoir near the northern end of the Bitter Lakes.[62] Meir confirmed the crossing of the waterway in a major address to the Knesset on October 16, insisting that the Arab attack had been "curbed" and that Israeli troops continued to shell Egyptian artillery and air defense units from the west bank of the Suez. On the Syrian front, said the prime minister, "we have overcome the aggressors and pushed them back across the cease-fire lines. The Syrian army has been severely mauled and its forces have crossed over to the other side of the cease-fire line."[63]

With the Arabs on the verge of defeat, Brezhnev quickly dispatched Kosygin to Cairo with a recommendation for Sadat to "consolidate the present situation," a clear indication that the Kremlin wanted the war ended as soon as possible. Much to Kosygin's dismay, Sadat initially insisted that the time for a cease-fire had not yet come; before any cease-fire went into effect, he wanted to establish a solid defense line east of Suez. He dismissed the penetration of Israeli troops to the West Bank of the Suez Canal as an "insignificant event" and a "political maneuver" of the Israelis. But as the Israeli threat to the Egyptian capital become more apparent, Sadat's tone began to change. By his third meeting with Kosygin on October 18, Sadat indicated that he was in favor of signing a "special Soviet-American binding agreement" that would commit Washington and Moscow to guarantee the borders of the warring sides and to carry out any measures aimed at implementing an eventual cease-fire agreement.[64]

Sadat's call for a Soviet-American agreement fell far short of the immediate cease-fire Kosygin had hoped to accomplish while in Cairo, but it offered enough signs of flexibility for Brezhnev to invite Kissinger to Moscow in an "urgent manner" to conduct "appropriate negotiations" regarding a cease-fire agreement.[65] For Kissinger, Brezhnev's invitation came as a blessing in disguise. He began to fear that the overwhelming turnaround in the military situation, fueled by American weapons, had "rattled" the Soviet leadership, which "may be tempted into some rash act of military intervention."[66] Negotiations with Brezhnev would also keep the issue out of the United Nations until he had the opportunity to shape an "acceptable outcome," and would give the Israelis at least another twenty-four to thirty-six hours to consolidate their positions on the battlefield before any cease-fire would take place.[67]

The Cease-Fire: Kissinger in Moscow

By the time that Kissinger and Dobrynin boarded the plane to Moscow at 2:00 a.m. on Saturday, October 20, Nixon's presidency lay in peril. Since the revelation in July 1973 that Nixon had installed a taping system throughout the White House, Executive Office Building, and at Camp David, he had engaged in a fierce legal battle for control of the tapes. After refusing subpoenas from Special Prosecutor Archibald Cox and Senator Sam Ervin, chairman of the Senate Watergate Committee, for copies of the taped conversations, and ignoring a decision by Judge John J. Sirica of the US Court of Appeals to make the tapes available to him for a decision on their use by a grand jury, Nixon, on October 19, worked out a compromise with the Senate Watergate Committee whereby Senator John C. Stennis agreed to review and summarize the tapes for the special prosecutor's office.[68]

With the "Stennis Compromise" in hand, the president ordered Cox to make no further effort to obtain tapes or other presidential documents. Cox quickly dismissed the compromise, insisting that Nixon's instructions violated the promises Attorney General Elliot Richardson made to the Senate during his confirmation hearings, when he assured the judiciary committee that Cox would have a free hand in conducting his investigation into the Watergate scandal. "For me to comply with those instructions," said Cox, "would violate my solemn pledge to the Senate and the country to invoke judicial process to challenge exaggerated claims of executive privilege. I shall not violate my promise."[69]

For Nixon, firing Cox seemed the only way to "rid the administration of the partisan viper we had planted in our bosom."[70] Thus, while Kissinger and Dobrynin were en route to Moscow, the president took the dramatic action of discharging Cox and accepting the resignations of Richardson and Deputy Attorney General William D. Ruckelshaus, both of whom refused to act on the president's orders to remove Cox. Nixon also abolished the Office of the Special Prosecutor and turned over to the Justice Department the entire responsibility for further investigation and prosecution of suspects and defendants in Watergate and related cases.[71]

A fierce reaction erupted in the wake of the "Saturday Night Massacre." Both Republicans and Democrats saw the move as a clear attempt to obstruct Cox's investigation and calls for Nixon's impeachment increased. The *New York Times* and the *Washington Post* ran lengthy editorials calling Nixon's actions a "brutal violation" of the pledges he had made in setting up the office of the special prosecutor.[72] James "Scotty" Reston, arguably the dean of the Washington press corps, described Nixon's actions as "devious and contemptuous of the courts, the Congress and the rights of others."[73] Even William Safire, Nixon's former speech writer, knew that Cox's removal opened up a Pandora's box: "The Department of Justice, an arm of the President, cannot properly investigate the President. Now is the time for the establishment of a joint House-Senate investigating committee, enabling Congress to raise the rumpus it is entitled to raise as a result of the Richardson confirmation double-cross."[74]

Had Nixon fully understood the political turmoil that would face him over the following ten months, he should have resigned then. Instead, he used the cover of the Middle East war to demonstrate that his ability to govern was unaffected by Watergate. On the evening of October 20, Nixon fired off two cables that would have important consequences for Kissinger's discussions in Moscow. The first message, sent directly to Brezhnev, informed the Soviet leader that Kissinger spoke with the president's "full authority" and that any commitment the secretary made during the course of their discussions had Nixon's "complete support."[75] On its surface, this seemed to be an innocent message. Kissinger later acknowledged that under most circumstances he would welcome such a commitment from the president.[76] But in this instance, the president had undercut the secretary of state's ability to stall during the negotiations by referring back to Washington for further instructions before he made any deal with the Soviet leader and left Brezhnev the impression that Washington and Moscow would unwillingly impose a settlement on Israel and its Arab neighbors.

The second telegram, sent to Kissinger, added pressure on the secretary of state to do more in Moscow than simply achieve a cease-fire agreement. Indeed, in a remarkable bout of clarity as events rapidly unfolded in Washington, Nixon argued that the end of the war presented the administration with its best opportunity to build a "lasting peace" between Arabs and Israelis. "Our greatest foreign policy weakness over the past four and a half years has been our failure to deal decisively with the Middle East crisis," the president argued. A number of factors had contributed to this failure, Nixon maintained, including the "intransigence" of the Israelis, the "unwillingness" of the Arabs to engage in discussions on a realistic basis, and the American preoccupation with Vietnam. All this had to change in his second term. "I now consider a permanent Middle East peace settlement to be the most important goal to which we must devote ourselves," the president declared. "I am convinced that history will hold us responsible if we let this opportunity slip by."[77]

For Kissinger, however, this was the wrong message to send to Brezhnev. His purpose in Moscow was to advance détente through a quick cease-fire agreement, before the war spun further out of control and drove Washington and Moscow closer to a confrontation, not to surprise the Soviets with gimmicks by attempting to impose a comprehensive peace in the Middle East. After digesting the contents of Nixon's telegrams, he sent a blistering cable back to his deputy, Brent Scowcroft, arguing that Nixon's letter to Brezhnev reflected "poor judgment" and made his position in Moscow "almost insoluble." He also told Scowcroft that he found the "tone and substance" of the president's instructions to him totally "unacceptable" and that he would continue with his agenda of pushing détente through a cease-fire agreement, "which I believe to be the appropriate course."[78]

Kissinger, of course, had grossly overreacted to Nixon's message, for neither telegram made his position in Moscow "insoluble." To the contrary, by the time he arrived at the Kremlin for his first meeting with Brezhnev

Secretary of State Kissinger is greeted by General Secretary Brezhnev inside the Kremlin on October 20, 1973. *(ITAR-TASS)*

late on October 20, the Israelis had left him with the upper hand in the negotiations by encircling the Egyptian Third Army and advancing its forces to the outskirts of Cairo. Brezhnev, in fact, admitted to Kissinger that the conflict had reached a "very acute" stage and stressed that their discussions should not be affected by the "tactical military situation," a clear reflection of his apprehension of the Israeli advances.[79]

Instead, the general secretary wanted to focus on improving the "special relationship" between the Soviet leaders and Nixon. Kissinger agreed. "There are many forces in the U.S. right now that are attempting to exploit the current crisis to destroy . . . [the] rapprochement between the United States and the Soviet Union," he said. "Therefore if we should succeed in this trip to develop a joint agreement that would bring an end to the war on reasonable terms it would be the best counterargument to these people who have claimed that we can no longer cooperate."[80]

The meeting with Brezhnev lasted until 11:30 p.m., with the agreement to resume negotiations on the details of a cease-fire the following day. When Kissinger returned to his guesthouse that evening, he had a message from the Egyptians pleading for a cease-fire "on the present lines" and indicating support for convening a peace conference with the object of reaching a fundamental settlement leading to the withdrawal of Israeli troops from Arab territory.[81] A similar appeal from Sadat reached the Kremlin around 4:00 a.m. in Moscow.[82] Although this was largely dictated by military events, it is no surprise that Sadat waited until Kissinger was in Moscow to finally "demand" an end to the war. By then, he had accomplished his political objectives of creating a crisis of détente and moving the Arab-Israeli dialogue to the forefront of the Soviet and American foreign policy agendas.

With the blessing of the Politburo to reach a quick cease-fire agreement, Brezhnev wasted little time getting down to details when his talks resumed with Kissinger at noon. In a matter of hours, the two rather easily hashed out a draft of a cease-fire resolution they would jointly submit to the UN Security Council at 9:00 p.m. in New York. The resolution called for: (1) a cease-fire "in place" to be carried out within twelve hours of the adopting of the Security Council Resolution; (2) a call for Security Council Resolution 242 to be implemented "in all its parts"; and (3) a provision for direct negotiations between the parties to start under "appropriate auspices." Brezhnev and Kissinger also reached a private understanding that "appropriate auspices" meant joint US-USSR leadership, and both countries would also push for an immediate exchange of all prisoners of war.[83]

As soon as the meeting ended, a jubilant Kissinger cabled Nixon with the details of the proposed agreement, leaving little doubt which side he believed emerged victorious from the negotiations. "This is a major accomplishment for the policy you initiated a week ago," he explained. "The settlement makes clear beyond any question that the U.S. is the dominant influence in the area without which nothing can be accomplished." For the Israelis, moreover, the agreement could only be interpreted as a "major victory," for the cease-fire left Israeli forces in both Syrian and Egyptian territory. Most important, he concluded, "We have faced down the Soviets for all the world to see."[84] The Security Council adopted Resolution 338 by a vote of fourteen to zero, with China abstaining.[85]

Without a doubt, Resolution 338 was one of Kissinger's crowning achievements as secretary of state. Although it contained only three operative paragraphs, the resolution not only ended the October War but offered both Arabs and Israelis a share of the "victory." By including a provision calling for the "full implementation" of Security Council Resolution 242, the Arabs could claim that Israel had to return to the 1967 boundaries, which gave them a "level of respectability" that was sorely lacking before the war, and it demonstrated that Israel would now have to depend on a combination of security and diplomacy to achieve its security.[86] For the Israelis, moreover, the cease-fire agreement left it with more territory than it possessed at the beginning of the war, increasing its leverage in future negotiations, and solved one of the problems that had plagued the Middle East for years—the Arabs' refusal to negotiate directly with the Israelis.

Most important, though, the cease-fire agreement preserved détente between the United States and the Soviet Union. "What we've done in the last two days is important not only to the Middle East but to US–Soviet relations and our whole foreign policy," Kissinger said to Foreign Minister Andrei Gromyko before departing for Tel Aviv on October 22.[87] Kissinger's jubilation, though, was premature. For although the crisis appeared to have ended, he would soon find out that its peak had yet to pass.

A "Tense" Visit in Israel

"Madame Prime Minister, we believe that this is a major achievement for you and for us and supportive of the brave fighting of your forces," Nixon wrote to Meir of the cease-fire agreement in advance of Kissinger's arrival in Tel Aviv on October 22. "It would leave your forces right where they are: There is absolutely no mention whatsoever of the word 'withdrawal' in the resolution." The president apologized for failing to discuss the details of the agreement with her, "but with the bloodshed continuing, with Israel in such a favorable position on the ground, with the risks increasing by the hour as substantial supplies are being poured in by both major powers, we felt it was imperative that an understanding be reached promptly."[88]

Meir refused to accept Nixon's assurances, however. She was furious with Kissinger for having agreed to a cease-fire without any prior consultation with her government and for not allowing Israel a few more days of fighting to destroy the Third Army and inflict a resounding and humiliating defeat on the Egyptians. "It was not a triumphal moment for small states," her foreign minister, Abba Eban, later wrote of having to swallow the Soviet-American agreement.[89] For Meir, the process was all too reminiscent of the events of 1957 when, under pressure from Eisenhower and Khrushchev, Israel was forced to withdraw its army from the Sinai Peninsula without receiving assurances from the Arab states that they would make peace in return.

As soon as Kissinger arrived at the Mossad "Guest House" in Herzliya, a short drive north from her office in Tel Aviv, Meir wasted little time getting to the heart of her concern: "Was there a secret US-Soviet deal to impose the 1967 borders?" she demanded to know. Kissinger denied the accusation forcefully, even offering to show Dinitz the verbatim protocols of the meeting as soon as he returned to Washington. But this did not appease Meir. She asked if there was a deal to explore "any other frontiers" and probed "all possible explorations of American duplicity" to ensure that this was not a repeat of 1957. "Israel's insecurity was so pervasive that even words were daggers," Kissinger recalled of his visit with the prime minister. "Golda knew very well that not even the attainment of its stated goals could compensate for the altered psychological balance."[90]

Kissinger spent much of the remainder of his time with the prime minister explaining why the agreement called for acceptance of Security Council Resolution 242, which Meir had made clear she would not fulfill. "To refuse reference to 242 would have been absolutely impossible in those conditions," he insisted. But even including the reference meant very little, he assured Meir. The ambiguous wording of 242 was such a "joke" in Kissinger's mind that this was something the Israelis should not fret over. "The phrases mean nothing," he said. "What it means is what is to be negotiated."

To allay concerns that the military would not have the opportunity to consolidate its positions on the battlefield, Kissinger assured the prime minister that the United States would understand if the Israelis felt they required additional time for military dispositions before the cease-fire took effect.[91]

"You won't get violent protests from Washington if something happens during the night, while I'm flying," he assured Meir. "Nothing can happen in Washington until noon tomorrow."[92] When he met with Israel's military leaders immediately following his meeting with Meir, he again reiterated that pledge. "That is in your domestic jurisdiction," he said in response to Dayan's complaint that he did not want to stop the Israeli advance. "I will be on an airplane."[93]

Kissinger's invitation to the Israelis to ignore the cease-fire resolution only fueled flame to the fire. As he flew back to Washington, Israeli forces advanced their positions on the west bank of the Suez Canal, cutting off the roads to Port Said and Suez and inching closer to Ismailia. Sadat complained bitterly to Vinogradov on October 23 that as a cosponsor of the cease-fire resolution the Soviets were obliged to take "all necessary steps" to see that Israel returned to the lines in effect when the parties agreed to the cease-fire,[94] but the Kremlin issued only a minor rebuke.

"This is absolutely unacceptable," Brezhnev wrote in a cable to Kissinger. "This looks like a flagrant deceit on the part of the Israelis." He suggested bringing the matter back to the Security Council to reaffirm the cease-fire decision and calling for a new resolution demanding that all forces be withdrawn to their positions at the moment the October 22 cease-fire resolution had passed.[95]

When the Israelis continued to advance their positions over Soviet and United Nations objections, however, Brezhnev appealed directly to Nixon, speaking of Israeli "treachery" and insisting that Soviet officials were "shocked" that the understanding reached in Moscow had been "ruptured" by the Israeli leadership. A similar appeal to Nixon came from Sadat pleading for "immediate" and "direct" American intervention, "even if that necessitates the use of forces," in order to guarantee the full implementation of the cease-fire resolution.[96] The Israelis denied responsibility for the cease-fire violations,[97] but the latest American intelligence reports confirmed that the Israeli action "reflected an effort definitely to isolate the Egyptians' southern salient."[98]

By the afternoon of October 23, Kissinger realized that he had erred in giving the Israelis the green light to advance their positions in violation of the Security Council resolution while he returned to Washington. The

Soviets, he knew, had been backed into a corner for refusing to enforce the cease-fire resolution they had helped steer through the United Nations. At Brezhnev's behest, Kissinger agreed to return to the United Nations that evening to secure another cease-fire resolution. The Security Council promptly adopted Resolution 339, reaffirming the principles in Resolution 338 and demanding a return to the cease-fire lines of October 22.[99]

When word reached Kissinger the following morning that the Israelis still refused to adhere to either of the Security Council resolutions, Kissinger called Dinitz in rage. "Look, Mr. Ambassador, we have been a strong support for you. But we cannot make Brezhnev look like a Goddamn fool in front of his own colleagues."[100] He demanded a cessation of all military activity and that Israeli forces remain in "defensive positions," and warned that if the fighting continued, the Kremlin would have no choice but to send in forces to uphold the cease-fire resolution and prevent the destruction of the Egyptian Third Army. "You know, there's a limit beyond which we can't go and one of them is we cannot make Brezhnev look like an idiot."[101]

The problem for Kissinger was that his warning came too late. Brezhnev had been compelled to action.

The Alert

The second UN Security Council cease-fire resolution had been in effect for less than thirty-six hours when, at 10:30 p.m. on the night of October 24, Admiral Thomas Moorer, chairman of the Joint Chiefs of Staff, received a telephone call from Lawrence Eagleburger, Kissinger's executive assistant, requesting his immediate presence at the White House Situation Room. Defense secretary Schlesinger and CIA director William Colby had also been summoned, as had Haig, Scowcroft, and Commander Jonathan T. Howe, Kissinger's military assistant on the National Security Council staff.[102]

Kissinger called the meeting in response to a letter Nixon just received from Brezhnev accusing Israel of "drastically" ignoring the Security Council's cease-fire agreement and "brazenly challenging" both the Soviet Union and the United States since it was their agreement in Moscow that constituted the basis for the Security Council resolution. To prevent further violations of the cease-fire and to demonstrate "to all those who are in favor of détente" the necessity of bringing the war to an immediate end, the general secretary proposed the establishment in Egypt of a joint Soviet-American military force to enforce the cease-fire resolution. But Brezhnev warned Nixon that his government would not stand idle in the face of continued Israeli aggression: "I'll say it straight. If you find it impossible to act jointly with us in this matter we should be faced with the necessity urgently to consider the question of taking appropriate steps unilaterally. We cannot allow arbitrariness on the part of Israel."[103]

Brezhnev's threat to intervene unilaterally in the conflict was a brilliant diplomatic ploy that caught Washington completely off guard. By offering to send to Egypt a small contingent of five to six thousand men, less than half of what they had in Egypt in 1972, Moscow could take credit for stopping the Israelis and regain much of the prestige that they had lost in the Arab world in recent years. Moreover, given the weak state that Nixon found himself in as a result of Watergate, it was fair for Kremlin leaders to reason that he would not counter the Soviet move by sending American troops to the Middle East and risk a confrontation with the Soviet Union.

The Nixon administration, however, was unwilling to take chances. Kissinger, in fact, called Brezhnev's threat of unilateral intervention in the region "one of the most serious challenges to an American President by a Soviet leader," which needed to be rejected in a manner that "shocked" the Soviets into abandoning any military action. If the United States agreed to a joint role with the Kremlin, Soviet troops would reenter Egypt with Washington's blessing and most likely would never leave. "Either we would be the tail to the Soviet kite in a joint power play against Israel, or we would end up clashing with Soviet forces in a country that was bound to share Soviet objectives regarding the cease-fire or could not afford to be perceived as opposing them," he later wrote.[104] He warned Dobrynin against the unilateral move, but the ambassador gave him no indication that the Soviets intended to back down in the face of Israel's continued aggression.[105]

Perhaps the more important consideration, however, was how the US response to Brezhnev's warning would affect the president's credibility in the face of his domestic problems. Accepting the Soviet offer of a joint force would clearly be seen by the Kremlin and its allies as a "passive" response in the face of an unambiguous threat and a clear signal to Moscow that Nixon had been so weakened by Watergate that the United States had to capitulate to Soviet demands. "They find a cripple facing impeachment and why shouldn't they go in there," Kissinger told Alexander Haig thirty minutes after receiving Brezhnev's letter. "I don't think the Soviets would have taken on a functioning President." Haig agreed: "I think we owe a lot to that."[106]

The decision of how to respond to Brezhnev's letter thus required a meeting of the government's most senior officials. The meeting began at 10:40 p.m. and took place in the White House Situation Room, with Kissinger as its chair. Kissinger originally wanted the meeting to convene at the State Department, but Haig prevailed on him to move it to the Situation Room to demonstrate White House control in the midst of the Watergate-related turmoil. Nixon did not attend the meeting, given that both Haig and Kissinger believed the president was "too distraught" from Watergate to participate in the discussion. But Nixon rarely attended WSAG deliberations, and no one present at the meeting felt it unusual that he did not show.[107]

Kissinger began the deliberations "quite upset," according to Moorer, as he passed around the exchanges that had occurred between Nixon and Brezhnev during the previous seventy-two hours. He explained that earlier in the day he had discussed with Dobrynin the "modalities" of the forthcoming negotiations, at which point everything seemed to be on track. The big question then became, "*Why did the Soviets suddenly reverse themselves and without any warning all day then 'bang' we receive the Brezhnev threat?*"[108]

Kissinger then offered three possibilities why the Soviet Union had made the dramatic move. First, he speculated that the Kremlin may have had this strategy in mind all along, beginning with the time when the Egyptian Third Army collapsed around October 13, and went through the "charade" of inviting him to Moscow with the intention of "seizing on any opportunity offered by the Israelis in violation of the ceasefire." Second, the Kremlin could have reached the conclusion that its prestige in the Arab world would take a major hit as its client had lost another war while the American client emerged victorious and had no choice but to intervene militarily. Third, Kissinger postulated, the Soviets felt they had been "tricked" by the Israelis who were guilty of "gross violations" of the cease-fire agreement and had no choice but to respond forcefully in support of their clients. Kissinger discounted the first possibility but felt a combination of the latter two would be a reasonable.

Admiral Moorer, who had numerous disagreements with Kissinger throughout the October War, was not so sure the first possibility could be dismissed. The continuous alert that Moscow had placed on their seven airborne divisions, along with the abrupt stand-down of the airlift, which could be reoriented to lift Soviet troops to Cairo, and the heavy sealift, which possibly could have been delivering weapons to be used in Egypt by the airborne forces when they arrived in that area, all indicated that this could have been part of a premeditated action on the part of the Soviets to reinsert their forces into the Middle East. But Moorer cautioned his colleagues about the dangers of rushing in to military action. *"The Soviets were correct in saying that the Israelis had violated the ceasefire,"* he emphasized, and the United States was not in a strong position to intervene militarily should the Soviets send forces to the region. Without support from its NATO allies, the United States had access to only one airfield—Lajes in the Azores—between the United States and Israel, making any direct confrontation on the ground with the Soviets very difficult. "In short," Moorer warned, *"the Middle East is the worse place in the world for the US to get engaged in a war with the Soviets."*[109]

Over the next two hours, the group debated the fundamental question: *"If the Soviets put in 10,000 troops into Egypt what do we do?"* A consensus emerged that the Soviets would begin an airlift at dawn and the United States would have to respond. Haig questioned whether this was a "rational plan" or "a move of desperation" as the Soviets watched their influence in the Middle East go down the drain as their Arab clients were once again on the verge of massive defeat. But, he argued, Moscow realized that it was losing ground in the region and wanted to "capitalize" on Nixon's Watergate problem, which "has served to weaken the President."[110]

Schlesinger and Colby strongly concurred with Haig. Both argued that the Soviets were using the crisis to put pressure on the United States or at least to "develop an excuse" to move in their own troops in the Middle East. Colby noted that the Soviets could recoup with the Arabs if they placed a major force in Cairo, which could be used essentially to establish a bridgehead. The Soviets, Schlesinger maintained, could now move into Egypt a relatively small force of five thousand men, take credit for stopping the Israelis, and regain their status in the Arab world. If the Soviets move, said Schlesinger, the United States should consider telling the Israelis to hit the Third Egyptian Army. When Kissinger asked: "What does 5,000 men in Cairo really mean?" Colby replied quickly: "It means the Soviets want a challenge and that, if they get in, they'll never get out."[111]

The thought of the superpowers sending forces to the Middle East left Kissinger "quite upset" about the future prospects of détente. If the Soviets wanted a cease-fire, they could have gotten an agreement that forced the Israelis back to the October 22 line without sending Soviet forces. He postulated that in the "thin margin" of the Politburo the hawks had prevailed over Brezhnev, forcing him to change course by sending his threatening letter to Nixon. Kissinger stressed that while he never "forced" détente, and he wanted to see US-Soviet relations emerge unscathed from this crisis, he could conclude only that the Soviet's overall strategy appeared to be one of "throwing détente on the table since we have no functional President." But Kissinger knew the serious consequences of what calling the Soviet bluff would entail: "If we do put Marines or troops into the Middle East it will amount to scrapping Détente and cutting off all relations with the Soviet Union. What did we do wrong?"[112]

After an hour of intense and often heated discussion, the group made a number of decisions, without the president, intended to show the Kremlin that Washington could still make responsible decisions concerning the use of force. The most important decision concerned placing American military forces on DEFCON III alert, the highest state of readiness for essentially peacetime conditions.[113] In case moving to the alert was not picked up quickly enough by decision-makers in Moscow, the WSAG also approved a number of more visible decisions that the Kremlin could not miss. At 12:20 p.m., Moorer alerted the 82nd Airborne Division for possible movement; at 12:25 p.m. orders were sent to the aircraft carrier *Franklin Delano Roosevelt* to move from the vicinity of Sicily to join the *USS Independence* south of Crete; the carrier *John F. Kennedy* and its task force were ordered to move from West Gibraltar to the Mediterranean; the Amphibious Ready Force was sent from Souda Bay; and seventy-five B-52s were recalled from Guam.[114]

Placing US forces on a worldwide alert and redeploying US aircraft carriers in the Mediterranean were likely to anger its European allies, but this hardly factored in the Americans' decision. Kissinger left the meeting around 1:00 a.m. to inform the British ambassador that the United States had moved to a "low level" military alert in response to Brezhnev's letter and would formally brief the North Atlantic Council in Brussels the following morning.[115] The British were naturally upset that they were not consulted before the decision, feeling that the United States had an obligation of prior notification given their shared military facilities in the United Kingdom and the normal close consultations between their two governments,[116] but they agreed that Brezhnev's warning's had to be taken seriously.

"Please tell Kissinger . . . I have long believed that the Russians could not accept another Arab humiliation," Foreign Secretary Sir Alec Douglas-Home wrote in a telegram back to Cromer in the early hours of October 25. "If Brezhnev really believes that this is imminent as a result of the Israeli bottling up the Egyptian forces at the Southern end of the Suez Canal, he may well feel obliged to intervene unilaterally to save the Egyptians as well as his own prestige and that of the Soviet Union."[117]

Still, both the foreign secretary and the prime minister maintained that the Americans did not have enough evidence of "aggressive Soviet intention," threatened or real, to justify moving to a worldwide nuclear alert.[118] "If the Soviets were in fact going to ferry a force into Egypt in order to attempt to persuade the Israelis to allow the Egyptian army to withdraw peacefully through some agreed corridor, or alternatively to force back the Israelis' armour so as to free the Egyptian beleaguered troops," Heath told his aides, "I do not see why such a nuclear alert should have deterred them." In his estimate, the United States "could not have used their missiles on an area in which the Israelis were so mixed up with the Egyptians, and surely not even the Russians could believe that the Americans would unleash the whole of their nuclear armoury for such a case."[119]

Instead of moving to a military alert, the British preferred a quick increase in the number United Nations truce observers and the beginning of negotiations envisioned in paragraph three of Resolution 338.[120] But the United States would not reverse its decision due to objections from the British or any of its NATO allies. "There was no middle position between alert and no alert," Kissinger insisted. "At issue were only readiness measures, not actions. In our perception . . . it was a clear emergency, and it fell to us to act as custodians of Western security."[121]

As it turned out, the alert had its desired effects. After receiving reports of the US military alert around 7:30 a.m. in Moscow, the Politburo met for more than four hours to discuss the "irresponsible" reaction from Washington. "All participants in the meeting understood that the conflict was heading toward a confrontation between the Soviet Union and the United States," said Victory Israelyan, a member of the Kremlin's Middle East task force, who attended the Politburo session. Brezhnev seemed particularly surprised that the alert could have been in response to his letter, which he believed stressed "joint" Soviet-American action in accordance with the understanding reached during Kissinger's visit to Moscow, while most of the other Politburo members expressed "indignation" that the Americans had prepared their troops for military action.[122]

Yet not one member of the Politburo believed that the Soviet Union should let the crisis escalate into a war with the United States. At one point, Defense Minister Grechko argued for placing Soviet forces on an increased level of readiness as a natural response to the American alert. But Grechko found little support for such action, and most members preferred political measures as the appropriate response. "Where is the brink, the line between peace, and a new nuclear war?" Foreign Minister Gromyko asked. "We have to act in accordance with the agreements with the Americans." Kosygin agreed: "It is not reasonable to become engaged in a war with the United States because of Egypt and Syria."[123]

Heeding the advice of the Politburo, and hoping to dampen down the crisis before it escalated further out of control, Brezhnev, on October 25, sent Nixon another letter, this time omitting any reference to his previous threat of unilateral intervention, nor did he even hint that the Soviets wanted to see forces from either side introduced into the region. Instead, the Soviet leader informed the president that he had dispatched to Egypt seventy Soviet "observers" with instructions to work in a "business-like operation" with a group of US representatives as soon as they arrived in Egypt. He also indicated Moscow's willingness to cooperate with the American side in taking other measures to ensure immediate implementation of Security Council Resolutions 338 and 339 and concluded the letter with the salutation "respectfully," a major change in tone from his previous letter.[124]

In Kissinger's view, Brezhnev's concession to back away from his earlier threat of unilateral intervention could only be seen as a major victory for the United States. Twenty minutes after receiving the general secretary's message from Dobrynin, he gleefully called Nixon with the news.

"Mr. President, you have won again," he said. "The Soviets have joined our resolution at the U.N. barring permanent members [from sending forces to the Middle East] after screaming like banshees."[125] To the president's chief of staff, he was equally emphatic. "We would have had a Soviet paratroop division in there this morning," he told Haig. "You know it, and I know it," Haig replied.[126]

In reality, though, the United States was no more "victorious" than the Kremlin. Rather, cooler heads simply prevailed. As the account of the Politburo meeting makes clear, the Soviet Union had no intention of sending forces to the Middle East. Nor did the United States, despite moving to DEFCON III, want to send troops to the region, deplete its reserves, and sink détente. Kissinger, in fact, sent several messages to the Israelis during the crisis indicating that although the United States would go to the brink, "it was not prepared to go over it." He pressed Meir to halt Israel's military advances and stated clearly that the United States could not allow the Egyptian army to be starved out by military action several days after a cease-fire had been agreed to by the United States and the Soviet Union. If this was Israel's policy, he said, the United States would have to "disassociate itself from it."[127]

By the end of the day on October 25, the crisis abated. The United Nations Security Council, in a unanimous vote, approved Resolution 340, which called for an immediate and complete cease-fire and for the parties to return to the positions occupied on October 22, 1973. The secretary-general also agreed to increase the number of UN military observers on both sides of the cease-fire lines and decided to use his authority to establish a United Nations Emergency Force.[128] During the day, Sadat also sent a back-channel message to Kissinger indicating his willingness to accept an international force as long as it was backed by the "full support" of the

Prime Minister Meir and Defense Minister Moshe Dayan (center) meeting with troops on the Golan Heights during the cease-fire. *(Ron Frenkel, Israel Government Press Office)*

United States and the Soviet Union. "We expect the force to be immediately dispatched to the area to assume its function before any delay results in incalculable and far-reaching consequences."[129]

The Israelis, understanding that they had pushed too far and were losing international support, agreed to the cease-fire at 4:00 a.m. on October 26, after a testy all-night cabinet meeting. Many on the Israeli right, led by Menachem Begin, criticized the decision to support the cease-fire rather than deliver the final blow to the Egyptian army, but the truth was that Israel had little hope for further military gains. "It would have been madly suicidal for us to pursue a subsidiary and sterile aim such as the capture of the Egyptian Third Army at the risk of Soviet intervention, American diplomatic hostility, and a huge Israeli casualty list," Foreign Minister Abba Eban later wrote. Sporadic fighting did erupt on October 26, as the Egyptians tried to break free from the surrounding Israeli forces, but persistent prodding from Kissinger, and an Israeli leadership reluctant to cause any further division in its relationship with the United States, kept its forces in the Sinai from retaliating.[130]

Even had the Israelis opted to continue the fighting, it would have done nothing to change the results of the conflict. By any military calculation, Israel had already won the war: its forces were deep into Egyptian territory, near the city of Suez; the Egyptian Third Army remained encircled and dependent on the United States for food, water, and eventual extrication; Israel's position on the Golan Heights had been fully restored and the Syrian army largely destroyed; and Israeli forces were twenty-five miles outside of Damascus. By comparison, no Israeli city was under threat by any Arab army, and with the American resupply of weapons and ammunitions continuing, the Israeli army remained vastly superior to the Arab forces.

But "victory" had different meanings. Egypt and Syria lost the war, but they were not humiliated, as they were in 1967. Through their battlefield success during the first week of conflict and by forcing the Israelis to rely on an American airlift to secure its victory, the Arabs had destroyed the myth of Israeli invincibility. According to Sadat, Egypt's "admirable" performance during the war "recovered all it had lost in the 1956 War and the 1967 defeat," and "restored self-confidence of our armed forces, our people, and our Arab nation."[131] Sadat could also claim victory in that, for him, the war was fought for largely political objectives. Viewed in this light, Egypt achieved most of its goals, not only by impelling US and Soviet diplomatic activity but also by moving the Israelis off their intransigent position of refusing to discuss the withdrawal of its forces from the occupied territories.

The change in the Israeli perception of the conflict was readily apparent during Meir's conversations in Washington with Nixon and Kissinger a week after the war. Gone from Meir was the cockiness of her previous meetings with the president, Secretary of State Rogers, and Kissinger. No longer did she insist that Israel would be unwilling to withdraw from Arab territory, nor did she speak of the "trauma of 1957" and complain about Arab leadership. "The war had devastated her," said Kissinger, after several meetings with the prime minister on November 1. Meir pressed hard for the release of all Israeli prisoners of war, and she made it clear that without the return of the POWs, Israel would be forced to break the cease-fire. But she also stressed the need for Israel never to face the "horror" it endured during the previous weeks.[132]

"Why the Arabs did it, I don't know," she told the president. "What they will have to do now is what we have wanted them to do right along—to sit down with us and to work out a peace agreement. . . . But this must be the last war."[133]

Conclusion: And the Meaning for Détente?

By the time the crisis was over, newspapers and periodicals were filled with commentary extolling how the successful mediation of the conflict by Washington and Moscow demonstrated the virtues of détente. "It is entirely wrong, we believe, to say that the very flowering of the crisis demonstrated how illusory or unworkable [was] détente," the *Washington Post* editorialized on October 26. "What is important now is to note, with sober thankfulness, that the relationship created by Mr. Nixon and Mr. Brezhnev in recent years served both of them well in their contest this week."[134]

Kissinger, too, found that in the October War détente had passed a significant test. It was hardly the point that détente had not prevented the crisis from erupting in the first place. After all, he argued, détente defined "not friendship but a strategy for a relationship between adversaries."[135] During his press conference on October 25 to explain the decision to place US forces on a worldwide alert, Kissinger made a strong case that while the United States and the Soviet Union remained ideological and political adversaries, both countries' nuclear arsenals meant that they had a "very special responsibility" to solve crises in a spirit of cooperation. "We—both of us—have a special duty to see to it that confrontations are kept within bounds that do not threaten civilized life," he stressed. "Both of us, sooner or later, will have to come to realize that the issues that divide the world today, and foreseeable issues, do not justify the unparalleled catastrophe that a nuclear war would represent."[136]

Critics of détente, especially in Congress, who believed that American officials were being "gulled" by the Soviets, simply missed the point, Kissinger maintained. Even though the administration had used détente to help end the war, US efforts to reduce Soviet influence in the Middle East were in fact making progress under the cover of détente. "An end to détente would have triggered the Soviets into political assault on us in the Middle

East that would, at a minimum, have greatly complicated our strategy," said Kissinger. "Détente was not a favor we did the Soviets. It was partly necessity; partly a tranquilizer for Moscow as we sought to draw the Middle East into closer relations with us at the Soviet's expense."[137]

Brezhnev also weighed in on the war's impact on Soviet-American relations. In a major speech delivered to the World Peace Congress in Moscow at the end of October, the general secretary insisted that the United States had acted irresponsibly by circulating "fantastic rumors" of Soviet plans for unilateral military intervention and had let Moscow down by allowing Israel to flaunt the terms of the cease-fire resolution on more than one occasion. But, he argued, the joint efforts by the United States and the Soviet Union to bring the war to an end showed that détente was irreversible. As a signal to the United States that the Soviets would not allow the recent military alert to threaten détente, Brezhnev indicated that his government would welcome Nixon to Moscow in 1974 and would take practical steps toward an East-West reduction of troops in Europe as early as 1975.[138]

Yet the war also demonstrated the limits of détente. Both superpowers could have brought the war to a quick end by calling for an immediate cease-fire in the UN Security Council. Instead, they chose to begin a massive airlift in weapons to their respective clients, prolonging the war and exacerbating tensions in Soviet-American relations. The following week, when the Soviets proposed sending a joint Soviet-American force to the region to end the conflict and threatened to dispatch Soviet troops unilaterally if Israel did not adhere to the Security Council's cease-fire resolution, Nixon and Kissinger chose to assume the worst in Brezhnev's motivations and placed US forces on military alert. "After all we have heard about the 'Hot Line' between the White House and the Kremlin, the trustful personal relationship between Secretary Kissinger and Ambassador Dobrynin of the Soviet Union, and the new 'partnership for peace' between the U.S. and the U.S.S.R.," Scotty Reston wrote in the New York Times the day after the crisis abated, "are we to believe that the only way Mr. Nixon can send Mr. Brezhnev the message is to put American forces all over the world on alert?"[139]

More important, it is impossible to ignore that the October War was in large part a product of Soviet-American relations and decision-making during the previous four and a half years and thus was a *consequence* of détente. After pleading with Soviet and American leaders for three years to abandon the "no war, no peace," situation that had solidified in the Middle East as a result of détente, Sadat felt compelled to launch an attack against Israel to move the superpowers off their frozen positions. In taking his country to war, however, and creating a crisis of détente, there can be no question that Sadat's strategy proved successful. Although he had suffered a near catastrophic defeat and the near destruction of the Egyptian Third Army, he accomplished in three weeks what he had been unable to accomplish in three years: moving the Arab-Israeli crisis to the forefront of American foreign policy and beginning the process that would lead to the return of the Sinai Peninsula to Egyptian hands.

Kissinger's Shuttle Diplomacy had begun.

Conclusion

Henry Kissinger's Boeing 707 touched down at the darkened Cairo airport just minutes before midnight, November 6, 1973. Almost two weeks had passed since he had negotiated the shaky cease-fire ending the fourth Arab-Israeli war, but tensions among Israel, Egypt, and Syria remained extremely high. Israeli forces continued to encircle Egypt's Third Army, an "intolerable affront to Egyptian honor," while President Anwar Sadat threatened to resume hostilities. A "grim mood" had enveloped Cairo with persistent fears of renewed fighting, *Washington Post* reporters Jim Hoagland and Murrey Marder wrote hours before the secretary of state's arrival in the ancient capital, but there was strong hope that Kissinger's talks with Sadat would touch off a long-range diplomatic process that would lead to a permanent settlement.[1]

As he stepped off the airplane, Kissinger waved courteously to a throng of reporters and television cameras who eagerly awaited a statement from the secretary of state, by now a bona fide superstar. In just a few years Kissinger had gone from a relatively obscure Harvard professor to having his face frequently emblazoned across the nation's leading newspapers and weekly periodicals. He was named *Time* magazine's "Man of the Year" in 1972, along with Richard Nixon, and received the 1973 Nobel Peace Prize for his efforts to end the Vietnam War. At the time of his nomination as secretary of state in September 1973, *Time* declared in a lengthy cover story on the Jewish émigré from Fürth, Germany, that Kissinger would emerge as a

"Super Secretary," uniquely equipped to "shake up the old systems" and reach his ambitious goals.[2]

Greeting the secretary at the airport was Ismail Fahmy, the recently appointed foreign minister, who had lived for many years in the United States while serving at the United Nations and was known to favor warmer relations with the West. Fahmy hurried Kissinger into a black Mercedes limousine that had once served as Nasser's personal vehicle and the two drove along a dark desert highway to the Nile Hilton, the headquarters of the American delegation. Two and a half years earlier, Secretary of State William Rogers had traveled the same roads and stayed at the same hotel on the eve of his first meeting with Anwar Sadat. Rogers left Cairo in May 1971 confident that in Sadat the United States had found a leader capable of making the difficult choices to broker peace with the Israelis. Yet two years later it was Sadat who started the October War. Kissinger knew the results of his talks would have to be better. "The mood was exuberant and . . . full of expectation," Kissinger later said. "One sensed a people yearning for peace and for a signal of hope."[3]

The following morning, after stopping for a brief tour of the Egyptian Museum, Kissinger took the short drive to Tahirah Palace in Heliopolis, a suburb of modern Cairo, for his first meeting with the Egyptian president. Sadat emerged dressed in a khaki military tunic, with an overcoat slung over his shoulder. He was "taller, swarthier, and more imposing" than Kissinger had expected but exuded "vitality and confidence." After exchanging the traditional greetings and pleasantries, Sadat ushered Kissinger into his large office with situation maps covering a wall. On one side were French windows overlooking a lawn in which wicker chairs had been placed in a semicircle for the benefit of the aides accompanying the two. "I have been longing for this visit," said Sadat enthusiastically to the secretary of state as he started filling a pipe. "I have a plan for you. It can be called the Kissinger Plan."[4]

During that first meeting with the secretary of state, Sadat discussed at length what drove him to war in October. For Sadat, the failure of the 1969 Rogers Plan convinced him that there would never be a "serious negotiation" so long as Israel equated security with military predominance. He explained to Kissinger how he had grown "disenchanted" with the Soviet

Secretary of State Kissinger and President Sadat in Cairo, November 7, 1973.
(Harry L. Koundakjian)

Union, as Moscow "prized" its relations with the United States above support of Egypt. The "bland" treatment of the Middle East question in the
communiqué of Nixon's 1972 summit in Moscow had removed any linger-
ing doubts about the Kremlin's commitment to helping Egypt, Sadat maintained, and he demanded the removal of Soviet troops from Egypt in July
1972 "because of the disrespect shown by Soviet leaders toward Egyptians."
Now that he had vindicated Egyptian honor, Sadat told Kissinger, he had
two objectives: to regain "my territory," that is to say, to restore the 1967
boundary in the Sinai, and to make peace.[5]

As he sat listening to Sadat, Kissinger quickly realized that he was in the
presence of a "unique leader" and a "remarkable man" whom he had underestimated since the moment Sadat had assumed power following Nasser's
death. "Sadat seemed free of the obsession with detail by which mediocre
leaders think they are mastering events, only to be engulfed by them,"
Kissinger wrote admiringly of the Egyptian president. Kissinger could not
tell during that first meeting whether it was possible to achieve peace, or

whether Sadat had the endurance for the "long journey" required to find out if the Israelis would cooperate. But there was no doubt in Kissinger's mind that Sadat represented the "best chance to transcend frozen attitudes that the Middle East had known since the creation of the State of Israel."[6]

Sadat, moreover, was equally impressed by the secretary of state. Although he had met with some of the world's most distinguished leaders during his many years in the Egyptian leadership, he believed that with Kissinger he was dealing with an entirely "new mentality" and a new political method. "For the first time, I felt as if I was looking at the real face of the United States, the one I had always wanted to see—not the face put on by [John Foster] Dulles, Dean Rusk, and [William] Rogers," said Sadat. "Anyone seeing us after that first hour in al-Tahirah Palace would have thought we had been friends for years."[7]

In less than three hours, Sadat and Kissinger had resumed diplomatic relations, which had been cut since the Six-Day War, and agreed to exchange ambassadors within two weeks. They also reached a deal on a "six-point program of action" calling for: (1) Egypt and Israel to observe the UN Security Council cease-fire; (2) discussions between Egypt and Israel to begin immediately on a return to the October 22, 1973, line and on the disengagement and separation of forces; (3) daily supplies of food, water, and medicine to be delivered without interference to the town of Suez; (4) no impediment to the movement of nonmilitary supplies to the East Bank; (5) United Nations checkpoints to replace Israeli checkpoints on the Cairo-Suez road; and (6) an exchange of prisoners of war to take place following the establishment of the UN checkpoints on the Cairo-Suez road. Egyptian and Israeli military representatives formally signed the agreement embodying the six-point program on November 11 in a tent erected at the "Kilometer 101" checkpoint on the Cairo-Suez road, marking the first major accord between Israel and an Arab country since the 1949 armistice agreements.[8]

But Sadat and Kissinger were not done. Two months later, on January 18, 1974, the secretary of state helped broker a more substantial agreement to disengage Egyptian and Israeli forces along the Suez Canal. Often referred to as Sinai I, the agreement provided for Israeli forces to withdraw about twenty miles east of the Canal to a line behind the strategic Mitla and Giddi mountain passes. Egyptian forces were reduced and restricted to an area eight miles east of the Canal, with the installation of a United Nations force as a buffer between the two armies. Although Sinai I was only "a first step" toward peace in the Middle East, as the text of the agreement said, and Israel's withdrawal appeared meager, it represented the first time that Israel had voluntarily agreed to withdraw from any of the Arab territory occupied in the 1967 war and signified the impact that the October War and Kissinger's forceful personality had on both Israelis and Egyptians.[9] "There was no difficulty in understanding one another," Sadat wrote in his autobiography of Kissinger. "Our agreement . . . marked the beginning of a relationship of mutual understanding with the United States culminating and crystallizing in what we came to describe as a 'Peace Process.' Together we started that process."[10]

The Kilometer 101 and Sinai I agreements certainly changed the relationship between Cairo and Washington and put Egypt on a path toward peace with Israel, but they also vindicated Sadat's strategy in launching the October War. For three years he had aggressively pushed the United States to move the Arab-Israeli negotiations to the forefront of its foreign policy agenda, only to see Nixon and Kissinger focus instead on Vietnam, China, and détente with the Soviets while relegating Egyptian and Israeli issues to a mere border dispute unworthy of significant White House involvement. By taking his country to war, Sadat fundamentally altered US policy and reignited the stalled political process. The negotiations that began in 1973 would, by the end of the decade, lead to the signing of the Egyptian-Israeli Peace Treaty, which returned the entire Sinai Peninsula to Egyptian hands. For Sadat, therefore, the war was an unparalleled success.

The same, however, could hardly be said of Syria's Hafez al-Asad. Egypt's acceptance of the cease-fire on October 22 caught Asad by surprise and left him embittered at Sadat for having misled him about Egypt's intentions entering the conflict.[11] Whereas Sadat went to war to begin a political process to win back the Sinai, Asad wanted to use the war to reclaim the Golan Heights militarily while inflicting as much damage on the Israelis in the process. Sadat's subterfuge had cost Syria in men and material, and left Syria weakened politically and militarily. Asad rationalized his acceptance of Resolution 338 by telling his people that the decision was based only on

Soviet assurances that Israel would withdraw from Arab territories and honor Palestinian rights, but it was clear the Syrian leader had no intention of turning the cease-fire into a meaningful peace agreement.[12]

The following month, in fact, at the Arab League summit in Algiers, Asad happily endorsed a declaration disavowing the agreements that ended the war. "The cease-fire in the field means in no way that the struggle has ended and that there can be imposed upon the Arab nation a solution not meeting its just goals," the declaration stated. So long as Israel remained on Arab territory, there would be neither "lasting peace nor true security." The Arabs also demanded Israel's withdrawal from the occupied territories and the "re-establishment" of full rights for Palestinians as the price of peace. "Unless these two conditions are fulfilled, it is illusory to expect anything in the Middle East except a worsening of the explosive situation and the start of a series of new confrontations."[13]

The declaration left the impression of Arab "solidarity" and convinced the Israelis that the Arabs had learned nothing from the war.[14] But in reality it was an empty gesture. For even Asad knew that without Egypt, no coalition of Arabs could defeat Israel military. Although he renewed attacks against the Israeli-occupied Golan Heights and refused to participate in the Geneva Peace Conference of December 1973, Asad was not irrational. He knew that Israel held all the cards and that only the United States could compel Israel to withdraw its forces. Asad, therefore, grudgingly welcomed Kissinger to Damascus in December 1973, the first time an American secretary of state had visited Syria in twenty years, and became an active, though at times a "prickly" and "tenacious" participant in Kissinger's shuttle diplomacy.[15]

Between December 1973 and May 1974, the secretary of state traveled to and from Damascus no fewer than twenty-six times and met with Asad for at least 130 hours.[16] "Since Asad was learning English at the same time," Kissinger recalled, "I teased him that he would be the only Arab leader who spoke English with a German accent."[17] All kidding aside, the negotiations were long and difficult and at several points verged on collapse. The Israelis insisted that Asad not get a better deal than the more reasonable Sadat and demanded the Syrian leader prohibit fedayeen attacks across the border as part of any agreement. For his part, Asad refused to become Israel's "frontier policeman"[18] and wanted a complete withdrawal of Israeli forces from the town of Quneitra as well as its three surrounding hills. It took Kissinger several weeks of artful diplomacy to bridge this very minor gap, including private guarantees that the United States interpreted any agreement to exclude guerrilla raids and that no Israelis forces or weapons would be stationed on the eastern slopes of the hills, but by the end of May 1974 an agreement had been reached.[19]

By any reasonable analysis, the Syrian-Israeli Separation of Forces agreement was modest; militarily, neither side accomplished much from its participation in Kissinger's negotiations. Israel agreed to return the town of Quneitra to Syrian hands and withdrew its forces to the post-1967 line in the Golan Heights, but it retained control of the Mount Hermon observation posts as well as the strategic hills immediately west of Quneitra. The Israelis also gained an expanded buffer zone between Israeli and Syrian armies to be patrolled by UN forces, as well as a "thinned out" zone on either side of the buffer.[20] "The well-publicized contest made Asad's reputation as a dogged champion of Syrian interests and as independent actor in Arab affairs," said biographer Patrick Seale. "But his gains on the ground were meager and the whole drama of the shuttle was no more than a classic example of Kissingerian hocus-pocus."[21]

The Syrian-Israeli disengagement accord fell far short of a formal peace agreement, and Syrian leaders remained miles away from recognizing Israel as a state. But there can be little doubt that the psychological acceptance of Israel had been advanced through Kissinger's diplomacy. Many Arab leaders viewed negotiations with Kissinger, even regarding Israel, as a bolster to their own prestige, and continued to meet with the secretary of state to discuss Middle East peace and the lifting of the Arab oil embargo. When the agreement was announced on May 31, all Arab states, except Libya, reported the news of the accord, and Israeli officials were repeatedly quoted in the Arab press throughout the negotiating process. "It has become natural for millions of Arabs to think of Israel as a country like any other," Henry Tanner of the New York Times concluded, "a thought many of them would not have accepted a year ago."[22]

For the Kingdom of Jordan, the war also had profound consequences. Although King Hussein refused to participate alongside Egypt and Syria, as he had in 1967, and Jordan emerged militarily unscathed from the conflict, the October War produced unprecedented momentum toward Palestinian statehood largely at Jordan's expense. Egypt, Yugoslavia, and the Soviet Union supported the creation of a Palestinian state on the West Bank and in Gaza, and many Arab states advocated for an independent Palestinian role in the peace negotiations.[23] "There can be no peace with justice unless the Arab Palestinian question is settled," Asad told Kissinger.[24] At the Algiers summit in November 1973, all Arab leaders except Hussein approved the Palestine Liberation Organization as the sole representative of the Palestinian people, while the Soviets appeared ready to recognize the PLO as a government-in-exile.[25]

Calls for a Palestinian state (or at least a government) posed an impossible dilemma for the king. As his biographer has astutely pointed out, "This put the Hashemite Kingdom in the untenable position of having to negotiate for the return of the West Bank with a view of handing it over to the PLO should the negotiations prove successful."[26] More important, the king feared that an independent West Bank would be a prelude to a Palestinian takeover of Jordan itself. Hussein agreed to consider a "United Arab Kingdom" composed of the East Bank, West Bank, and Gaza, but even this scenario had its problems. With more than 2.5 million Palestinians loyal to the PLO, as opposed to 500,000 East Bankers, the Palestinians would demand more autonomy and gradually chip away at Hashemite control. "The King, if he can maintain the support and loyalty of the Jordan Arab Army which is overwhelmingly composed of East Bankers, could, in the short run, keep control of such a state," US ambassador to Jordan Dean Brown concluded, "but it is difficult to imagine that he could do so over a long period of time."[27]

Hussein's best prospect to hold on to his kingdom was a quick agreement with the Israelis that would restore most of the West Bank to Jordan, but the National Religious party, a coalition partner in Israel's government, opposed giving up *any* West Bank territory, and the king did not reap the benefits of Kissinger's shuttle diplomacy. Despite promising Hussein on October 19 a "crucial role" in any postwar political process, Kissinger instead focused his efforts almost entirely on the more pressing issue of separating Arab and Israeli forces in the Sinai and in the Golan Heights.[28] "I was sympathetic [to the king]," Kissinger said, "but [an Israeli-Jordanian shuttle] was futile while a new Israeli coalition was being formed, including a party that opposed any territorial change on the West Bank."[29]

The failure to include the king in the postwar political process and help return the West Bank to Hashemite control had lasting repercussions on Jordan's strategic position in the region and for US-Jordan relations. With Jordan effectively shut out of the "peace process" by the United States, the king began an "open flirtation" with the Soviet Union, which he once publicly accused of trying to wreck the United Nations,[30] and he gravitated toward radical Arab regimes hostile to US interests. The king repaired his relations with President Asad by supporting Syrian intervention in the Lebanese civil war and joining the Syrian leader in rejecting the US-brokered Camp David Accords in 1978.[31] And Hussein forged a new strategic partnership with Saddam Hussein's Iraq to offset the growing strength of an expansionist Israel. As Prince Talal bin Muhammad, the king's nephew, has commented: "His Majesty saw Iraq as providing the Arabs with strategic parity with the Israelis to enable us to resume negotiations from a position of strength. . . . Israel would then be forced to come to the negotiating table. We would be able to negotiate from a position of equality rather than inferiority."[32] Not until the mid-1990s, after Iraq's defeat in the Persian Gulf War, did Hussein fully repair his relationship with the United States.

The war produced mixed results for Israel. Militarily, Israel emerged from the war much stronger than the Arab states. Despite Israel's loss of more than 400 tanks and 102 warplanes, the United States agreed to resupply its ally with more than $2.2 billion worth of military hardware, including the immediate transfer of 46 A4 aircraft and 34F4Es, 172 M60 tanks, 400 Maverick missiles, 81 TOW antitank launchers, and 8 CH53 helicopters from the Marine Corps.[33] Combined with tanks and weapons captured from the Arab armies during the war, Israeli arsenals were near their prewar levels within a matter of months. Relative to the Egyptian and Syrian armies, which were largely destroyed and took years to rebuild, there can be little doubt that the war left Israel as the dominant military power in the region.[34]

Psychologically, however, it is difficult to exaggerate the traumatic impact the war had on the mentality of Israeli leaders. One member of the Labor Party described it in Hebrew as *r'idat ha'adamah*—the Earthquake—an apt description for the way it shook the foundations of Israel's defense policies.[35]

No longer could the "conception" of the Arabs' military weakness, especially in the air, preclude them from launching an effective attack. Nor could Israeli officials believe that possession of the occupied territories made Israel safer. "The halo of supremacy and the political and military premise that Israel is stronger than the Arabs, that they would be defeated should they dare to start a war, did not hold true," Defense Minister Moshe Dayan admitted during the war. "My theory was that it would take them the whole night to erect bridges, which we would manage to disable using our armoured vehicles. But it turned out that it was not easy to disable them. Sending tanks to the battle front was very costly. We never expected that."[36]

The Earthquake also shattered the confidence of many Israelis in their political and military leaders. Shortly after the war ended, antigovernment demonstrations erupted across the country that conveyed widespread dissatisfaction with the present leadership, whose hard-line policies against the Arabs were viewed as outdated and had led Israel into a needless war. During one demonstration outside of Golda Meir's office in Jerusalem, Motti Ashkenazi, a thirty-three-year-old graduate student at Hebrew University, who at the outbreak of the war commanded an outpost on the Bar-Lev Line in the Sinai and witnessed thirty-two of his men killed in action, held a placard that captured the sentiment of Israel's younger generation: "GRANDMA, YOUR DEFENSE MINISTER IS A FAILURE AND 3,000 OF YOUR GRANDCHILDREN ARE DEAD." For Ashkenazi, as with so many other Israelis, the failures at the beginning of the war demonstrated the need for a new and younger generation of leaders. "The government and the people are on different planets," he said. "They have adopted a psychology of we-versus-they. That is what has to change."[37]

But Ashkenazi was not alone. Even highly decorated military officers and members of the Knesset demanded accountability for the leadership's failure to anticipate the Arab attack on Yom Kippur. Major General Ariel Sharon, who came out of retirement to command the successful assault across the Suez Canal that helped trap Egypt's Third Army, led the charge against his superiors. "What happened to us should not have happened," said Sharon, referring to being caught off guard on October 6. "We should have been better prepared for an Egyptian crossing. It is a pity that it happened, but it happened, and I won't accept any excuse."[38] Ezer Weizman, former chief of the air force, concurred: "At certain levels of the military hierarchy there was an insensibility that caused a lack of proper readiness for war. . . . Let us have no mercy on who is found guilty of mistakes, failures or misdoings."[39] The bulk of the criticism, though, was reserved for Dayan. In November, more than sixty Labor Party members, including former senior army officers, signed a petition calling for the defense minister's resignation, citing Israel's alleged unpreparedness for the October War and "mismanagement" for its conduct.[40]

Bowing to public pressure, Meir agreed to set up an inquiry commission to assess responsibility for Israel's preparedness failure. Chaired by the president of the Israeli supreme court, Justice Shimon Agranat, the commission members were asked to determine why civilian and military officials failed to draw the proper conclusions from Arab war preparations and to evaluate the general preparedness of the IDF to fight, especially on October 5, the day before hostilities began.[41] "There was something wantonly masochistic about this definition," said Foreign Minister Abba Eban. "Here was a war that begun in failure and that had ended in triumph, and yet the government, which had shared both the failure and the triumph, decided to investigate the former and not the latter."[42] Still, the commission served a useful purpose. Understanding that the investigations would take months to complete, the commission gave Meir "breathing space" to keep her government intact until the Knesset elections on December 31, at which time the Israeli public would have its say as to whether the leadership should remain.[43]

Meir's Labor "alignment" managed to retain 51 of 120 Knesset seats (down from 56), but the parliamentary election results indicated visible signs that confidence in Meir's government had declined markedly. The right-wing Likud Party, Labor's chief opposition, increased its membership by 25 percent—from 31 to 39 seats—riding the popularity of Ariel Sharon. Shulomit Alomi, an archenemy of Meir who campaigned on an antiestablishment platform, broke from Labor to run as the head of her own list, the Civil Rights Movement, and unexpectedly carried three seats with her. And despite being asked to form a new government, Meir struggled to piece together a coalition that could deliver peace with the Arabs.[44]

After three months of bitter interparty squabbling, including threats from Dayan not to join the next cabinet, Meir cobbled together a fragile coalition consisting of Labor, the National Religious Party, and the Independent Liberal Party, but the government was short-lived. On April 2, 1974, the Agranat Commission submitted its preliminary conclusions to the cabinet. Although the report cleared Meir and Dayan of any "direct responsibility" for Israel's unpreparedness on Yom Kippur, many Israelis were outraged that the commission made scapegoats of army chief of staff Lieutenant General David Elazar and army intelligence chief Major General Eliyahu Zeira. It was simply unreasonable to harshly punish the generals, while their direct superiors, Dayan and Meir, were exonerated. The report set off another wave of antigovernment demonstrations, deeply divided Israel's ruling Labor party, and doomed Meir's coalition government. "I can no longer bear the burden. . . . It is beyond my strength," said Meir on April 10 as she announced her resignation as prime minister. "I have reached the end of the road. . . . I am sorry this brings down the whole government.[45]

Meir's successor, Yitzhak Rabin, former chief of staff and ambassador to Washington, pledged to be flexible on reaching an accommodation with the Arabs, but the momentum had largely run out for further disengagement agreements. For Rabin, the peace process had to be more than just a series of Israeli withdrawals; peace must come with security and that meant that the Arab states must recognize Israel as a state, agree to minor adjustments in their borders, and provide guarantees for Israel's security.[46] "Any further agreement that does not contain a meaningful political component will not be a further step toward peace," he told President Nixon during a meeting in Israel on June 16, 1974.[47]

The problem for Rabin was that neither Kissinger nor President Gerald Ford, who replaced Nixon in August 1974, believed that an overall settlement was within reach. Kissinger felt that such an approach would lead to "deadlock," while Ford characterized it as "utopian."[48] The impasse compelled Rabin, who did not want to lose American support, to accept another limited disengagement similar to Sinai I. It took nearly eight months of tedious negotiations and another successful round of Kissinger's shuttle diplomacy to complete, but Rabin reluctantly agreed in September 1975 to withdraw further east in the Sinai, beyond the Mitla and Giddi passes, in exchange for an expanded UN buffer zone, American-controlled electronic early warning stations, and Egyptian commitments to "nonbelligerency" and a peaceful resolution of the Arab-Israeli conflict. With the completion of Sinai II, Kissinger's active involvement in the Middle East, a product of the October War, effectively came to an end.[49]

Kissinger's shuttle diplomacy eased Arab-Israeli tensions and put Egypt on a path toward permanent peace with Israel, but it also marked an effective end of Soviet-American cooperation in the Middle East and further demonstrated that détente would have its limits. Instead of using the US-Soviet framework that had produced the cease-fire ending the war to conduct the postwar negotiations, Kissinger unilaterally launched his Shuttle Diplomacy, ensuring that the Soviets would reap none of the benefits that came from ending the Israeli occupation. True, the December 1973 Geneva conference in which the Egyptians and Israelis convened for the first time since the end of the war,[50] was held under the joint auspices of the Soviet Union and the United States, but even the participants at the conference could see through Kissinger's transparent ploy to "pacify" the Soviets by letting them be part of the game without providing them with any role in the negotiations.[51] Following Geneva, Kissinger abandoned any pretext of involving the Soviets in the Middle East negotiations.

By the time the secretary of state had concluded the second disengagement agreement with Egypt in 1975, he had accomplished the goal the Nixon administration had set out from nearly day one, which sought to reduce the Soviet influence in the Middle East and to "produce a stalemate until Moscow urged compromise or until, even better, some moderate Arab regime decided that the route to progress was through Washington."[52] But at what cost?

With the Soviets facing the deterioration of their strategic position in the Arab world all to the benefit of the United States, they had little incentive to help Washington conclude peace agreements that would bring additional Arab states further into the American sphere of influence, and they were less inclined to cooperate with future administrations on the Middle East. It should come as no surprise that in 1978, Ambassador Dobrynin, a strong advocate of US-Soviet détente, recommended that the Kremlin throw a "wrench" into the Carter administration's game plan in the Middle East by revealing the "hypocrisy" of the United States in trying to show that it was equally close to the interests of the Arabs and Israel and to "more actively use the contradiction between the American imperialistic interests in the Middle East (oil, investment in Saudi Arabia, etc.) and Israeli-Zionist interests (open territorial expansion at the Arabs' expense)."[53]

The Soviets also took aggressive steps in the mid- to late 1970s to reclaim the strategic ground they had lost in the Middle East as a result of détente. Coinciding with its deteriorating relationship with Cairo and the expulsion of its military presence from Egypt, Moscow accelerated military aid to Aden, providing a twenty-million-dollar arms deal in 1972 and doubling it the following year. Also in 1972, Moscow signed a Treaty of Friendship and Cooperation with the Baath party in Iraq and assisted Baghdad with the nationalization of its oil. It later provided Iraq with enough arms to double the size of its armed forces by 1975.[54] And in 1978, the Soviets supported the coup in the People's Democratic Republic of Yemen (South Yemen) that brought to power Abd al-Fattah Ismail, first leader of the Yemeni Socialist party, which gave Moscow important air facilities in the Persian Gulf.[55]

The resurgence of the Soviet military presence in the Middle East, combined with its activities in Afghanistan[56] and the Horn of Africa,[57] not only demonstrated the limits of US-Soviet cooperation but signaled the impending decline of détente. President Jimmy Carter's warning to the Soviets in his 1980 State of the Union address that he would view any attempt by any "outside force" to gain control of the Persian Gulf region as "an assault on the vital interests of the United States of America," which would be "repelled by any means necessary, including military force," echoed the language of the Truman and Eisenhower Doctrines, extended containment to the Persian Gulf, and brought a return to traditional Cold War politics.[58]

All this is not to say that détente did not have its benefits. Certainly, détente produced the ABM and SALT treaties, helping to limit the size of US and Soviet nuclear arsenals; it brought about the Quadripartite Agreement, which removed Berlin as a frequent crisis point in the Cold War; and it led to the 1975 Conference on Security and Cooperation in Europe, which produced the Helsinki Accords, a wide-ranging series of agreements on economic, political, and human rights issues.[59] Moreover, détente improved overall US-Soviet relations by reducing the potential for major superpower conflict in many areas of the world. Nevertheless, détente was not a monolithic policy; its application and effect varied depending on the context. Nowhere was this truer than in the Middle East. As American and Soviet leaders pursued détente, their policies undermined progress toward an Arab-Israeli peace settlement and in so doing helped trigger the October War. Finally, as the peacemaking effort got under way, Nixon and Kissinger dispensed with any pretense of US-Soviet cooperation in a deliberate effort to seize the opportunity to establish preeminence in the Middle East. Clearly, competition would persist. The Cold War would continue. Détente had its limits.

Introduction

1. Henry Kissinger, *Crisis: The Anatomy of Two Major Foreign Policy Crises* (New York: Simon and Schuster, 2003), 13–14.
2. Telegram 7766 from Tel Aviv, Oct. 6, 1973, NARA, NPMS, NSCF, box 610, CF, ME, Israel, vol. 12.
3. *YoU*, 451–453.
4. Ibid., 459.
5. Kissinger-Dobrynin Telcon, Oct. 6, 1973, 6:40 a.m., NARA, NPMS, HAK Telcons, box 22.
6. Ibid. Kissinger's other calls to Dobrynin on October 6 came at 7:46 a.m., 9:20 a.m., 9:25 a.m., 11:25 a.m., 3:50 p.m., 5:45 p.m., 6:20 p.m., 7:20 p.m., and 9:10 p.m. Kissinger, *Crisis*, 15–84.
7. Richard M. Nixon to Anwar Sadat, Oct. 25, 1973, NARA, NPMS, NSCF, box 1175, HHSF, Middle East War.
8. Dobrynin, *In Confidence*, 292.
9. *YoU*, 600.
10. "... And the Meaning for Détente," *WP*, Oct. 26, 1973, A26; "From Cuba to Suez," *NYT*, Oct. 26, 1973, 42.
11. *YoU*, 600.
12. On Kissinger's role during the October War and "shuttle diplomacy," see Walter Isaacson, *Kissinger: A Biography* (New York: Simon and Schuster, 1992), 511–545; Robert Schulzinger, *Henry Kissinger: Doctor of Diplomacy* (New York: Columbia University Press,), 150–162; William P. Bundy, *A Tangled Web: The Making of Foreign Policy in the Nixon Presidency* (New York: Hill and Wang, 1998), 428–472; Raymond L. Garthoff, *Détente and Confrontation: American-Soviet Relations from Nixon to Reagan* (Washington, DC: Brookings Institution, 1994), 413. Kenneth W. Stein,

Heroic Diplomacy: Sadat, Kissinger, Carter, Begin, and the Quest for Arab-Israeli Peace (New York: Routledge, 1999); Jussi Hanhimaki, *The Flawed Architect: Henry Kissinger and American Foreign Policy* (New York: Oxford University Press, 2004), 302–331; Robert Dallek, *Nixon and Kissinger: Partners in Power* (New York: HarperCollins, 2007), 520–533; Jeremi Suri, *Henry Kissinger and the American Century* (Cambridge, MA: Harvard University Press, 2007), 257–269; Alistair Horne, *Kissinger: 1973, The Crucial Year* (New York: Simon and Schuster, 2009), 226–265.

13. Hanhimaki, *Flawed Architect*, 303; Bundy, *Tangled Web*, 442–443; Richard Ned Lebow and Janice Gross Stein, *We All Lost the Cold War* (Princeton, NJ: Princeton University Press, 1994), 198–290.

14. William B. Quandt, *Decades of Decision: American Policy Towards the Arab-Israeli Conflict, 1967–1976* (Berkeley: University of California Press, 1977). In the revised edition of this study, updated to include discussion of the Carter, Reagan, Bush, and Clinton administrations, Quandt changed the name of this chapter from "Standstill Diplomacy" to "Kissinger's Diplomacy: Stalemate and War, 1972–73." See William B. Quandt, *Peace Process: American Diplomacy in the Arab-Israeli Conflict Since 1967* (Washington, DC: Brookings Institution, 2001), 98–129. For a more recent interpretation of the stalemate during this period, see Salim Yaqub, "The Politics of Stalemate: The Nixon Administration and the Arab-Israeli Conflict, 1969–1973," in Nigel J. Ashton, ed., *The Cold War in the Middle East: Regional Conflict and the Superpowers, 1967–1973* (London: Routledge, 2007), 35–58.

15. David A. Korn, *Stalemate: The War of Attrition and Great Power Diplomacy in the Middle East, 1967–1970* (Boulder, CO: Westview, 1992); Richard B. Parker, *The Politics of Miscalculation in the Middle East* (Bloomington: Indiana University Press, 1993), 125–163; Yaacov Bar-Siman-Tov, *The Israeli-Egyptian War of Attrition, 1969–1970: A Case Study of Limited Local War* (New York: Columbia University Press, 1980); Benny Morris, *Righteous Victims: A History of the Zionist-Israeli Conflict, 1881–2001* (New York: Vintage, 2001), 347–386.

16. Dima Adamsky, "Disregarding the Bear: How US Intelligence Failed to Estimate the Soviet Intervention in the Egyptian-Israeli War of Attrition," *Journal of Strategic Studies* 28 (2005): 803–831; Dima Adamsky, "'Zero-Hour for the Bears': Inquiring into the Soviet Decision to Intervene in the Egyptian-Israeli War of Attrition, 1969–70," *Cold War History* 6, no. 1 (2006): 113–136; Dima Adamsky and Uri Bar Joseph, 'The Russians Are Not Coming': Israel's Intelligence Failure and Soviet Military Intervention in the 'War of Attrition,'" *Intelligence and National Security* 21, no. 1 (2006): 1–25; Isabella Ginor, "'Under the Yellow Arab Helmet Gleamed Blue Russian Eyes': Operation *Kavkaz* and the War of Attrition, 1969–70," *Cold War History* 3, no. 1 (2002): 127–156. Valerii Safonov, ed., *Grif sekretno sniat. Kniga ob uchastii sovetskikh voennosluz-. hashchikh v Arabo-Izrail'skom konflikte* [Secret classification removed: A book on the participation of Soviet military servicemen in the Arab-Israeli conflict] (Moscow: Sovet veteranov boevykh deistvii v. Egipte, 1997); V. M. Vinogradov, *Diplomatiia: liudi I sobytiia: iz zapisok posla* (Rossiiskaia

politicheskaia entsiklopediia, 1998) [Diplomacy: People and events: From an ambassador's notes (Russian political encyclopedia, 1998)].

17. Vladislav M. Zubok, *A Failed Empire: The Soviet Union in the Cold War from Stalin to Gorbachev* (Chapel Hill: University of North Carolina Press, 2007), 192–264; Melvyn P. Leffler, *For the Soul of Mankind: The United States, the Soviet Union, and the Cold War* (New York: Hill and Wang, 2007); Keith Nelson, *The Making of Détente: Soviet-American Relations in the Shadow of Vietnam* (Baltimore: Johns Hopkins University Press, 1993).

18. Patrick Seale, *Asad: The Struggle for the Middle East* (Berkeley: University of California Press, 1989), 208; Saad el Shazly, *The Crossing of the Suez* (San Francisco: American Mideast Research, 1980), 245–246.

19. Richard M. Nixon to William P. Rogers, Feb. 4, 1969, NARA, RG 59, Secretary/Undersecretary Lot Files, WPR, box 25.

20. Thanks to Doug Little and Galia Golan for helping me better articulate this key point.

Chapter One From Confrontation to Negotiation, January–September 1969

1. Alfred Friendly, "Flight over Sinai Deserts Witness to Egypt's Disaster," *WP*, June 11, 1967; "Routed Egyptians Rove Sinai; Israelis Describe Fall of Strait," *NYT*, June 12, 1967; Michael B. Oren, *Six Days of War: June 1967 and the Making of the Modern Middle East* (New York: Oxford University Press, 2002), 46.

2. Mohamed Heikal, *The Road to Ramadan* (New York: Quadrangle, 1975), 83–90.

3. Joseph W. Grigg, "Sees Israeli Blitz Over Syria," *CT*, June 12, 1967; Charles Mohr, "Mop Up in Syria," *NYT*, June 12, 1967: James Feron, "Youth in Kibbutz Describe Attack," *NYT*, June 11, 1967.

4. Joe Alex Morris Jr., "Bethlehem Road Littered by War," *LAT*, June 9, 1967; "Bethlehem Area Littered with Remnants of War," *NYT*, June 9, 1967.

5. Seth S. King, "Along with Terrain, Israel Gets Burden of 900,000 Refugees," *NYT*, June 8, 1967.

6. "Friends Deserted, Hussein Laments," *WP*, June 9, 1967.

7. Nigel Ashton, *King Hussein of Jordan: A Political Life* (New Haven: Yale University Press, 2008), 120.

8. On the Six-Day War, see Oren, *Six Days of War*; Tom Segev, *1967: Israel, the War, and the Year that Transformed the Middle East* (New York: Metropolitan Books, 2007); Eric Hammel, *Six Days in June: How Israel Won the 1967 Arab-Israeli War* (New York: Scribner's, 1992); Donald Neff, *Warriors for Jerusalem: The Six Days That Changed the Middle East* (Brattleboro, VT: Amana Books, 1988); David Kimche and Dan Bawly, *The Sandstorm: The Arab-Israeli War of June 1967: Prelude and Aftermath* (London: Secker and Warburg, 1968); Richard B. Parker, ed., *The Six Day War* (Gainesville: University of Florida Press, 1997); and Samir A. Mutawi, *Jordan in the 1967 War* (Cambridge: Cambridge University Press, 1987).

9. Harry C. McPherson Jr. to President Johnson, June 11, 1967, *FRUS*, 1964–1968, vol. 19, doc. 263.

10. Terrence Smith, "Israelis Weep and Pray Beside the Wailing Wall," *NYT*, June 8, 1967.

11. "Middle East: The Quickest War," *Time*, June 16, 1967.

12. David W. Lesch, *The Arab-Israeli Conflict: A History* (New York: Oxford University Press, 2007), 214.

13. McPherson to Johnson, June 11, 1967; Oren, *Six Days of War*, 314; J. Y. Smith, "Dayan Would Keep Major Conquests," *WP*, June 12, 1967.

14. McPherson to Johnson, June 11, 1967.

15. "Israel Won't Give Up Gains of War: Eshkol," *CT*, June 13, 1967.

16. Avi Shlaim, *The Iron Wall: Israel and the Arab World* (New York: W. W. Norton, 2000), 251.

17. Statement to the Knesset by Prime Minister Eshkol, June 12, 1967, *IFR*, 1947–1974, The Six-Day War, doc. 23.

18. A text of the Khartoum Resolution can be found in Lesch, *Arab-Israeli Conflict*, 223–224; David Larsen, "Israel Attacks Arab Khartoum Resolution," *LAT*, Sept. 4, 1967; Shlaim, *Iron Wall*, 258–259.

19. A text of Resolution 242 can be found in Lesch, *Arab-Israeli Conflict*, 222–223; "Resolution on the Mideast," *NYT*, Nov. 23, 1967; Oral History Interview with Undersecretary of State Joseph J. Sisco, Mar. 19, 1990, ADST.

20. Message from Premier Kosygin to President Johnson, June 10, 1967, *FRUS*, 1964–1968, vol. 19, doc. 243; Oren, *Six Days of War*; Isabella Ginor, "The Russians Were Coming: The Soviet Military Threat in the 1967 Six-Day War," *Middle East Review of International Affairs* 4, no. 4 (2000): 44–59.

21. Abba Eban, *Personal Witness: Israel Through My Eyes* (New York: G. P. Putnam's Sons, 1992), 424.

22. "Highlights from the Kosygin Speech," *LAT*, June 20, 1967; David A. Korn, *Stalemate: The War of Attrition and Great Power Diplomacy in the Middle East, 1967–1970* (Boulder, CO: Westview, 1992), 25.

23. Korn, *Stalemate*, 53–57.

24. Alvin Rubinstein, *Red Star on the Nile: The Soviet-Egyptian Influence Relationship Since the June War* (Princeton, NJ: Princeton University Press, 1977), 30.

25. Memorandum of Conversation, Sept. 4, 1968, *FRUS*, 1964–1968, vol. 20, doc 245.

26. Nixon to Rogers, May 26, 1971, NARA, RG 59, Secretary/Undersecretary Lot Files, WPR, box 25; Richard M. Nixon, *RN: The Memoirs of Richard Nixon* (New York: Grosset and Dunlap, 1978), 477. On the American response to the Holocaust, see David Wyman, *The Abandonment of the Jews: America and the Holocaust, 1941–1945* (New York: Pantheon Books, 1984).

27. Douglas Little, *American Orientalism: The United States and the Middle East Since 1945*, 3rd ed. (Chapel Hill: University of North Carolina Press, 2008); Salim

Yaqub, *Containing Arab Nationalism: The Eisenhower Doctrine and the Middle East* (Chapel Hill: University of North Carolina Press, 2004).

28. Little, *American Orientalism*, 94–96; Warren Bass, *Support Any Friend: Kennedy's Middle East and the Making of the U.S.-Israel Alliance* (New York: Oxford University Press, 2003).

29. Little, *American Orientalism*, 77, 96.

30. Notes of a Meeting with President Lyndon B. Johnson and Foreign Minister Abba Eban at the White House, May 26, 1967, ISA, RG 130, MFA, 6853/1.

31. Fawaz A. Gerges, "The 1967 Arab-Israeli War: US Actions and Arab Perceptions," in David W. Lesch, ed., *The Middle East and the United States: A Historical and Political Reassessment*, 4th ed. (Boulder, CO: Westview, 2007), 163–164.

32. Nixon, *Memoirs*, 283.

33. Nixon to Rogers, May 26, 1971.

34. Nixon, *Memoirs*, 477.

35. Nixon to Rogers, May 26, 1971.

36. Nixon, *Memoirs*, 345.

37. "Text of Nixon's Statement to G.O.P. Platform Panel on the War," NYT, Aug. 2, 1968.

38. Editorial Note, FRUS, 1969–1976, vol. 1, doc. 6; "Text of Nixon's Acceptance Talk," LAT, August 9, 1968.

39. *Public Papers of the Presidents of the United States: Richard Nixon, 1969* (Washington, DC: GPO, 1970), 3–4.

40. Herbert S. Parmet, *Richard Nixon and His America* (Boston: Little, Brown, 1990), 111–113.

41. Allen Weinstein, *Perjury: The Hiss-Chambers Case* (New York: Knopf, 1978), 242; Conrad Black, *Richard Nixon: A Life in Full* (New York: Public Affairs, 2007), 129–135.

42. Roger Morris, *Richard Milhous Nixon: The Rise of an American Politician* (New York: Henry Holt, 1990), 581; "Down from the Highest Mountaintop," *Time*, Aug. 19, 1974.

43. Haynes Johnson, "Turbulent Career Summed Up in a Word," WP, April 23, 1994.

44. Nixon, *Memoirs*, 208–209.

45. Address by Richard M. Nixon to the Bohemian Club, July 29, 1967, FRUS, 1969–1976, vol. 1, doc. 2; Nixon, *Memoirs*, 284–285.

46. Nixon, *Memoirs*, 344; Anatoly Dobrynin, *In Confidence: Moscow's Ambassador to America's Six Cold War Presidents* (New York: Times Books, 1995), 201.

47. Nixon Address to the Bohemian Club, July 29, 1967; George C. Herring, *America's Longest War: The United States and Vietnam, 1950–1975*, 3rd ed. (New York: McGraw Hill, 1996), 163–164.

48. Nixon, *Memoirs*, 345.

49. William Taubman, *Khrushchev: The Man and His Era* (New York: W. W. Norton, 2003), 435–439; Aleksandr Fursenko and Timothy Naftali, *Khrushchev's Cold War: The Inside Story of an American Adversary* (New York: W. W. Norton, 2006), 226–232.

50. Robert Dallek, *An Unfinished Life: John F. Kennedy, 1917–1963* (Boston: Little Brown, 2003), 614–620; Richard Reeves, *President Kennedy: Profile of Power* (New York: Simon and Schuster, 1993), 548–552.

51. Thomas Alan Schwartz, *Lyndon Johnson and Europe* (Cambridge, MA: Harvard University Press, 2003), 135–136, 181–182.

52. Jeremi Suri, *Power and Protest: Global Revolution and the Rise of Détente* (Cambridge, MA: Harvard University Press, 2003), 44–61, 73–79, 216–226.

53. Suri, *Power and Protest*, 2.

54. Memorandum of Conversation, Jan. 2, 1969, NARA, NPMS, NSCF, box 725, CF, EUR, USSR, Contacts with the Soviets Prior to January 20, 1969; Memorandum of Conversation, Dec. 18, 1968, *FRUS*, 1964–1968, vol. 14, doc. 335.

55. John Lewis Gaddis, *Strategies of Containment: A Critical Appraisal of Postwar American National Security Policy* (New York: Oxford University Press, 1982), 290; *WHY*, 61–62.

56. "The President's News Conference," Jan. 27, 1969, *Public Papers: Nixon*, 1969, 18.

57. Briefing Paper, Jan. 14, 1969, *FRUS*, 1969–1976, vol. 12, doc. 2.

58. Tcherniakov-Ellsworth Memcon, Dec. 30, 1968, NARA, NPMS, NSCF, HAKOF, HAK Administrative and Staff Files—Transition, Robert Ellsworth. Tcherniakov officially presented the plan to Rusk the same day. For a record of the conversation between Rusk and Tcherniakov, see *FRUS*, 1964–1968, vol. 20, doc. 374.

59. NSC Interdepartmental Group Study on the Middle East, Jan. 30, 1969, NARA, NPMS, H-Files, box H-20.

60. Editorial Note, *FRUS*, 1969–1976, vol. 12, doc. 9.

61. Nixon to Kosygin, Mar. 26, 1969, NARA, NPMS, NSCF, box 433, Backchannel, Beam Instructions.

62. Nixon to Rogers, Feb. 4, 1969, NARA, RG 59, Secretary/Undersecretary Lot Files, WPR, box 25.

63. Dobrynin, *In Confidence*, 201.

64. Ibid.

65. A full text of Gromyko's July 10 speech before the Supreme Soviet is in *The Current Digest of the Soviet Press*, vol. 21, Aug. 6, 1969, 6–10.

66. Lorenz M. Luthi, *The Sino-Soviet Split: Cold War in the Communist World* (Princeton, NJ: Princeton University Press, 2008), 46–79; Sergey Radchenko, *Two Suns in the Heavens: The Sino-Soviet Struggle for Supremacy* (Palo Alto, CA: Stanford University Press, 2009); Chen Jian, *Mao's China and the Cold War* (Chapel Hill: University of North Carolina Press, 2000), 49–84.

67. Chen, *Mao's China*, 240–241.

68. See *FRUS*, 1969–1976, vol. 17, doc. 15, n. 2; William I. Hitchcock, *The Struggle for Europe: The Turbulent History of a Divided Continent, 1945 to the Present* (New York: Doubleday, 2002), 296.

69. Kissinger to Nixon, July 23, 1969, *FRUS*, 1969–1976, vol. 12, doc. 71.

70. National Intelligence Estimate, Aug. 12, 1969, ibid., doc. 73.

71. William Burr, "Sino-American Relations, 1969: The Sino-Soviet Border War and Steps towards Rapprochement," *Cold War History* 1, no. 3 (2001): 73–112.

72. Kissinger to Nixon, July 26, 1969, *FRUS*, 1969–1976, vol. 12, doc. 61.

73. Helms to Rogers, July 14, 1969, ibid., doc. 66.

74. Vladislov M. Zubok, *A Failed Empire: The Soviet Union in the Cold War from Stalin to Gorbachev* (Chapel Hill: University of North Carolina Press, 2007), 207; Transcript of Leonid Brezhnev's Telephone Conversation with Alexander Dubcek, Aug. 13, 1968, NSA.

75. Schwartz, *Lyndon Johnson and Europe*, 219.

76. Zubok, *Failed Empire*, 220.

77. National Intelligence Estimate, Feb. 27, 1969, *FRUS*, 1969–1976, vol. 12, doc. 21.

78. Excerpts from "An Assessment of the Course of Foreign Policy and the State of Soviet-American Relations" (approved by the Politburo), Sept. 16, 1968, in Dobrynin, *In Confidence*, 643.

79. Dobrynin, *In Confidence*, 184.

80. Sonnenfeldt to Kissinger, Jan. 28, 1969, *FRUS*, 1969–1976, vol. 12, doc. 7.

81. Tcherniakov-Ellsworth Memcon, Dec. 30, 1968; Rostow to Johnson, Dec. 31, 1968, *FRUS*, 1964–1968, vol. 20, doc. 374.

82. Memorandum of Conversation, Jan. 2, 1969, NARA, NPMS, NSCF, box 725, CF, EUR, USSR, Contacts with the Soviets Prior to January 20, 1969; Kissinger to Nixon, Jan. 4, 1969, ibid., HAKOF, box 66, CF, USSR, Soviet Contacts; *WHY*, 127–128.

83. *Public Papers: Nixon, 1969*, 1–4.

84. Editorial Note, *FRUS*, 1969–1976, vol. 12, doc. 12.

85. Note from the Soviet Leadership to President Nixon, undated, NARA, RG 59, Central Files, 1967–1969, POL 1 US-USSR.

86. Nixon-Dobrynin Memcon, From the Diary of Anatoly Dobrynin, Feb. 17, 1969, *Soviet-American Relations: The Détente Years, 1969–1972*, ed. David C. Geyer et al. (Washington, DC: US Department of State, 2007), 14–18 (hereafter cited as *Soviet-American Relations*); Dobrynin, *In Confidence*, 203–204; *WHY*, 143, 354; Jussi Hanhimaki, *The Flawed Architect: Henry Kissinger and American Foreign Policy* (New York: Oxford University Press, 2004), 38–40.

87. Memorandum of Conversation, Feb. 17, 1969, NARA, RG 59, Central Files, 1967–1969, POL 1 US-USSR.

88. *WHY*, 11.

89. Nixon-Kissinger Recording, Nov. 13, 1972, *FRUS*, 1969–1976, vol. 2, doc. 347.

90. On restructuring the NSC system, see ibid., doc. 11. See also John Prados, *Keeper of the Keys: A History of the National Security Council from Truman to Bush* (New York: William Morrow, 1991), 265–276; and WHY, 46–48.

91. Memorandum of Conversation, From the Diary of Anatoly Dobrynin, Feb. 17, 1969, *Soviet-American Relations*, doc. 6.

92. Quotations from Robert Dallek, *Nixon and Kissinger: Partners in Power* (New York: HarperCollins, 2007), 171; and Jeremi Suri, *Henry Kissinger and the American Century* (Cambridge, MA: Harvard University Press, 2007), 252. For other authors who support this view, see Hanhimäki, *Flawed Architect*, 94; Isaacson, *Kissinger*, 511; William B. Quandt, *Peace Process: American Diplomacy in the Arab-Israeli Conflict Since 1967* (Washington, DC: Brookings Institution, 2001), 57; and Bundy, *Tangled Web*, 126.

93. Nixon, *Memoirs*, 477.

94. Suri, *Kissinger and the American Century*, 562.

95. Quoted in Isaacson, *Kissinger*, 562. See also Dallek, *Nixon and Kissinger*, 171.

96. Suri, *Kissinger and the American Century*, 252–253.

97. Leonard Garment, *Crazy Rhythm: From Brooklyn and Jazz to Nixon's White House, Watergate, and Beyond* (New York: Times Books, 1997), 181; William Safire, *Before the Fall: An Inside View of the Pre-Watergate White House* (New York: Doubleday, 1975), 565–567.

98. Anwar al-Sadat, *In Search of Identity: An Autobiography* (New York: Harper and Row, 1978).

99. Nixon, *Memoirs*, 477.

100. Dallek, *Nixon and Kissinger*, 114.

101. Korn, *Stalemate*, 154.

102. WHY, 351.

103. Kissinger to Nixon, March 5, 1969, in WHY, 356.

104. Ibid., 364–365.

105. "Transcript of Nixon's Program on Television Introducing His Cabinet Members," *NYT*, Dec. 12, 1968, 37. For evidence on the early relationship between Nixon and Rogers, see Richard M. Nixon, *Six Crises* (Garden City, NY: Doubleday, 1962); Morris, *Richard Milhous Nixon*, 411–413, 824–827; and William P. Rogers, Oral History Interview, June 28, 1968, NARA, RG 59, Lot Files, WPR, box 11.

106. Seymour M. Hersh, *The Price of Power: Kissinger in the Nixon White House* (New York: Summit Books, 1983), 32.

107. Joseph J. Sisco, interview with the author, Mar. 5, 2001; Oral History Interviews, Undersecretary of State Joseph J. Sisco, Nov. 6, 1971, Mar. 19, 1990, ADST; Korn, *Stalemate*, 144–146; Kathleen Teltsch, "Forceful Diplomat," *NYT*, July 16, 1969, 2; David Stout, "Joseph Sisco, 85, Dies; Top Mideast Envoy," *NYT*, Nov. 24, 2004.

108. WHY, 349.

109. Nixon-Kissinger Recording, Apr. 20, 1971, NARA, NPMS, WHT, conversation no. 483-4.
110. Telegram from Ambassador Dobrynin to Soviet Foreign Ministry, Mar. 13, 1969, *Soviet-American Relations*, doc. 14.
111. Ibid.
112. Eban, *Personal Witness*, 481; Golda Meir, *My Life* (London: Weidenfeld and Nicolson, 1975), 306–308.
113. *WHY*, 568.
114. Kissinger-Rabin Memcon, Mar. 4, 1969, NARA, NPMS, NSCF, HAKOF, box 134, CF, ME Rabin-Kissinger, 1969–1970; *WHY*, 355; Yitzhak Rabin, *The Rabin Memoirs*, expanded ed. (Berkeley: University of California Press, 1996), 144–146.
115. Rabin, *Memoirs*, 147–148.
116. Eban-Rogers Meeting No. 1 and No. 3, Mar. 12, 14, 1969, ISA, RG 130, MFA, 4780/2; Telegram 38852 to Tel Aviv, Mar. 13, 1969, NARA, NPMS, NSCF, box 1170, HHSF, Middle East Settlement, US-USSR Talks, January 20–April 30, 1969; Rabin, *Memoirs*, 146–147; *WHY*, 359.
117. Eban-Rogers Meeting, March 13, 1969, ISA, RG 130, MFA, 4780/2.
118. Shlaim, *Iron Wall*, 289; "Life on the Bar-Lev Line," *Time*, June 22, 1970; Raymond H. Anderson, "Egypt Terms 1967 Cease-Fire Plan Void; Israel Appeals to U.N. to Enforce the Agreement," *NYT*, Apr. 24, 1969.
119. Kissinger-Fawzi Memcon, Apr. 10, 1969, NPMS, NSCF, box 134, CF, ME, Rabin-Kissinger, 1969–1970.
120. Henry A. Kissinger, "Foreword," *Soviet-American Relations*, x.
121. Korn, *Stalemate*, 151.
122. Kissinger to Nixon, June 13, 1969, *Soviet-American Relations*, doc. 23. Memorandum of Conversation, Apr. 7, 1970, NARA, NPMS, NSCF, box 711, CF, EUR, USSR.
123. Dobrynin-Nixon Memcon, From the Diary of Anatoly Dobrynin, Oct. 20, 1969, *Soviet-American Relations*, doc. 34.
124. Saunders to Kissinger, Mar. 30, 1969, *FRUS*, 1969–1976, vol. 12, doc. 30.
125. Kissinger-Dobrynin Memcon, Apr. 14, 1969, NARA, NPMS, NSCF, box 489, PTF Dobrynin/Kissinger, 1969.
126. Rogers to Nixon, Apr. 23, 1969, NARA, NPMS, H-Files, box H-022, NSC Meeting 4/25/69—Middle East.
127. Ibid.
128. NSC Meeting Minutes, Apr. 25, 1969, NARA, NPMS, H-Files, box H-109. See also William B. Quandt, *Decades of Decision: American Policy Towards the Arab-Israeli Conflict, 1967–1976* (Berkeley: University of California Press, 1977), 85–86.
129. The meetings between Sisco and Dobrynin took place on May 6, 8, and 12 and are recorded in Department of State Telegrams to Moscow, 71012, 72809, and

75822, respectively. NARA, RG 59, Lot Files, Secretary/Undersecretary, JJS, box 28; Saunders to Kissinger, May 8, 1969, *FRUS*, 1969–1976, vol. 12, doc. 44; Saunders to Kissinger, May 10, 1969, ibid., doc. 46; Saunders to Kissinger, May 14, 1969, ibid., doc. 47.

130. Telegram 75035 to Moscow, May 12, 1969, NARA, RG 59, Lot Files, Secretary/Undersecretary, JJS, box 28; Telegram 75822 to Moscow, May 13, 1969, ibid.

131. Saunders to Kissinger, May 14, 1969.

132. Telegram 71862 to Moscow, May 8, 1969, NARA, NPMS, NSCF, box 725, CF, EUR, Sisco-Dobrynin Talks, Part II, 1969; Saunders to Kissinger, May 14, 1969.

133. Saunders to Kissinger, May 14, 1969.

134. Saunders to Kissinger, May 8, 1969.

135. Thomas Hughes to Rogers, June 11, 1969, *FRUS*, 1969–1976, vol. 12, doc. 54.

136. Telegram 99315 to Moscow, June 18, 1969, NARA, NPMS, NSCF, box 649, CF, ME, Middle East Negotiations, June 1969. See also Korn, *Stalemate*, 155.

137. Saunders to Kissinger, June 20, 1969, NARA, NPMS, NSCF, box 649, CF, ME, Middle East Negotiations, June 1969.

138. Ibid.

139. Ibid.

140. Telegram 3463 from Moscow, July 14, 1969, NARA, NPMS, NSCF, box 710, CF, EUR, USSR; Saunders to Kissinger, July 18, 1969, *FRUS*, 1969–1976, vol. 12, doc. 69; Korn, *Stalemate*, 156.

141. Telegram 3463 from Moscow, July 14, 1969.

142. Sisco's discussions with Vinogradov are recorded in Department of State Telegrams 3501, 3503, 3546, and 3547 from Moscow. His meeting with Gromyko on July 17 is recorded in Department of State Telegram 3566 from Moscow, NARA, NPMS, NSCF, box 653, CF, ME, Sisco Middle East Talks, April–June 1969; "U.S. and Soviet Plans on Mideast Show Some Accord but Many Differences," *NYT*, Oct. 19, 1969. See also Quandt, *Decades of Decision*, 87–88.

143. Sisco's July 18 conversation with Jarring is reported in Department of State Telegram 2045 from Stockholm, NARA, NPMS, NSCF, box 653, CF, ME, Sisco Middle East Talks, April–June 1969; Bernard Gwertzman, "Sisco Wins No Gain on Soviet in Mideast," *NYT*, July 18, 1969.

144. Korn, *Stalemate*, 156–157.

145. WHY, 367.

146. Korn, *Stalemate*, 157.

147. Editorial Note, *FRUS*, 1969–1976, vol. 12, doc. 78.

148. Korn, *Stalemate*, 156.

149. Theodore L. Elliot to Kissinger, Sept. 10, 1969, NARA, RG 59, Central Files, 1967–1969, box 1838.

150. Excerpts of Minutes from NSC Meeting, Sept. 11, 1969, *FRUS*, 1969–1976, vol. 12, doc. 78.

151. Telegram 4174 from Moscow, Aug. 11, 1969, NARA, RG 59, Central Files, 1967–69, POL 1 US-USSR.

Chapter Two The Rogers Plan, October–December 1969

1. Address by the Honorable William P. Rogers Before the 1969 Galaxy Conference on Adult Education, Sheraton Park Hotel, Washington, DC, Dec. 9, 1969, *DSB*, vol. 62, January 5, 1970, 7–11 (hereafter cited as Rogers Address 1969).

2. Richard B. Parker, *The Politics of Miscalculation in the Middle East* (Bloomington: Indiana University Press, 1993), 1; Peter Grose, "Mideast 1: A U.S. Plan for Steps Toward Peace," *NYT*, Dec. 14, 1969; David A. Korn, *Stalemate: The War of Attrition and Great Power Diplomacy in the Middle East, 1967–1970* (Boulder, CO: Westview, 1992), 161.

3. Telegram 4640 from Tel Aviv, Dec. 23, 1969, NARA, NPMS, NSCF, box 605, CF, ME, Israel, vol. 3; Abba Eban, *An Autobiography* (New York: Random House, 1977), 464; Kissinger-Rabin Memcon, Nov. 17, 1969, NARA, NPMS, NSCF, HAKOF, box 134, CF, ME, Rabin-Kissinger, 1969–1970. Rabin's remarks on the Rogers Plan were based on the text of the "Fundamental Principles," not the speech by Secretary Rogers; Peter Grose, "U.S. Proposals on Mideast Are Disclosed by Rogers," *NYT*, Dec. 10, 1969; Raymond H. Anderson, "Egyptians Cold to Rogers Speech," ibid., Dec. 12, 1969, 14.

4. Richard M. Nixon, *RN: The Memoirs of Richard Nixon* (New York: Grosset and Dunlap, 1978), 478–479.

5. Article by Marilyn Berger in the *Washingtonian*, January 1970, NARA, RG 59, Lot Files, Secretary/Undersecretary, WPR, 1969–1973, box 13; Max Frankel, "The Nixon Team After One Year," *NYT*, Dec. 14, 1969.

6. *WHY*, 370.

7. Golda Meir, *My Life* (London: Weidenfeld and Nicolson, 1975), 13; Israel Shenker, "Peace and Arab Acceptance Were Goals of Her Five Years as Premier," *NYT*, Dec. 9, 1978.

8. Meir, *My Life*, 350–352.

9. Moshe Dayan, *Story of My Life* (New York: Morrow, 1976), 442–443; Abba Eban, *Personal Witness: Israel Through My Eyes* (New York: G. P. Putnam's Sons, 1992), 476–477.

10. Meir, *My Life*, 306–308.

11. Ibid., 372–373.

12. Prime Minister's Meeting with Secretary of State Rogers, Sept. 30, 1969, ISA, MFA, 5968/11.

13. Record of Conversation among Wilson, Stewart, and Meir, June 17, 1969, 12:45 p.m., TNA, PREM 13/2736.

14. Korn, *Stalemate*, 165–171.
15. Ibid.
16. Telegram 16383 to Tel Aviv, Sept. 26, 1969, NARA, RG 59, Central Files, 1967–1969, box 1838, POL 27-14 ARAB-ISR.
17. George C. Denney to Harold Saunders, Oct. 10, 1969, NARA, NPMS, NSCF, box 1155, HHSF; Thomas Hughes to Dean Rusk, Mar. 6, 1968, ibid.; Yitzhak Rabin, *The Rabin Memoirs*, expanded ed. (Berkeley: University of California Press, 1996), 154–155; Benny Morris, *1948: A History of the First Arab-Israeli War* (New Haven: Yale University Press, 2008), 375–391.
18. Mahmoud Riad, *The Struggle for Peace in the Middle East* (New York: Quartet Books, 1982), 107–108; "Riad Affirms Cairo Views on Middle Eastern Accord," *NYT*, Sept. 25, 1969.
19. Minutes of Conversation at Cabinet Room, Sept. 25, 1969, ISA, MFA, 5968/11; Telegram 16383 to Tel Aviv.
20. Prime Minister's Meeting with Secretary of State Rogers, Sept. 30, 1969.
21. Meir-Kissinger Telcon, Sept. 27, 1969, 5:20 p.m., NARA, NPMS, HAK Telcons, box 2; Meir, *My Life*, 386–394; Rabin, *Memoirs*, 153–154; Nixon, *Memoirs*, 478; *WHY*, 370–371.
22. Nixon-Kissinger Telcon, Sept. 27, 1969, 4:40 p.m., 5:45 p.m., NARA, NPMS, HAK Telcons, box 2. See also Jussi Hanhimaki, *The Flawed Architect: Henry Kissinger and American Foreign Policy* (New York: Oxford University Press, 2004), 94.
23. William P. Rogers to Richard M. Nixon, Oct. 14, 1969, NARA, NPMS, NSCF, box 1169, HHSF.
24. Joint US-USSR Working Paper: Fundamental Principles for an Israel-UAR Settlement, Oct. 9, 1969, ibid.
25. Fundamental Principles for an Israel-Jordan Settlement, Oct. 9, 1969, ibid.; Rogers to Nixon, Oct. 14, 1969.
26. Rogers to Nixon, Oct. 14, 1969.
27. Kissinger-Sisco Telcon, Oct. 14, 1969, 12:10 p.m., NARA, NPMS, HAK Telcons, box 2; *WHY*, 371–372.
28. Korn, *Stalemate*, 157–158.
29. Harold Saunders, interview with the author, Oct. 19, 2009; Saunders to Kissinger, Oct. 22, 1969, NARA, NPMS, NSCF, box 1169, HHSF.
30. Saunders to Kissinger, Oct. 22, 1969.
31. Saunders to Kissinger, Oct. 27, 1969, NARA, NPMS, NSCF, box 1169, HHSF.
32. Memorandum of Conversation with the President, Oct. 27, 1969, Yale University, Sterling Memorial Library, Dean Acheson Papers, Group 1087, RG 4, box 68, folder 173; Acheson-Kissinger Memcon, Dec. 29, 1969, ibid.
33. Nixon-Kissinger-Dobrynin Memcon, Oct. 20, 1969, 3:30 p.m., *FRUS*, 1969–1976, vol. 12, doc. 93.
34. Ibid.

35. Henry Kissinger, *Ending the Vietnam War: A History of America's Involvement in and Extrication from the Vietnam War* (New York: Simon and Schuster, 2003), 101–103.

36. Nixon-Kissinger Telcon, Oct. 25, 1969, 11:50 a.m., NARA, NPMS, HAK Telcons, box 2.

37. *WHY*, 372.

38. Telegram 182821 from Washington, NARA, NPMS, NSCF, box 650, CF, MENF, July–October 1969.

39. Ibid.

40. The content of the October 2 *Pravda* editorial was reported in Department of State Telegram 173218 from Washington, NARA, RG 59, Central Files, 1967–1969, box 1838.

41. Telegram 6227 from Moscow, Nov. 6, 1969, NARA, NPMS, NSCF, box 650, CF, ME, MENF, July–October 1969.

42. Joseph J. Sisco to William P. Rogers, Nov. 6, 1969, NARA, RG 59, Lot Files, Secretary/Undersecretary Lot Files, JJS, box 27, Two Power Talks, 10/28/69 Demarche.

43. Draft Speech for Secretary on Middle East, Nov. 6, 1969, ibid.

44. Sisco to Rogers, Nov. 6, 1969.

45. Rogers to Nixon, Nov. 15, 1969, NARA, RG 59, Lot Files, Secretary/Undersecretary Lot Files, JJS, box 27, Two Power Talks, 10/28/69 Demarche.

46. Kissinger-Sisco Telcon, Dec. 4, 1969, 11:48 am, NARA, NPMS, HAK Telcons, box 3.

47. Kissinger to Nixon, Dec. 9, 1969, NARA, NPMS, NSCF, box 644, CF, ME, General, vol. 2; *WHY*, 374.

48. Kissinger to Nixon, Nov. 11, 1969, NARA, NPMS, NSCF, box 1169, HHSF.

49. Riad, *Struggle for Peace in the Middle East*, 110–111.

50. Kissinger-Rabin Memcon, Nov. 17, 1969.

51. Kissinger-Sisco Telcon, Dec. 4, 1969, 11:48 a.m.; Oral History Interview with Saunders, Nov. 24, 1993, ADST.

52. Rogers Address, Dec. 9, 1969, 7–11.

53. Ibid.

54. "Call to Reason in the Middle East," *NYT*, Dec. 11, 1969; "Fair Guidelines for a Middle East Settlement," *WP*, Dec. 11, 1969; Grose, "Mideast 1."

55. For details of Kissinger's Shuttle Diplomacy and the Camp David Accords, see William B. Quandt, *Peace Process: American Diplomacy in the Arab-Israeli Conflict Since 1967* (Washington, DC: Brookings Institution, 2001), 130–204.

56. NSC Meeting Minutes, Dec. 10, 1969, NARA, NPMS, H-Files, box H-109.

57. Ibid.

58. Ibid.

59. Ibid.

60. "Humphrey Scores Mideast Plan," *NYT*, Dec. 12, 1969; Peter Grose, "U.S. Says Soviet Makes Propaganda on Mideast," ibid., Dec. 16, 1969.

61. Riad, *Struggle for Peace in the Middle East*, 107.
62. James Feron, "Israel Criticizes Rogers Position," NYT, Dec. 11, 1969.
63. Telegram 209262 to Tel Aviv, NARA, NPMS, NSCF, box 605, CF, ME, Israel, vol. 3.
64. Leonard Garment to Kissinger, Dec. 20, 1969, NARA, NPMS, NSCF, box 1169, HHSF.
65. Paper Prepared in the Israeli Ministry of Foreign Affairs, "A Few Observations on the Rogers Statement," ISA, RG A, Previously Classified Material, 7023/5.
66. Rabin, *Memoirs*, 160–161.
67. Ibid., 159.
68. Policy Background: An Analysis of the US Mideast Peace Plan, Dec. 24, 1969, Embassy of Israel, Washington, DC, NARA, RG 59, Lot Files, Secretary/Undersecretary Lot Files, JJS, box 28, Four Power Talks Resumed, November–December 1969; Rabin, *Memoirs*, 161.
69. Rabin, *Memoirs*, 162.
70. Telegram 211998 from Washington, Dec. 24, 1969, NARA, NPMS, NSCF, box 1169, HHSF.
71. Ibid.
72. Telegram 4640 from Tel Aviv, Dec. 23, 1969.
73. Sisco to Rogers and Richardson, Jan. 9, 1970, ibid.
74. Saunders to Kissinger, Dec. 31, 1969, NARA, NPMS, NSCF, box 1151, HHSF.
75. Kissinger-Dobrynin Memcon, Dec. 29, 1969, NARA, NPMS, NSCF, box 489, PTF, Dobrynin/Kissinger, 1969.
76. Quoted in Richard B. Parker, ed., *The October War: A Retrospective* (Gainesville: University Press of Florida, 2001), 29.
77. Dobrynin, *In Confidence*, 210–211.
78. Oral History Interview with Ambassador Alfred Leroy Atherton, Jr., Summer 1990, ADST.
79. Parker, *October War*, 29–30.
80. Kissinger-Dobrynin Memcon, Dec. 29, 1969.
81. Dean Acheson to Kissinger, Dec. 29, 1969, Yale University, Sterling Memorial Library, Dean Acheson Papers, Group 1087, RG 4, box 68, folder 173.
82. Joseph J. Sisco, interview with the author, Mar. 5, 2001; Oral History Interview with Undersecretary of State Joseph J. Sisco, Mar. 19, 1990, ADST.

Chapter Three The First Soviet Threat, January–May 1970

1. Avi Shlaim and Raymond Tanter, "Decision Process, Choice, and Consequences: Israel's Deep Penetration Bombing of Egypt, 1970," *World Politics* 30 (1978): 483–516.

2. David A. Korn, *Stalemate: The War of Attrition and Great Power Diplomacy in the Middle East, 1969–1970* (Boulder, CO: Westview, 1992), 176–178; Richard B. Parker, *The Politics of Miscalculation in the Middle East* (Bloomington: Indiana University Press, 1993), 143; Yaacov Bar-Siman-Tov, *The Israeli-Egyptian War of Attrition, 1969–1970: A Case Study of Limited Local War* (New York: Columbia University Press, 1980), 134–135. See map 2.

3. Korn, *Stalemate*, 178.

4. Rabin's telegrams to Jerusalem can be found in ISA, MFA, 9360/1, 5969/1, 5969/2.

5. Rabin to Jerusalem, Sept. 19, 1969, quoted in Yitzhak Rabin, *The Rabin Memoirs*, expanded ed. (Berkeley: University of California Press, 1979), 151–152.

6. Korn, *Stalemate*, 173–174; Abba Eban, *Personal Witness: Israel Through My Eyes* (New York: G. P. Putnam's Sons, 1992), 484.

7. Ezer Weizman, *On Eagles' Wings* (London: Weidenfeld and Nicolson, 1976), 271–272.

8. Shlaim and Tanter, "Decision Process, Choice, and Consequences"; Eban, *Personal Witness*, 482–483.

9. Quoted in Bar-Siman-Tov, *Israeli-Egyptian War of Attrition*, 123; Rabin, *Memoirs*, 165; Korn, *Stalemate*, 176–183; Avi Shlaim, *The Iron Wall: Israel and the Arab World* (New York: W. W. Norton, 2000), 291–292; Shlaim and Tanter, "Decision Process, Choice, and Consequences"; "Israel and Egypt Renew Air Raids," *NYT*, Jan. 7, 1970.

10. Korn, *Stalemate*, 180–181; Bar-Siman Tov, *Israeli-Egyptian War of Attrition*, 134–135; James Feron, "Israeli Jets Raid U.A.R. Army Depot in a Cairo Suburb," *NYT*, Jan. 14, 1970; Kissinger to Nixon, "Further Background on the Kosygin Letter," Feb. 6, 1970, NARA, NPMS, NSCF, box 711, CF, EUR, USSR, vol. 7.

11. William Hyland to Kissinger, June 8, 1970, *FRUS*, 1969–1976, vol. 12, doc. 163.

12. Andrei Gromyko to Politburo, Apr. 6, 1970, quoted in Anatoly Dobrynin, *In Confidence: Moscow's Ambassador to America's Six Cold War Presidents* (New York: Times Books, 1995), 212.

13. Henry A. Kissinger, "Foreword," *Soviet-American Relations: The Détente Years, 1969–1972*, ed. David C. Geyer et al. (Washington, DC: US Department of State, 2007) (hereafter cited as *Soviet-American Relations*), ix–xviii.

14. Dobrynin, *In Confidence*, 204–205.

15. Kissinger-Dobrynin Memcon, July 9, 1970, NARA, NPMS, NSCF, box 489, PTF, Dobrynin/Kissinger, 1970.

16. Ibid.; Kissinger, "Foreword," ix.

17. Alexei Kosygin to Nixon, Jan. 31, 1970, NARA, NPMS, NSCF, box 340, SF, Dobrynin/Kissinger, 1970; Rogers-Kissinger Telcon, Jan. 31, 1970, 9:20 p.m., NARA, NPMS, HAK Telcons, box 4; Kissinger to Nixon, Feb. 1, 1970, NARA, NPMS, NSCF, box 489, PTF, Dobrynin/Kissinger, 1970.

18. Kosygin to Nixon, Jan. 31, 1970; *WHY*, 560–561.

19. Dima P. Adamsky, "'Zero-Hour for the Bears': Inquiring into the Soviet Decision to Intervene in the Egyptian-Israeli War of Attrition, 1969–1970," *Cold War History* 6, no. 1 (2006): 115.

20. On the Soviets, see Michael B. Oren, *Six Days of War: June 1967 and the Making of the Modern Middle East* (New York: Oxford University Press, 2002); Yaacov Ro'i, ed., *The Soviet Union and the June 1967 Six Day War* (Palo Alto, CA: Stanford University Press, 2008); and Isabella Ginor and Gideon Remez, *Foxbats over Dimona: The Soviets' Nuclear Gamble in the Six-Day War* (New Haven: Yale University Press, 2008).

21. Mohamed Heikal, *The Road to Ramadan* (New York: Quadrangle, 1975), 83–90.

22. Adamsky, "'Zero-Hour for the Bears,'" 124; Isabella Ginor, "'Under the Yellow Arab Helmet Gleamed Blue Russian Eyes': Operation *Kavkaz* and the War of Attrition, 1969–70," *Cold War History* 3, no. 1 (2002): 127–156.

23. Hyland to Kissinger, June 8, 1970.

24. Kissinger to Nixon, Feb. 6, 1970, NARA, NPMS, NSCF, box 711, CF, EUR, USSR, vol. 7. Although the memo has been declassified in full at NARA, reference to the intercepted conversation was omitted in the recent publication of the memo in *FRUS*, 1969–1976, vol. 12, 379–380. In a memorandum to Kissinger on February 5, Helmut Sonnenfeldt of the NSC staff concluded that "the interesting intercept of the Brezhnev-Grechko conversation . . . suggests an emotional reaction to the killing of Soviet officers, and indicates Brezhnev's personal involvement in drafting the [Kosygin] letter." Ibid.

25. Rogers to Nixon, Feb. 2, 1970, NARA, NPMS, NSCF, box 340, SF, Dobrynin/ Kissinger, 1970.

26. Kissinger to Nixon, "Message from Kosygin," Feb. 1, 1970, NARA, NPMS, NSCF, box 489, PTF, Dobrynin/Kissinger, 1970. See also Robert Dallek, *Nixon and Kissinger: Partners in Power* (New York: HarperCollins, 2007), 220.

27. Kissinger to Nixon, Feb. 6, 1970, *FRUS*, 1969–1976, vol. 12, 380–383.

28. Kissinger to Nixon, Feb. 4, 1970, NARA, NPMS, NSCF, box 711, CF, EUR, USSR, vol. 7.

29. Nixon to Kosygin, Feb. 4, 1970, NARA, NPMS, NSCF, box 765, PC, Kosygin.

30. "Nixon's Report to Congress on Foreign Policy," *NYT*, Feb. 19, 1970.

31. Minutes of Washington Special Actions Group Meeting, Feb. 9, 1970, NARA, NPMS, NSCF, H-Files, box H-114, WSAG Minutes (Originals), 1969–1970.

32. National Intelligence Estimate, Mar. 5, 1970, *FRUS*, 1969–1976, vol. 12, 414–432.

33. Minutes of Washington Special Actions Group Meeting, Feb. 11, 1970, ibid., 384–389.

34. Kissinger to Nixon, Feb. 10, 1970, NARA, NPMS, NSCF, box 711, CF, EUR, USSR, vol. 7.

35. Kissinger-Dobrynin Memcon, From the Diary of Anatoly Dobrynin, Feb. 10, 1970, *Soviet-American Relations*, 123–125; WHY, 562.

36. Ibid.

37. Ibid.

38. Telegram 738 from the Embassy in the Soviet Union, Feb. 11, 1970, NARA, NPMS, NSCF, box 711, CF, EUR, USSR, vol. 6.

39. Rabin to Meir, Feb. 13, 1970, ISA, MFA, 9360/3; Telegram 023085 to Tel Aviv, Feb. 13, 1970, NARA, RG 59, Central Files, 1970–1973, POL 27 ARB-ISR.

40. Rabin-Kissinger Telcon, Mar. 17, 1970, 10:10 p.m., NARA, NPMS, HAK Telcons, box 4.

41. "Text of Five Messages Sent by Soviet Union on Fighting in Middle East," *NYT*, Nov. 6, 1956; William Jorden, "Moscow Aroused," *NYT*, Nov. 6, 1956.

42. Isabella Ginor, "The Russians Were Coming: The Soviet Military Threat in the 1967 Six-Day War," *Middle East Review of International Affairs* 4, no. 4 (2000): 44–59.

43. Adamsky, " 'Zero-Hour for the Bears,' " 115.

44. Dobrynin to the USSR Ministry of Foreign Affairs, Mar. 22, 1970, AVP RF, f. 059a, op. 7, p. 13, d. 8, l. 102–109, courtesy US Department of State.

45. Adamsky, " 'Zero-Hour for the Bears,' " 124; Dima Adamsky and Uri Bar Joseph, 'The Russians Are Not Coming': Israel's Intelligence Failure and Soviet Military Intervention in the 'War of Attrition,' " *Intelligence and National Security* 21, no. 1 (2006): 1–2.

46. Mahmoud Riad, *The Struggle for Peace in the Middle East* (New York: Quartet Books, 1982), 112–114.

47. Ginor, " 'Under the Yellow Arab Helmet,' " 127–156.

48. Telegram USUN 356, Mar. 6, 1970, NARA, RG 59, Central Files, 1970–1973, box 2064, POL 27-14 ARAB-ISR, 3/1/70.

49. Gromyko's instructions to Dobrynin were attached to a Soviet memorandum of conversation between Kissinger and Dobrynin on March 10. See *Soviet-American Relations*, doc. 50, n. 4.

50. Kissinger-Dobrynin Memcon, Mar. 10, 1970, NARA, NPMS, NSCF, box 489, PTF, Dobrynin/Kissinger, 1970.

51. Kissinger to Nixon, Mar. 13, 1970, NARA, NPMS, NSCF, box 711, CF, EUR, USSR, vol. 7.

52. Kissinger-Rabin Memcon, Mar. 12, 1970, NARA, NPMS, NSCF, HAKOF, box 134, CF, ME, Rabin-Kissinger, 1969–1970, vol. 1; *WHY*, 568–569; Rabin, *Memoirs*, 169.

53. Kissinger-Rabin Memcon, Mar. 17, 1970, NARA, NPMS, NSCF, HAKOF, box 134, CF, ME, Rabin-Kissinger, 1969–1970, vol. 1; Rabin-Kissinger Telcon, Mar. 17, 1970, 10:10 p.m.

54. Nixon to Kissinger, Mar. 17, 1970, NARA, NPMS, NSCF, box 652, CF, ME, Negotiations.

55. Kissinger to Nixon, Mar. 18, 1970, NARA, NMPS, NSCF, box 652, CF, ME, vol. 2, March–May 1970.

56. Conversation Between the President and Israeli Ambassador Rabin, Mar. 18, 1970, NARA, NPMS, NSCF, box 612, CF, Israel.
57. Ibid.; Rabin, *Memoirs*, 171–173.
58. *WHY*, 570.
59. Kissinger-Dobrynin, Mar. 20, 1970, 2:15 p.m., NARA, NPMS, NSCF, box 489, PTF, Dobrynin-Kissinger, 1970, vol. 1 [pt. 2].
60. Kissinger-Dobrynin Soviet Memcon, From the Diary of Anatoly Dobrynin, Mar. 20, 1970, *Soviet-American Relations*, 138–139.
61. Kissinger-Dobrynin Memcon, Mar. 20, 1970, 2:15 p.m., NARA, NPMS, NSCF, box 489, PTF, Dobrynin/Kissinger, 1970.
62. The President's News Conference of 21 March 1970, *Public Papers of the Presidents of the United States: Richard Nixon, 1970* (Washington, DC: GPO, 1971), 289–290.
63. Richard Nixon, *RN: The Memoirs of Richard Nixon* (New York: Touchstone, 1980), 480.
64. Telegram from Anatoly Dobrynin to the USSR Ministry of Foreign Affairs, Mar. 22, 1970, AVP RF, f. 059a, op. 7, p. 13, d. 8, 1. 102–109, courtesy US Department of State.
65. Memorandum for the Record, Mar. 25, 1970, *FRUS, 1969–1976*, vol. 12, 451–452.
66. "Transcript of President's News Conference on Foreign and Domestic Matters," *NYT*, Mar. 22, 1970; *WHY*, 464–465; Dallek, *Nixon and Kissinger*, 190–192.
67. Nixon's instructions were written on the bottom of a memorandum from Kissinger on Mar. 19, 1970. See *FRUS, 1969–1976*, vol. 6, doc. 205, n. 1.
68. Alexander Haig to Kissinger, Apr. 3, 1970, ibid., 753–756.
69. Kissinger informed Rogers of the president's decision in a telephone conversation on April 21. Rogers replied that he believed Nixon was "making decisions off the drop of a hat. We can make a good case for helping them [the Cambodians] but we should do it openly." Ibid., 838.
70. Nixon to Kissinger, Apr. 22, 1970, NARA, NPMS, NSCF, PPS, box 2, Memorandum from the President, January–December 1970, April 1970. See also *WHY*, 1484.
71. Kissinger-Dobrynin Memcon, From the Diary of Anatoly Dobrynin, Apr. 10, 1970, *Soviet-American Relations*, 145–148.
72. Korn, *Stalemate*, 197.
73. "Excerpts from Brezhnev's Speech on Arms Talks and Other Foreign Policy Issues," *NYT*, Apr. 15, 1970, 17; Jim Fazio to Kissinger, Apr. 14, 1970, NARA, NPMS, NSCF, box 711, CF, EUR, USSR, vol. 7.
74. Kissinger-Rabin Memcon, Apr. 24, 1970, NARA, NPMS, NSCF, box 606, CF, ME, Israel, vol. 4, March 1–May 21, 1970.
75. Telegram 064278 to Tel Aviv, ibid.
76. Meir to Nixon, Apr. 27, 1970, ibid.

77. "Policy Background: The Soviet Union Assumes Combatant Role Against Israel," Embassy of Israel, Washington, DC, Apr. 29, 1970, NARA, NPMS, NSCF, box 606, CF, ME, Israel, vol. 4, March 1–May 21, 1970; "Text of the Israeli Statement on Russians," NYT, Apr. 30, 1970, 8.

78. Kissinger-Rabin Memcon, Apr. 30, 1970, NARA, NPMS, NSCF, HAKOF, box 134, Rabin/Kissinger, vol. 1.

79. "The More Perilous Crisis," NYT, May 13, 1970; "Relief for Egypt, Anxiety for Israel," Time, May 11, 1970; James Reston, "Washington: And Now the Middle East Again," NYT, Apr. 29, 1970; "Reports from U.A.R. Confirm Role of Russian Pilots," NYT, May 1, 1970, 10; "For U.S. The Pilots Are a Dangerous Challenge," NYT, May 3, 1970; Stephen Kidman, "Soviets' Growing Role in Egypt Is Linked to Global Policy," WP, May 3, 1970.

80. Saunders to Kissinger, May 7, 1970, NARA, NPMS, H-Files, box H-044, Meeting Files, 1969–1974, Senior Review Group Meetings, folder 4, Review Group–Middle East 5/21/1970.

81. Ibid.

82. Kissinger-Sisco Telcon, May 11, 1970, 10:40 a.m., NARA, NPMS, HAK Telcons, box 5.

83. Kissinger to Nixon, May 12, 1970, NARA, NPMS, NSCF, box 645, CF, ME, General, vol. 3.

84. "Relief for Egypt, Anxiety for Israel," Time, May 11, 1970.

85. Hyland to Kissinger, June 8, 1970.

86. WHY, 573.

Chapter Four Crisis on the Suez, June–September 1970

1. "A Conversation with the President About Foreign Policy," July 1, 1970, Public Papers of the Presidents of the United States: Richard Nixon, 1970 (Washington, DC: GPO, 1971), 557.

2. William Hyland to Kissinger, June 8, 1970, NARA, NPMS, NSCF, box 712, CF, USSR, vol. 8, May 1970–July 1970.

3. Kissinger-Rabin Memcon, Aug. 5, 1970, 5:30 p.m., NARA, NPMS, NSCF, box 134, Kissinger-Rabin, 1969–1970; Mohamed Heikal, The Road to Ramadan (New York: Quadrangle, 1975), 93; Mahmoud Riad, The Struggle for Peace in the Middle East (New York: Quartet Books, 1982), 139.

4. Said K. Aburish, Nasser: The Last Arab (New York: St. Martin's, 2004), 258; C. L. Sulzberger, "Nasser III: Man Behind the Mask," NYT, Apr. 3, 1961; "Nasser's Legacy: Hope and Instability," Time, Oct. 12, 1970.

5. "Nasser Going to Soviet for Medical Treatment," NYT, July 25, 1968; Heikal, Road to Ramadan; Riad, Struggle for Peace in the Middle East, 141–145; Anwar el-Sadat, In Search of Identity: An Autobiography (New York: Harper and Row, 1978), 200.

6. "Vice Presidency Post Re-Established in UAR," *NYT*, Dec. 21, 1969; Sadat, *In Search of Identity*, 196.

7. Sadat, *In Search of Identity*, 198–199.

8. "The Second United States Initiative," June 19, 1970, *IFR*, vols. 1–2: 1947–1974, The War of Attrition and Ceasefire, doc. 16; Telegram 096867 to Tel Aviv, June 19, 1970, NARA, NPMS, NSCF, box 1155, HHSF; David A. Korn, *Stalemate: The War of Attrition and Great Power Diplomacy in the Middle East, 1967–1970* (Boulder, CO: Westview, 1992), 246.

9. Rogers to Nixon, "Next Steps in the Middle East," June 9, 1970, NARA, NSCF, box 1155, HHSF, US Peace Initiative for the Middle East, June 10–July 23 [1970], vol. 1.

10. Telegram from Soviet Embassy in Washington to USSR Ministry of Foreign Affairs, June 8, 1970, AVP RF, f. 0129, op. 54, p. 405, d. 5, 1. 230–240, courtesy US Department of State.

11. Extract from President Nasser's May 1 Speech, NARA, NPMS, NSC Files, box 636, UAR, vol. 4, May 1–July 31, 1970; Kissinger to Nixon, "Nasser's 'Appeal' to You—A New Diplomatic Initiative," May 12, 1970, ibid.; Korn, *Stalemate*, 245.

12. Heikal, *Road to Ramadan*, 93.

13. Korn, *Stalemate*, 252.

14. Mohamed Heikal, *The Sphinx and the Commissar: The Rise and Fall of Soviet Influence in the Middle East* (New York: Harper and Row, 1978), 200; Riad, *Struggle for Peace in the Middle East*, 139–140; Kissinger to Nixon, "The Soviet Leaders Speak Out," June 25, 1970, *FRUS*, 1969–1976, vol. 12, 530.

15. Bernard Gwertzman, "Nasser in Soviet for Vital Talks," *NYT*, June 30, 1970.

16. Riad, *Struggle for Peace in the Middle East*, 144.

17. Ibid., 145.

18. Telegram from Soviet Embassy in Washington to USSR Ministry of Foreign Affairs, June 8, 1970, AVP RF, f. 0129, op. 54, p. 405, d. 5, 1. 230–240, courtesy US Department of State.

19. Telegram from the Soviet Embassy in Washington to the USSR Ministry of Foreign Affairs, From the Diary of Anatoly Dobrynin, July 16, 1970, courtesy US Department of State.

20. Riad, *Struggle for Peace in the Middle East*, 147.

21. John L. Hess, "Nasser Accepts U.S. Plan, But Won't Yield 'One Inch,'" *NYT*, July 24, 1970; Korn, *Stalemate*, 253.

22. Rogers's July 23 conversation with Dobrynin was reported in Department of State Telegram and other posts and can be found in the NARA, NPMS, NSCF, box 1155, HHSF, U.S. Peace Initiative for the Middle East, June 10–July 23 [1970], vol. 1; Bernard Gwertzman, "Soviet Appears to Back Nasser's Positive Reply on U.S. Cease-fire Plan," *NYT*, July 25, 1970.

23. Kissinger to Nixon, June 9, 1970, NARA, NPMS, NSCF, box 1155, HHSF, U.S. Peace Initiative for the Middle East, June 10–July 23 [1970], vol. 1.

24. John Freeman to Sir Dennis Greenhill, June 6, 1970, TNA, FCO 73/131, Various Papers, 1970, Sir Dennis Greenhill.

25. Excerpts of Minutes of NSC Meeting on the Middle East, June 10, 1970, *FRUS, 1969–1976*, vol. 12, 512–513.

26. Ibid., 513.

27. H. R. Haldeman, *The Haldeman Diaries: Inside the Nixon White House* (New York: G. P. Putnam's Sons, 1994), Aug. 17, 1970.

28. Kissinger-Dobrynin Memcon, June 10, 1970, 7:30 p.m.–1:00 a.m., NARA, NPMS, NSCF, box 489, PTF, Dobrynin/Kissinger, 1970.

29. Kissinger-Dobrynin Soviet Memcon, From the Diary of Anatoly Dobrynin, 10 June 1970, *Soviet-American Relations: The Détente Years, 1969–1979*, ed. David C. Geyer et al. (Washington, DC: US Department of State, 2007), 14–18 (hereafter cited as *Soviet-American Relations*), 159–165.

30. Kissinger to Nixon, June 16, 1970, quoted in *WHY*, 577–578.

31. Ibid.

32. Ibid.

33. Murrey Marder, "U.S. Seeking to Oust Soviet Units in Egypt," *WP*, July 3, 1970; Marvin Kalb and Bernard Kalb, *Kissinger* (Boston: Little, Brown, 1974), 192–193; *WHY*, 579–580; Murrey Marder, "Clarifies Goal of 'Expelling' Soviets," *WP*, July 4, 1970.

34. Kissinger-Sisco Telcon, July 10, 1970, 3:45 p.m., NARA, NPMS, HAK Telcons, box 5.

35. "On 'Expelling' the Russians from the Middle East," *WP*, July 7, 1970.

36. Joseph Kraft, "Stiffening of Near East Stand Reveal Nixon Team Fissure," *WP*, July 9, 1970.

37. Telegram 109223 to Tokyo, July 9, 1970, NARA, NPMS, NSCF, box 1155, HHSF, U.S. Peace Initiative for the Middle East, June 10–July 23 [1970], vol. 1.

38. Kissinger-Rabin Memcon, June 22, 1970, 5:30–5:50 p.m., NARA, NPMS, NSCF, HAKOF, box 134, CF, ME, Rabin-Kissinger, 1969–1970.

39. Korn, *Stalemate*, 255–256.

40. Kissinger-Rabin Memcon, June 22, 1970, 5:30–5:50 p.m.

41. Ibid.

42. Nixon-Kissinger Telcon, June 22, 1970, 5:45 p.m., NARA, NPMS, HAK Telcons, box 5.

43. Telegram 3325 from Tel Aviv to Secretary of State, June 26, 1970, NARA, NPMS, NSCF, box 1155, HHSF, vol. 6.

44. Statement to the Knesset by Prime Minister Meir, June 29, 1970, *IFR*, vols. 1–2: 1947–1974, The War of Attrition and Ceasefire, doc. 17.

45. Ibid.; Raymond H. Anderson, "U.S. Proposals for Mideast Peace Rebuffed by Nasser," *NYT*, June 26, 1970.

46. Kissinger-Rabin Memcon, Aug. 5, 1970, 5:30 p.m., NARA, RG 59, Central Files 1970–73, POL 17 ISR-US.

47. Korn, *Stalemate*, 230.
48. Yitzhak Rabin, *The Rabin Memoirs*, expanded ed. (Berkeley: University of California Press, 1996), 178.
49. Kissinger-Rabin Memcon, July 8, 1970, 12:44–1:02 p.m., NARA, NPMS, NSCF, HAKOF, box 134, CF, ME, Rabin-Kissinger, 1969–1970.
50. Ibid.
51. Minutes of the NSC Special Review Group Meeting, July 9, 1970, 2:35–3:50 p.m., NARA, NPMS, H-Files, box 111, SRG Minutes Originals 1970 [3 of 5].
52. Riad to Rogers, July 22, 1970, NARA, NPMS, NSCF, box 1157, HHSF, Middle East–Jarring Talks; Korn, *Stalemate*, 231.
53. Nixon to Meir, July 23, 1970, NARA, NPMS, NSC Files, box 756, PC, Nixon-Meir.
54. Ibid.
55. Telegram 119832 to Tel Aviv, July 25, 1970, NARA, NPMS, NSCF, box 1155, HHSF, Middle East–Jarring Talks; Rabin, *Memoirs*, 179.
56. Haig to Kissinger, "Telephone Call from Rabin," July 29, 1970, NARA, NPMS, NSCF, box 607, CF, ME, Israel, vol. 5, 22 May 1970–30 July 1970.
57. Abba Eban, *Personal Witness: Israel Through My Eyes* (New York: G. P. Putnam's Sons, 1992), 490.
58. Memorandum for the Record, "Israeli Aircraft Down Four Soviet Piloted MiG-21s," July 30, 1970, NARA, NPMS, NSCF, box 607, CF, ME, Israel, vol. 5, 22 May 1970–30 July 1970.
59. Israel Accepts the United States Initiative-Government Statement, July 31, 1970, *IFR*, vols. 1–2: 1947–1974, The War of Attrition and Ceasefire, doc. 18.
60. Eban, *Personal Witness*, 491; Korn, *Stalemate*, 257–258.
61. Rabin to Rogers, Aug. 4, 1970, ISA, MFA, 6854/8.
62. Theodore L. Elliot to Kissinger, Aug. 6, 1970, NARA, NPMS, NSCF, box 1155, HHSF; Rabin, *Memoirs*, 180–181; Korn, *Stalemate*, 260–261.
63. Rabin-Sisco Telcon, Aug. 6, 1970, ISA, MFA, 6854/8.
64. Korn, *Stalemate*, 261.
65. Oral History Interview with Joseph J. Sisco, Mar. 19, 1990, ADST; Rabin, *Memoirs*, 180–181.
66. Rabin, *Memoirs*, 180–181.
67. Ibid.
68. Ibid. See also Oral History Interview with Ambassador Alfred Leroy Atherton, Jr., Summer 1990, ADST.
69. Rabin, *Memoirs*, 181.
70. Executive Secretary to Kissinger, Aug. 7, 1970, NARA, RG 59, Central Files, 1970–1973, POL 27 ARAB-ISR.
71. Kissinger-Rabin Memcon, Aug. 6, 1970, 10:00 p.m., NARA, NPMS, NSCF, HAKOF, box 134, CF, ME, Rabin-Kissinger, 1969–1970.
72. Ibid.; Rabin, *Memoirs*, 182.

73. Kissinger-Atherton Telcon, Aug. 6, 1970, 10:30 p.m., NARA, NPMS, NSCF, box 6, Chronological File.

74. Ibid. See also Oral History Interview with Atherton, Summer 1990.

75. Kissinger-Sisco Telcon, Aug. 6, 1970, 11:30 p.m., NARA, NPMS, HAK Telcons, box 6, Chronological File.

76. Kissinger-Rabin Memcon, Aug. 6, 1970, 10:00 p.m.

77. Rogers-Kissinger Telcons, Aug. 7, 1970, 12:00 p.m., 12:30 p.m., NARA, NPMS, HAK Telcons, box 6, Chronological File.

78. Kissinger-Rabin Memcon, Aug. 6, 1970, 10:00 p.m.

79. Ibid.

80. Nixon to Meir, Aug. 9, 1970, ISA, MFA, 6854/8.

81. The text of the cease-fire agreement is printed as app. E in Korn, *Stalemate*, 287; "Text of U.S., Israeli, U.A.R., and Thant Statements," *NYT*, Aug. 8, 1970; Hedrick Smith, "Cease-Fire in Effect Along Suez; Israel and Egypt Police Zone; Initial Talks Begin at U.N.," *NYT*, Aug. 8, 1970.

82. Korn, *Stalemate*, 287.

83. Broadcast to the Nation by Prime Minister Meir, Aug. 7, 1970, *IFR*, vols. 1–2: 1947–1974, The War of Attrition and Ceasefire, doc. 21.

84. Raymond H. Anderson, "Egypt Emphasizes Security," *NYT*, Aug. 8, 1970.

85. Richard M. Nixon, *RN: The Memoirs of Richard Nixon* (New York: Grosset and Dunlap, 1978), 482–483.

86. Kissinger-Rabin Memcon, Aug. 15, 1970, 10:00 a.m., NARA, NPMS, NSCF, HAKOF, box 134, CF, ME, Rabin-Kissinger, 1969–1970; Korn, *Stalemate*, 264–265.

87. Telegram 2303 from Washington to the Foreign and Commonwealth Office, Aug. 6, 1970, TNA, PREM 15/123; Telegram 2317 from Washington to London, Aug. 7, 1970, ibid.

88. Riad, *Struggle for Peace in the Middle East*, 151.

89. Korn, *Stalemate*, 264; Rabin, *Memoirs*, 182; Telegram 4252 from Tel Aviv to Washington, Aug. 10, 1970, NARA, RG 59, Central Files, 1970–1973, box 2642, POL UAR-USSR.

90. FCO Telegram 1761 from London, Aug. 8, 1970, TNA, PREM 15/123; Telegram 1356 to Nicosia, Aug. 9, 1970, NARA, RG 59, Central Files, 1970–1973, box 2642, POL UAR-USSR.

91. According to Telegram 135412 to Cairo, the State Department selected the name for the mission, as well as the "slug" for all messages dealing with the high-altitude U-2 missions "to reflect our role as impartial observer of ceasefire and in deeper sense to symbolize total evenhandedness that has always characterized United States Arab-Israeli policy." NARA, RG 59, Central Files, 1970–1973, box 2642, POL UAR-USSR.

92. Telegram 128590, Aug. 8, 1970, NARA, NPMS, NSCF, box 1155, HHSF, Middle East–Jarring Talks; "Egypt Pushing Missile Buildup, Israel Charges," *LAT*, Aug. 15, 1970.

93. Sisco to Rogers, Aug. 15, 1970, NARA, RG 59, Central Files, 1970–1973, box 2068, POL 27-14 Arab-Israeli, 8/1/1970–9/5/1970; Kissinger to Nixon, n.d., NARA, NPMS, H-Files, box H-029, folder 4, NSC Meeting–Middle East, 9/1/1970.

94. I. McCluney to Peter Moon, "Middle East Ceasefire Surveillance," Aug. 21, 1970, TNA, PREM 15/123.

95. Nixon-Kissinger Telcon, Aug. 29, 1970, 11:45 a.m., NARA, NPMS, HAK Telcons, box 6.

96. Rabin to Meir, Aug. 14, 1970, ISA, MFA, 6854/8.

97. Rabin-Kissinger Memcon, Aug. 15, 1970, 10:00 a.m., NARA, NPMS, NSCF, HAKOF, box 134, CF, ME, Rabin-Kissinger, 1969–1970.

98. Meir to Rogers, Aug. 19, 1970, ISA, MFA, 6854/8.

99. WHY, 589.

100. Frank Shakespeare to Nixon, Sept. 2, 1970, NARA, NPMS, NSCF, box 713, CF, EUR, USSR, vol. 9.

101. Sisco to Rogers, Aug. 31, 1970, NARA, RG 59, Central Files, 1970–1973, POL 27-14 Arab-Israeli; WHY, 590.

102. Nixon, Memoirs, 482–483.

103. WHY, 591; Sisco to Rogers, Aug. 31, 1970; Haldeman Diaries, Sept. 1, 1970.

104. Riad, Struggle for Peace in the Middle East, 152.

105. Telegrams 951, 953 from Cairo to FCO, Sept. 5, 1970, TNA, PREM 15/123.

106. Telegram 5076 from Moscow, Sept. 3, 1970, FRUS, 1969–1976, vol. 12, 610.

107. Sisco to Rogers and Kissinger, Sept. 5, 1970, NARA, NPMS, NSCF, box 713, CF, EUR, USSR, vol. 9.

108. Rogers-Haig Telcon, Sept. 4, 1970, 2:55 p.m., NARA, NPMS, HAK Telcons, box 6.

109. Israel Suspends Its Participation in the Jarring Talks, Interview with Prime Minister Meir, Sept. 21, 1970, IFR, vols. 1–2: 1947–1974, The War of Attrition and Ceasefire, doc. 23; Peter Grose, "Israel Pulls Out of Peace Parlay Until Missiles Go," NYT, Sept. 7, 1970.

110. Telegram from the Department of State to the Embassy in the Soviet Union, Sept. 6, 1970, FRUS, 1969–1976, vol. 24, doc. 199.

111. Paper Prepared by the NEA Working Group in the Department of State Operations Center, ibid., doc. 208.

112. Nigel Ashton, King Hussein of Jordan: A Political Life (New Haven: Yale University Press, 2008), 138.

113. Paul T. Chamberlin, "Preparing for Dawn: The United States and the Global Politics of Palestinian Resistance, 1967–1975" (PhD diss., Ohio State University, 2009).

114. On Eisenhower's decision to send forces to the Middle East in 1957, see Salim Yaqub, Containing Arab Nationalism: The Eisenhower Doctrine and the Middle East (Chapel Hill: University of North Carolina Press, 2004); and Douglas Little,

American Orientalism: The United States and the Middle East Since 1945, 3rd ed. (Chapel Hill: University of North Carolina Press, 2008).

115. *WHY*, 602. A summary of the meeting can be found in *FRUS, 1969–1976*, vol. 24, doc. 209, n. 2.

116. Minutes of a Combined Washington Special Actions Group and Review Group Meeting, Sept. 9, 1970, 11:40 a.m.–12:35 p.m., ibid., doc. 214.

117. Kissinger to Nixon, "Options in Jordan," Sept. 16, 1970, *FRUS, 1969–1976*, vol. 24, doc. 247.

118. Minutes of a Combined Washington Special Actions Group and Review Group Meeting, Sept. 9, 1970, 11:40 a.m.–12:35 p.m.

119. *WHY*, 612.

120. Nixon-Kissinger Telcon, Sept. 17, 1970, 9:00 a.m., NARA, NPMS, HAK Telcons, box 6.

121. Telegram from the Department of State to the Embassy in Jordan, Sept. 13, 1970, *FRUS, 1969–1976*, vol. 24, doc. 234.

122. Kissinger to Nixon, "Jordan/Hijacking Situation," Sept. 16, 1970, ibid., doc. 248.

123. Avi Shlaim, *Lion of Jordan: The Life of King Hussein in War and Peace* (New York: Knopf, 2008), 330.

124. Telegram 4887 from Amman, Sept. 17, 1970, NARA, NPMS, NSCF, box 615, CF, ME, Jordan, vol. 5; Minutes of a Washington Special Actions Group Meeting, Sept. 17, 1970, 3:20–3:45 p.m., *FRUS, 1969–1976*, vol. 24, doc. 260; Eric Pace, "Hussein's Tanks Clearing Guerrillas from Amman; U.S. Alert Stepped Up," *NYT*, Sept. 18, 1970.

125. Prime Minister Golda Meir's Conversation with Secretary of State William P. Rogers, Sept. 18, 1970, ISA, MFA, 5968/11.

126. Kissinger to Nixon, "The Jordan Situation—6:30 P.M. Sunday, September 20," Sept. 20, 1970, *FRUS, 1969–1976*, vol. 24, doc. 280; Minutes of a National Security Council Meeting, Sept. 21, 1970, ibid., doc. 299.

127. Kissinger to Nixon, "The Situation in Jordan," Sept. 19, 1970, ibid., doc. 272.

128. Telegram from the Embassy in Jordan to the Department of State, Sept. 21, 1970, ibid., doc. 284, emphasis added.

129. Nixon, *Memoirs*, 483.

130. Rogers-Kissinger-Sisco Telcon, Sept. 20, 1970, 10:10 p.m., *FRUS, 1969–1976*, vol. 24, doc. 285.

131. Kissinger-Nixon Telcon, Sept. 20, 1970, ibid., doc. 286.

132. Rabin-Kissinger Telcon, Sept. 20, 1970, 10:35 p.m., ibid., doc. 287; Rabin, *Memoirs*, 186–187.

133. Rabin, *Memoirs*, 186–187.

134. Kissinger-Rabin Telcon, Sept. 20, 1970, *FRUS, 1969–1976*, vol. 24, doc. 289.

135. Nixon-Kissinger Telcon, Sept. 21, 1970, 5:30 a.m., ibid., doc. 292; Kissinger to Nixon, "The Situation in Jordan," Sept. 21, 1970, ibid., doc. 305.

136. Shlaim, *Lion of Jordan*, 335.
137. Intelligence Memorandum Prepared in the Central Intelligence Agency, *FRUS*, 1969–1976, vol. 24, doc. 325.
138. Kissinger-Rabin Telcon, Sept. 21, 1970, ibid., doc. 301.
139. Nixon-Kissinger Telcon, Sept. 21, 1970, 5:30 a.m.
140. Telegram from the Department of State to the Embassy in Israel, Sept. 21, 1970, ibid., doc. 306.
141. Nixon-Kissinger Telcon, Sept. 21, 1970, 5:30 a.m.
142. Minutes of Washington Special Actions Group Meeting, Sept. 20, 1970, 7:10–9:15 p.m., Sept. 20–21, 1970, midnight–12:40 a.m., *FRUS*, 1969–1976, vol. 24, docs. 281, 290; *WHY*, 622; Shlaim, *Lion of Jordan*, 334.
143. Minutes of a National Security Council Meeting, Sept. 21, 1970, *FRUS*, 1969–1976, vol. 24, doc. 307.
144. Kissinger to Nixon, "Meeting on Jordan," Sept. 22, 1970, *FRUS*, 1969–1976, vol. 24, doc. 315.
145. Shlaim, *Lion of Jordan*, 338.
146. Nixon to Kissinger, "The Situation in Jordan," Sept. 23, 1970, *FRUS*, 1969–1976, vol. 24, doc. 316; Saunders to Kissinger, "The Situation in Jordan," Sept. 23, 1970, ibid., doc. 322.
147. Minutes of a National Security Council Meeting, Sept. 23, 1970, ibid., vol. 24, doc. 318; Nixon to Kissinger, "The Situation in Jordan," Sept. 23, 1970, ibid., doc. 316.
148. Kissinger to Nixon, "Jordan Situation Report," Sept. 28, 1970, *FRUS*, 1969–1976, vol. 24, doc. 330; Raymond H. Anderson, "Hussein, Arafat Sign Arab Pact to End Clashes," *NYT*, Sept. 28, 1970.
149. Kissinger to Nixon, "The Situation in Jordan," Sept. 28, 1970, *FRUS*, 1969–1976, vol. 24, doc. 330.
150. Shlaim, *Lion of Jordan*, 342–343.
151. Kissinger–Dobrynin Soviet Memcon, From the Diary of Anatoly Dobrynin, Oct. 6, 1970, *Soviet-American Relations*, 200–201.

Chapter Five Fighting for Sadat, October 1970–August 1971

1. Robert Stephens, *Nasser: A Political Biography* (London: Penguin, 1971); Salim Yaqub, *Containing Arab Nationalism: The Eisenhower Doctrine and the Middle East* (Chapel Hill: University of North Carolina Press, 2004), 31–34.
2. Nixon-Rogers Recording, May 19, 1971, NARA, NPMS, WHT, conversation no. 510–4.
3. Sadat to Nixon, Dec. 24, 1970, NARA, NPMS, NSCF, box 763, PC, U.A.R.-Sadat, vol. 1.
4. Kirk Beattie, *Egypt During the Sadat Years* (New York: Palgrave, 2000), 13–15; Anwar el-Sadat, *In Search of Identity: An Autobiography* (New York: Harper and Row, 1978), 4–28.

5. Ibid.
6. Laila Morsy, "The Military Clauses of the Anglo-Egyptian Treaty of Friendship and Alliance, 1936," *International Journal of Middle East Studies* 16, no. 1 (1984): 67–97.
7. Anwar el-Sadat, *Revolt on the Nile* (New York: J. Day, 1957).
8. Sadat, *In Search of Identity*, 107–108; Beattie, *Egypt During the Sadat Years*, 18–21.
9. David Hirst and Irene Benson, *Sadat* (London: Faber and Faber, 1981), 100.
10. Beattie, *Egypt During the Sadat Years*, 34.
11. Sadat, *In Search of Identity*, 196.
12. Saunders to Kissinger, Sept. 28, 1970, NARA, NPMS, NSCF, box 636, CF, ME, UAR, vol. 5.
13. Kissinger to Nixon, Oct. 12, 1970, ibid.
14. Vadim Kirpichenko, *Razvedka: litsa I lichnosti* (Intelligence: faces and personalities) (Moscow: Geiia, 2001), 114.
15. Andrei Gromyko, *Memoirs* (New York: Doubleday, 1990), 271.
16. Quoted in Mohamed Heikal, *The Sphinx and the Commissar: The Rise and Fall of Soviet Influence in the Middle East* (New York: Harper and Row, 1978), 216–217.
17. For more on Dulles's decision to withdraw American financial support for the Aswan Dam project see, Peter Hahn, *The United States, Great Britain, and Egypt, 1945–1956: Strategy and Diplomacy in the Early Cold War* (Chapel Hill: University of North Carolina Press, 1991), 202–205; Diane B. Kunz, *The Economic Diplomacy of the Suez Crisis* (Chapel Hill: University of North Carolina Press, 1991), 65–72; and Yaqub, *Containing Arab Nationalism*, 46–47.
18. Nixon to Rogers, May 26, 1971, NARA, RG 59, Secretary/Undersecretary Lot Files, WPR, box 25.
19. Raymond H. Anderson, "Sadat Tells Cairo Deputies He'll Follow Nasser Policy," *NYT*, Oct. 8, 1970.
20. C. L. Sulzberger, "Nasserism Without Nasser," *NYT*, Oct. 16, 1970.
21. Isabella Ginor, "'Under the Yellow Arab Helmet Gleamed Blue Russian Eyes': Operation *Kavkaz* and the War of Attrition, 1969–70," *Cold War History* 3, no. 1 (2002): 127–156; Max Frankel, "Russian Airmen Believed Flying in U.A.R.," *NYT*, Apr. 29, 1970, 1.
22. Mohamed Heikal, *Road to Ramadan* (New York: Quadrangle, 1975), 122.
23. Kissinger to Nixon, Oct. 12, 1970, NARA, NPMS, NSCF, box 636, CF, ME, UAR, vol. 5.
24. Alvin Rubinstein, *Red Star on the Nile: The Soviet-Egyptian Influence Relationship Since the June War* (Princeton, NJ: Princeton University Press, 1977), 133–136.
25. Telegram 2262 from Cairo, Oct. 3, 1970, NARA, NPMS, NSCF, box 637, CF, UAR, vol. 6. Interview with Elliot Richardson as seen in *The Fifty Years War: Israel and the Arabs* (New York: Public Broadcasting Service, 1998), disc 2.

26. Telegram 2262 from Cairo, Oct. 3, 1970. See also Beattie, *Egypt During the Sadat Years*, 53.
27. Sadat to Nixon, Dec. 24, 1970.
28. Beattie, *Egypt During the Sadat Years*, 56–57.
29. FBIS 72, Feb. 5, 1971, NARA, NPMS, NSCF, box 1160, HHSF.
30. Peter Grose, "Israeli Cabinet Disputes Dayan," *NYT*, Nov. 23, 1970; Grose, "Dayan Suggests New Truce Pact, *NYT*, Nov. 27, 1970.
31. Jarring handed an Aide Memoire, Feb. 8, 1971, NARA, NPMS, NSCF, box 1160, HHSF.
32. Telegram 328 from Cairo, Feb. 16, 1971, ibid.
33. Rabin to Meir, Feb. 8, 1971, ISA, MFA, 6810/8; Telegram 263 from Cairo, Feb. 8, 1971, NARA, NPMS, NSCF, box 1160, HHSF.
34. "Sabry Removed by Sadat from Vice President's Job," *NYT*, May 3, 1971; Sadat, *In Search of Identity*, 222; Beattie, *Egypt During the Sadat Years*, 63.
35. Sadat, *In Search of Identity*, 223–224; Beattie, *Egypt During the Sadat Years*, 62–73.
36. Telegram 990 from Cairo, May 3, 1971, NARA, NPMS, NSCF, box 637, CF, UAR, vol. 6.
37. Haig to Nixon, May 7, 1971, ibid.
38. Rogers to Nixon, Nov. 17, 1970, ibid.
39. Rogers-Dobrynin Memcon, From the Diary of Anatoly Dobrynin, Dec. 24, 1970, Department of State, Office of the Historian, Russian-American Project Special Collection.
40. Rabin to Meir, Feb. 12, 1971, ISA, MFA, 6810/8.
41. The Jarring Initiative and the Response, Feb. 8, 1971, *IFR*, 1947–1974, vol. 2, 950–951.
42. Record of Conversation Between Rabin and Rogers, Feb. 24, 1971, ISA, RG A, Previously Classified Material, 7021/4; Addendum to Conversation with Secretary Rogers, Feb. 24, 1971, ibid.; Rabin, *Rabin Memoirs*, 194.
43. NSC Meeting Recording, Feb. 26, 1971, NARA, NPMS, WHT, conversation no. 48–4. A written record of the meeting can be found ibid., H-Files, box H-110.
44. Ibid.
45. The written record of the conversation attributes this line to Rogers. However, a close examination of the tape recording clearly indicates that the statement was made by President Nixon, not Secretary Rogers.
46. NSC Meeting Recording, Feb. 26, 1971.
47. Memorandum for the Record, Mar. 10, 1971, NARA, NPMS, NSCF, box 647, CF, ME, General, vol. 8, 1971 [3 of 3]; Kissinger to Nixon, Mar. 9, 1971, ibid., box 129, HAKOF, CF, ME; Nixon-Kissinger Recording, NARA, NPMS, WHT, conversation no. 464–17.
48. Interview of Secretary of State William P. Rogers by Elizabeth Drew for Public Broadcasting Service Program 30 *Minutes With . . .*, Mar. 9, 1971, NARA, RG 59, Secretary/Undersecretary Lot Files, WPR, box 16.

49. Nixon-Rogers Recording, Apr. 19, 1971, NARA, NPMS, WHT, conversation no. 2–4.
50. Nixon-Haldeman-Zeigler Recording, Apr. 26, 1971, ibid., conversation no. 488–6.
51. For records of Dulles meetings in Cairo in 1953, see *FRUS, 1952–1954*, vol. 9, 2065–2073.
52. Adele Rogers to Rogers Family, May 15, 1971, Personal Papers of William and Adele Rogers, Bethesda, MD.
53. Nixon-Rogers Recording, Apr. 22, 1971, NARA, NPMS, WHT, conversation no. 486–7. A written record of the conversation can be found ibid., POF, Memorandum for the President's File, box 84, Apr. 22, 1971. See also H. R. Haldeman, *The Haldeman Diaries: Inside the Nixon White House* (New York: G. P. Putnam's Sons, 1994), Apr. 22, 1971.
54. The Rogers Plan is discussed in chapter 2. For a text of Rogers's December 9 speech in which he launched his Middle East peace plan, see "Address by the Honorable William P. Rogers Before the 1969 Galaxy Conference on Adult Education, Sheraton Park Hotel, Washington, DC, Dec. 9, 1969, *DSB* 62, Jan. 5, 1970, 7–11.
55. Nixon-Rogers Recording, Apr. 22, 1971.
56. Nixon-Rogers Recording, May 10, 1971, NARA, NPMS, WHT, conversation no. 496–13.
57. David A. Korn, *Stalemate: The War of Attrition and Great Power Diplomacy in the Middle East, 1967–1970* (Boulder, CO: Westview, 1992), 210. In Korn's book, the figures are erroneously given in the billions instead of millions.
58. Nixon-Rogers Recording, May 10, 1971.
59. Nixon-Rogers Recording, May 19, 1971.
60. Ibid.
61. Nixon-Rogers Recording, May 10, 1971.
62. Ibid.
63. Interview with Joseph J. Sisco, Mar. 5, 2001. Sisco expressed these comments in a meeting with Rabin immediately on his return to Washington. Rabin, *Rabin Memoirs*, 200.
64. Adele Rogers to Rogers Family, May 15, 1971.
65. Nixon-Rogers Recording, May 10, 19, 1971.
66. Minutes of Conversation Between Meir and Rogers, May 6, 1971, 5:15 p.m., ISA, MFA, 9360/13.
67. Ibid.
68. Quoted in Meir's Statement to the Knesset, Feb. 9, 1971, *Israel's Foreign Relations, 1947–1974*, vol. 2, 956–957.
69. Minutes of Conversation Between Meir and Rogers, May 6, 1971, 5:15 p.m.
70. Nixon-Rogers Recording, May 10, 1971.
71. Minutes of Conversation Between Meir and Rogers, May 6, 1971, 5:15 p.m.

72. Adele Rogers to Rogers Family, May 15, 1971.
73. Telegram 2919 from the Embassy in Italy, May 8, 1971, NARA, NPMS, NSCF, box 657, CF, ME, Nodis/Cedar/Plus, vol. 2.
74. Consultations Prior to Conversations with Secretary Rogers, May 7, 1971, ISA, MFA, 9360/13.
75. Minutes of a Meeting Among Dayan, Dinitz, Sisco, and Atherton, May 7, 1971, ibid.
76. Main Points of Conversation Between Dayan and Sisco, May 7, 1971, ISA, RG A, Previously Classified Material, 7038/9; Saunders to Kissinger, May 17, 1971, NARA, NPMS, NSCF, box 1163, HHSF.
77. Minutes of a Meeting Among Dayan, Dinitz, Sisco, and Atherton, May 7, 1971.
78. Consultations Prior to Conversations with Secretary Rogers, May 7, 1971; Abba Eban, *An Autobiography* (New York: Random House, 1977), 475–476.
79. Main Points of Prime Minister's Talk with Rogers, May 7, 1971, ISA, RG A, Previously Classified Material, 7038/9.
80. Ibid.
81. Telegram 2919 from the Embassy in Italy to the Department of State, May 8, 1971.
82. In telegram 1103 from Cairo, May 9, 1971, Sisco relayed the details of his two-hour private meeting with President Sadat to Secretary Rogers. He first pointed out that Sadat "laid great stress in several different ways on two cardinal points: why he must have Egyptian troops across the canal; and why he needs a commitment to the international border in the context of an overall political settlement." Sadat also offered an "alternative proposal" for the United States to consider: "A limited number of UAR troops crossing the canal, with a specified limited amount and type of arms, with a wide 50 kilometer buffer zone between the two sides, with limited arms on the Israeli side of the new line." In connection with the ideas on the Russians which Sadat had earlier told Rogers, Sisco added: "I just want to confirm to your interpretation of what he said to you is absolutely correct. He reiterated this to me in plain language." NARA, NPMS, NSCF, box 1162, HHSF.
83. Nixon-Rogers Recording, May 10, 1971, NARA, NPMS, WHT, conversation no. 496–13.
84. Telegram 2919 from the Embassy in Italy to the Department of State, May 8, 1971.
85. Ibid.
86. Nixon-Rogers Recording, May 19, 1971.
87. On May 20, 1971, President Nixon announced that the United States and the Soviet Union had agreed to work out an ABM agreement and "certain measures with respect to the limitation of offensive strategic weapons." For provisions of the agreement, see Raymond L. Garthoff, *Détente and Confrontation: American-Soviet Relations from Nixon to Reagan* (Washington, DC: Brookings Institution, 1994), 167–170.

88. Nixon-Haldeman-Ehrlichman Recording, May 10, 1971, NARA, NPMS, WHT, conversation no. 496–16.

89. Nixon to Rogers, May 26, 1971, NARA, RG 59, Secretary/Undersecretary Lot Files, WPR, box 25. The memorandum was dictated by the president in the Oval Office on May 26, 1971. A partial recording of Nixon's dictation of the memo can be found in NARA, NPMS, WHT, conversation no. 505–2. Major portions of the dictation inexplicably remain classified while the memo is declassified in full. In a conversation with Haldeman on June 1, Kissinger complained about not being informed of the details of the president's memorandum. Haldeman wrote in his diary: Kissinger "thinks Rogers is engaged in secret negotiations, that the P[resident] knows about it and isn't telling Henry. So he asked me to ask the P[resident] what he sent to Rogers last week via military aide, which the P[resident] mentioned to Rogers on the phone while both Henry and I were in there, and also the direct question: is Rogers conducting a secret negotiation that K[issinger] doesn't know about. Henry says if he is, then he, Henry, will have to quit, that he can't tolerate something of that sort." Haldeman, *Haldeman Diaries*, June 1, 1971.

90. Nixon to Rogers, May 26, 1971.

91. Ibid.

92. Vladislov M. Zubok, *A Failed Empire: The Soviet Union in the Cold War from Stalin to Gorbachev* (Chapel Hill: University of North Carolina Press, 2007), 192–226.

93. Telegram from the Soviet Embassy in Washington, From the Diary of Anatoly Dobrynin, Feb. 14, 1971, Department of State, Office of the Historian, Russian-American Project Special Collection.

94. Memorandum for the President's Files, Jan. 28, 1971, NARA, NPMS, NSCF, box 490, PTF, Dobrynin/Kissinger, 1971.

95. Telegram from the Soviet Embassy in Washington, Jan. 31, 1971, Department of State, Office of the Historian, Russian-American Project Special Collection.

96. Telegram from the Soviet Embassy in Washington, Feb. 24, 1971, ibid.

97. Sadat, *In Search of Identity*, 221.

98. Kirpichenko, *Razvedka*, 114–117; Victor Israelyan, *On the Battlefields of the Cold War: A Soviet Ambassador's Confession* (University Park: Pennsylvania State University Press, 2003), 168. See also Christopher Andrew and Vasili Mitrokhin, *The World Was Going Our Way: The KGB and the Battle for the Third World* (New York: Basic Books, 2005), 154–155.

99. Kirpichenko, *Razvedka*, 114–117.

100. Quoted in Heikal, *Sphinx and the Commissar*, 227.

101. The text of the treaty was reprinted in the *NYT*, 28 May 1971. See also Rubinstein, *Red Star on the Nile*, 143–153; Galia Golan, *Soviet Policies in the Middle East: From World War II to Gorbachev* (Cambridge: Cambridge University Press, 1990),

77–79; and Mahmoud Riad, *The Struggle for Peace in the Middle East* (New York: Quartet Books, 1982), 204–206.

102. The Brezhnev Doctrine, CWIHP, Virtual Archive, Brezhnev Doctrine.

103. Matthew Ouimet, *The Rise and Fall of the Brezhnev Doctrine in Soviet Foreign Policy* (Chapel Hill: University of North Carolina Press, 2003), 9–33.

104. Quoted in Wilson to the Secretary of State for Foreign and Commonwealth Affairs, June 7, 1971, TNA, FCO 39/977.

105. Meeting of Presidium of USSR Supreme Soviet, June 28, 1971, TNA, FCO 39/977.

106. "The U.S.S.R. Gains in Egypt," NYT, May 30, 1971.

107. "Moscow and Cairo Sign Up for 15 Years," WP, May 29, 1971.

108. WHY, 1284.

109. R. A. Beaumont to A. D. Parsons, June 23, 1971, TNA, FCO 39/977.

110. Diplomatic Report no. 325/71, June 7, 1971, ibid.

111. Nixon-Rogers Recording, May 28, 1971, NARA, NPMS, WHT, conversation no. 3–166.

112. Ibid.

113. Telegram 1311 from Cairo, May 29, 1971, NARA, NPMS, NSCF, box 1163, HHSF.

114. Telegram 1639 from Cairo, July 6, 1971, ibid., box 134, CF, ME, Rabin-Kissinger 1971, vol. 2.

115. Kissinger to Nixon, June 26, 1971, NARA, NPMS, H-Files, box H-031.

116. Nixon-Rogers Recording, May 31, 1971, NARA, NPMS, WHT, conversation no. 3–203.

117. Nixon-Kissinger Recording, May 19, 1971.

118. Kissinger-Dobrynin Memcon, June 8, 1971, NARA, NPMS, NSCF, box 491, PTF, Dobrynin-Kissinger, 1971, vol. 5.

119. Ibid.

120. Nixon-Kissinger Recording, June 12, 1971, NARA, NPMS, WHT, conversation no. 518–3.

121. Records of Conversations between Rabin and Kissinger, May 25, June 4, 1971, ISA, MFA, 9352/3.

122. Nixon-Kissinger Recording, June 12, 1971.

123. Memorandum for the Record, NSC Meeting on the Middle East and South Asia, July 16, 1971, San Clemente, NARA, NPMS, H-Files, box H-110.

124. Ibid.

125. Joseph J. Sisco, interview with the author, Mar. 5, 2001.

126. Interview with Sisco as seen in the *Fifty Years War*, disc 2; Oral History Interview with Undersecretary of State Joseph J. Sisco, Mar. 19, 1990, ADST.

127. Minutes of Meeting between Meir and Sisco, Aug. 4, 1971, ISA, RG A, Previously Classified Material, 7029/6.

128. Minutes of Meeting between Meir and Sisco, July 30, 1971, ISA, RG A, Previously Classified Material, 7029/7; Sisco interview, Mar. 5, 2001.

129. Rabin, *Rabin Memoirs*, 201.
130. Minutes of Meeting between Meir and Sisco, July 30, 1971.
131. Ibid.
132. Ibid.

Chapter Six The Race to the Summit, September 1971–May 1972

1. Richard M. Nixon, *RN: The Memoirs of Richard Nixon* (New York: Grosset and Dunlap, 1978), 103–106.
2. Thomas W. Zeiler, "Nixon Shocks the World," paper presented to the Workshop on Unpeaceable Exchange: Trade and Conflict in the Global Arena, 1000–2000, University of Lisbon, July 17, 2010; Judith Stein, *Pivotal Decade: How the United States Traded Factories for Finance in the Seventies* (New Haven: Yale University Press, 2010).
3. "Transcript of the President's News Conference on Foreign and Domestic Affairs," *NYT*, Oct. 13, 1971.
4. *Public Papers of the Presidents of the United States: Richard Nixon, 1969* (Washington, DC: GPO, 1970), 67.
5. Memorandum from Kissinger for the President's File, Oct. 12, 1971, *FRUS*, 1969–1976, vol. 14, doc. 2.
6. Quoted in Anatoly Dobrynin, *In Confidence: Moscow's Ambassador to America's Six Cold War Presidents* (New York: Times Books, 1995), 209.
7. Memorandum of Conversation, From the Diary of Anatoly Dobrynin, Jan. 23, 1971, *Soviet-American Relations: The Détente Years, 1969–1972*, ed. David C. Geyer et al. (Washington, DC: US Department of State, 2007) (hereafter cited as *Soviet-American Relations*), doc. 116; *WHY*, 833; Dobrynin, *In Confidence*, 214–215.
8. Memorandum from Kissinger for the President's File, Oct. 12, 1971.
9. Editorial Note, ibid., doc. 43.
10. *WHY*, 1287.
11. Memorandum for the President's File, NARA, NPMS, NSCF, box 492, PTF, Dobrynin/Kissinger, 1971. An audio recording of this meeting can be found ibid., WHT, conversation no. 580–20.
12. Memorandum of the One-on-One Conversation between A. A. Gromyko and US President Nixon in Washington, Sept. 29, 1971, AVP RF, f. 0129, op. 55, p. 411, d. 2, l. 60–69, courtesy US Department of State; Nixon-Gromyko Recording, Sept. 29, 1971, NARA, NPMS, WHT, conversation no. 580–20; Nixon-Kissinger Recording, Sept. 30, 1971, ibid., conversation no. 581–2.
13. Memorandum of the One-on-One Conversation between A. A. Gromyko and U.S. President Nixon in Washington, Sept. 29 1971.
14. *WHY*, 838.
15. Nixon-Kissinger Recording, Sept. 30, 1971.

16. *WHY*, 1288; Nixon-Kissinger Telcon, Oct. 1, 1971, 9:40 a.m., NARA, NPMS, HAK Telcons, box 1.
17. Kissinger-Gromyko-Dobrynin Memcon, Sept. 30, 1971, NARA, NPMS, NSCF, box 492, PTF, Dobrynin/Kissinger, 1971.
18. Kissinger-Gromyko-Dobrynin Memcon, Sept. 30, 1971, *Soviet-American Relations*, 476–481.
19. The Soviet-Egyptian Treaty of Friendship and Cooperation is discussed in chapter 4. The text of the treaty was reprinted in the *NYT*, May 28, 1971.
20. Extract from Protocol No. 12 of the Politburo Meeting, Aug. 5, 1971, printed in Primakov, *Russia and the Arabs*, 266.
21. Secret Conversation with the Russians, Aug. 29, 1971, ISA, RG A, Previously Classifed Material, 7037/17; Minutes of a Meeting with Moshe Dayan, Aug. 31, 1971, ibid.; Primakov, *Russia and the Arabs*, 267–274.
22. Primakov, *Russia and the Arabs*, 274.
23. Rogers-Kissinger Telcons, Aug. 7, 1970, 12:00 p.m., 12:30 p.m., NARA, NPMS, HAK Telcons, box 6. For more on the disagreements between Rogers and Kissinger over the Aug. 7, 1970, cease-fire agreement, see chapter 4.
24. Terrance Smith, "Foreign Policy: Decision Power Ebbing at State Department," *NYT*, Jan. 18, 1971; Terrance Smith, interview with the author, February 2005.
25. Nixon-Kissinger Recording, Mar. 9, 1971, NARA, NPMS, WHT, conversation no. 464–17.
26. Memorandum of Conversation, From the Diary of Anatoly Dobrynin, Oct. 9, 1971, *Soviet-American Relations*, doc. 210.
27. Gromyko-Kissinger Memcon, Sept. 30, 1971, ibid., doc. 206.
28. Ibid., 204.
29. Yitzhak Rabin, *The Rabin Memoirs*, expanded ed. (Berkeley: University of California Press, 1996), 204–206.
30. "Soviet and Egyptian Options as of the Egyptian-Soviet Summit Meeting," October 1971, ISA, RG A, Previously Classified Material, 7053/12.
31. Conversation Between Meir and Rogers, Dec. 2, 1971, ISA, MFA, 5968/21.
32. Nixon-Meir Recording, Dec. 2, 1971, NARA, NPMS, WHT, conversation no. 628–16; Nixon-Kissinger Recording, Dec. 2, 1971, ibid., conversation no. 628–2; Rabin, *Memoirs*, 206–208; *WHY*, 1289.
33. Rabin, *Memoirs*, 209.
34. *WHY*, 1289.
35. Brezhnev to Nixon, Jan. 17, 1972, NARA, NPMS, NSCF, box 493, PTF, Dobrynin/Kissinger, 1972.
36. Telegram from Soviet Embassy in Washington to USSR Ministry of Foreign Affairs, Feb. 20, 1972, AVP RF, f. 59a, op. 7, p. 13, d. 9, l. 341–347, courtesy US Department of State.
37. Ibid.

38. Dobrynin, *In Confidence*, 244–245; WHY, 1124–1140.
39. Kissinger to Nixon, Apr. 19, 1972, *FRUS*, 1969–1976, vol. 14, doc. 125, emphasis added.
40. Nixon to Kissinger, Apr. 20, 1972, NARA, NPMS, WHSF, PPF, box 74, PSF, April 1972, Kissinger Trip to Moscow, emphasis in original; WHY, 1154.
41. Memorandum of Conversation, Apr. 22, 1972, *FRUS*, 1969–1976, vol. 14, doc. 141, n. 5.
42. Kissinger-Gromyko Memcon, Apr. 23, 1972, ibid., doc. 150; Kissinger-Gromyko Memcon, Apr. 23, 1972, *Soviet-American Relations*, doc. 309.
43. Ibid.
44. Kissinger-Brezhnev Memcon, Apr. 24, 1972; Kissinger-Brezhnev Memcon, Apr. 24, 1972, *Soviet-American Relations*, doc. 312; Kissinger to Haig, Apr. 24, 1972, *FRUS*, 1969–1976, vol. 14, doc. 163.
45. WHY, 1151.
46. Brezhnev to Nixon, May 1, 1972, *FRUS*, 1969–1976, vol. 14, doc. 181, emphasis in original.
47. Rogers to Nixon, May 1, 1972, NARA, RG 59, Central Files, 1970–73, POL US–USSR.
48. Anwar el-Sadat, *In Search of Identity: An Autobiography* (New York: Harper and Row, 1978), 227, 286.
49. Notes on a Conversation with the Egyptian Prime Minister, Feb. 3, 1972, TNA, FCO 39/1217.
50. "Fog Over Suez," *Time*, Jan. 31, 1972.
51. Sadat, *In Search of Identity*, 286.
52. The account of Sadat's conversation in Moscow, Feb. 2, 3, 1972, is based on the account Sadat provided Josip Broz Tito during meeting in Brioni, Feb. 4, 5, 1972, CWIHP.
53. Mahmoud Riad, *The Struggle for Peace in the Middle East* (New York: Quartet Books, 1982), 227.
54. Sadat, *In Search of Identity*, 288.
55. Yugoslav Notes About the Talks of the President of the Republic with the President of the Arab Republic of Egypt Anwar al-Sadat, Feb. 4, 5, 1972, in Brioni, CWIHP.
56. Riad, *Struggle for Peace in the Middle East*, 224–225.
57. Ceausescu-Sadat Memcon, Apr. 6, 1972, CWIHP *Bulletin* no. 16, 542–543.
58. Ceausescu-Sadat Memcon, Cairo, Apr. 3, 1972, ibid., 541.
59. Minutes of First Meeting Between Meir and Ceausescu, May 5, 1972, 9:30–13:30, ISA, RG A, Previously Classified Material, 7099/16. The minutes were written by Simcha Dinitz based on what was read to him by the interpreter the following day; Handwritten Notes of Meeting Between Meir and Ceausescu, May 5, 1972, ibid.; Notes of Meeting Between Meir and Ceausescu, May 5, 1972, Bucharest, ibid., RG 130, MFA, 5256/1; Meir later discussed her conversation with Ceausescu during a

meeting with Nixon, Mar. 1, 1973. A record of that conversation can be found in *FRUS*, 1969–1976, vol. 25, doc. 35.

60. Golda Meir, *My Life* (London: Weidenfeld and Nicolson, 1975), 400–401.
61. Nixon-Meir Memcon, Mar. 1, 1973, *FRUS*, 1969–1976, vol. 25, doc. 35.
62. Mohamed Heikal, *The Road to Ramadan* (New York: Quadrangle, 1975), 169.
63. Soviet-Egyptian Joint Communiqué, Apr. 30, 1972, TNA, FCO 39/1217.
64. Editorial Note, *FRUS*, 1969–1976, vol. 14, doc. 43.
65. J. R. Young to Malcolm A. Holding, May 30, 1972, TNA, FCO 17/1647.
66. Ismail Fahmy, *Negotiating for Peace in the Middle East* (Baltimore: Johns Hopkins University Press, 1983), 6–7.
67. Ibid.
68. Young to Holding, May 30, 1972.
69. Ibid.
70. Fahmy, *Negotiating for Peace in the Middle East*, 5–9.
71. Notes of Meeting Between Tito and Ghaleb, May 23, 1972, CWIHP.
72. Kissinger to Nixon, May 22, 1972, *FRUS*, 1969–1976, vol. 14, doc. 256.
73. Ibid.
74. Nixon, *Memoirs*, 619.
75. Hedrick Smith, "Crowds on Nixon's Route Kept Subdued," *NYT*, May 23, 1972; *WHY*, 1206.
76. Nixon-Haig Recording, May 2, 1972, NARA, NPMS, WHT, conversation no. 717–20; Nixon-Kissinger Recording, May 3, 1972, ibid., conversation no. 718–9.
77. Dobrynin, *In Confidence*, 252–253.
78. Kissinger to Nixon, undated, *FRUS*, 1969–1976, vol. 14, doc. 232.
79. For details of the negotiations at the summit, see *FRUS*, 1969–1976, vol. 14; the Soviet records can be found in *Soviet-American Relations*, chap. 10. See also Dobrynin, *In Confidence*, 251–257; *WHY*, 1202–1257; and Nixon, *Memoirs*, 609–621.
80. Richard M. Nixon, *U.S. Foreign Policy for the 1970s*, vol. 4: *Shaping a Durable Peace*, A Report to the Congress (Washington: GPO, 1973), 37.
81. *WHY*, 1246.
82. Paper Prepared by the National Security Council Staff, May 16, 1972, *FRUS*, 1969–1976, vol. 14, doc. 231.
83. Memorandum of Conversation, May 26, 1972, ibid., doc. 284.
84. "Basic Provisions for a Final Settlement in the Middle East," NARA, NPMS, NSCF, box 73, HAKOF, CF, EUR, USSR.
85. *WHY*, 1246.
86. Memorandum of Conversation, May 26, 1972, *Soviet-American Relations*, doc. 368.
87. *WHY*, 1247.
88. Ibid.
89. Memorandum of Conversation, May 28, 1972, NARA, NPMS, NSCF, box 73, HAKOF, CF, EUR, USSR.

90. *WHY*, 1247.
91. Memorandum of Conversation, May 28, 1972, *FRUS*, 1969–1976, vol. 14, doc. 293.
92. *Public Papers of the Presidents of the United States: Richard Nixon, 1972* (Washington, DC: GPO, 1973), 635–642.
93. *WHY*, 1247–1248.
94. Raymond L. Garthoff, *Détente and Confrontation: American-Soviet Relations from Nixon to Reagan* (Washington, DC: Brookings Institution, 1994), 325.
95. "Rules for Coexistence," *NYT*, May 30, 1972.
96. *WHY*, 1248.
97. Sadat, *In Search of Identity*, 229.

Chapter Seven Bombshells and Backchannels, June 1972–February 1973

1. "Get Out! Egypt Tells Russians," *LAT*, July 18, 1972.
2. "Russians Go Home," *NYT*, July 19, 1972; "Russians Go Home," *Time*, July 31, 1972; "An Astonishing Turn in Cairo," *WP*, July 19, 1972; "Friction on the Nile," *LAT*, July 19, 1972.
3. Rogers to Nixon, July 20, 1972, NARA, NPMS, NSCF, box 1168, HHSF, Middle East Talks.
4. FCO Telegram no. 1118 from Cairo, July 31, 1972, TNA, FCO 39/1265.
5. Statement to the Knesset by Prime Minister Meir, July 26, 1972, *Israel's Foreign Relations*, 1947–1974, vols. 1–2; Telegram 4840 from Tel Aviv, July 26, 1972, NARA, NPMS, NSCF, box 1168, HHSF, Middle East Talks.
6. Brezhnev to Nixon, July 20, 1972, NARA, NPMS, NSCF, box 494, PTF, Dobrynin/Kissinger 1972; Kissinger-Dobrynin Memcon, July 20, 1972, ibid.
7. *WHY*, 1297; Nixon-Kissinger Recording, July 25, 1972, NARA, NPMS, WHT, conversation no. 752–6.
8. *WHY*, 1296.
9. Rogers to Nixon, July 20, 1972.
10. Ihsan A. Hijazi, "Domestic Pressure on Sadat Reported," *NYT*, July 19, 1972.
11. FCO Telegram no. 1118 from Cairo, July 31, 1972, TNA, FCO 39/1265.
12. Rogers to Nixon, July 20, 1972.
13. Anwar el-Sadat, *In Search of Identity: An Autobiography* (New York: Harper and Row, 1978), 230–231.
14. Speech by President Anwar Sadat to the 24 July Session of the ASU National Congress, July 24, 1972, NARA, NPMS, NSCF, box 1168, HHSF, Middle East Talks.
15. Telegram 1135 from Moscow, July 21, 1972, TNA, FCO 39/1217.
16. Nixon-Rogers Recordings, May 10, 19, 1971, NARA, NPMS, WHT, conversation nos. 496–13 and 501–4. See chapter 5.
17. Anwar el-Sadat, "Where Egypt Stands," *Foreign Affairs* 51, no. 1 (1972): 114–123.

18. Yugoslav Notes About the Talks of the President of the Republic with the President of the Arab Republic of Egypt Anwar al-Sadat, Feb. 4, 5, 1972, in Brioni, CWIHP; Sadat, *In Search of Identity*, 228; Alvin Rubinstein, *Red Star on the Nile: The Soviet-Egyptian Influence Relationship Since the June War* (Princeton, NJ: Princeton University Press, 1977), 170–180.
19. FCO Telegram 1049, July 20, 1972, TNA, FCO 39/1217.
20. The Message Addressed by President Sadat to President Leonid Brezhnev, Aug. 30, 1972, reprinted in Sadat, *In Search of Identity*, 317–324 (app. 1).
21. Speech by President Anwar Sadat to the 24 July Session of the ASU National Congress, July 24, 1972.
22. Sadat, *In Search of Identity*, 231.
23. Telegram 1135 from Moscow to London, July 21, 1972, TNA, FCO 39/1217.
24. Hijazi, "Domestic Pressure on Sadat Reported."
25. FCO Telegram 1062, July 21, 1972, TNA, FCO 39/1217; William Dullforce, "Egyptian Editor Says War Impasse Threatens Soviet Position in Country," *NYT*, June 17, 1972.
26. Saad el Shazly, *The Crossing of the Suez* (San Francisco: American Mideast Research, 1980), 159–160.
27. Ibid., 162–163.
28. Sadat, *In Search of Identity*, 229–230; Mahmoud Riad, *The Struggle For Peace in the Middle East* (New York: Quartet Books, 1982), 230; V. M. Vinogradov, "Toward a History of Soviet–Egyptian Relations," in M. S. Meyer et al., eds., *Then, in Egypt: Soviet Aid to Egypt in the Military Confrontation with Israel* (in Russian) (Moscow: Asia and Africa Institute, 2001), 19.
29. FCO Telegram 1049, July 20, 1972; Rubinstein, *Red Star on the Nile*, 188–189.
30. The Message Addressed by President Sadat to President Leonid Brezhnev, Aug. 30, 1972.
31. "Summary of Sadat Talk on Soviet Ties," *NYT*, July 19, 1972; Rubinstein, *Red Star on the Nile*, 189.
32. Mohamed Heikal, *The Road to Ramadan* (New York: Quadrangle, 1975), 118–119.
33. Speech by President Anwar Sadat to the 24 July Session of the ASU National Congress.
34. Yitzhak Rabin, *The Rabin Memoirs*, expanded ed. (Berkeley: University of California Press, 1996), 214.
35. Kissinger-Dobrynin Memcon, July 20, 1972, NARA, NPMS, NSCF, box 494, PTF; WHY, 1295.
36. Kissinger-Dobrynin Telcon, July 20, 1972, 9:45. a.m., NARA, NPMS, HAK Telcons, box 15.
37. Nixon to Brezhnev, July 27, 1972, NARA, NPMS, NSCF, box 131, CF, ME, Egypt/Ismail, vol. 4.

38. Henry Kissinger, *Diplomacy* (New York: Simon and Schuster, 1994), 739.
39. *WHY*, 1296.
40. Rogers to Nixon, July 20, 1972.
41. Ibid.
42. Alan Urwick to FCO, July 21, 1972, TNA, FCO 39/1217.
43. Cairo Letter no. 23/72, Call on Admiral Ivliev, Nov. 14, 1972, TNA, FCO 1217; Isabella Ginor and Gideon Remez, "The Origins of a Misnomer: The 'Expulsion' of Soviet Advisers from Egypt in 1972," in Nigel J. Ashton, ed., *The Cold War in the Middle East: Regional Conflict and the Superpowers, 1967–1973* (London: Routledge, 2007), 138.
44. Sadat, *In Search of Identity*, 320–324.
45. The Message Addressed by President Sadat to President Leonid Brezhnev, Aug. 30, 1972.
46. Heikal, *Road to Ramadan*, 199.
47. Adams to Douglas-Home, Mar. 20, 1973, TNA, FCO 93/235; Sadat-Ceausescu Memcon, Cairo, Apr. 3, 1972, CWIHP.
48. Sadat, *In Search of Identity*, 287.
49. Heikal, *Road to Ramadan*, 200.
50. *WHY*, 1293.
51. Green to Department of State, June 20, 1972, NARA, NPMS, NSCF, box 638, CF, ME, Arab Republic of Egypt (UAR), vol. 7, 1972; Memorandum of Conversation Between Neville I. Marzwell, a.k.a. Nabil I. Marzouk, and Jay P. Freres, USINT Cairo, May 30, 1972, ibid. Further information on the Marzwell contacts can be found in Department of State Telegrams 1640 from Cairo and 100611 from Washington, NARA, RG 59, Central Files, 1970–73, POL 27-14 ARAB-ISR.
52. Memorandum of Conversation Between Marzwell, and Freres, USINT Cairo, May 30, 1972.
53. Memorandum of Conversation Between Neville I. Marzwell, a.k.a. Nabil I. Marzouk, Marshall W. Wiley, DPO, USINT Cairo, and Jay P. Freres, USINT Cairo, June 15, 1972, NARA, NPMS, box 638, CF, ME, Arab Republic of Egypt (UAR), vol. 7, 1972 [2 of 2]; Telegram 1807 from Cairo, June 20, 1972, ibid. In the telegram Green relates that Marzwell briefed US officials in Cairo on June 14, but the memorandum of conversation indicates that the conversation took place on June 15.
54. Green to Department of State, June 20, 1972.
55. *WHY*, 1298.
56. Ibid.
57. Ibid., 1299.
58. Ibid., 1300.
59. Timothy Naftali, *Blind Spot: The Secret History of American Counterterrorism* (New York: Basic Books, 2005), 54–56.

60. Simon Reeve, *One Day in September: The Full Story of the 1972 Munich Olympic Massacre and the Israeli Revenge Operation "Wrath of God"* (New York: Arcade, 2000), 152–167.

61. "Israelis Report Raid in Lebanon," *NYT*, Feb. 21, 1973.

62. Kissinger-Rabin Memcon, Feb. 22, 1973, NARA, NPMS, NSCF, box 135, HAKOF, Rabin/Dinitz, Sensitive Memcons, 1973.

63. Rabin, *Memoirs*, 215.

64. Mohamed Heikal, *Secret Channels: The Inside Story of Arab-Israeli Peace Negotiations* (London: HarperCollins, 1996), 175.

65. British biographical sketch of Hafez Ismail, undated, TNA, PREM 15/1484; Gratton to Forrester, Feb. 1, 1973, ibid.; *YoU*, 212; Henry Tanner, "Egyptian to Visit U.S. to Give View," *NYT*, Feb. 18, 1973; Bernard Gwertzman, "Nixon and Rogers See a Cairo Aide," *NYT*, Feb. 24, 1973.

66. Kissinger to Nixon, Feb. 23, 1973, NARA, NPMS, NSCF, box 131, HAKOF, ME, Egypt/Ismail, vol. 2.

67. Sadat to Nixon, Feb. 18, 1973, *FRUS*, 1969–1976, vol. 25, doc. 21.

68. Richard M. Nixon, *RN: The Memoirs of Richard Nixon* (New York: Grosset and Dunlap, 1978), 786–787.

69. Heath-Nixon Memcon, Feb. 2, 1973, TNA, PREM 15/1764.

70. Nixon-Haig Recording, Jan. 23, 1973, NARA, NPMS, WHT, conversation no. 404–6.

71. Nixon Diary Entry, Feb. 3, 1973, printed in Nixon, *Memoirs*, 786–787.

72. Nixon to Rogers, May 26, 1971, NARA, RG 59, Secretary/Undersecretary Lot Files, WPR, box 25.

73. Kissinger to Nixon, Feb. 23, 1973.

74. Nixon, *Memoirs*, 786–787.

75. Kissinger to Nixon, Feb. 23, 1973, emphasis in original.

76. Nixon-Ismail Recording, Feb. 23, 1973, NARA, NPMS, WHT, conversation no. 862–10; Nixon-Ismail Memcon, Feb. 23, 1973, *FRUS*, 1969–1976, vol. 25, doc. 26.

77. Adams to Douglas-Home, Mar. 20, 1973, TNA, FCO 93/235.

78. Rogers-Ismail Memcon, Feb. 23, 1973, NARA, NPMS, NSCF, HAKOF, box 131, CF, ME, Egypt/Ismail, vol. 3; Adams to Douglas-Home, Mar. 20, 1973; *YoU*, 212.

79. Kissinger to Nixon, Feb. 23, 1973, emphasis in original; *YoU*, 212.

80. Kissinger-Ismail Memcon, Feb. 25, 1973, NARA, NPMS, NSCF, HAKOF, box 131, CF, ME, Egypt/Ismail, vol. 3.

81. Kissinger-Rabin Memcon, Feb. 22, 1973.

82. Ibid.

83. *YoU*, 213.

84. Kissinger-Ismail Memcons, Feb. 25, 26, 1973, NARA, NPMS, NSCF, HAKOF, box 131, CF, ME, Egypt/Ismail, vol. 3.

85. Kissinger to Nixon, Mar. 6, 1973, ibid., vol. 4.
86. Kissinger-Ismail Memcon, Feb. 25, 1973.
87. Summary of Conversation, Feb. 27, 1973, ISA, MFA, 9352/2.
88. Kissinger-Ismail Memcon, Feb. 25, 1973.
89. Kissinger to Nixon, Mar. 6, 1973.
90. Kissinger-Ismail Memcon, Feb. 25, 1973.
91. Sadat, *In Search of Identity*, 288.
92. Ibid.; Kissinger to Nixon, Mar. 6, 1973.
93. Kissinger to Nixon, Mar. 6, 1973.
94. *YoU*, 215–216.
95. Sadat, *In Search of Identity*, 288.
96. Kissinger-Ismail Memcon, Feb. 25, 1973.
97. Kissinger-Ismail Memcon, Feb. 26, 1973, ibid.
98. President Sadat's Interview with Arnaud De Borchgrave, Apr. 10, 1973, TNA, FCO, 93/235.
99. Sadat, *In Search of Identity*, 288–289.
100. Adams to Douglas-Home, Mar. 20, 1973, TNA, FCO 93/235.
101. Ibid.
102. Kissinger to Nixon, Mar. 6, 1973; Minutes of Meeting Between Meir, Kissinger, and Rabin, Feb. 28, 1973, ISA, MFA, 9352/2.
103. Nixon and Kissinger Recording, Feb. 26, 1973, *FRUS*, 1969–1976, vol. 25, doc. 29.
104. Minutes of Meeting Between Meir, Kissinger, and Rabin, Feb. 28, 1973; Summary of Conversation, Feb. 27, 1973, ibid.; Nixon-Kissinger Recording, Feb. 28, 1973, *FRUS*, 1969–1976, vol. 25, doc. 32.
105. Rabin, *Memoirs*, 215–216.
106. Minutes of Meeting Between Meir, Kissinger, and Rabin, Feb. 28, 1973.
107. Nixon-Meir Memcon, Mar. 1, 1973, NARA, NPMS, NSCF, box 1026, Presidential/ HAK Memcons, January–March 1973; *YoU*, 220.
108. President Sadat's Interview with Arnaud De Borchgrave, Apr. 10, 1973.
109. Sadat, *In Search of Identity*, 238.
110. Kissinger to Richardson, Mar. 2, 1973, *FRUS*, 1969–1976, vol. 25, doc. 37.
111. President Sadat's Interview with Arnaud De Borchgrave, Apr. 10, 1973.
112. Memorandum from NSC Staff, undated, doc. 1 in William Burr, ed., "The October War and U.S. Policy: Electronic Briefing Book," NSA. The paper was most likely drafted May 3–19, 1973.
113. Kissinger to Nixon, Mar. 30, 1973, *FRUS*, 1969–1976, vol. 25, doc. 42; Henry Tanner, "Sadat Takes over the Premiership," *NYT*, Mar. 27, 1973.
114. Schlesinger to Kissinger, Apr. 16, 1973, *FRUS*, 1969–1976, vol. 25, doc. 50.
115. Kissinger-Dinitz Memcon, Mar. 30, 1973, ibid., doc. 43.
116. President Sadat's Interview with Arnaud De Borchgrave, Apr. 10, 1973.

Chapter Eight The Contradictions of Leonid Brezhnev, March–October 5, 1973

1. "The Soviets: A Mix of Caution and Optimism," *Time*, Nov. 22, 1982.
2. Memorandum for the Record, Oct. 16, 1964, *FRUS*, 1964–1968, vol. 14, doc. 54.
3. Vladislav M. Zubok, *A Failed Empire: The Soviet Union in the Cold War from Stalin to Gorbachev* (Chapel Hill: University of North Carolina Press, 2007), 194–195.
4. WHY, 527; Anatoly Dobrynin, *In Confidence: Moscow's Ambassador to America's Six Cold War Presidents* (New York: Times Books, 1995), 212.
5. Kissinger to Nixon, Mar. 27, 1971, NARA, NPMS, NSCF, box 714, CF, EUR, USSR, vol. 12.
6. Kissinger to Nixon, Apr. 10, 1971, ibid., vol. 13.
7. Peter Osnos, "The Apparatchik Who Led the Soviet Board of Directors," WP, Nov. 12, 1982.
8. Zubok, *Failed Empire*, 203.
9. Ibid., 202; Melvyn P. Leffler, *For the Soul of Mankind: The United States, the Soviet Union, and the Cold War* (New York: Hill and Wang, 2007), 237; *SALT II and the Growth of Mistrust*, Conference No. 2 of the Carter-Brezhnev Project, May 6–9, 1994, NSA.
10. Richard M. Nixon, *RN: The Memoirs of Richard Nixon* (New York: Grosset and Dunlap, 1978), 613.
11. YoU, 242.
12. Kissinger to Nixon, undated, *FRUS*, 1969–1976, vol. 14, doc. 232.
13. Report Prepared by Yuri Andropov, KGB, May 7, 1973, CWIHP, The Mitrokhin Archives, About the Middle East, folder 81, The Chekist Anthology; Christopher Andrew and Vasili Mitrokhin, *The World Was Going Our Way: The KGB and the Battle for the Third World* (New York: Basic Books, 2005), 158–159.
14. Kissinger to Nixon, June 14, 1973, *FRUS*, 1969–1976, vol. 25, doc. 70.
15. YoU, 228.
16. Ibid., 228–235; Dobrynin, *In Confidence*, 278–279.
17. Kissinger to Nixon, undated.
18. YoU, 229–334.
19. Report Prepared by Yuri Andropov, KGB, May 7, 1973.
20. Memorandum of Conversation, May 7, 1973, *FRUS*, 1969–1976, vol. 25, doc. 53.
21. Ibid.; YoU, 461.
22. YoU, 282.
23. Kissinger-Gromyko Memcon, May 8, 1973, NARA, NPMS, NSCF, HAKOF, box 75, CF, EUR, USSR.
24. Nixon-Kissinger Recording, May 16, 1973, *FRUS*, 1969–1976, vol. 25, doc. 58.
25. Kissinger to Nixon, June 14, 1973.
26. Kissinger-Dinitz Memcon, June 14, 1973, NARA, NPMS, NSCF, HAKOF, box 135, Rabin/Dinitz Sensitive Memcons, 1973.

27. Dobrynin, *In Confidence*, 288.
28. Brezhnev to Nixon, May 13, 1973, *FRUS, 1969–1976*, vol. 25, doc. 56.
29. Keith W. Olson, *Watergate: The Presidential Scandal That Shook America* (Lawrence: Kansas University Press, 2003), 90–91; Stanley Kutler, *The Wars of Watergate: The Last Crisis of Richard Nixon* (New York: Norton, 1992), 323–357; Stephen Ambrose, *Nixon: Ruin and Recovery, 1973–1990* (New York: Simon and Schuster, 1991), 179–201; Richard Reeves, *President Nixon: Alone in the White House* (New York: Simon and Schuster, 2001), 592–603; Carl Bernstein and Bob Woodward, "Dean Alleges Nixon Knew of Cover-Up Plan," WP, June 3, 1972.
30. *YoU*, 77–78, 289.
31. Nixon, *Memoirs*, 877; Dobrynin, *In Confidence*, 271.
32. Brezhnev's remarks were relayed by Brandt to Prime Minister Meir during a meeting in Jerusalem in June 1973. Dinitz informed Kissinger of the remarks on June 15, saying that "Brandt said to the Prime Minister that Brezhnev doesn't put importance on Watergate. He sees it as an anti-Communist plot. . . . Mrs. Meir wanted me to pass this on." NARA, NMPS, NSCF, HAKOF, box 135, Rabin-Dinitz Sensitive Memcons, 1973.
33. Dobrynin, *In Confidence*, 270–271; *YoU*, 287.
34. Brezhnev to Nixon, Feb. 22, 1973, NARA, NPMS, NSCF, PTF, box 495, Dobrynin/ Kissinger, 1973; Nixon, *Memoirs*, 875.
35. Premier Alexei Kosygin's 1967 visit to the United States, during which he met with President Lyndon Johnson at Glassboro, New Jersey, was officially to the United Nations.
36. Dobrynin, *In Confidence*, 281.
37. "The Nine Pacts of Brezhnev's Visit," NYT, June 25, 1973; Dobrynin, *In Confidence*, 281–282.
38. *YoU*, 286–301; Nixon, *Memoirs*, 879–882; Dobrynin, *In Confidence*, 281–286.
39. Dobrynin, *In Confidence*, 277.
40. Nixon-Brezhnev Memcon, June 23, 1973, NARA, NPMS, NSCF, HAKOF, box 75; Brezhnev Visit, June 18–25, 1973, Memcons.
41. Kissinger-Gromyko Memcon, June 23, 1973, ibid.; *YoU*, 295–296; Robert Dallek, *Nixon and Kissinger: Partners in Power* (New York: HarperCollins, 2007), 493.
42. Ibid.
43. *YoU*, 295–296. For the text of the joint communiqué issued on June 25, see *Public Papers of the Presidents of the United States: Richard Nixon, 1973* (Washington, DC: GPO, 1974), 611–619.
44. *YoU*, 297.
45. Nixon, *Memoirs*, 883–884.
46. *YoU*, 297; Nixon, *Memoirs*, 884.
47. *YoU*, 297.

48. Nixon, *Memoirs*, 612–613; *YoU*, 297. A record of Nixon's meeting at Brezhnev's dacha on May 24, 1972, can be found in *FRUS, 1969–1976*, vol. 14, doc. 271.

49. Dobrynin, *In Confidence*, 288.

50. Memorandum from Henry Kissinger for the President's Files, June 23, 1973, *FRUS, 1969–1976*, vol. 25, doc. 73; Telegram no. 2060, July 1, 1973, TNA, PREM 15/1933.

51. Memorandum from Henry Kissinger for the President's Files, June 23, 1973, *FRUS, 1969–1976*, vol. 25, doc. 73.

52. Ibid.

53. Ibid.; Telegram no. 2060, July 1, 1973, TNA, PREM 15/1933.

54. Memorandum from Henry Kissinger for the President's Files, June 23, 1973, *FRUS, 1969–1976*, vol. 25, doc. 73.

55. Nixon, *Memoirs*, 884–885.

56. Telegram no. 2060, 1 July 1973, TNA, PREM 15/193.

57. *YoU*, 297.

58. Ibid., 298; Dobrynin, *In Confidence*, 288.

59. Nixon, *Memoirs*, 885.

60. Memorandum from Henry Kissinger for the President's Files, June 23, 1973.

61. Saunders to Kissinger, "Message from King Hussein," May 17, 1973, *FRUS, 1969–1976*, vol. 25, doc. 61; Précis of National Intelligence Estimate, May 17, 1973, ibid., doc. 59; Editorial Note, ibid., doc. 65.

62. Schlesinger to Kissinger, "Israeli Estimates of Egypt's Present Military Intentions," May 5, 1973, ibid., doc. 52; Uri Bar-Joseph, *The Watchman Fell Asleep: The Surprise of Yom Kippur and Its Sources* (Albany: State University of New York, 2005), 67–69; Abba Eban, *Personal Witness: Israel Through My Eyes* (New York: G. P. Putnam's Sons, 1992), 516–517.

63. Dobrynin, *In Confidence*, 288.

64. Telegram no. 2060, July 1, 1973.

65. Nixon, *Memoirs*, 885.

66. Memorandum from Henry Kissinger for the President's Files, June 23, 1973.

67. Dobrynin, *In Confidence*, 288.

68. Nixon-Kissinger Telcon, Oct. 14, 1973, 9:04 a.m., NARA, NPMS, HAK Telcons, box 23.

69. *YoU*, 297–298.

70. US-USSR Communiqué, June 26, 1973, PREM 15/1933, TNA.

71. *YoU*, 299.

72. Ismail Fahmy, *Negotiating for Peace in the Middle East* (Baltimore: Johns Hopkins University Press, 1983), 6.

73. Urwick to Craig, July 3, 1973, TNA, FCO 93/43.

74. Heikal, *Road to Ramadan*, 205–206.

75. Bone to Nixon, July 24, 1973, TNA, FCO 94/43.

76. Soviet Oral Note in the Name of the Ambassador, July 19, 1973, NARA, NPMS, NSCF, HAKOF, box 72, CF, EUR, U.S.-USSR; Kissinger to Nixon, July 21, 1973, ibid.; Bone to Nixon, July 24, 1973.

77. Anwar el-Sadat, *In Search of Identity: An Autobiography* (New York: Harper and Row, 1978), 242.

78. Saad el Shazly, *The Crossing of the Suez* (San Francisco: American Mideast Research, 1980), 24–39; Sadat, *In Search of Identity*, 249–251; Rabinovich, *The Yom Kippur War: The Epic Encounter That Transformed the Middle East* (New York: Random House, 2004), 25–30.

79. Heikal, *Road to Ramadan*, 181.

80. Patrick Seale, *Asad: The Struggle for the Middle East* (Berkeley: University of California Press, 1989), 197.

81. Memorandum from NSC Staff, undated, doc. 1 in William Burr, ed., "The October War and U.S. Policy: Electronic Briefing Book," NSA. The paper was most likely drafted May 3–19, 1973. Jim Hoagland, "Cairo Aglow, War Effort Fades," WP, Mar. 26, 1973.

82. Henry Tanner, "Sadat's New Powers: Image of a Man Clearing the Deck," *NYT*, Mar. 31, 973.

83. Gladstone to Williams, Aug. 7, 1973, TNA, FCO 93/43.

84. Ibid.

85. Vinogradov's Version of October Events, Apr. 24, 1974, TNA, FCO 93/561.

86. Gamassy's Lectures on October War, Oct. 1, 1974, ibid.

87. Brown to Kissinger, "Hussein on His Private Talk with Sadat," Sept. 19, 1973, NARA, NPMS, Mandatory Review Opening 2008, temporary box 7.

88. Avi Shlaim, *Lion of Jordan: The Life of King Hussein in War and Peace* (New York: Knopf, 2008), 366–367; Rabinovich, *Yom Kippur War*, 49–51.

89. Shlaim, *Lion of Jordan*, 366–367.

90. Cline to Kissinger, "Syrian Military Intentions," Sept. 30, 1973, NARA, NPMS, NSCF, box 1173, HHSF, MENF.

91. Telegram from the Embassy in Israel to the Department of State, Oct. 1, 1973, NARA, NPMS; Moshe Dayan, *Story of My Life* (New York: Morrow, 1976), 469.

92. JCS Telegram 1448 to Washington, Oct. 2, 1973, *FRUS*, 1969–1973, vol. 25, doc. 92, n. 2.

93. Memorandum of Conversation, Sept. 28, 1973, NARA, NPMS, NSCF, HAKOF, box 71, CF, EUR, USSR; Sonnenfeldt to Kissinger, Oct. 10, 1973, *FRUS*, 1969–1976, vol. 25, doc. 151.

94. "Vinogradov's Version of October Events," Oct. 20, 1974, TNA, FCO 93/561; Sadat, *In Search of Identity*, 246; Victor L. Israelyan, *Inside the Kremlin During the Yom Kippur War* (University Park: Pennsylvania State University Press, 1997), 10.

95. Israelyan, *Inside the Kremlin*, 10–11.

96. Ibid., 3.

97. *YoU*, 465; "The Performance of the Intelligence Community Before the Arab-Israeli War of October 6, 1973: A Preliminary Post-Mortem Report," Dec. 20, 1973, *FRUS*, 1969–1976, vol. 25, doc. 412.

98. *YoU*, 465–467.

99. *FRUS*, 1969–1976, vol. 25, doc. 97; *YoU*, 466.

100. "Fear of Détente, Small Hope for a Settlement," *Time*, Oct. 22, 1973.

101. *YoU*, 469–470.

102. Kissinger-Haig Telcon, Oct. 6, 1973, 10:35 a.m., NARA, NPMS, HAK Telcons, box 22.

103. Note from Soviet Leadership to Nixon and Kissinger, Oct. 6, 1973, *FRUS*, 1969–1976, vol. 25, doc. 108.

Chapter Nine The Crisis of Détente: October 1973

1. *The Commission of Inquiry—The Yom Kippur War, an Additional Partial Report: Reasoning and Complement to the Partial Report of April 1, 1974* (in Hebrew), 7 vols. (Jerusalem: GPO, 1974, hereafter cited as Agranat), 71; "Sirens Break Solemnity of Israel's Yom Kippur," *LAT*, Oct. 7, 1973; "Black October, Old Enemies at War Again," *Time*, Oct. 15, 1973.

2. Consultations in the Prime Minister's Bureau, Oct. 6, 1973, 8:05 a.m., ISA, Special Collection on the Yom Kippur War.

3. Abraham Rabinovich, *The Yom Kippur War: The Epic Encounter That Transformed the Middle East* (New York: Random House, 2004), 85–169; Patrick Seale, *Asad: The Struggle for the Middle East* (Berkeley: University of California Press, 1989), 202.

4. Telegram from the Polish Embassy in Cairo, Oct. 7, 1973, Polish Foreign Ministry Archives, Warsaw, courtesy of J. Hershberg. I thank Aleksandra Dybkowska, an undergraduate student at the City College of New York, for her translation assistance; Diplomatic Report 86/74 from Cairo, Jan. 7, 1974, TNA, FCO 93/561.

5. Dinitz-Kissinger Memcon, Oct. 9, 1973, *FRUS*, 1969–1976, vol. 25, doc. 132; Consultations in the Prime Minister's Bureau, Oct. 7, 1973, 1:40 p.m., ISA, Special Collection on the Yom Kippur War.

6. Consultations in the Prime Minister's Bureau, Oct. 7, 1973, 2:50 p.m., ISA, Special Collection on the Yom Kippur War.

7. Department of State Middle East Task Force, Situation Report no. 8, Oct. 7, 1973, William Burr, ed., "The October War and U.S. Policy, Electronic Briefing Book," doc. 19, NSA; Kissinger-Dinitz Memcon, Oct. 7, 1973, 8:20 p.m., NARA, RG 59, Records of Henry Kissinger, 1973–1977, box 25, cat C 1974 Arab-Israeli War.

8. Minutes of Meeting with Prime Minister Meir, Oct. 7, 1973, 1:40 p.m.

9. Telegram from the Polish Embassy in Cairo, Oct. 8, 1973, Polish Foreign Ministry Archives, Warsaw, courtesy of J. Hershberg, translation by Aleksandra Dybkowska.

10. Ismail to Kissinger, Oct. 7, 1973, *FRUS, 1969–1976*, vol. 25, doc. 116.
11. Golda Meir, *My Life* (London: Weidenfeld and Nicolson, 1975), 440–441; Richard B. Parker, ed., *The October War: A Retrospective* (Gainesville: University Press of Florida, 2001), 94; Rashid Khalidi, *Sowing Crisis: The Cold War and the American Dominance in the Middle East* (Boston: Beacon Press, 2009), 126–133; FCO Telegram 497 to Cairo and Washington, Oct. 19, 1973, TNA, PREM 15/1766.
12. Seale, *Asad*, 208; Saad El Shazly, *The Crossing of the Suez* (San Francisco: American Mideast Research, 1980), 245–246; Avi Shlaim, *The Iron Wall: Israel and the Arab World* (New York: W. W. Norton, 2000), 319; Rabinovich, *Yom Kippur War*, 10–16; Parker, *October War*, 129.
13. *YoU*, 479.
14. *Ibid.*, 637.
15. Anwar el-Sadat, *In Search of Identity: An Autobiography* (New York: Harper and Row, 1978), 255.
16. *YoU*, 460.
17. Kissinger-Dobrynin Telcon, Oct. 6, 1973, 6:40 a.m., NARA, NPMS, HAK Telcons, Box 22.
18. Kissinger-Dobrynin Telcon, Oct. 6, 1973, 7:20 p.m., ibid. Kissinger's other calls to Dobrynin that day came at 7:46 a.m., 9:20 a.m., 9:25 a.m., 11:25 a.m., 3:50 p.m., 5:45 p.m., 6:20 p.m., and 9:10 p.m. Henry Kissinger, *Crisis: The Anatomy of Two Major Foreign Policy Crises* (New York: Simon and Schuster, 2003), 15–84.
19. *YoU*, 468.
20. Kissinger-Huang Chen Memcon, Oct. 6, 1973, Burr, "The October War and U.S. Policy," doc. 72.
21. Kissinger-Dobrynin Telcon, Oct. 6, 1973, 9:35 a.m., NARA, NPMS, HAK Telcons, Box 22; *YoU*, 471.
22. Victor L. Israelyan, *Inside the Kremlin During the Yom Kippur War* (University Park: Pennsylvania State University Press, 1997), 30–39.
23. Quoted in Richard Ned Lebow and Janice Gross Stein, *We All Lost the Cold War* (Princeton, NJ: Princeton University Press, 1994), 182.
24. Israelyan, *Inside the Kremlin*, 32–33.
25. "Sadat Reveals Moscow Pressure on Egypt to Accept Ceasefire to End October War," Mar. 29, 1973, TNA, FCO 93/561; "Vinogradov's Version of October Events," Oct. 20, 1974, ibid.; Israelyan, *Inside the Kremlin*, 39; Sadat, *In Search of Identity*, 252–253.
26. Israelyan, *Inside the Kremlin*, 31–33.
27. Lebow and Stein, *We All Lost the Cold War*, 186.
28. Message from the Soviet Union Leadership to Nixon and Kissinger, Oct. 6, 1973, *FRUS, 1969–1976*, vol. 25, doc. 106; Brezhnev to Nixon, Oct. 7, 1973, ibid., doc. 118; Kissinger-Dobrynin Telcon, Oct. 8, 1973, 9:54 a.m., NARA, NPMS, HAK Telcons, box 22.

29. Henry Kissinger, "Moral Purposes and Foreign Policy Choices," *DSB* 69, Oct. 29, 1973, 525–531.

30. Ibid.

31. Kissinger-Dinitz Telcon, Oct. 9, 1973, 1:45 a.m., NARA, NPMS, HAK Telcons, box 22.

32. Minutes of Meeting with Prime Minister Meir, Oct. 9, 1973, 8:05 a.m., ISA, Special Collection on the Yom Kippur War.

33. Kissinger-Dinitz Memcon, Oct. 9, 1973, 8:20–8:40 a.m., NARA, RG 59, Records of Henry Kissinger, E-5403, box 25, Arab-Israeli War.

34. Memorandum of Conversation, Oct. 7, 1973, *FRUS*, 1969–1976, vol. 25, doc. 113.

35. Kissinger-Dinitz Telcon, Oct. 8, 1973, 1:14 p.m., NARA, NPMS, HAK Telcons, box 22.

36. Ibid.; *YoU*, 491–492.

37. Memorandum of Conversation, Oct. 9, 1973, *FRUS*, 1969–1976, vol. 25, doc. 133.

38. Ibid.

39. Ibid.

40. Quandt to Kissinger, Oct. 9, 1973, ibid., doc. 137.

41. Agnew resigned the vice presidency Oct. 10, 1973, under allegations of extortion, bribery, and income-tax violations during his tenure as governor of Maryland.

42. Memorandum of Conversation, Oct. 9, 1973, 4:45 p.m., *FRUS*, 1969–1976, vol. 25, doc. 138.

43. Richard M. Nixon, *RN: The Memoirs of Richard Nixon* (New York: Grosset and Dunlap, 1978), 924; Memorandum of Conversation, Oct. 10, 1973, *FRUS*, 1969–1976, vol. 25, doc. 143.

44. William B. Quandt, "Soviet Policy in the October 1973 War," A Report Prepared for the Office of the Assistant Secretary of Defense/International Security Affairs by the Rand Corporation, May 1976.

45. Kissinger-Schlesinger Telcon, Oct. 10, 1973, 7:15 p.m., NARA, NPMS, HAK Telcons, box 22.

46. Schlesinger-Moorer Telcon, Oct. 10, 1973, *FRUS*, 1969–1976, vol. 25, doc. 142, emphasis in original.

47. Diary Entry of the Chairman of the Joint Chiefs, Oct. 10, 1973, ibid., doc. 143.

48. Ibid.

49. FCO Telegram 3183, Oct. 12, 1973, TNA, PREM 15/1765.

50. Record of Conversation Between Foreign and Commonwealth Secretary and Dr. Kissinger, Oct. 13, 1973, TNA, PREM/1765; Telegram 132200Z from FCO to Washington, Oct. 13, 1973, ibid.; Douglas-Home-Kissinger Telcon, Oct. 13, 1973, 3:35 p.m., *Crisis*, 232–233.

51. Record of a Meeting at Chequers, Oct. 13, 1973, 7 p.m., TNA, PREM 15/1765.

52. Douglas-Home-Kissinger Telcon, Oct. 13, 1973, 3:35 p.m., NARA, NPMS, HAK Telcons, box 22; Telegram 3209 to London, Oct. 13, 1973, TNA, PREM 15/1765.

53. Telegram 130630Z from Washington, Oct. 13, 1973, ibid.

54. FCO Telegram 3208, Oct. 12, 1973, TNA, PREM 15/1765.

55. Ibid.

56. Memorandum of Conversation, Oct. 12, 1972, *FRUS*, 1969–1976, vol. 25, doc. 164.

57. Richard B. Parker, ed., *The October War: A Retrospective* (Gainesville: University Press of Florida, 2001), 158.

58. Moorer-Goodpaster Telcon, Oct. 15, 1973, 9:20 a.m., *FRUS*, 1969–1976, vol. 25, doc. 183; *YoU*, 525; Minutes of a Washington Special Actions Group Meeting, Oct. 15, 1973, 10:08–11:08 a.m., *FRUS*, 1969–1976, vol. 25, doc. 184.

59. Editorial Note, *FRUS*, 1969–1976, vol. 25, doc. 198.

60. *YoU*, 873; Judith Stein, *Pivotal Decade: How the United States Traded Factories for Finance in the 1970s* (New Haven: Yale University Press, 2010), 81–82.

61. Minutes of a Washington Special Actions Group Meeting, Oct. 15, 1973, 10:08–11:08 a.m.

62. David W. Lesch, *The Arab-Israeli Conflict: A History* (New York: Oxford University Press, 2007), 249; Seale, *Asad*, 213.

63. Statement to the Knesset by Prime Minister Meir, Oct. 16, 1973, *IFR*, vols. 1–2, 1947–1974, Yom Kippur War and Its Aftermath, doc 7.

64. Israelyan, *Inside the Kremlin*, 95–110.

65. Kissinger-Dobrynin Telcon, Oct. 19, 1973, 11:04 p.m., NARA, NPMS, HAK Telcons, box 23.

66. Cromer to Douglas-Home, Oct. 20, 1973, TNA, PREM 15/1766.

67. *YoU*, 542.

68. Stanley I. Kutler, *The Wars of Watergate: The Last Crisis of Richard Nixon* (New York: W. W. Norton, 1990), 383–414; Keith W. Olson, *Watergate: The Presidential Scandal That Shook America* (Lawrence: University Press of Kansas, 2003), 103–122; "Judge Sirica's Order," *NYT*, Aug. 30, 1973.

69. John M. Crewdson, "Prosecutor Firm," *NYT*, Oct. 20, 1973; James Doyle, *Not Above the Law: The Battles of Watergate Prosecutors Cox and Jaworski* (New York: William Morrow, 1977).

70. Nixon, *Memoirs*, 929.

71. Kutler, *Wars of Watergate*, 383–414; Keith W. Olson, *Watergate: The Presidential Scandal That Shook America* (Lawrence: University Press of Kansas, 2003), 103–122; Carroll Kilpatrick, "President Obolishes Prosecutor's Office; FBI Seals Records," *WP*, Oct. 21, 1973.

72. "Justice Undone," *WP*, Oct. 21, 1973; "The Tape Cover-up," *NYT*, Oct. 21, 1973.

73. James Reston, "Moral and Legal Tangle," *NYT*, Oct. 21, 1973.

74. William Safire, "The Big Play," *NYT*, Oct. 22, 1973.

75. Nixon to Brezhnev, Oct. 22, 1973, NARA, NPMS, NSCF, HAKOF, box 70, CF, EUR, USSR, vol. 7.

76. Interview with Kissinger as seen in *The Fifty Years War: Israel and the Arabs* (New York: Public Broadcasting Service, 1998), disc 2.

77. Scowcroft to Kissinger, Oct. 20, 1973, NARA, NPMS, NSCF, HAKOF, box 39, HAK Trip—Moscow, Tel Aviv, London, Oct. 20–23, 1973, TOHAK 1–60.

78. Kissinger to Scowcroft, Oct. 21, 1973, *FRUS*, 1969–1976, vol. 25, doc. 218.

79. Brezhnev-Kissinger Memcon, Oct. 20, 1973, NARA, NPMS, NSCF, HAKOF, box 76, CF, EUR, USSR, Kissinger Trip to Moscow, Tel Aviv, London, October 20–22, 1973; Scowcroft to Nixon, Oct. 20, 1973, *FRUS*, 1969–1976, vol. 25, doc. 217.

80. Brezhnev-Kissinger Memcon, Oct. 20, 1973.

81. Telegram to HAK32557, Oct. 21, 1973, NARA, NPMS, NSCF, HAKOF, box 76, CF, EUR, USSR, Kissinger Trip to Moscow, Tel Aviv, London, October 20–22, 1973.

82. Israelyan, *Inside the Kremlin*, 129–132.

83. Memorandum of Conversation, Oct. 21, 1973, 12:00–4:00 p.m., NARA, NPMS, NSCF, HAKOF, box 76, CF, EUR, USSR, Kissinger Trip to Moscow, Tel Aviv, London, October 20–22, 1973; Kissinger to Scowcroft, Oct. 21, 1973, *FRUS*, 1969–1976, vol. 25, doc. 220.

84. Kissinger to Scowcroft, Oct. 21, 1973.

85. Security Council Resolution 338, Oct. 22, 1973, *IFR*, vols. 1–2: 1947–1974, The Yom Kippur War and Aftermath, doc. 8.

86. Minutes of the Secretary of State's Staff Meeting, Oct. 23, 1973, 4:35 p.m., NARA, RG 59, Transcripts of Secretary of State Kissinger's Staff Meetings, 1973–1977, box 1.

87. Memorandum of Conversation, Oct. 22, 1973, *FRUS*, 1969–1976, vol. 25, doc. 227.

88. Nixon to Meir, Oct. 21, 1973, ibid., doc. 226.

89. Abba Eban, *Personal Witness: Israel Through My Eyes* (New York: G. P. Putnam's Sons, 1992), 536.

90. Kissinger-Meir Memcon, Oct. 22, 1973, 1:35–2:15 p.m., NARA, NPMS, NSCF, box 76, CF, ME; *YoU*, 564–565.

91. Memorandum of Conversation, Oct. 22, 1973, 2:30–4:00 p.m., *FRUS*, 1969–1976, vol. 25, doc. 232.

92. Kissinger-Meir Memcon, Oct. 22, 1973, 1:35–2:15 p.m.

93. Minutes of Luncheon Meeting Among Kissinger, Meir, Allon, Dayan, Eban, and Rabin, Oct. 22, 1973, 3:00 p.m., ISA, RG A, Previously Classified Material, 7244/17; Minutes of Post-Luncheon Meeting, Oct. 22, 1973, 4:15 p.m., ibid.

94. Telegram from the Polish Embassy in Cairo, Oct. 23, 1973, Polish Foreign Ministry Archives, Warsaw, courtesy of J. Hershberg, translation by Aleksandra Dybkowska; Israelyan, *Inside the Kremlin*, 154–155.

95. Brezhnev to Kissinger, Oct. 23, 1973, *FRUS*, 1969–1976, vol. 25, doc. 239.

96. Sadat to Nixon, Oct. 23, 1973, ibid., doc. 246.

97. Kissinger-Dinitz Telcon, Oct. 23, 1973, 11:04 a.m., NARA, NPMS, HAK Telcons, box 23.

98. Ray Cline to Kissinger, Oct. 24, 1973, Burr, "The October War and U.S. Policy," doc. 67.

99. The text of UN Resolution 339 can be found in the *NYT*, Oct. 24, 1973.
100. Kissinger-Dintiz Telcon, Oct. 24, 1973, 9:22 a.m., NARA, NPMS, HAK Telcons, box 23.
101. Kissinger-Dintiz Telcon, Oct. 24, 1973, 9:32 a.m., ibid.
102. Memorandum for the Record, Oct. 24/25, 1973, *FRUS*, 1969–1976, vol. 25, doc. 267.
103. Brezhnev to Nixon, Oct. 24, 1973, NARA, NPMS, NSCF, box 69, HAKOF, CF, EUR, USSR, Dobrynin/Kissinger, 1973.
104. *YoU*, 583–584.
105. *WHY*, 584–585; Anatoly Dobrynin, *In Confidence: Moscow's Ambassador to America's Six Cold War Presidents* (New York: Times Books, 1995), 300–301.
106. Kissinger-Haig Telcon, Oct. 24, 1973, 10:20 p.m., NARA, NPMS, HAK Telcons, box 23.
107. Ibid.; *YoU*, 585.
108. Memorandum for the Record, Oct. 24/25, 1973, emphasis in original.
109. Ibid., emphasis in original.
110. Ibid.
111. Ibid.
112. Ibid.
113. Ibid.; *YoU*, 587–588.
114. Memorandum for the Record, Oct. 24/25, 1973; *YoU*, 588.
115. Telegram 3328 to London, Oct. 25, 1973, TNA, PREM 15/1766; Message from Lord Cromer in Washington at 6:15 a.m., Oct. 25, 1973, ibid.; Kissinger-Cromer Telcon, Oct. 25, 1973, 1:03 a.m., NARA, NPMS, HAK Telcons, box 23.
116. Note to the Prime Minister on US Facilities in UK, Oct. 25, 1973, TNA, PREM 15/1766.
117. Telegram 2143 to Washington, Oct. 25, 1973, ibid.
118. Note to the Prime Minister on US Alert, undated, TNA, PREM 15/1382.
119. Prime Minister to Lord Bridges, Oct. 28, 1973, ibid.
120. Telegram 2143 to Washington, Oct. 25, 1973.
121. *YoU*, 713.
122. Israelyan, *Inside the Kremlin*, 179–180.
123. Ibid.
124. Brezhnev to Nixon, Oct. 25, 1973, NARA, NPMS, NSCF, HAKOF, box 70, CF, EUR, USSR, Exchange of Notes Between Kissinger and Dobrynin, vol. 8; Kissinger-Dobrynin Telcon, Oct. 25, 1973, 2:40 p.m., ibid., HAK Telcons, box 23; *YoU*, 597.
125. Nixon-Kissinger Telcon, Oct. 25, 1973, 3:05 p.m., NARA, NPMS, HAK Telcons, box 23.
126. Kissinger-Haig Telcon, Oct. 25, 1973, 2:35 p.m., ibid.
127. Eban, *Personal Witness*, 538.

128. Security Council Resolution 340, Oct. 25, 1973, *IFR*, vols. 1–2: 1947–1974, The Yom Kippur War and Aftermath, doc. 14; The United Nations Emergency Force—A Report by Secretary General Waldheim-AB-42–221073, Oct. 26, 1973, ibid., doc. 15.
129. Ismail to Kissinger, Oct. 25, 1973, *FRUS*, 1969–1976, vol. 25, doc. 273.
130. Eban, *Personal Witness*, 541; Department of State's Middle East Task Force Situation Report, Oct. 26, 1973, 12:00 p.m., NARA, NPMS, NSCF, box 1175, HHSF; Kissinger-Dinitz Telcon, Oct. 26, 1973, 4:15 p.m., NARA, NPMS, HAK Telcons, box 23.
131. Sadat, *In Search of Identity*, 249.
132. Minutes of the Meeting of the Prime Minister of Israel and the Secretary of State, held at Blair House, Nov. 1, 1973, ISA, MFA, 5973/5; Memorandum of Conversation, Nov. 1, 1973, 12:10 p.m., *FRUS*, 1969–1976, vol. 25, doc. 304.
133. Memorandum of Conversation, Nov. 1, 1973.
134. "And the Meaning for Détente," WP, Oct. 26, 1973.
135. *YoU*, 600.
136. "Kissinger News Conference Text," *LAT*, Oct. 26, 1973; *YoU*, 594.
137. *YoU*, 594.
138. "Excerpts from the Address by Soviet Party Leader Brezhnev to a Session of the World Peace Congress," *NYT*, Oct. 27, 1973; Hedrick Smith, "Moscow Critical," *NYT*, Oct. 27, 1973.
139. James Reston, "A Crisis a Day," *NYT*, Oct. 26, 1973.

Conclusion

1. Henry Tanner, "Kissinger in Cairo for Talks with Sadat," *NYT*, Nov. 7, 1973; Jim Hoagland and Murrey Marder, "Kissinger in Cairo," *WP*, Nov. 7, 1973; *YoU*, 632–635.
2. "A Super Secretary to Shake Up State," *Time*, Sept. 3, 1973.
3. *YoU*, 633,
4. Ibid., 636–637; Editorial Note, Nov. 7, 1973, *FRUS*, 1969–1976, vol. 25, doc. 322.
5. *YoU*, 637.
6. Ibid., 638.
7. Anwar el-Sadat, *In Search of Identity: An Autobiography* (New York: Harper and Row, 1978), 291.
8. Editorial Note, Nov. 7, 1973; David W. Lesch, *The Arab-Israeli Conflict: A History* (New York: Oxford University Press, 2007), 251.
9. "Text of the Disengagement Agreement," *NYT*, Jan. 19, 1974; "Israel, Egypt Sign Accord; Kissinger Will Go to Syria," *LAT*, Jan 18. 1974.
10. Brent Scowcroft to Nixon, Nov. 7, 1973, NARA, NPMS, NSCF, box 639, CF, ME, Arab Republic of Egypt, vol. 10; Sadat, *In Search of Identity*, 267–268, 291–292.

11. Patrick Seale, *Asad: The Struggle for the Middle East* (Berkeley: University of California Press, 1989), 220–221.

12. Intelligence Note Prepared in the Bureau of Intelligence and Research, Nov. 2, 1973, *FRUS*, 1969–1976, vol. 25, doc. 309.

13. "Text of Arab Declaration After the Arab Leaders' Meeting," *NYT*, Nov. 29, 1973; William Tuohy, "Arab Peace Price: Israel Pullout, Full Palestinian Rights," *LAT*, Nov. 29, 1973.

14. Henry Tanner, "The Arab World: New Solidarity in a Mideast Changed by the Fighting in October," *NYT*, Nov. 29, 1973.

15. *YoU*, 783, 781.

16. Seale, *Asad*, 244; Lesch, *Arab-Israeli Conflict*, 252–253.

17. *YoU*, 781.

18. Seale, *Asad*, 245.

19. William B. Quandt, *Peace Process: American Diplomacy in the Arab-Israeli Conflict Since 1967* (Washington, DC: Brookings Institution, 2001), 152–153; Seale, *Asad*, 244–247; *YoU*, 1094–1110.

20. Quandt, *Peace Process*, 152–153.

21. Seale, *Asad*, 244.

22. Henry Tanner, "A Pact that Could Reshape the Arab World," *NYT*, June 1, 1974.

23. Paul T. Chamberlin, "Preparing for Dawn: The United States and the Global Politics of Palestinian Resistance, 1967–1975" (PhD diss., Ohio State University, 2009).

24. Memorandum of Conversation, Dec. 15, 1973, *FRUS*, 1969–1976, vol. 25, doc. 393.

25. Saunders and Quandt to Kissinger, Nov. 23, 1973, ibid., doc. 355.

26. Nigel Ashton, *King Hussein of Jordan: A Political Life* (New Haven: Yale University Press, 2008), 182.

27. Telegram from the Embassy in Jordan to the Department of State, Dec. 6, 1973, *FRUS*, 1969–1976, vol. 25, doc. 374.

28. Telegram from the Department of State to the Embassy in Jordan, Oct. 19, 1973, ibid., doc. 207.

29. *YoU*, 847–848.

30. "Excerpts from Speech by King Hussein," *NYT*, Oct. 3, 1960. A full text of Hussein's speech can be found in *Uneasy Lies the Head: An Autobiography of H.M. King Hussein of Jordan* (London: Heinemann, 1962), 200–207; *YoU*, 787.

31. Ashton, *King Hussein of Jordan*, 193–209.

32. Avi Shlaim, *Lion of Jordan: The Life of King Hussein in War and Peace* (New York: Knopf, 2008), 419; Ashton, *King Hussein of Jordan*, 210–229.

33. Schlesinger to Nixon, Nov. 1, 1973, *FRUS*, 1969–1976, vol. 25, doc. 304; Abraham Rabinovich, *The Yom Kippur War: The Epic Encounter That Transformed the Middle East* (New York: Random House, 2004), 496–497.

34. Rabinovich, *Yom Kippur War*, 496–497.

35. Terence Smith, "The First Israeli Revolution: The October War Changed Everything," *NYT*, Dec. 30, 1973.

36. *Al-Ahram Weekly On-line*, Oct. 9–15, 2008, Issue no. 917.

37. Terence Smith, "Dayan Is Subject of Rare Protest," *NYT*, Feb. 18, 1974; Rabinovich, *Yom Kippur War*, 499–500; Elinor Burkett, *Golda* (New York: HarperCollins, 2008), 337–338.

38. Charles Mohr, "Israeli General Assails Superiors," *NYT*, Nov. 9, 1973; William Tuohy, "Israeli War Tactics Disputed," *LAT*, Nov. 11, 1973; "The Generals Wage Another War," *Time*, Nov. 26, 1973.

39. "Israel War Heroes Urge Probe of Early Defeats," *LAT*, Nov. 3, 1973.

40. "Dayan to Stay: Golda Party Avoids Rift," *CT*, Nov. 29, 1973.

41. Pnina Lahav, *Judgment in Jerusalem: Chief Justice Shimon Agranat and the Zionist Century* (Berkeley: University of California Press, 1997), 227–229.

42. Abba Eban, *Personal Witness: Israel Through My Eyes* (New York: G. P. Putnam's Sons, 1992), 555.

43. Rabinovich, *Yom Kippur War*, 501.

44. Susan Hattis Rolef, "The Domestic Fallout of the Yom Kippur War," in P. R. Kumaraswamy, ed., *Revisiting the Yom Kippur War* (New York: Frank Cass, 2000), 181–182.

45. "Excerpts from Israeli Report and Elazar Letter," *NYT*, Apr. 4, 1974; Lahav, *Judgment in Jerusalem*, 229–231; "Mrs. Meir Resigning: 'I Have Reached the End of the Road,'" *CT*, Apr. 11, 1974.

46. *YoU*, 1137.

47. Yitzhak Rabin, *The Rabin Memoirs*, expanded ed. (Berkeley: University of California Press, 1996), 244.

48. Ibid., 245.

49. Lesch, *Arab-Israeli Conflict*, 256.

50. Syria did not participate at Geneva. For more on the Geneva Conference, see *YoU*, 747–798; and Quandt, *Peace Process*, 138–141.

51. Richard B. Parker, ed., *The October War: A Retrospective* (Gainesville: University Press of Florida, 2001), 249.

52. *WHY*, 1279.

53. Political Letter of Soviet Ambassador to the United States Anatoly Dobrynin to the USSR Ministry of Foreign Affairs, July 11, 1978, CWIHP, US-Soviet Relations.

54. Galia Golan, *Soviet Policies in the Middle East: From World War II to Gorbachev* (Cambridge: Cambridge University Press, 1990), 167.

55. Ibid., 228–243.

56. In December 1979, Soviet troops invaded Afghanistan to preserve a shaky Communist government and to expand its influence in South Asia. Brezhnev in particular feared that a Communist defeat at the hands of Muslim guerrillas would damage Soviet prestige worldwide and that the adjacent Muslim areas of the USSR

would be destabilized. See Odd Arne Westad, *The Global Cold War: Third World Interventions and the Making of Our Times* (Cambridge: Cambridge University Press, 2005), 316–326.

57. After failing to broker a ceasefire between Ethiopia and Somalia over the disputed Ogaden region of Somalia, the Soviet Union lent its military support to Ethiopia, prompting the United States to support Somalia in response. Gebru Tareke, "The Ethiopia-Somalia War of 1977 Revisited," *International Journal of African Historical Studies* 33 (2000): 635–667; Westad, *Global Cold War*, 273–287.

58. Terrence Smith, "Carter Warns U.S. Would Use Armed Force to Repel a Soviet Thrust at Persian Gulf," *NYT*, Jan. 24, 1980; Olav Njolstad, "Shifting Priorities: The Persian Gulf in U.S. Strategic Planning in the Carter Years," *Cold War History* 4, no. 3 (2004): 21–55; William E. Odom, "The Cold War Origins of the U.S. Central Command," *Journal of Cold War Studies* 8, no. 2 (2006): 52–82.

59. On the Helsinki Accords, see Sarah B. Snyder, *Human Rights Activism and the End of the Cold War: A Transnational History of the Helsinki Network* (New York: Cambridge University Press, 2011); and Mike Bowker and Phil Williams, *Superpower Détente: A Reappraisal* (London: Royal Institute of International Affairs, 1988), 63.

INDEX